Border Crossings

By the same author

Ideology and Power

Chartism

The Approach of War, 1938–1939

The Limits of Foreign Policy: The West, the League and the Far Eastern Crisis of 1931–1933

Allies of a Kind: The United States, Britain and the War Against Japan, 1941–1945

Racial Aspects of the Far Eastern War of 1941–1945

The Issue of War: States, Societies and the Far Eastern Conflict of 1941–1945 (paperback edn: *The Far Eastern War*)

American Political Culture and the Asian Frontier, 1943–1973

The East Asian Institute of Columbia University

The East Asian Institute is Columbia University's centre for research, education, and publication on modern East Asia. The Studies of the East Asian Institute were inaugurated in 1962 to bring to a wider public the results of significant new research on modern and contemporary East Asia.

Border Crossings

Studies in International History

CHRISTOPHER THORNE

Basil Blackwell
in association with the East Asian Institute,
Columbia University

British Library Cataloguing in Publication Data
Thorne, Christopher
Border crossings: studies in international
history.
1. International relations   2. World
politics—1900-1945
I. Title
303.4′ 82′0904   JX1391
ISBN 0-631-16062-0

Library of Congress Cataloging in Publication Data
Thorne, Christopher C.
Border crossings.
Includes index.
1. World politics—1919-1932.   2. World politics—
1933-1945.   I. Title.
D727.T525   1988   909.82   87-35462
ISBN 0-631-16062-0

Typeset in 10 on 12 pt Baskerville
by DMB Typesetters (Oxford)
Printed in Great Britain

for
Philip Whitting, GM
scholar, teacher and friend

Contents

Preface

The essays contained in this collection are presented as they were first written, with the exception of slight amendments to two concluding paragraphs (which seemed appropriate with a wider readership in mind) and the addition of a number of references to relevant works that have appeared during the intervening years. My thanks are due to the editors of those journals in which the previously published pieces originally appeared for allowing me to reissue them in this form; my thanks also to those who invited me to contribute the two conference papers that are being printed here for the first time.

Those many institutions and individuals who have contributed greatly to my cross-border inquiries – across the United States and Western Europe; in India, Australia, New Zealand and Japan – will forgive me if I do not name them separately here, as I have already done in the particular books for which their help was given. I do wish, however, to make special mention of Columbia University's East Asian Institute, whose association with the present volume is a happy reminder of the valuable contacts that I have been able to make within its doors over the years, and in particular to express my gratitude to two of its members: Dr Carol Gluck, who encouraged me to proceed with this collection, and Dr Dorothy Borg, who has long occupied a unique place in the study of United States–East Asian relations.

There is one further scholar whom I must name in connection with this series of essays, reflecting as it does a lengthy period of historical investigation. When I left Oxford after graduating in 1958, my formal education at an end, it was my good fortune to begin working under the aegis of Philip Whitting. Both as a student of Byzantine numismatics and as a teacher of exceptionally able young Londoners, he had already established a well-nigh legendary reputation; and for me his example quickly dispelled any temptation there might have been to assume other than that the pursuit of understanding was only just beginning. In him, scholarly values and standards were and have remained exemplified; from him, I received and have continued to receive encouragement without stint. If I have been excited by and at the same time less than satisfied with the kind of work represented in this present collection, it is because of attitudes which he more than anyone brought out in me. And it is to him, therefore, with great affection and esteem, that the following record of cross-border inquiries is dedicated.

Christopher Thorne

Part I

Approaches to International History

1

Introduction

In December 1926, 'Five Bewildered Freshmen' of Cornell University wrote to their campus newspaper to confess a matter which disturbed them greatly: after engaging for no less than two months in academic pursuits, they found themselves none the wiser as to 'what it was all about'. The young men were offered reassurance, however, in an ensuing letter to the same journal by the distinguished Cornell historian, Carl L. Becker. The students, he suggested, had clearly benefited already from their courses by being 'unsettled', by being prompted to ask the question 'What is it all about?' 'That is a pertinent question,' he added. 'I have been asking it for 35 years, and I am still as bewildered as they are.'[1]

The essays that follow are offered in a spirit akin to that displayed by Becker: one, if not of bewilderment, of awareness that the benefits of a lengthy study of twentieth-century international history have lain more in a greater awareness of questions than in the acquisition of a set of hard-and-fast 'answers'. Such questions relate both to particular historical topics and issues and to those matters of philosophy, perspective and technique that accompany the attempt to write history of any kind. In this connection, I have taken 'border crossings' as the title of the collection as reflecting not simply the essential element in international relations (together with my own numerous entries and departures in the quest for archival material pertaining to that subject), but also attempts made, *ambulando*, to learn and profit from other disciplines surrounding the central, historical one upon which my inquiries have been based.

In his *What is History?*, E. H. Carr has written of 'a revolution in our conception' of the subject, as it has 'become possible for the first time . . . to imagine a whole world consisting of peoples who have in the fullest sense

1 M. Kammen (ed.), *'What Is the Good of History?' Selected Letters of Carl L. Becker, 1900–1945* (Ithaca, NY, 1973), pp. 109–11.

entered into history'.[2] Such a change may reflect the ethnocentric limitations of our past imaginings as much as those developments which have tended towards the interdependence of all nations. Certainly, however, those who seek to study the history of recent international relations, and who are not content to restrict their focus and their aetiologies simply to one small corner of the complex web of connections involved, now find themselves facing, as well as challenges of a quantitative kind (massive archival collections scattered across countries and continents; the plurality of relevant cultures and languages), others pertaining to the boundaries of the discipline itself. Or so it has seemed to me, at least, and at the risk of intruding the personal unduly I will briefly indicate the directions which my interests and questionings have taken over the past 30 years or so, in order to provide an author's context for the various exercises that follow.

By the time my university education had come to an end, I had been introduced to the study of international affairs only up to the outbreak of the First World War, and only on the basis of historical narratives – some of them outstanding, of course, for qualities of precision and thoughtfulness, as with the works of G. P. Gooch, say, or Luigi Albertini. In those days, moreover, the very notion of moving the study of the past into more recent times, of 'contemporary history', as it was coming to be called, was still dismissed in some academic quarters as being at odds with the requirements of true scholarship. It is worth recalling how comparatively recently the subject area has become a respectable one, so to speak, thanks not least to the fine work of such individuals as Alan Bullock, Michael Howard, James Joll and Peter Calvocoressi in Britain, Pierre Renouvin in France, Karl-Dietrich Bracher in Germany and Hosoya Chihiro in Japan. Perhaps it is in the United States, though, that the subject of recent international affairs has attracted most attention; and although in my view the rapid expansion of this area of study has been accompanied (as in Britain) by certain less than admirable practices to which I shall refer below, outstanding contributions have been made by such scholars as Ernest May and Walter LaFeber, John Fairbank and Lloyd Gardner. (As a further and recent example of what can be achieved in the study of controversial governmental activities very close to our own time, one could refer to, say, Walter McDougall's survey of the domestic and international politics of the US and Soviet space programmes, . . . *The Heavens and the Earth*.[3])

My own inquiries into contemporary international history were prompted in the first instance by a desire to learn more about the Munich episode in

2 E. H. Carr, *What is History?* (Harmondsworth, 1964), pp. 148–9. Cf., for example, E. R. Wolf, *Europe and the People Without History* (Berkeley, Ca, 1982).
3 W. A. McDougall, . . . *The Heavens and the Earth. A Political History of the Space Age* (New York, 1985).

particular, by the well-known controversy that surrounded the publication of A. J. P. Taylor's *The Origins of the Second World War*, and by the availability of those volumes of British and German diplomatic documents that formed the basis of my own subsequent book *The Approach of War, 1938–1939*. When the opportunity came to undertake further writing, however (that is, when I left the BBC in 1968), I chose to turn away from that European theatre which had constituted the limits of virtually my entire education up to that point, and to begin learning about the Western presence in Asia: more particularly, to explore that Far Eastern crisis of 1931–3 which – so I frequently read – had formed the point of departure for the 'slide' which culminated in the Second World War. This new line of study was also prompted by the knowledge that the British official archives for the years in question had recently been opened to researchers. The subject quickly called for additional archival labour much further afield, however, as it became apparent that Britain's presence and policies in Asia were bound up with those of the other European imperial powers (herein lay the beginnings of my special connection with matters Dutch) and, above all, of the United States. The study of Western dealings with various Asian states and nations thus came to be interwoven with that of intra-Western affairs, not least Anglo-American relations and including the positions and policies of those occidental outposts in the South Pacific, Australia and New Zealand.

From the outset, of course, there were limits to what one could hope to achieve. For example, my inability to read either Chinese or Japanese (a disability which I rightly suspected would prove to be lasting) meant that the focus of my work, and the nature of any historical contribution I might be able to make, must lie mainly on the Western side of the international affairs in question. Moreover, even within the Western states alone, the sheer mass of archival material that was now becoming available (in The Hague and Canberra, for example, as well as in London, and from Washington, DC, to California) was well-nigh overwhelming – particularly if one was seeking to bring together such matters as military, economic, and so-called 'high political' affairs, which I believed had too often been studied within separate compartments. Meanwhile, there arose the further requirement – essential, as I saw it – of learning something of not merely the governments but the societies, Asian and Western alike, that had been involved in these events; of achieving a better appreciation of what it was, for example, that made American society and the American body politic so different in many essentials from those more familiar ones of Northwest Europe; of seeking to make some, small progress beyond the Western-centred approach to history that had largely formed the basis of my reading and thinking up till then.

Geographical and temporal extensions of the learning process were thus accompanied by others of a disciplinary kind: by the need to profit from the work of cultural, intellectual and economic historians, among others; from studies of political scientists involving, besides specific regimes and systems, the underlying political cultures and concepts that had been impinging upon international affairs.[4] I also came to take notice of perspectives and questions of a broader kind still that were being raised mainly by political-science students of international relations. By nature – and perhaps also as a consequence of the formal education I experienced – I am inclined to think more readily in terms of the particular than of the general; to take note of the contingent and the exceptional; to be sceptical alike of grand theories concerning the historical process and of attempts to reduce the play of politics and relations among untidy, inconsistent human beings to formulae or to 'games' that can be re-run under laboratory conditions and their outcomes predicted. Like Theodore Zeldin,[5] I am conscious that 'to be a historian is to study the rise and fall of theories', and that 'the demand for theories, ideologies and "frameworks" is strong and insistent precisely because they are always inadequate when they try to grapple with the complexities of human nature'. I doubt the possibility of establishing 'a science of politics modeled after the methodological assumptions of the natural sciences',[6] and, like Stanley Hoffmann, whom I quote to this effect in essay number 3 below, am inclined to think that the most the social sciences can expect to achieve, in regard to a repeated activity such as war, is to 'show . . . the limits of our knowledge . . . [and to] provide tools for the analysis of concrete situations'.

None the less, it has not seemed to me acceptable to follow the practice of many historians and simply ignore questions concerning the general and the possible connections between it and the particular. When studying, say, the origins of this or that international conflict, could one be sure that there was nothing to be learned from inquiries made into the causes of war as a recurring phenomenon? Might not the course of events between certain states at this or that time have been influenced by the overall configuration and properties of the international system in general during the period concerned? Even if a monocausal economic explanation of, say, the apogée and decline of Western imperialism in Asia appeared simplistic, had not certain long-term and underlying processes, shaped in part at least by systems of production and exchange, done much to establish the conditions

---

4 For a recent example of what I have in mind, see L. W. Pye, *Asian Power and Politics. The Cultural Dimension of Authority* (Cambridge, Mass., 1985): and see essay number 3 below.
5 T. Zeldin, *France, 1848–1945*, 2 vols (Oxford, 1973–7), Introduction. And see for example, the reflections of Carl Becker in his *Everyman His Own Historian* (New York, 1935).
6 D. Easton, *A Framework For Political Analysis* (Englewood Cliffs, NJ, 1965), p. 8.

within which immediate confrontations were occurring? Or, to take a final illustration of the general in terms of human behaviour patterns, might not an examination of the perceptions of another nation that had been entertained by a particular set of foreign-policy-makers, and of the ways in which alternative courses of action abroad have been considered, be furthered by drawing upon the work being done by social psychologists on the general processes by which images are formed or changed, or the dynamics of group decision-making under stress? And so forth.

This is not to say, of course, that when I began to move outwards in such directions (encouraged by my membership of an international relations, and not solely international history, group at the University of Sussex) I found the potentially relevant offerings of political- and social-scientists in every instance either helpful or impressive in their own right. If a good deal of what one might term the traditional study of diplomatic history now appeared to me to be somewhat narrowly conceived,[7] so, too, did the development of general theories (about international systems, for example) on the part of some political scientists seem to have become an end in itself: divorced from the complexities provided by historical evidence; riding high into a quasi-theological stratosphere; delivered in an unlovely tongue; in some cases accompanied by seemingly super-rational exercises in mathematics whose complexity, it transpired, formed the basis for conclusions regarding political processes that were remarkable only for their banality.

It was not a matter of chance that the greater part of these confident, would-be 'scientific' demonstrations of how international relations actually worked – and how they could be better controlled in the future – were emerging during these years from the United States: from a society in which it was widely believed that the time had come to re-order the world on the basis of American values and in the American image; from a culture that fostered the belief that there were precise answers and solutions to all questions and problems, and from a people who, having seen the much-proclaimed wisdom and experience of the Europeans come to nought once again in the 1930s, now had the added incentive of the need to forestall a nuclear doom when it came to getting things right for humankind where others had repeatedly failed. As a consequence (and to some degree reflecting the underlying reasons for the contemporary failures of successive Washington administrations in their dealings with Central America and Southeast Asia, for example), much of the work in question in the 1950s and 1960s was ethnocentric,[8] tending to project US assumptions,

7 The very label, 'diplomatic history', that is still widely attached to university courses in the United States, should in my view be discarded as encouraging the retention of an unduly narrow focus.

8 Strictly speaking, of course, this term will not do in relation to so multi-ethnic a society as that of the United States; but 'Americano-centric' or 'nationally centred' are clumsy.

values, experiences and (idealized) patterns of social development as being relevant to all of heterogeneous humanity. The very focus of many of the students involved upon 'decision-making' and the management of crisis situations also derived from a view of the nature of international affairs that was culture-bound and dangerously limited.[9]

None the less, I had no wish to align myself with those international historians who, being able to point to offerings of a facile or pretentious kind by individuals in other disciplines, then proceeded to dismiss all contributions from across the border as worthless. It seemed to me, to take a specific example, that if attempts by political scientists to construct 'models' of foreign policy decision-making tended to focus attention upon the atypical occasion, to overlook the ongoing (and often unspectacular) nature of international affairs, and to leave unanswered the question of the relative significance to be attached to this or that element in the shaping of the policy at issue, they could provide, none the less (particularly as refined by a student such as Michael Brecher, for example, and of course by one's immediate historical material itself),[10] at least a check-list, so to speak, of perspectives and questions to be brought to bear upon the complex inter-actions between two or more governments and the societies they claimed to represent. And if, like Hedley Bull among others, I found overstated certain claims that the development of a 'world-system' had rendered obsolete and misleading a focus upon the actions of states, it seemed evident, none the less, that one should examine 'transnational politics' from perspectives that embraced actors other than governments, look at configurations besides those created by inter-state alliances, say, and ask questions concerning the dynamics and properties of the system as a whole – including (with Hedley Bull himself) ones relating to the presence or otherwise of the attributes of an 'international society'.[11]

9 See, for example, the critiques developed by Stanley Hoffmann in Part II of his *Gulliver's Troubles, or the Setting of American Foreign Policy* (New York, 1968), by Hoffmann again in his article, 'An American Social Science: International Relations', *Daedalus*, vol. 106 no. 3, summer 1977, and by Michel Crozier, 'Decision-Making America', in his *The Trouble with America* (Berkeley, Ca, 1984). See also the observations of Edmund Stillman and William Pfaff, in their *Power and Impotence. The Failure of America's Foreign Policy* (New York, 1966, p. 45): 'American political science as a discipline has even in recent years interested itself in developing theoretical "models" and "systems" on the example of economic mathematics, whose tendency, whatever their other merit, is to eliminate the need for specific understanding or intimate data and intuition in studying foreign affairs. The significance of this is borne out by the common experience of American soldiers, officials, businessmen, and tourists abroad. Only infrequently do Americans really enter into the texture of a foreign society.'

10 M. Brecher *et al.*, 'A framework for research on foreign policy behavior'. *Journal of Conflict Resolution*, March, 1969, and *The Foreign Policy System of Israel* (Oxford, 1972), pp. 1–20.

11 Cf., for example, H. Bull, *The Anarchical Society. A Study of Order in World Politics* (London, 1977); R. O. Keohane and J. S. Nye, *Transnational Relations and World Politics* (Cambridge, Mass., 1970) and *Power and Interdependence. World Politics in Transition* (Boston, 1977); R. O.

As a final comment upon the sometimes bitter exchanges that surrounded the examination of international relations in the 1960s and 1970s, upon the 'contending approaches' to the subject, as they were described at the time, I would add that in my view there were and are still to be found among traditionally conceived historical studies, and within their own terms alone, features as open to criticism as those displayed in neighbouring fields. Here, too, there has been cultural bias.[12] Here, too, American students of international history have tended to mirror the parochialism and sense of primacy widespread among their own society by approaching world affairs on the basis of numerous bilateral relationships, each one radiating outwards from the United States at the centre.[13] Or again, in Britain, for example, to entitle an archival monograph, not 'Foreign Office and Cabinet dialectic in the shaping of British policy towards Venusia, 1935–6' (a subject entirely worthy of a doctoral thesis), but 'Anglo-Venusian relations in the age of the dictators' is to be as pretentiously misleading in its way as to suggest that one can measure the reasons why wars occur to three places of decimals. To foster a competitive scramble to seize upon and photocopy wholesale the latest batch of official documents to be released for public viewing, then swiftly to publish historical 'scoops' on the basis of these materials or (more hazardous still) those relatively few, spectacular items obtained under the Freedom of Information Act no more exemplifies the pursuit of scholarship than does the quest (so prominent in the 1960s and 1970s) to 'sell' one's social-science model for the analysis and shaping of affairs to the power-brokers of Washington, DC.

Happily, the markedly negative phase of 'contending approaches' to the study of international affairs appears now to have given way to a greater readiness to acknowledge the possible complementarity of the various disciplines involved. As indicated in the essay number 2, and again in the third of the series, like others before me I suspect that individual personality and need, and not solely unalloyed academic debate, play their part in such

Keohane, *After Hegemony. Cooperation and Discord in the World Political Economy* (Princeton, NJ, 1984) and (ed.) *Neorealism and its Critics* (New York, 1986); S. Strange (ed.), *Paths to International Political Economy* (London, 1984); H. Bull and A. Watson (eds), *The Expansion of International Society* (Oxford, 1984), and R. W. Cox, 'Social forces, states and world orders: Beyond international relations theory', *Millennium: Journal of International Studies*, Summer, 1981. Also essay number 3 below.

12 See, for example, P. A. Cohen, *Discovering History in China: American Historical Writing on the Recent Chinese Past* (New York, 1984).

13 See the comment of Louis Hartz: 'The truth is, the American historian at practically every stage has functioned quite inside the nation: he has tended to be an erudite reflection of the limited social perspectives of the average American himself'. *The Liberal Tradition in America. An Interpretation of American Political Thought Since the Revolution* (New York, 1955), p. 29. And see B. D. Karl, 'History and social science: the paradox of American utopianism', in N. Hagihara, A. Iriye, G. Nivat and P. Windsor (eds), *Experiencing the Twentieth Century* (Tokyo, 1985), p. 281.

matters. Certainly, it was above all personal inclination that prompted me to persist with my own research on an essentially individual basis, however much its widening scope might seem to suggest some form of group endeavour. I needed to, and did, lean heavily on generous colleagues who, for example, helped guide my early steps into the history and politics of various Asian societies; but even apart from considerations of personality, the endeavour to achieve a synthesis within a single mind has always seemed to me to be central to the nature of historical inquiry, and a collaborative basis (unfruitfully essayed on one occasion) thus unsatisfactory.

Not that the process of individual inquiry has become any easier with an increase in mere knowledge, derived over the years from archival and printed sources. The establishment of one set of tentative 'answers' within a particular perspective and addressed to a particular set of events has usually served only to open up further perspectives and more difficult questions regarding the crucial matter of causality. Like James Joll, whom I quote to this effect in the third essay in this collection, there have been moments when I have rather wistfully supposed that the possession of a single, systematic and overarching set of epistemological and philosophical principles would render this particular problem of causal connections more tractable (which is not to suggest that the best of Marxist historiography, say, as distinct from vulgar-Marxist exercises in economic determinism, is in any way facile). Like him, however, I do not enjoy such a faith or *Weltanschauung*, and am thus often left with uncertainty and no more than a range of possible explanations for the historical developments in question.

As for the particular course my work has taken, there has been a degree of logical development involved: from the Western–Japanese confrontation of the early 1930s into that of 1941–5; outwards from there into the Anglo-American relations of the time (here surveyed in broad terms in essay number 4), and also the social patterns and processes within the nations caught up in the onset and course of the Far Eastern conflict as a whole; on again, into the final phase of what K. M. Panikkar has termed 'the era of Western dominance' in Asia, centring upon the American attempt, and failure, to shape the future of that part of the world. (The final essay in this collection, for example, represents an attempt to establish certain links of a societal kind between developments before and during the Second World War and this more recent phase of international affairs.)

I have no doubt that the times through which I myself have been living have played their part in increasing my receptivity to material encountered along the way concerning such dimensions of my subjects as the racial one, examined within a limited framework in essay number 12, and in broader terms in my Raleigh Lecture for the British Academy, *Racial Aspects of the Far Eastern War of 1941–45*. At the same time, the element of chance or the suggestions of others have frequently directed my attention towards particular material or topics within the overall scope of my interests. Thus, for example, it was a lunch-time conversation with my colleague Rupert Wilkinson which led me to a wicker hamper in a cellar in Princeton, and there to the manuscript diary (now available to researchers in the splendid Archive Centre of Churchill College, Cambridge) which his father had kept whilst serving as a liaison officer with General MacArthur in the Philippines and Australia (see essay number 7 below). Or again, it was an invitation from the Council of the Royal Institute of International Affairs in London, to examine their unopened archives and report on the potential value for historical research of the material therein, that created the opportunity for the small study contained in essay number 8, and an invitation to survey Anglo-American relations over a lengthy period on the occasion of the fortieth anniversary of Churchill's 'Iron Curtain' speech at Fulton, Missouri, that led to the writing of essay number 4. The attempt in essay number 3 to step back and ask questions about the degree of mutual assistance (or mutual neglect) achieved by students of, respectively, sociology and international relations was prompted both by the problems I had encountered whilst writing *The Issue of War* and, more immediately, by the holding of a conference to mark the retirement of my friend and colleague Tom Bottomore from his Chair in the former discipline. The contrastingly small-scale sketch, in essay number 11, of one young man's ideas and actions amid the Indian scene of 1940 had its origins, on the other hand, in a 'border crossing' of the more obvious kind: in a visit to New Delhi, where, while working for other purposes on the papers of Jawaharlal Nehru, I stumbled across the letters which lay at the centre of the bizarre episode in question.

Whatever occasioned them in immediate terms, all the essays in this collection reflect what E. H. Carr has termed a series of 'reciprocal actions' between evidence and interpretation.[14] The two which immediately follow are particularly concerned with noting some of the underlying assumptions and approaches which have shaped various 'actions' of this kind in regard to particular aspects of recent international history and particular issues in international relations. The questions involved have of course been raised in the past by scholars such as Isaiah Berlin, Pieter Geyl and Fernand Braudel: questions pertaining for example to the part played by the predispositions of the individual student, to the validity or otherwise of what is claimed to be 'theory-free' 'narrative history', and to the relationship between history and a neighbouring discipline – in this case, sociology – towards which the pursuit of the question 'why' has carried me in recent years.

14 Carr, *What is History*, pp. 29–30.

2

International Relations and the Promptings of History

History is too important to be left to the historians. An individual or a society lacking an awareness of the past is as deprived as those who remain strangers to the world of imaginative literature. Moreover, anyone tempted to rely totally upon the pronouncements of professional historians for their ideas about earlier events still has to choose (even though the process is not always a conscious one) from among a wide range of versions and verdicts emanating from the ranks of those historians themselves.

And yet when this has been said, it is possible to suggest nevertheless that private individuals and public figures alike are wont to summon up the past in order to bolster some current perception or conviction, and to do so with a confidence that they would not dream of doing in the fields of, say, theoretical physics or linguistics. On occasion, of course, the public personage concerned may appear to the world at large to be particularly well qualified to engage in the flourishing of historical evidence, thus, perhaps, gaining for the *bêtise* in question a still wider currency.[1] Alternatively, a large proportion of an entire society can sometimes be observed reaching into the past in heavy-handed fashion. Thus, the multifarious outpourings recently occasioned in West Germany by the one-

This essay is a revised version of the opening address delivered to the annual conference of the British International Studies Association held at the University of Sussex in December 1981. The writer's colleague at Sussex, John MacLean, kindly provided helpful comments on the draft version. The essay is reproduced from *Review of International Studies*, 9 (1983), pp. 123–35.

1 Thus, for example, Henry Kissinger's assertion that 'it was not evil intentions but mediocrity' that brought about the First World War, as 'military decisions ran away with political judgements' serves as a reminder of how out of touch he is with historical scholarship. *Washington Review of Strategic and International Studies*, vol. I, no. 1 and *The Times*, 19 December 1977. See also Stanley Hoffmann's invaluable antidote to Kissinger's *White House Years*, 'The Case of Dr Kissinger', *New York Review of Books*, 6 December 1979.

hundred-and-fiftieth anniversary of a politically inspired mass demonstration in the Rhineland Palatinate led one journalist to observe that 'for Germans, history is not so much a series of events as a magic mirror where everyone sees what he wants'.[2]

It was precisely this widespread tendency for history to be used – or, more often, abused – by all and sundry that prompted both the not entirely frivolous thought of sub-titling the spoken version of this essay, 'Clio as call-girl', and the reference on that occasion to Genet's *The Balcony*, wherein Madam Irma, keeper of the brothel she calls her 'House of Illusions', finds that 'each individual, when he rings the bell and enters, brings his own scenario, perfectly thought out'.

The intention was, and remains here, to proceed from these grave allusions to reflections on three related topics: the variety of occasions and circumstances in which concepts of history and perceptions of its 'lessons' or its future 'judgements' have apparently played some part in the attitudes and actions of individuals, groups, and even, in a broad sense, entire societies over an event or issue of international significance; some possible lines along which research into such phenomena might be pursued; and some of the problems that could be encountered *en route*.[3]

There would seem to be sufficient evidence to suggest that the attitudes and actions of those involved in the shaping of international relations may be influenced by the promptings of history at a number of levels and in a variety of circumstances. The mental processes of an individual policy-maker, for example, may encompass material of this kind in relation to the aspirations with which he or she approaches international politics as a whole or a particular issue, to the identifying of specific goals, and/or to the choice of means to be adopted. Perceptions of the past can help shape policies of a long-term kind (as in the case of de Gaulle, for example); they can also, as over the invasions of South Korea in 1950 and of Afghanistan in 1980, provide speedy guidance in a crisis. Not least (as we shall see in

---

2 *The Times*, 26 May 1982. And see, e.g., Carl L. Becker in his *Everyman His Own Historian* (New York, 1935): 'The past is a kind of screen upon which each generation projects its vision of the future' (p. 170).

3 Thus, it is not the intention to focus upon the historical dimensions involved in specific international issues such as those centred upon Palestine or Northern Ireland, nor to explore in detail the perceptions attached to those dimensions in any particular case. For an admirable treatment of, for example, the Palestine issue before 1948 see C. Sykes, *Cross Roads to Israel* (London, 1965); or again, on the perception of a senior US analyst that the Soviet invasion of Afghanistan represented victory for them in 'the Great Game' dating back to the nineteenth century, see *The Times*, 31 December 1979.

relation to the two world wars), they can seem to offer a means of creating a better, safer world when the existing one has fallen into chaos and destruction.

If we can perhaps make the general observation that what we are dealing with in terms of process is the 'defining of a situation', the significance of which has been emphasized by social psychologists working in the field of international relations,[4] it can be suggested at the same time that what are involved in terms of input are not only perceptions of specific historical events but – whether articulated or not – underlying concepts of history as a whole. And when we come to examine examples of the particular promptings that can ensue, a further, fairly crude distinction can be made between, on the one hand, an awareness of history yet to be written: in other words, promptings of a forward-looking nature; and on the other a belief in the current relevance of some past event or trend: promptings, that is, derived from looking backwards, even though the glance is directed with present and future issues in mind.

Apparently confident appeals to 'the judgement of history' are often to be heard from politicians and others seeking to establish the profound correctness of their reading of a current situation. It is rare, however, for those who invoke that judgement of Clio to acknowledge (indeed, even to recognize, one suspects) that such a cry begs more questions than it settles. What exactly is meant by the statement that 'history' will prove the correctness of this or that policy? Is the implication that 'success' (measured by what criteria and over what period?) will be seen to have followed from the course being advocated? It is being asserted that documentary or other evidence not currently open to inspection will eventually supply a complete and unequivocal justification? Is the anticipation that future historians will be so at one in their approving judgement that the issue will be removed from the realms of doubt and dispute? When Churchill (whose preparations during the Second World War for the eventual writing of his own account of that conflict have evoked from one scholar the comment that 'Events and their planned history marched hand in hand'[5]) observed wryly that he did not fear the judgement of history as he intended to indite it himself, he was in effect undermining part of the rhetorical edifice commonly erected by politicians of all shades – himself included.

No one was more conscious of 'making history' than Churchill. Here

---

4 See, for example, D. G. Pruitt, 'Definition of the situation as a determinant of international action', in H. Kelman (ed.), *International Behavior* (New York, 1966). And see R. Jervis, *Perception and Misperception in International Politics* (Princeton, NJ, 1976), ch. 6, 'How decision-makers learn from history'.

5 J. H. Plumb, 'The historian', in A. J. P. Taylor et al., *Churchill: Four Faces and the Man* (Harmondsworth, 1973), p. 147.

again, however, he is but one of many prominent figures whose perceptions of this kind give rise to the question of whether and if so in what ways they influenced behaviour and decisions. 'The destruction of the tea [at Boston] is so bold, so daring, so firm, intrepid and inflexible', wrote John Adams in his diary in December 1773, 'and it must have important consequences so lasting, that I can't but consider it as an Epoch in History.'[6] Were his own actions during the revolution thereafter in some way shaped to accord with the mightiness of the occasion? Or again, to what extent was Trotsky sustained throughout the turmoil and hazards of 1917 and afterwards by the conviction that he was helping to bring about and secure 'the classic revolution of history'?[7]

Predictions as to what 'history will say' have also been employed on numerous occasions as a lever against others within international as well as domestic political contexts. 'The statesman who returns from the war', warned a Liberal leader in the Reichstag in January 1918, '. . . without Belgium in hand, without the Flanders coastline freed from England's power, without the line of the Meuse in our control, will go down in history as the gravedigger of German prestige'.[8] More succinctly, on 11 June 1940, as the onrush of Hitler's forces threatened to sweep away one of the great powers of Europe, the French Prime Minister, Reynaud, resorted to a similar tactic in conversation with Churchill: 'No doubt history will say the Battle of France was lost through lack of aircraft'.[9]

Churchill's rejoinder on that occasion: 'And through lack of tanks' (in retrospect, not an acute analysis: in numbers, the French and British tanks were actually superior to the German in 1940; it was the scattered distribution of the French armour that was crucial in this respect), did not mean that he was indifferent to considerations of the kind Reynaud had raised. Indeed, a few weeks earlier he had himself urged his Cabinet colleagues in London to agree to the dispatch to France of six more RAF fighter squadrons on the grounds that 'it would not look good historically if [the French] requests were denied and their ruin resulted'.[10] During the same, dramatic series of events General Weygand, too, was looking ahead to 'history' as he argued that one, last, battle should be fought, not in the belief that it could lead to victory, but in the desire 'to save the honour of the French flag'.[11] The concept of honour in a historical setting was likewise to weigh heavily with Admiral Yamamoto Isoroku, after he had

6 Quoted in F. Brodie, *Thomas Jefferson: an Intimate History* (London, 1974), p. 98.
7 See John Reed, *Ten Days That Shook the World* (London, 1961), e.g. pp. 117, 180.
8 Quoted in M. Balfour, *The Kaiser and His Times* (Harmondsworth, 1975), p. 388.
9 A. Horne, *To Lose a Battle* (Harmondsworth, 1979), p. 634.
10 Ibid., p. 448.
11 Ibid., p. 609.

become aware of the failure to deliver Japan's declaration of war immediately before the carrier-borne planes struck at Pearl Harbor, thus, as he saw it, tarnishing the reputation of the Imperial Navy on what Roosevelt described as a day that would 'live in infamy'.[12]

A concern for the verdict of history on an individual, as well as a national, reputation is also frequently to be encountered, of course. If its medieval manifestations are epitomized in the eleventh century *Chanson de Roland*,[13] its potential international consequences in more modern times can be indicated by reference to Napoleon who, in H. A. L. Fisher's phrase, 'would imagine himself one of Plutarch's heroes', and whose expedition to Egypt was undertaken with an eye on Alexander the Great and in the belief that 'great celebrity can be won only in the East'.[14] More recently, we find Eden in Moscow in October 1944, faced with Churchill's readiness to accept Stalin's demand that Lvov should go to the Soviet Union and not to a reconstituted Poland, enquiring of his aides: 'If I give way over Lvov, shall I go down in the history books as an appeaser?'[15] Or again, one can instance Kennedy, Johnson and Nixon, each in his own way concerned not to become the president who had lost a war and 'lost' Vietnam.[16] And in Johnson's case, it seems, in addition, that his decision not to stand for re-election in 1968 owed something to the desire to enhance his eventual place in history: 'If the American people don't love me, their descendants will'.[17]

Considerations of this forward-looking kind have often been accompanied in the minds of public figures by the belief that a peering in the opposite direction, so to speak, into already-recorded history, would help

12 H. Agawa, *The Reluctant Admiral: Yamamoto and the Imperial Navy*, trans. J. Bester (Tokyo, 1979), pp. 259, 271. It would be interesting to explore, for example, the extent to which Japanese perceptions of a need to 'work their passage' back to international respectability after the events of 1937–45 have influenced their foreign relations, policies and behaviour.

13 'Ill tales of me shall no man tell, say I', declares Roland; and of the weapons he and Oliver bear: 'Ne'er shall base ballad be sung of them in hall!' *The Song of Roland*, trans. D. L. Sayers (Harmondsworth, 1957), lines 1016, 1466. Concepts of the present as history in the making, including the notion of fame, have obviously been bound up with changing concepts of time. For an example of relevant studies, see R. J. Quinones, *The Renaissance Discovery of Time* (Cambridge, Mass., 1972).

14 H. A. L. Fisher, *Napoleon* (London, 1960), pp. 7, 47, 137, 203.

15 D. Carlton, *Anthony Eden* (London, 1981), p. 246. For an early suggestion that Eden's behaviour over Suez was influenced less by memories of his strong rôle in the 1930s than by an inner awareness that his popular reputation as a firm 'anti-appeaser' lacked foundation see C. Thorne, 'Nationalism and public opinion in Britain', *Orbis;* vol. 10, no. 4, 1967.

16 See, e.g. D. Ellsberg, 'The quagmire myth', in his *Papers on the War* (New York, 1972); L. H. Gelb and R. K. Betts, *The Irony of Vietnam: The System Worked* (Washington, DC, 1979).

17 D. Kearns, *Lyndon Johnson and the American Dream* (London, 1976), p. 344. And see L. Berman, *Planning a Tragedy. The Americanization of the War in Vietnam* (New York, 1982), pp. 114ff.

guide their steps through current obstacles and perplexities to success and a secure niche in the temples of fame. One recent example has been provided by President Carter, anxiously thumbing through the first volume of Churchill's history of the Second World War and establishing in his mind as a means of resolving the uncertainties and frustrations surrounding the Soviet invasion of Afghanistan a 'parallel' with Hitler's occupation of the Rhineland in 1936. [18]

It is important to recall, however, that politicians who seek instruction from the past in this fashion are joining a company that includes over the centuries numerous historians themselves. [19] 'It will be enough for me', declares Thucydides in the first chapter of his *Peloponnesian War*,

if these words of mine are judged useful by those who want to understand clearly the events which happened in the past and which (human nature being what it is) will, at some time or other and in much the same way, be repeated in the future. My work . . . was done to last for ever. [20]

To Macaulay, history was 'a compound of poetry and philosophy' which 'impresses general truths on the mind by a vivid representation'. In short, the past has been seen by many of those devoted to its study as (to use a phrase of Burke's) 'a great volume unrolled for our instruction'. [21]

Moreover, historians with a particular interest in the recent past have frequently been only too happy to contribute their findings, 'lessons' and all, directly to the policy-making process itself. In a valuable essay that should be read in conjunction with the present one, [22] Donald Watt has analysed this phenomenon in terms of the planning for post-war security that was conducted in Britain and the United States between 1914 and 1918, and again between 1939 and 1945. On both sides of the Atlantic, not

18 See *The Times*, 12 April 1980, and the comments of the present writer in the correspondence columns of that newspaper, 16 April 1980.
19 Moreover, even historians who (rightly, in the view of the present writer) emphasize, in Hugh Trevor-Roper's words, that 'history is full of surprises' and that 'no men are more surprised than those who believe they have discovered its secret' are not thereby precluded from acknowledging at the same time that (again to quote Trevor-Roper) 'historians of every generation, . . . unless they are pure antiquaries, see history against the . . . controlling background of current events'. H. Lloyd-Jones et al. (ed.), *History and Imagination* (London, 1981), pp. 358–9, 367.
20 Thucydides, *History of the Peloponnesian War*, trans. R. Warner (Harmondsworth, 1954), pp. 24–5.
21 T. B. Macaulay, essay (1828) on Hallam's *Constitutional History*, in *Critical and Historical Essays* vol. I (London, 1873); *Selections from the Speeches and Writings of Edmund Burke* (Routledge, London, n.d.), p. 221.
22 D. C. Watt, 'Every war must end: War-time planning for post-war security in Britain and America in the wars of 1914–18 and 1939–45. The roles of historical example and of professional historians', *Transactions of the Royal Historical Society*, 5th series, vol. 28, 1978.

only did views of the historical process as a whole and on the lessons to be learnt from past errors figure prominently in the business of preparing for peace; professional historians themselves came forward to pronounce on such matters as eagerly as those streams of social scientists were in later years to pour through National Airport, Washington DC, *en route* to selling their insights into the making of a better world.[23]

One must note in passing, nevertheless, that whether pronounced in a private or a public capacity, such perceptions of 'lessons' and 'patterns' have frequently embraced what other historians (faced, for example, with the 'Whig interpretation') have come to regard as myth rather than fact.[24] In some instances, too, the underlying conceptions of history involved have entailed a spurning of the 'might-have-beens' and an open or implied identifying of what actually happened (or what is seen as having happened) as having been, in effect, inevitable: the manifestation of some inexorable process.[25]

Such notions of history, whoever they have belonged to, have also frequently been accompanied by the conviction that a knowledge and understanding of the past demonstrates above all the special or 'chosen' status and role of one particular section of mankind. That section may comprise a single nation (the English; the Japanese; the Jews; the Germans) or society (post-independence America); it may embrace a wider segment still of the world's population ('Europeans', or 'Asians'), supposedly homogenous in some crucial respect; or again, it may be identified in terms of a smaller company whose self-proclaimed, unique insights into the historical process provide the justification for the adoption of the élitist role of 'enlightened vanguard'.

The accompanying liturgy is all too familiar in its arrogance: the heralding of 'the thousand-year Reich', of 'the American century', of 'the

23 On history, historians and war-time planning, see, e.g., J. Headlam-Morley, *A Memoir of the Paris Peace Conference, 1919* (London, 1972); P. A. Reynolds and E. J. Hughes, *The Historian as Diplomat: Charles Kingsley Webster and the United Nations, 1939–1946* (London, 1977); M. S. Sherry, *Preparing for the Next War: American Plans for Post-war Defense, 1941–1945* (New Haven, Conn., 1977); Thorne, 'Chatham House, Whitehall and Far Eastern issues, 1941–1945', essay number 8 below.

24 See, e.g. Plumb's comments on Churchill's view of English history, in *Churchill: Four Faces and the Man.*

25 On this, compare, for example, the approach of E. H. Carr, as explicitly stated in his *What is History?* (London, 1961) and the argument of Trevor-Roper (Lloyd-Jones, *History and Imagination*, pp. 364–5) that 'history is not merely what happened: it is what happened in the context of what might have happened.' And for contrasting approaches to the international crisis over Czechoslovakia in 1938, see, e.g., E. H. Carr, *The Twenty Years Crisis, 1919–1939* (London, 1940), pp. 14, 28, 192–4, 274, 278, 281–3, and P. Calvocoressi and G. Wint, *Total War* (London, 1972) pp. 74ff, and 92–6. See also Isaiah Berlin, *Historical Inevitability* (London, 1954).

Asian century'; the promptings and justifications of 'manifest destiny', of a *'mission civilisatrice'*, of hakkō ichiu ('the eight corners of the world under one roof').[26] When Sir John Seeley (Regius Professor of Modern History in the University of Cambridge during the latter part of the nineteenth century, but one who, it is evident, would have had a contribution to make within the British International Studies Association had that body then existed) set out to discover by what he termed 'scientific' historical methods 'great truths having . . . scientific generality and momentous political bearings', and in particular 'the laws by which states rise, expand, prosper and fall', he happily revealed at the same time the explanation for that 'mighty phenomenon' which most occupied his mind: 'the diffusion of our race and the expansion of our state'.[27]

If we take the present century alone, there have been numerous occasions when perceived 'lessons' and 'parallels' from history have apparently played a part either in an immediate international context or within a domestic political contest, the outcome of which has had consequences of an international kind as well. The triumph of Stalin over Trotsky, for example (and thus of the policy of 'socialism in one country' over that of 'permanent revolution'), owed something, it seems, to the tendency of the Bolshevik leadership to draw analogies with the French Revolution, and hence to their perception of Trotsky as the likely instigator of a 'Bonapartist' coup.[28] Probably no 'lesson' has gained wider currency and had greater consequences, however, than the one put forward by many commentators during and after the Second World War, and by Churchill most notably: that that war had been 'unnecessary', and that the build-up of aggression during the 1930s, far from having been inevitable, could have been avoided had the requisite degree of understanding and resolution been present among the peoples and governments of the democracies. 'It is my purpose', wrote Churchill at the outset of his history of that conflict, '. . . to show how easily the tragedy of the Second World War could have been prevented.'[29]

26 See, e.g. V. G. Kiernon, *The Lords of Human Kind* (Harmondsworth, 1972); D. Hay, *Europe: the Emergence of an Idea* (Edinburgh, 1957); E. O. Reischauer, *The Japanese* (Cambridge, Mass. 1977); C. Thorne, *Racial Aspects of the Far Eastern War of 1941–1945* (London, 1982); G. Mosse, *The Crisis of German Ideology* (New York, 1964); A. K. Weinberg, *Manifest Destiny* (Baltimore, 1935); J. L. Talmon, *The Origins of Totalitarian Democracy* (London, 1955); H. Tinker, *Race, Conflict and the International Order* (London, 1977).

27 J. R. Seeley, *The Expansion of England* (London, 1925; first published 1883), pp. 1, 3, 10, 156.

28 Trotsky himself had perceived the same danger in others. See L. Schapiro, *The Communist Party of the Soviet Union* (London, 1960), p. 267; I. Deutscher, *The Prophet Armed: Trotsky, 1921–1929* (Oxford, 1970) pp. 457ff.

29 W. S. Churchill, *The Gathering Storm* (London, 1950), p. 16.

The widespread acceptance of this thesis, together with a readiness to refer to it when faced with the need to define a subsequent international situation and to settle upon an appropriate response, was evident in London during the early stages of the Suez crisis of 1956 – and not simply where Eden and his fellow-conspirators were concerned.[30] In Washington, Truman, for one, was quick to reach for analogies with the 1930s at the onset of the Korean crisis and in the context of his general conviction that, as he expressed it later, 'when we are faced with a situation, we must know how to apply the lessons of history in a practical way'. Those lessons, he assured an interviewer, provided a clear guide to the 'right principles' of action.[31] Those same alleged lost opportunities during the 1930s for halting the spread of aggression and avoiding the necessity for a full-scale, great-power conflict were again used as a significant point of reference by American policy-makers at various stages of the US involvement in Southeast Asia.[32] They also helped shape the pattern of relations between president and Congress during the post-war years.[33]

It is sometimes possible to obtain a more detailed view of a policy-maker's application of historical material to current situations. Kennedy's handling of the Cuban missile crisis, for example, was influenced, it seems, by his having read shortly beforehand Barbara Tuchman's study of the onset of war in 1914, *The Guns of August*.[34] As for Truman, the picture of the 1930s which formed the basis of his reasoning contained at least one important feature – his view of the notorious Stimson–Simon exchanges over the Far Eastern crisis in 1932 – that was quite simply erroneous.[35] Here, too, in citing in support of certain 'right principles' of action a false or at least highly questionable version of past events, he was far from being alone. The confident prescriptions handed out for the benefit of mankind by Lord Cecil in 1941, for example, in his book *A Great Experiment*, rested in part on a treatment of that same Far

---

30 See, e.g., H. Thomas, *Suez* (Harmondsworth, 1970); L. D. Epstein, *British Politics in the Suez Crisis* (London, 1964).

31 H. S. Truman, *Memoirs: Year of Decisions* (Garden City, 1955), p. 121; G. Paige, *The Korean Decision* (New York, 1968), pp. 23, 114.

32 See Gelb and Betts, *Irony of Vietnam*, and Ernest May's fine study, *'Lessons' of the Past* (New York, 1973).

33 See A. Schlesinger, *The Imperial Presidency* (London, 1974).

34 G. T. Allison, *Essence of Decision* (Boston, 1971), p. 218.

35 Thus, Truman was convinced that during the Far Eastern crisis of 1931-3, the Secretary of State, Henry Stimson, had vainly proposed to Britain and others that sanctions should be placed upon Japan. Cf. B. Baruch, *The Public Years* (New York, 1960), p. 368, and C. Thorne, *The Limits of Foreign Policy: the West, the League and the Far Eastern Crisis of 1931–1933* (London, 1972), ch. 7.

Eastern crisis, the simplistic nature of which is shown up not least by a study of his own private correspondence of the time. [36]

It is perhaps worth adding that looking to history when considering policy options has not been confined to Western or great-power leaders in recent times. It is interesting, for example, to find both Jawaharlal Nehru and President Manuel Quezon of the Philippines concluding in private whilst their respective countries remained under imperial control that the events surrounding the destruction of Czechoslovakia and Poland in 1938–9 provided a lesson that would be relevant to their own circumstances when independence had been achieved: that for a small or even medium-sized state to attempt to build up its armed forces was merely to invite the hostile attention of greater powers. As Nehru put it, 'unless you arm to the same strength [as those powers], then your arms will be of no avail'; or, in Quezon's words: 'What is the use of an expensive and highly-trained army, if a Great Power decides to conquer a small one?' [37]

Quezon, of course, was to die before the Philippines ceased (at least in formal terms) to be a dependency of the United States. As for Nehru, his actions after 1947 were to depart somewhat from the course suggested by these earlier musings. [38] This shift of emphasis, however, serves as a reminder that the promptings of history, like the dictates of conscience, [39] are likely to form but one among many and often contending consider-ations in the minds and discussions of those who shape a state's policies.

These, then, are simply a few examples of occasions when individuals involved in the conduct of international affairs have apparently been influenced by their perceptions of past events, or of history yet to be written, or of the historical process in its entirety. And while, as already indicated, some work has been done on this phenomenon, notably by Professor May, there is surely a need (whether there is an *opportunity*

36 See 'Viscount Cecil, the Government and the Far Eastern-crisis of 1931', essay number 9 below. Similarly, the critical observations of F. P. Walters in his *History of the League of Nations* (London, 1967) concerning the behaviour of the principal governments represented at Geneva in 1931–2 are in contradiction to the urgent advice that he himself, as *chef de cabinet* of the Secretary General, Drummond, was sending to the latter from Tokyo at the time. See Thorne, *The Limits of Foreign Policy*, p. 182.

37 Clapper Cable (n.d. 1942) on talks with Nehru, Raymond Clapper Papers (Library of Congress), box 36; Sayre memo. of conversation with Quezon, 8 January 1940, Francis B. Sayre Papers (Library of Congress), box 7.

38 See, e.g. N. Maxwell, *India's China War* (Harmondsworth, 1972).

39 For an example of a foreign policy decision taken on grounds of principle and conscience, yet reversed shortly afterwards by the same body, see 'The quest for arms-embargoes: Failure in 1933', essay number 10 below.

depends in Britain on whether postgraduate studies and faculty research activities can survive the current onslaught of the barbarians) for further investigation into the elements, processes and consequences involved.

It would be interesting, for example, to explore as one possible significant variable the concepts of history underlying a large number of selected cases. Some indication of the kinds of questions that would arise has been given above, and clearly the person conducting the research would need to be at home in wide areas of intellectual and social history, as well as historiography.

Had the men – and, very occasionally, women – who come before us in some past international context imbibed in their formative years the beliefs, say, of a Leopold von Ranke or a Lord Acton (the latter, in Michael Howard's splendid phrase, 'insatiably persistent in his quest for more knowledge, continually frustrated in his quest for more light'),[40] that history could and should be written 'as it actually was' and that a 'definitive' or 'ultimate' version was becoming attainable?[41] Had they accepted as axiomatic the idea that history represents a process of some kind, and that there lies within it a 'key' which can reveal the patterns of the present and future as well? Did particular perceptions of history-as-process lie within that nineteenth century 'liberal descent' recently illuminated by John Burrow?[42] Did they centre upon, say, a belief in the inevitability of progress?[43] Did they embrace 'certainties' involving the mastery of man over his environment through science and technology,[44] or the inevitability and rightness of imperial conquest,[45] or the ability of man to abolish war?[46] Did they elevate the concept of freedom,[47] the institution of the state,[48] the

40 *Times Literary Supplement*, 7 August 1980.
41 See, for example, the 'Introductory Note' to volume 1 of the *Cambridge Modern History* (Cambridge, 1903), an undertaking planned by Lord Acton. On Ranke, see, e.g., the essay on him written for the Historical Association by H. Liebeschütz (London, 1954).
42 J. Burrow, *A Liberal Descent: Victorian Historians and the English Past* (Cambridge, 1981).
43 Exemplified by Macaulay, for example: 'History is full of the signs of this natural progress of society . . . We see the wealth of nations increasing, and all the arts of life approaching nearer and nearer to perfection, in spite of the grossest corruption and the wildest profusion on the part of rulers.' Essay on Southey's *Colloquies on Society* (1830) in *Critical and Historical Essays*. See, in general, R. Nisbet, *History of the Idea of Progress* (New York, 1980).
44 See, e.g., I. F. Clarke, *The Pattern of Expectation* (London, 1979).
45 See, e.g., M. Howard, 'Empire, race and war in pre-1914 Britain', in Lloyd-Jones, *History and Imagination*.
46 See, e.g., M. Howard, *War and the Liberal Conscience* (London, 1978) and J. V. Nef, *War and Human Progress* (London, 1950).
47 See, e.g., that celebrated Washington document of 1950, N.S.C.68: 'The idea of freedom is the most contagious idea in history.' T. H. Etzold and J. L. Gaddis, *Containment: Documents on American Policy and Strategy, 1945–1950* (New York, 1980), p. 388.
48 For example, Hegel: 'World history goes on within the realm of the Spirit . . . The State is the definitive object of world history proper, [being] the idea of Spirit in the externality of

destiny of a single people,[49] or the inevitable triumph on history's 'battlefield of incarnate ideas'[50] of a particular section of society, its opponents to be subjected, in Trotsky's phrase, to 'the sweep of the broom of history'?[51] Or did those perceptions involve patterns of a cyclical, rather than a linear, kind, their implications, perhaps, providing grounds for pessimism rather than for belief in a golden age to come?[52] Did they incorporate convictions about relationships between the study and writing of history on the one hand and racial and cultural aspects of international power politics on the other?[53] And so on.

Questions of this nature also point towards the idea of exploring for possible variations along another axis: that is, in terms of differing societies and political cultures. Here, too, the work of social psychologists would be relevant,[54] as would the findings of those who have inquired into the teaching of history to the young.[55] Again, however, the understanding required in our notional student would extend further still. It would need to cover, for example, the ways in which the study of history have played a part in the contemporary politics of various societies: of late-medieval Florence, say,[56] or within nineteenth-century Europe[57] and twentieth-century Africa.[58] And beyond such particular occasions and developments lie the challenging issues of a society's very interest in and sense of history,[59]

---

human will and its freedom.' *Reason in History*, trans. R. S. Hartman (Indianapolis, 1953), pp. 16, 20, 40, 53, 61, 69, 89. The relevance to our subject of the debate surrounding Karl Popper's *The Poverty of Historicism* (London, 1957) is obvious.

49 See, e.g., H. Kohn, *The Mind of Germany: the Education of a Nation* (London, 1961), and Mosse, *Crisis of German Ideology*.

50 I. Berlin, *Karl Marx* (London, 1948), p. 131. For a summary of the Ayatollah Khomeini's teachings on historical necessity as one of the 'four prisons' in which mankind finds itself but from which an individual can achieve liberation – in this particular respect, by an understanding of how historical forces operate, see *The Times*, 8 July 1981.

51 In June 1982, President Reagan resorted to a metaphor akin to Trotsky's broom: the 'ash-heap of history', reserved for Communism and, presumably, all 'failures' as judged from California.

52 See, e.g., O. Spengler, *The Decline of the West: Form and Actuality*, trans. C. F. Atkinson (London, 1926), pp. 21, 39.

53 For example, cf. E. W. Said, *Orientalism* (London, 1978), and the formidable riposte of Bernard Lewis, 'The question of orientalism', *New York Review of Books*, 24 June 1982.

54 See, e.g., W. A. Scott, 'Psychological and social correlates of international images', in Kelman, *International Behavior*, and Jervis, *Perception and Misperception*.

55 See, e.g., F. Fitzgerald, *America Revised: History Schoolbooks of the Twentieth Century* (New York, 1980).

56 See, e.g., D. Hay, *The Italian Renaissance in its Historical Context* (Cambridge, 1970), p. 122.

57 See, e.g., H. Kohn, *The Idea of Nationalism* (New York, 1961).

58 See, e.g., T. L. Hodgkin, *Nationalism in Colonial Africa* (London, 1956), pp. 172ff. On such issues in general, see A. Bozeman, *Politics and Culture in International History* (Princeton, NJ, 1960).

59 See H. Butterfield, *The Origins of History* (London, 1981).

together with the changes that apparently can occur in that respect;[60] of
the place occupied by concepts of history within a society's entire
value-system;[61] of the relationship between a society's political culture and
its approaches to and actions within the international arena.[62]

If differing concepts of history and differing political cultures, then, appear
to offer two possible lines of further inquiry, it would be wrong to ignore
variations in terms of the individual. Ernest May has already brought out,
for example, the formative part played in the shaping of the ideas of the
men responsible for US policies in the post-war years by the political
developments they had witnessed during the 1930s.[63] In this context,
obviously, one might well need to distinguish among past episodes in which
an individual had participated in some central role (as in the cases of Cecil
and Eden referred to above), others which had simply been 'lived through',
so to speak, and others again encountered subsequently in literature or
through word of mouth (Jewish memories of the Nazi holocaust, for
example, or Palestinian memories of the events of 1948).

Even so, individuals who have shared a single experience can look back
upon it in very differing ways, and our notional inquiry into the processes
involved in the promptings of history would probably need to address itself
also to the personalities of those concerned.[64] But – mild provocation now
follows – would even this be sufficient? Does individual character become a
proper object for study only in terms of those whose actions on the international stage form our starting-point? Given that any sustained explanation
of the phenomenon under discussion is likely to embrace, directly or indirectly,
the work of both historians and social scientists, might it not be appropriate
if we were to allow our reflections upon the part played by personality to
extend to those professionally observing and commenting upon man's
behaviour, past and present?

60 See, e.g., J. H. Plumb's suggestions concerning the declining role of history in British
politics, in *Churchill: Four Faces and the Man*, p. 123.
61 On the USA in this respect, especially in terms of its foreign relations, see e.g. the relevant
material in N. Graebner, *Ideas and Diplomacy: Readings in the Intellectual Traditions of American
Foreign Policy* (New York, 1964), and S. Hoffmann, *Gulliver's Troubles* (New York, 1968),
chap. 5.
62 In addition to the material on Germany and the USA cited above, see, in terms of
China's foreign relations, C. P. Fitzgerald, *The Chinese View of Their Place in the World*
(London, 1969).
63 May, *'Lessons' of the Past*, p. 84; W. I. Cohen, *Dean Rusk* (Totowa, NJ, 1980).
64 Note, in addition to the relevant studies by social psychologists, the idea lying at the heart
of Marcel Proust's *A la Récherche du Temps Perdu*, that a subconscious memory, unencumbered
by the clutter of sensations surrounding an event itself, constitutes supreme reality.

At this point it becomes necessary to allude, though certainly not to return, to that essentially sterile debate bearing the label 'contending approaches to international relations'. It is relevant to the topic under discussion to recall that among the objections that can be raised to the 'scientific-versus-historical' basis upon which many of those exchanges were conducted there stands the wide range of assumptions and methods to be found among historians working in the field of international affairs, as elsewhere.[65] In addition, it is worth emphasizing that if it has tended to be historians who have been quick to point out abuses of history committed by social scientists in the pursuit of some grand design or other,[66] historians have also been prominent among those criticizing the intellectual poverty of, for example, what is claimed to be an a-theoretical, and hence somehow objective, 'narrative' form of their art.[67]

Indeed, it will be suggested below that in terms of the philosophical and epistemological bases of their work, the position of certain historians is a good deal closer to that of some of their social-scientist colleagues than to that of others ostensibly engaged in the same trade as themselves. At the same time, however, it would be foolish for our imagined student of the promptings of history to ignore dissimilarities among the disciplines that he or she is likely to encounter along the way: differences and their attendant difficulties which have been acknowledged by, among others, historians whose own work has entailed a strong sympathy for and close involvement with neighbouring realms of intellectual inquiry.[68]

65 As Keith Thomas has recently observed in his review of Lawrence Stone's *The Past and the Present* (*Times Literary Supplement*, 30 April 1982), history is likely to remain 'a loose confederation of jealously independent topics and techniques'.
66 A good example of such abuse is provided by Daniel Bell's *The Cultural Contradictions of Capitalism* (New York, 1976), the theses of which are supported by reference to the experiences of 'the West' over several centuries in terms that are often far-removed from much of European history, being based, it would seem, on a projection of aspects of the American past.
67 See, e.g., the Preface of Arthur Marder's *Old Friends, New Enemies: the Royal Navy and the Imperial Japanese Navy;* also the present writer's review of the book in the *Times Literary Supplement*, 4 December 1981, and the general arguments of Fernand Braudel in *On History* (London, 1980), p. 4 and passim.
68 See, e.g. the comments of Braudel (*On History*, p. 50) on what he sees as 'the crux of the debate between historians and sociologists'. Note also the conclusion arrived at by Andrew Shonfield: that 'the closer one gets to the problems of the real world, the more insistent the need for the genuinely interdisciplinary effort'; but that at the same time, 'the more one departs from the simplification of explanatory models drawn from a particular discipline . . . [the less likely one is] to arrive at the kind of scientific truth which can be used for the purposes of prediction.' R. Morgan (ed.), *The Study of International Affairs* (London, 1972), p. 9. See also the review by Frank Parkin (*TLS*, 23 July 1982) of Philip Abrams, *Historical Sociology* (London, 1982).

Moreover, although debates among students of international relations have for the most part taken on a more constructive character since the stage battles of the 1960s, we would probably do well to recognize the possibility that perceptions, currently widespread, of a world moving rapidly towards some form of large-scale disaster may help to magnify again differences of an interdisciplinary nature. In other words, it seems possible, at least, that current apocalyptic visions of trends in world politics may renew among some sections of those studying international relations the strength of post-1945 impulses to acquire precise 'answers', scientific 'truths' and a capacity to predict;[69] and that such a development would contrast markedly with that emphasis, widely to be found among today's historians, upon the subjectivity of the student, the limits to his powers of understanding, and the significance of the contingent in the realm of human affairs.

To be a historian, [writes Theodore Zeldin in the Preface to his much acclaimed *France, 1848–1945*] is to study the rise and fall of theories . . . The demand for theories, ideologies and 'frameworks' is strong and insistent precisely because they are always inadequate when they try to grapple with the complexity of human nature. Our knowledge of man is still far too rudimentary to allow wide generalisations . . . [70]

And yet when due notice has been taken of both inherent differences of approach and potentially diverging trends among those intellectual disciplines with a bearing on international relations, it remains impossible to base such distinctions upon the notion of a single category that covers the work of all historians in the field. Between, say, a Toynbee and a Trevor-Roper,[71] or a Gabriel Kolko and a Theodore Zeldin (in each pairing the

69 In part, this quest may be seen as merely another form taken by the longstanding Western liberal belief that war can and should be eradicated: in other words, as a mutation of that 'idealist' approach to the problems of international relations which had predominated between the wars and which practitioners of the 'scientific' approach now castigate. (See M. Howard, *War and the Liberal Conscience*.) The impulsion to discover the 'laws' of international relations no doubt also owed much to the horrors of 1937–45 and the prospect of nuclear annihilation; to those 'can-do' features of American political culture which emphasize the possibility of finding precise answers to any problem; and to an increased readiness among Europeans, their confidence diminished by the two world wars, to look across the Atlantic for new and dynamic approaches to the problems facing mankind.

70 See also the position of a scholar who has blended in his work strategic studies and intellectual, political and social history: 'I am an unrepentant historian and not a social scientist. I think in terms of analogies rather than theories, of process rather than structure, of politics as the realm of the contingent rather than of necessity.' Michael Howard, *Studies in War and Peace* (London, 1970), p. 13.

71 See, e.g., H. R. Trevor-Roper, 'Arnold Toynbee's millennium', *Encounter*, June 1957.

former perceiving in history large-scale patterns and overriding causal processes) lies a conceptual distance greater than that between, say, a Kolko and a Kaplan[72] – or, come to that, between a Toynbee and a Trotsky.[73]

Faced, then, with such profound differences among historians, past and present, as well as between some historians and social scientists, should not our notional student of the promptings of history take account of the personalities of those whose work crosses his path, in addition to the characters of the political figures from the past who come under review? Behind the cut and thrust of cardboard blades in the battle of the 'contending approaches to international relations', beneath that odour of pretentiousness, indispensable to the second-rate and the insecure, which clings like some strident after-shave lotion to the academic body as a whole, are there not to be found those who are disposed, whether by nature or by nurture or both, to be believers, and others inclined from the outset towards agnosticism?

Among the believers and would-be-believers, of course, will be those who have the capacity to acknowledge and respond creatively to evidence that fails to square with even all-encompassing theory; among the agnostics will be those who, within what they see as the limits to human understanding, seek to base their own fallible and transient judgements on rigorous professional standards: to strive for objective subjectivity, one might say. Among the agnostics, too, there will be those who choose to adopt a holistic perspective when it appears appropriate to the search for a better under-standing of the past or the present. Nor is a simple dichotomy likely to be tenable beyond the stage of advancing the initial hypothesis. Nevertheless, if that hypothesis does have some substance, then within the spectrum, rather, of predispositions to which we are referring, there will be significant differences that are marked at one end by an inclination towards perceptions involving patterns, explanations and convictions of an all-embracing kind. Whether the focus of belief sits in Rome, lies in Highgate cemetery, or awaits the assembling of some body of knowledge wherein mankind may finally comprehend and control the processes of international relations, the predisposition will be towards the complete rather than the partial; towards certainty, not doubt.[74]

72 See, e.g., J. and G. Kolko, *The Limits of Power* (New York, 1972); M. A. Kaplan, *System and Process in International Politics* (New York, 1957).

73 That is, Trotsky as the author of that remarkable work, *History of the Russian Revolution* (New York, 1932).

74 See, e.g., Pieter Geyl's observation on his fellow-Dutch historian, the Marxist Jan Romein: 'Romein finds uncertainty unbearable, and because he hears his soul cry out that the certainty without which it feels itself lost *must* exist. So he goes out to seek, and (as indeed it is written) he finds.' *Encounters in History* (London, 1963), p. 242. Several of the essays in this

The personalities of those who study history and international relations, then, may have to be numbered among the problems to be encountered in any attempt to examine the ways in which notions about the past have influenced the making of current policies. Certainly, the entire subject is one on which there remain wide differences of basic assumptions even among those who appear to think in a not dissimilar fashion on other matters. During the initial stages of the Soviet invasion of Afghanistan, a distinguished US economist who was a colleague and friend of the writer's at the Netherlands Institute for Advanced Study asked with much anxiety and earnestness: 'You're a historian of the 1930s: when's the moment [i.e., during what he, like many of his compatriots, saw as the beginning of a carefully-planned Soviet drive to the Gulf] we must fight?' It is one of the ironies of our time that when many historians apparently accept, with Theodore Zeldin, that their discipline 'is a means of becoming aware of the subjectivity of one's outlook'[75] and with Trevor-Roper that 'no men are more surprised than those who believe they have discovered [history's] secret', among politicians, social scientists and the plain-interested there still flourishes the expectation of finding 'lessons', 'truths' or 'laws' in a past recorded by those historians themselves. The arrival, not the journey, matters.

---

collection of Geyl's are relevant to the topic under discussion here. Note that Romein was, in Geyl's words, 'a fervent admirer of Toynbee; ibid., p. 357. See also Isaiah Berlin, *The Hedgehog and the Fox. An Essay on Tolstoy's View of History* (London, 1953), and the reflections of Carl Becker in *Everyman His Own Historian*, in *Detachment and the Writing of History* (Ithaca, NY, 1958), and in M. Kammen (ed.), *'What is the good of history?'. Selected Letters of Carl L. Becker, 1900–1945* (Ithaca, NY, 1973).
75 Zeldin, *France, 1848–1945.*

3

Societies, Sociology and the International: Some Contributions and Questions, with Particular Reference to Total War

If Anthony Giddens is to be believed, sociologists as a species are 'chronically subject to self-doubt'.[1] All the more reason, therefore, for emphasizing at the outset that the essay which follows stems above all from a sense of inadequacy on the part of a historian: from an awareness of limitations in terms of concepts and perspectives, as well as of knowledge; an awareness that has grown *pari passu* with the attempt over a lengthy period to combine with the study of relations among states at the official level, in peace and war, a greater understanding of the societies involved and the interrelationships that have existed across national and state boundaries at that deeper level.[2] It is commonly argued, of course, that, in Peter Burke's words, 'despite the existence of a few bilinguals . . . sociologists and historians still do not speak the same language';[3] and indeed, Weber's contrasting of the 'greater precision of concepts' of the one discipline with the 'fullness of concrete content' of the other does not appear entirely to have lost its relevance. Even Philip Abrams, when persuasively submitting that 'in terms of their fundamental preoccupations, history and sociology

This essay was first published in a volume to mark the retirement of Tom Bottomore from his Chair of Sociology at the University of Sussex: W. Outhwaite and M. Mulkay (eds), *Social Theory and Social Criticism* (Oxford, Basil Blackwell, 1987). Warm thanks are due to Ron Dore, Rosemary Foot, Tony Giddens, John MacLean and William Outhwaite for commenting helpfully on the original draft.

1 A. Giddens, *The Class Structure of the Advanced Societies* (London, 1973), p. 13.
2 Cf. Thorne, *The Approach of War, 1938–1939* (London, 1967), and subsequent studies of Western–Far Eastern relations: *The Limits of Foreign Policy* (London, 1972); *Allies of a Kind* (London, 1978); and *The Issue of War* (London, 1985; re-issued in p.b., London, 1986, as *The Far Eastern War*).
3 P. Burke, *Sociology and History* (London, 1980), p. 14.

are and always have been the same thing', acknowledges that 'the methodological compulsions of sociologists incline them to begin with explanation in principle almost as fastidiously as historians tend to begin with colligation'.[4] Even that most sociologically minded of historians, Fernand Braudel, discerns persisting tensions that arise from the 'violent' contraints of historical time, from which, as he sees it, the sociologist tends to escape 'by concentrating either on the instant, which is always present, as if suspended somewhere above time, or else on repeated phenomena which do not belong to any age'.[5]

There are problems of accommodation which remain to be acknowledged, in other words, even when one has dismissed as intellectually impoverished the notion, explicitly or implicitly advanced by some historians, that what they term 'narrative history' is a form of objective method,[6] or when one has discounted sociological sermons constructed on the basis of historical distortion, such as Bell's *Cultural Contradictions of Capitalism*. At the same time, however, it would be wrong to proceed on the basis of a simple dichotomy between the two disciplines. The range of philosophies, approaches and methods to be encountered among historians, for example, is vast, and in such respects a good many of them (not least those of 'hedgehog' rather than 'fox' predisposition, to employ Isaiah Berlin's categorization) are closer to social scientists than they are to various fellow-historians.[7] Moreover, there is surely much force in Abrams's contention that 'Sociology must be concerned with eventuation, because that is how structuring happens. History must be theoretical, because that is how structuring is apprehended'; force, too, in the same writer's observations that 'most practical explanation in both history and sociology tends to be a tightly constructed melange of explanation in principle and explanation in detail, with a more or less generous measure of colligation stirred in as well'.[8] At the very least, one can point to the work of Barrington Moore, Peter Laslett and others and acknowledge, as does Peter Burke himself,

---

4 P. Abrams, *Historical Sociology* (Shepton Mallet, 1982), pp. x, 221. And see C. Lloyd, *Explanation in Social History* (Oxford, 1986), pp. 15ff and passim.
5 F. Braudel, *On History*, trans. S. Matthews (London, 1980), pp. 48–50. Cf. R. Aron, *Peace and War. A Theory of International Relations*, trans. R. Howard and A. B. Fox (London, 1966), pp. 177–80.
6 See, for example, the Preface to Arthur Marder's *Old Friends, New Enemies: the Royal Navy and the Imperial Japanese Navy* (Oxford, 1981), and the present author's comments in *Times Literary Supplement*, 4 December 1981. Also, Abrams, *Historical Sociology*, chs 7 and 10.
7 I. Berlin, *The Hedgehog and the Fox. An Essay on Tolstoy's View of History* (London, 1953). And see essay number 2 in this volume.
8 Abrams, *Historical Sociology*, pp. x, 211. And see Lloyd, *Explanation in Social History*, pp. 314–15 and T. Skocpol (ed.) *Vision and Method in Historical Sociology* (Cambridge, 1984).

that in the 1950s and 1960s, after a prolonged estrangement, 'sociology and history began to converge'.[9]

If there continue to be difficulties surrounding any such convergence, it is not to be wondered at if they appear to be particularly great where international contexts and perspectives are concerned, embracing as they do the additional problems of both comparative sociology and the highly contentious discipline – or is it simply a 'field', a meeting-place for many disciplines?[10] – of international relations. And it may be that such inherent difficulties have accounted in part for the extent to which neglect has existed on both sides: neglect of sociological issues and perspectives by those students of contemporary international history who fail to pursue the 'why' of foreign policy-making beyond the doors of cabinets and foreign ministries,[11] or who move outside such dialectical processes merely to provide a sketch of the immediate domestic 'background' against which policy was formulated, or who ignore even the possibility that there has come to exist during the past hundred years or so, if not longer, a network of relations and processes among and transcending national societies, both affecting and being affected by the course of international politics as conducted at the formal level of governments and international organizations; neglect and distortion also on the part of those sociologists who pass over the parts played by war and military power generally in the formation and perpetuation of states,[12] or who, as Giddens describes them, treat

9 Burke, *Sociology and History*, p. 28. And see the 'sociological approach' to the analysis of international relations adopted by Robert Gilpin in his *War and Change in World Politics* (Cambridge, 1981).

10 See, for example, W. Eberhard, *Conquerors and Rulers. Social Forces in Medieval China* (Leiden, 1965), ch. 1, 'the initial reflections in L. W. Pye, *Asian Power and Politics. The Cultural Dimensions of Authority* (Cambridge, Mass., 1985); and K. E. Knorr and J. N. Rosenau (eds), *Contending Approaches to International Relations* (Princeton, NJ, 1969).

11 As late as 1960, A. E. Campbell could describe as 'still dominant' that 'tradition of historiography, long-established . . . that diplomatic history can be studied as a thing apart, and that the relations of nation-states proceed with little reference to . . . the emotions and the private interests of the people who live in them', *Great Britain and the United States, 1895–1903* (London, 1960), p. 1.

12 For recent exceptions to this tendency, see Michael Mann's essay, 'Capitalism and militarism', in M. Shaw (ed.), *War, State and Society* (London, 1984); C. Creighton and M. Shaw (eds), *The Sociology of War and Peace* (London, 1987); and A. Giddens, *The Nation-State and Violence* (Cambridge, 1985), pp. 22ff, 103ff. Also R. Pettman, *State and Class: A Sociology of International Affairs* (London, 1979). There are, of course, numerous other works, long considered basic to the study of international relations, which are relevant: for example, K. N. Waltz, *Man, the State and War. A Theoretical Analysis* (New York, 1959); Q. Wright. *A Study of War* (2 vols, Chicago, 1942). Social–psychological explorations which could be of interest to sociologists entering the field include H. C. Kelman (ed.), *International Behavior* (New York, 1966); and R. Jervis, *Perception and Misperception in International Politics* (Princeton, NJ, 1976).

' "external" ' factors as no more than an ' "environment" to which the society [concerned] had to "adapt" ', rather than as an inherent element in the processes of continuity and change.[13] (Miles Kahler goes so far as to suggest that 'contemporary social science has surrounded societies with a theoretical insulation from the intrusion of the external'.)[14]

One could speculate further on what has brought about this degree of mutual neglect. On the sociological side, for example, if it is indeed true that, as Christopher Dandeker has asserted in a recent article,[15] 'the analysis of warfare remains on the periphery of social theory', or that, in the words of the *Macmillan Student Encyclopedia of Sociology*, sociological responses to the question of the effects of major twentieth-century wars on social structures have as yet been only 'varied and fragmentary',[16] is this to be attributed in part, as Tony Giddens has suggested,[17] to the long-term influence of sociological concepts arrived at by major students in the field in an era of comparative peace, internationally speaking? (The *Communist Manifesto*, it will be recalled, proclaimed that 'national differences and antagonisms between peoples' were 'daily more and more vanishing'; and Comte and Spencer, among others, could declare that the spread of 'indus-trially organized societies' would foster the extension of such a process.) Or is the neglect to be understood, rather, as simply one consequence of what Aron has summarized as a general rejection by the 'Western empirical sociologists' of our day of 'global sociological interpretations of the modern age' as lying beyond 'the present possibilities of science'?[18]

Yet we should not overstate either nineteenth-century sociological complacency about international conflict or the subsequent neglect by scholars of this and other sociological aspects of international relations. After all, Marx and Engels, for example, in the period following the publi-cation of the *Manifesto*, went on to set out what W. B. Gallie has termed 'the first sociology of war ever devised', and the same author has also gathered together the evidence to demonstrate the remarkable extent to which Engels

13 Giddens, *Class Structure*, p. 265. By way of contrast, Eberhard, for one, emphasizing transnational connections in both the modern and pre-modern eras, has propounded a 'layer theory' of social analysis in which 'there are no local "social systems". There is only humanity as such: the social world of man' (*Conquerors and Rulers*, pp. 11–12). For the development of Giddens's own theses, see his *The Nation-State and Violence*, pp. 84, 263.

14 M. Kahler, *Decolonization in Britain and France: the Domestic Consequences of International Relations* (Princeton, NJ, 1984), p. 17.

15 C. Dandeker, 'Warfare, planning and economic relations', *Economy and Society*, vol. 12, no. 1, February 1983.

16 See the entry under 'militarism' by Michael Mann. (I owe this and the preceding reference to William Outhwaite. C.T.)

17 A. Giddens, *A Contemporary Critique of Historical Materialism*, vol. 1 (London, 1981), p. 177.

18 R. Aron, *Main Currents in Sociological Thought*, vol. 2, trans. R. Howard and H. Warner (Harmondsworth, 1970), p. 271.

in his later writings foresaw (like I. S. Bloch not long afterwards) the fearful totality and destructiveness of conflict among the modern major powers.[19] One can point also to the general propositions regarding the relationship between the intrinsic nature of domestic societies on the one hand and their external stance and behaviour on the other that have subsequently been put forward by a variety of sociologists: by Durkheim and Veblen, obviously, and by Sorokin, for example, in the third volume of his *Social and Cultural Dynamics*;[20] by Mumford in terms of, *inter alia*, the 'bellicose' characteristics he descried in the societies of his 'paleotechnic phase' of history,[21] and by Mills in terms of the predilections he attributed to the 'Overdeveloped Society' in 'the Fourth Epoch';[22] by Rosa Luxemburg among others on the roots and impulsions of militarism in particular,[23] and by Harold Lasswell (both before and after the defeat of the Axis powers) concerning the development, internal dynamics and external stance of a 'garrison state' that was not, he emphasized, ' "by definition" non-democratic'.[24] Particular mention should also be made of the propositions concerning 'determinants and constraints' in the engendering of war advanced by Aron, the one scholar of note in recent times to have made substantial contributions in the two fields of sociology and international relations.[25]

Moreover, a number of sociologists and other social scientists have also advanced less generalized analyses regarding those characteristics of particular states that have a bearing upon their external relations: Weber, for one, in his reflections on the Germany of his own day;[26] Maruyama and

19 W. B. Gallie, *Philosophers of War and Peace: Kant, Clausewitz, Marx, Engels, and Tolstoy* (Cambridge, 1978), ch. 4; and see V. Kubálková and A. Cruickshank *Marxism and International Relations* (Oxford, 1985). On Bloch, see, for example, J. F. C. Fuller, *The Conduct of War, 1789-1961* (London, 1961) ch. 7; also I. F. Clarke, *Voices Prophesying War, 1763-1984* (Oxford, 1966).

20 P. A. Sorokin, *Social and Cultural Dynamics, vol. 3: Fluctuations of Social Relationships, War and Revolution* (New York, 1937).

21 L. Mumford, *Technics and Civilization* (London, 1946), pp. 264-5. Cf., for example, J. U. Nef, *War and Human Progress* (London, 1950); R. Caillois, *Bellone, ou la pente de la guerre* (Brussels, 1963); W. H. McNeill, 'The industrialization of war', *Review of International Studies*, vol. 8, 1982.

22 For example, C. Wright Mills, 'Culture and politics in the Fourth Epoch', and 'The decline of the left', in L. Horowitz (ed.), *Power, Politics and People. The Collected Essays of C. Wright Mills* (New York, 1963).

23 See the general survey by V. R. Berghahn, *Militarism. The History of an International Debate* (Leamington Spa, 1981).

24 H. D. Lasswell, 'The garrison state', *American Journal of Sociology*, vol. 46, no. 4, 1941; Lasswell, 'The garrison state hypothesis today', in S. P. Huntington (ed.), *Changing Patterns of Military Politics* (Glencoe, IU, 1962).   25 Aron, *Peace and War*, pt 2.

26 M. Weber: for example, 'The Prussian junkers', in S. N. Eisenstadt (ed.), *Max Weber on Charisma and Institution Building* (Chicago, 1963); and see in the same collection Weber's suggestions regarding 'the origins of discipline in war', in 'Meaning of discipline'.

Fukutake, in their sociopolitical examinations of Japan before and during the Second World War;[27] Veblen and Barrington Moore, on both Germany and Japan from the latter half of the nineteenth century onwards (the former, of course, resting his arguments in part on the premiss that 'machine technology' and 'the exact sciences' were bound up '[in] the nature of cause and effect' with 'the modern drift toward free or popular institutions');[28] Jeffrey Herf, on the contribution to Nazism's external drives made by a 'reactionary modernism' that was itself 'a specifically German response to a universal dilemma of societies facing the consequences of the industrial and French revolutions';[29] Mills, again, together with Stanley Hoffmann and others who have sought to relate the foreign policy of the United States since 1945 to the major properties of American society (not least, the emergence of the 'military–industrial complex') and American political culture.[30]

Here, indeed, is one area in which 'sociology and history have begun to converge', for a number of historians, too – not least William Appleman Williams and other scholars designated 'revisionist' – have been seeking to establish the socioeconomic bases of modern American external policies and assumptions, including, in Richard Drinnon's study *Facing West*, 'the historical link between American racism and expansionism'.[31] The same kind of historical exploration has also been conducted during the past 25 years or so in regard to the external behaviour of other states, most notably Germany before and during the First World War.[32] And if we turn our

27 M. Maruyama, *Thought and Behaviour in Modern Japanese Politics*, ed. I. Morris (London, 1963); T. Fukutake, *The Japanese Social Structure: its Evolution in the Modern Century*, trans. R. Dore (Tokyo, 1982). See also, for example, M. B. Jansen (ed.), *Changing Japanese Attitudes Toward Modernization* (Princeton, NJ, 1965).

28 T. Veblen, *Imperial Germany and the Industrial Revolution* (New York, 1915) and *An Enquiry into the Nature of Peace and the Terms of its Perpetuation* (New York, 1917); Barrington Moore, *Social Origins of Dictatorship and Democracy: Lord and Peasant in the Modern World* (London, 1967), pp. 305, 313, 433.

29 J. Herf, *Reactionary Modernism. Technology, Culture and Politcs in Weimar and the Third Reich* (Cambridge, 1984).

30 See C. Thorne, *American Political Culture and the Asian Frontier, 1943–1973* (London, 1988). Also, for example, Mills, 'The structure of power in American society'; 'The conservative mood', and 'Culture and politics: the Fourth Epoch', in Horowitz, *Power, Politics and People*; S. Hoffmann, *Gulliver's Troubles, or The Setting of American Foreign Policy* (New York, 1968); *Primacy or World Order* (New York, 1978); and *Dead Ends* (Cambridge, Mass., 1983). See also the survey in Berghahn, *Militarism*, ch. 5; and cf. Z. Brzezinski, *Between Two Ages, America's Role in the Technetronic Era* (New York, 1970).

31 R. Drinnon. *Facing West. The Metaphysics of Indian-Hating and Empire Building* (New York, 1980). And see, for example, R. W. Rydell, *All the World's a Fair: Visions of Empire at American International Expositions, 1876–1916* (Chicago, 1984). W. A. Williams, *The Roots of the Modern American Empire* (New York, 1969); and also *Empire as a Way of Life* (New York, 1980).

32 See, in particular, F. Fischer, *Germany's Aims in the First World War* (London, 1967); and

attention towards, so to speak, arrows that are pointing in the opposite direction, towards, that is, the impact of external events and developments on the structures and attitudes within domestic societies, then here, too, it will be sufficient to recall, for example, the work of E. P. Thompson on the making of the English working class in the era of the French Revolution,[33] and of Arthur Marwick, Gordon Wright and others on Britain and other European societies during the two world wars.[34] Recent and detailed contributions include those of Duncan Gallie on the differing effects of those international conflicts on working-class radicalism in Britain and France respectively,[35] Miles Kahler on the consequences of the British and French retreats from empire for particular groups within the two metropolitan societies,[36] and Alan Ware on the part played by the Vietnam War in the decline of Democratic Party organization in the United States.[37] Reference should obviously be made also, within this broad category, to the wide variety of studies concerning the social consequences of imperial rule, whether in regard to, say, 'patterns of dominance' generally (to employ the title of Philip Mason's book on the subject),[38] or to changes in contacts and interrelationships among sections of a colonized people;[39] to the material

---

War of Illusions (London, 1973); also, V. R. Berghahn, *Germany and the Approach of War in 1914* (London, 1973), and for an analysis of British foreign policy in its social context in the same period, Z. S. Steiner, *Britain and the Origins of the First World War* (London, 1977).

33 E. P. Thompson, *The Making of the English Working Class* (London, 1964). See also C. Emsley, *British Society and the French Wars, 1793–1815* (London, 1979).

34 For example, A. Marwick, *The Deluge: British Society and the First World War* (London, 1965); and *Britain in the Century of Total War* (London, 1968); G. Wright, *The Ordeal of Total War, 1939–1945* (New York, 1968); also E. J. Leed, *No Man's Land: Combat and Identity in World War One* (Cambridge, 1979); R. Fussell, *The Great War in Modern Memory* (London, 1975); R. Wohl *The Generation of 1914* (London, 1980); J. M. Halpern, 'Farming as a way of life: Yugoslav peasant attitudes', in J. F. Karcz (ed.), *Soviet and East European Agriculture* (Berkeley, Ca., 1967).

35 D. Gallie, *Social Inequality and Class Radicalism in France and Britain* (Cambridge, 1983), ch. 12 and pp. 267–8.

36 Kahler, *Decolonization in Britain and France*.

37 A. Ware, *The Breakdown of Democratic Party Organization, 1940–1980* (Oxford, 1985), pp. 91ff. And see, for example, Kenneth Morgan's judgement on the domestic consequences – if only indirectly, social in part – of the greatly enlarged defence commitment accepted by the British Labour government in January 1951 at the urging of Washington and following the intervention of Chinese forces in the Korean War: '[It] marked a profound watershed in British political history. It instilled new elements of pressure and division within the government and the party. Its political and financial implications were to dominate British public affairs for a decade to come'. *Labour in Power, 1945–1951* (Oxford, 1985), p. 435; also the thesis developed by Joel Krieger in his *Reagan, Thatcher, and the Politics of Decline* (Cambridge, 1986).

38 P. Mason, *Patterns of Dominance* (London, 1970).

39 See, for example, G. W. Skinner, 'The nature of loyalties in rural Indonesia', in I. Wallerstein (ed.), *Social Change: the Colonial Situation* (New York, 1966).

consequences of the introduction from outside of a money economy,[40] or to the social–psychological dimensions of the colonial situation and its legacies.[41]

In the second part of the present essay, questions will be raised in the specific and illustrative context of the Second World War concerning some of the challenges and difficulties that continue to face those studying the interactions between the external and the domestic, none the less. Meanwhile, particular mention should be made of the reflections on such problems offered by Theda Skocpol, who contends that modern social revolutions need to be linked to 'the internationally uneven spread of capitalist economic development and nation-state formation on a world scale'.[42] Skocpol's respect for the confusion and untidiness of the past will commend itself to those historians who are given to emphasizing what Margaret Mead has termed 'the unique event in all its uniqueness'.[43] (Arguing that 'international relations have intersected with pre-existing class and political structures to promote and shape divergent as well as similar changes in various countries', she is consequently cautious as to the possibility of generalizing from the causal links that she advances in the specific cases of France, Russia and China.) It is also likely that many early-modern historians would share her view that Wallerstein's depiction of the emergence of a 'modern world-system' in the sixteenth century embodies an unacceptable reductionism,[44] together with a certain manipulation of the historical evidence.[45]

40 For example, W. F. Wertheim and J. S. Giap, 'Social change in Java, 1900–1930', in Wallerstein, *Social Change*; and Wertheim, *Indonesian Society in Transition* (The Hague, 1964).
41 For example, O. Mannoni, *Prospero and Caliban: the Psychology of Colonization*, trans. P. Powesland (New York, 1964); and A. Memmi, *Portrait du Colonisé* (Paris, 1973).
42 T. Skocpol, *States and Social Revolutions. An Introduction to the Analysis of a Political Phenomenon* (Cambridge, 1972); and, for a study of international responses to other peoples' revolutions, L. C. Gardner, *Safe for Democracy. The Anglo-American Response to Revolution, 1913–1923* (New York, 1984).
43 M. Mead, 'Anthropologist and historian: their common problems', in *Anthropology: A Human Science* (Princeton, NJ, 1964).
44 In the context of more recent times, too, Giddens's observation is appropriate: 'The world system is not only formed by transnational economic connections and interdependencies, but also by the global system of nation-states, neither of which can be exhaustively reduced to the other', *Nation-State and Violence*, pp. 161ff. On divisions among Marxist analysts themselves in this context, see Kubálková and Cruickshank, *Marxism and International Relations*, ch. 10.
45 I. Wallerstein, *The Modern World-System. Capitalist Agriculture and the Origins of the Capitalist World-Economy in the Sixteenth Century* (New York, 1974); T. Skocpol, 'Wallerstein's world capitalist system: a theoretical and historical critique', *American Journal of Sociology*, vol. 82, March 1977. See also Kubálková and Cruickshank, *Marxism and International Relations*, and C. Ragin and D. Chirot, 'The World System of Immanuel Wallerstein: Sociology and Politics in History', in Skocpol (ed.), *Vision and Method in Historical Sociology*.

With Wallerstein's work we have come to a perspective that transcends the two foci mentioned so far (that is, the influence of the domestic on foreign policy, and the impact of the external on the domestic – these being accompanied by the debate, so beloved by some German historians and political scientists in particular, regarding the *Primat der Aussenpolitik* or *der Innenpolitik*). It is a perspective, also, that transcends the conventional ordering of the modern world, for historical and other heuristic purposes, into states and the relations among them, concentrating, rather, on 'the articulation of the *processes* of the world-scale division and integration of labor', as well as 'the *processes* of state-formation and deformation', this articulation providing, it is argued, 'an account, at the most general level, for . . . the patterns and features of modern social change'.[46] To ignore such 'processes that transcend separable cases, moving through and beyond them and transforming them as they proceed', asserts the anthropologist Eric Wolf in his parallel study, *Europe and the People Without History*, is to be left with 'concepts like "nation", "society", and "culture" [which] name bits and threaten to turn names into things'; it is to overlook the 'totality of interconnected processes' which brought into being 'the social system of the modern world', and which alone enable us 'to make analytic sense of all societies, including our own'.[47]

The particular objections – sociological, historical or anthropological – that can and will be brought against such a perspective and analysis are doubtless numerous. And many students, including the present writer, will incline towards Philip Abrams's submission that the potential of historical sociology lies less in 'imposing grand schemes of evolutionary development on the relationship of the past to the present' than in developing a ' "middle range" idiom of practical explanation', which seeks to connect the general with the particular.[48] Moreover, where the development of 'world capitalism' itself is concerned, it could well be that Skocpol's own tentative alternative picture will prove more fruitful a hypothesis than the one advanced by Wallerstein: a picture consisting of 'intersecting structures (such as class structures, trade networks, state structures, and geopolitical systems) involving varying and autonomous logics and different, though overlapping, historical times, rather than a single all-encompassing system that comes into being in one stage and then remains constant in its essential patterns until capitalism meets its demise'.

46 T. K. Hopkins and I. Wallerstein (eds), *World-Systems Analysis: Theory and Methodology* (Beverley Hills, Ca., 1982), p. 12.
47 E. R. Wolf, *Europe and the People without History* (Berkeley, Ca, 1982), preface and introduction.
48 Abrams, *Historical Sociology*, pp. 16, 70, 224. Cf., for example, J. MacLean, 'Political theory, international theory, and problems of ideology', *Millennium: Journal of International Studies*, vol. 10, 1981.

One does not have to subscribe to the Marxist paradigm, however (should one now say 'one of the Marxists' paradigms'?), or be entirely committed to the dominance of a holistic perspective and analysis in one form or another, in order to derive stimulus and insight from attempts such as those of Wallerstein and Wolf to understand the dynamics of a world of peoples whose vastly increased interdependence in modern times has come to be acknowledged on all sides. (A. J. Latham, for example, while emphasizing less the exploitation of non-Western peoples than the 'liberation of the energies of Asians and Africans' by 'the market-widening effects of [European enterprise]', has none the less sought to demonstrate that Asia in general, and China and India above all, had become crucial to the international economy during the 50 or so years before the First World War.)[49] Likewise, an inherent scepticism (whether from nature or nurture or both) regarding the possibility of constructing a satisfactory general theory need not prevent one from acknowledging the intellectual benefits that can accrue from attempts to proceed in that direction also.[50]

It is to be regretted that such issues and socioeconomic dimensions of international relations receive only occasional attention in the collection of essays (of considerable interest in other respects) edited by the late Hedley Bull and Adam Watson, *The Expansion of International Society*.[51] In other words, one might have expected that contemporary international historians other than those specifically addressing themselves to topics like Patrick O'Brien's 'Europe in the World Economy' would consider, if only to demonstrate its weaknesses and limitations, the 'world-system' analytical perspective; that a considerable number of the essays in such a volume would find it profitable to explore, for example, contentions of the kind advanced by Giddens, for one, that 'the nation-state replaces the city as the "power container" shaping the development of capitalist societies as the old city – countryside symbiosis becomes dissolved';[52] that they would need to take cognizance of Ernest Gellner's thesis – so markedly different in its focus from those predominantly ethnic-centred studies that have long held the field – that the roots of modern nationalism have lain 'in the distinctive structural requirements of industrial society', and that 'the age of transition to industrialism was bound to be an age of nationalism, a period of turbulent readjustment, in which either political boundaries, or cultural ones, or both, were being modified, so as to satisfy the new nationalist imperative'.[53]

49 A. J. Latham, *The International Economy and the Underdeveloped World, 1865–1914* (London, 1978). For another non-Marxist approach, see T. Smith, *The Pattern of Imperialism. The United States, Great Britain, and the Late-Industrializing World since 1815* (Cambridge, 1981).
50 See, for example, the concluding section of Kahler, *Decolonization in England and France*.
51 H. Bull and A. Watson (eds), *The Expansion of International Society* (Oxford, 1984).
52 A. Giddens, *A Contemporary Critique of Historical Materialism*, vol. 1 (London, 1981), pp. 11–13.   53 E. Gellner, *Nations and Nationalism* (Oxford, 1983), pp. 35, 40.

Students of the 'high politics' and history of recent international relations will also need at least to note in passing (if only as a part of the intellectual history of the time) those 'modernization' theories which implicitly have rested in many cases on the notion that 'to modernize' is a requirement of 'progress', and that, in the words of one critic, 'all social change is progressive, organic, linear';[54] theories which in some instances embraced the belief that détente between the super-powers would develop as a consequence of the 'convergence' of their two societies, and which Marion Levy sought to bring to bear on international relations in two somewhat turgid volumes, lacking in empirical material, *Modernization and the Structure of Societies*;[55] theories, again, which in certain instances appear to have owed something to an American ethnocentrism and parochialism that was reflected also in much of that country's foreign policy of the time. For all his acknowledgement that 'social conditions, as well as the way in which science and technology are socially applied, vary enormously', Zbigniew Brzezinski, for example, remained convinced in 1970 that 'the rest of the world learns what is in store for it by observing what happens in the United States', and that American society was 'having the greatest impact on all other societies, prompting far-reaching cumulative transformation in their outlook and mores'. 'It is only a matter of time', he proclaimed, 'before students at Columbia University and, say, the University of Teheran will be watching the same lecture simultaneously.'[56]

Brzezinski's are by no means the only set of post-war sociological assumptions, of course, that, when viewed in retrospect, bear the strong imprint of the particular period in which they were written, as well as of

54 See, for example, the comments of M. H. Hunt in W. I. Cohen (ed.), *New Frontiers in American–East Asian Relations* (New York, 1983), and of P. A. Cohen, *Discovering History in China. American Historical Writings on the Recent Chinese Past* (New York, 1984). Also E. Gellner, *Thought and Change* (London, 1964), ch. 1. In contrast to Gellner's own 'neo-Episodic' focus on industrialization and the consequential 'crucial transformation of our time . . . of beetles (i.e. relatively alien beings and societies) into men (i.e. forms of life akin to our own)' – the reference is of course to Kafka's *Metamorphosis* – see the observation of Eberhard, *Conquerors and Rulers*, p. 17: 'If . . . the term "traditional society" means nothing but "non-industrialized" society, we classify all societies into two classes on the basis of a single criterion – a procedure which is scientifically untenable. Social scientists in the distant future might even regard the development of industries as only one, and not even the most important, factor in the total changes of mankind between 1000 and 2000 AD.'

55 M. J. Levy, *Modernization and the Structure of Societies: A Setting for International Affairs*, 2 vols (Princeton, NJ, 1966).

56 Brzezinski, *Between Two Ages*, pp. 22, 31, 277–8. Cf. Stanley Hoffmann's comments on American 'craving for simplicity' in the country's external relations in general, in *Dead Ends*, passim. On the belief in the 1920s that European and other societies would be 'Americanized', see F. Costigliola, *Awkward Dominion. American Political, Economic and Cultural Relations with Europe, 1919–1933* (Ithaca, NY, 1984).

personal inclination. The same can be said of, for instance, the optimistic analysis of 'a pluralistic international system' that was drawn up by Talcott Parsons in 1960–1.[57] Emphasizing that 'the institutionalization of normative culture . . . is not an either–or proposition, but a matter of degree', Parsons, too, found grounds for hope for 'the gradual evolution of a more stable international order' in not merely the 'nexus of solidary relationships which cross-cut the divisions on the basis of "national" interest', but in 'a genuine value-consensus . . . which runs deep' and which, as he saw it, was focused upon 'the valuation of modernization' and 'certain fundamental universal significancies of Western culture'.

Twenty-five years on, and given, *inter alia*, the resurgence of Islam as a major force in international affairs, together with the demonstrated antipathy of a significant portion of mankind not simply to the United States as a power, but also to the mores of American society,[58] one wonders whether Parsons would have introduced a number of qualifications to his thesis a second time around. Nevertheless, Ronald Dore, too, continues to find grounds for perceiving 'a movement towards a world society', a society which can be seen as complementary to the development of 'a society of states', and which is being fostered, in his view, by 'a diffusion of fellow-feeling' that is inherent in the 'world culture', Western in essence, that links middle-class life-styles around the globe.[59] For Adda Bozeman, in contrast, who finds it 'hard to fathom a "world culture"', the evidence

---

57 T. Parsons, 'Order and community in the international social system', in J. N. Rosenau (ed.), *International Politics and Foreign Policy. A Reader in Research and Theory* (New York, 1961). Cf. Abrams's question (*Historical Sociology*, p. 127) regarding 'just how far Parsons has any sort of serious scholarly interest in history as distinct from his obviously very serious commitment to celebrating his own society'.

58 Not that such reactions are new, of course; nor have they been confined to the 'Third World'. See, for example, D. Strauss, *Menace in the West. The Rise of French Anti-Americanism in Modern Times* (Westport. Conn., 1978).

59 R. Dore, 'Unity and diversity in world culture', in Bull and Watson, *Expansion of International Society*. For Reinhold Niebuhr's 1930 vision of a 'world community', see Costigliola, *Awkward Dominion*, p. 267. Note also David Riesman in his late 1950s 'reconsideration' of *The Lonely Crowd* (S. M. Lipset and L. Lowenthal (eds), *Culture and Social Character. The Work of David Riesman Reviewed* (New York, 1961), pp. 443–4): 'The most important passion left in the world is not for distinctive practices, cultures, and beliefs, but for certain achievements – the technology and organization of the West – whose immediate consequence is the dissolution of all distinctive practices, cultures, and beliefs. If this is so then it is possible that the cast of national characters is finished.' Likewise, Arnold Toynbee argued in his introduction to the 1964 printing of Walter Prescott Webb's *The Great Frontier* (Austin, Texas): 'The Western orientation of the leaders of the non-Western liberation movements is remarkable. Their objective in struggling so persistently to throw off the domination of the Western peoples turns out to have been to go Western themselves, in a radical way . . . [and to join] a new society [which] is going to be a world society united by a common allegiance to a modern world civilization . . . based, to begin with, on the Western way of life.'

points, rather, 'to a plurality of frames of reference' and to the significance of the fact that 'the majority of non-Western and non-Communist states . . . have not accepted certain crucial Western norms'. 'We do not have . . . a globally meaningful system', she concludes, 'because the world society consists today as it did before the nineteenth century of a plurality of diverse political systems, each an outgrowth of culture-specific concepts.'[60]

Amid such contrasting readings of the contemporary world, there clearly lie issues of the utmost importance for sociologists and students of international relations alike. Also evident is the need in this as in other contexts to proceed on the basis of terms that are clearly defined and agreed among those debating the issues in question. The sense in which Bozeman here employs the term 'system', for instance, is well removed from that adopted by many analysts of international relations, among whom Aron, to take one example, defines 'an international system' as 'the ensemble constituted by political units that maintain regular relations with each other and that are all capable of being implicated in a generalized war'.[61] Or again, with the Dore thesis in mind, it is worth recalling that in the 1930s Robert Park was identifying a 'culture' as 'the function of groups who can act collectively', being contrasted by him with a 'civilization', which he took to describe 'an aggregate of people who use the same artefacts and who have no solidarity at all'.[62]

Beyond this matter of definition, there are a number of initial historical premises that also require examination. For example, Bull and Watson open their collection of essays with the proposition that what has been happening in the past hundred years or so is the expansion of an 'international society of European states' and its transformation into 'the global international society of today'.[63] In doing so, they take such a 'society' to consist of states which not only form a system, but 'have established by

60 A. Bozeman, 'The international order in a multicultural world', in Bull and Watson, *Expansion of International Society*. And see her *Politics and Culture in International History* (Princeton, NJ, 1960) and *The Future of Law in a Multicultural World* (Princeton, NJ, 1971). Also Pye (*Asian Power and Politics*, p. 342): 'The degree to which cultures converge during the process of modernization is significant since they are all participating in the spread of a world culture based on advanced technology. Yet political cultures will always have a strongly parochial dimension because every political system is anchored in its distinctive history, and the central political values of loyalty and patriotism and the phenomenon of national identity mean that differences are certain to persist, *and possibly even to increase*, with modernization.' (Emphasis added.)

61 Aron, *Peace and War*, p. 94. And see, for example, Giddens, *Nation-State and Violence*, pp. 276–7.

62 R. E. Park, 'Culture and civilization', in *Race and Culture* (New York, 1950). Cf. Gellner, *Thought and Change*, pp. 153–7, and for examples of contrasting usages, Thorne, *The Issue of War*, pp. 69–70.

63 Bull and Watson, *Expansion of International Society*, p. 1.

dialogue and consent common rules and institutions for the conduct of their relations, and recognise their common interest in maintaining these arrangements'. One may ask, however, to what extent within Europe itself such a society existed from, say, Bismarckian times onwards. Is there not some weight in Aron's observation that 'the homogeneity of the European system in the nineteenth century was superficial',[64] and were not the differences in question reflected before 1914 in a severely limited acknowledgement, in some quarters, of 'common interests' and 'common rules'? How is the assertion that Voltaire's 'commonwealth divided into several states' remained a predominantly European 'international society . . . until the Second World War' to be reconciled with the phenomena and international consequences of Nazism and fascism (the former mentioned but once in the volume, the latter not at all)? Does not the historical evidence – from both before and after the 1939–45 war – suggest that while what has emerged is indeed, in Giddens's words, 'an inter-societal system that is truly global in scope', the process of creation, as he again summarizes it, 'is a dialectical one which both unifies and fragments'?[65]

For the international historian in particular, moreover, there remains the problem of establishing specific causal relationships between the inter-societal system and international politics; between, also, the properties and dynamics of a single society and the external stance and policies of the state in question. How far, in this respect, is it possible to discern and demonstrate interconnections that take us beyond simply a description of what Paul Kennedy, in his study of the domestic context of Britain's foreign policies since the mid-nineteenth century, terms 'background influences'?[66] Arno Mayer is one historian who has attempted to construct a major exercise of this kind, in which he seeks to demonstrate, in his *The Persistence of the Old Regime*, 'that the Great War of 1914 . . . was an outgrowth of the latter-day remobilization of Europe's *anciens régimes*'; that that conflict was essentially 'an instrument of domestic politics', designed to preserve the 'material, social and cultural pre-eminence' of the old elites.[67] But quite apart from the unconvincing generalizations that Mayer includes within the development of his argument (can one really lump, say, Russia and Austria–Hungary together with the Britain of the 1900s, when asserting that 'the economic and social carriers of bourgeois liberalism remained relatively weak and supine'? How can one begin to square with the

64 Aron, *Peace and War*, p. 318.
65 Giddens, *Contemporary Critique*, p. 168; and *Class Structure*, p. 264.
66 P. Kennedy, *The Realities Behind Diplomacy. Background Influences on British External Policy, 1865–1980* (London, 1981).
67 A. J. Mayer, *The Persistence of the Old Regime. Europe to the Great War* (London, 1981), pp. 4, 15, 305 and passim.

evidence regarding the situation that obtained within the Liberal Ministry in London the insistence that a 'predilection for war' was 'pervasive', not simply in Berlin, but 'in all cabinets of the major powers'?),[68] the actual connection between the postulated social dynamics on the one hand and foreign-policy decision-making on the other is nowhere addressed.

In other words, Mayer, too, in the event stops short of accepting a challenge that is indeed a formidable one. As James Joll puts it in the conclusion of his own survey of the origins of the First World War:

Each of the crucial decisions was taken within a specific institutional and social framework. They were conditioned by a wide range of assumptions about the behaviour of individuals and governments and by values resulting from long cultural and political traditions as well as from the social and economic structure of each country. The problem of these ever-widening circles of causation is that the attempt to find a general explanation for the outbreak of war is likely to get lost in a vast number of possible causes so that it is difficult to know where to stop if one is not to be left with explanations of such remoteness and generality that one still finds oneself without an adequate understanding of why this particular war broke out at that particular moment.[69]

Joll goes on to reflect that 'perhaps this means resigning ourselves to a kind of two-tier history': a history of 'the broad lines of social and economic development', on the one hand, revealing long-term patterns within which 'even so revolutionary a development as the First World War' becomes 'only a minor episode, a small irregularity on the graph'; and, on the other, a history of 'the world in which the decisions of individual leaders, whatever their origins, can affect the lives and happiness of millions and change the course of history for decades'.

Of course (as was acknowledged earlier in the passing reference to Isaiah Berlin's distinction between 'hedgehog' and 'fox'), underlying both this question of the relationship between what Mills termed 'the microscopic' and 'the molecular'[70] and the contrasts of perspective and interpretation that have been alluded to above there lie philosophical and epistemological issues that are fundamental. (Joll himself observes somewhat wistfully that 'the attraction of a Marxist theory of history is that it appears to offer an explanation for a very wide range of phenomena in terms of a comparatively small number of basic factors'.) In this respect it will suffice here to draw attention to the contrast between the approaches and assumptions of, for example, Wallerstein and Aron regarding the international

68 Ibid., pp. 45, 321. Cf. Steiner, *Britain and the Origins of the First World War*.
69 J. Joll, *The Origins of the First World War* (London, 1984), pp. 204–5.
70 Mills, 'Two types of social science research', in Horowitz, *Power, Politics and People*.

scene – the latter's as exemplified in the chapter of *Peace and War* entitled 'In search of a pattern of change'; or of Wolf and Hoffmann, the latter asserting in *The State of War* that 'the best social science can do, in dealing with a problem such as war, is to accomplish a . . . doubly modest task. On the one hand it can show . . . the limits of our knowledge. On the other . . . it can provide tools for the analysis of concrete situations . . . The social scientist's hierarchy of causes cannot but be largely subjective.'[71] To start from such a basis, of course, is to render a presentation of the 'totality of interconnected processes' that have created 'the social system of the modern world' an achievement beyond reach. Is it, then, to be judged myopic, or faint-hearted – or an exercise in realism, to be set alongside that concentration upon 'middle-range' exercises which Abrams has envisaged for historical sociology in general?

So far in this essay, frequent, though brief, reference has been made to the phenomenon of war, particularly to that form described as 'total'. And for the societies involved, such periods of upheaval have made the intrusion of the external more apparent than at any other time. Indeed, so evident is the international challenge and pressure that is placed upon the structure, institutions, fabric, values and morale of a domestic society in such a period[72] that the choice of the years 1939–45 as a complement to the foregoing general survey, from which to illustrate more concretely some of the historical–sociological questions and issues that can arise, perhaps needs to be accompanied by the rider that the international perspective involved is not one to be abandoned once the guns fall silent. Certainly, one gains the impression that the advent of the Second World War aroused among sociologists in general an interest in the impact of the external that was not to be sustained in post-war years. Thus, quite apart from the monitoring and planning that was soon being conducted within official circles with regard to social issues in a changing world,[73] the *American Journal of Sociology*, for example, even before Pearl Harbor, was carrying

71 S. Hoffmann, *The State of War. Essays on the Theory and Practice of International Politics* (London, 1965), pp. 273–4. See, for example, Hoffmann, 'The long road to theory', in Rosenau, *International Politics and Foreign Policy*; and C. Wright Mills, *The Sociological Imagination* (New York, 1959), p. 150: 'We do not know any universal principles of historical change, because the mechanisms of change . . . vary with the social structure we are examining.' In general, see Lloyd, *Explanation in Social History*.
72 See, for example, Giddens, *Nation-State and Violence*, pp. 232ff.
73 See, for example, I. McLaine, *Ministry of Morale. Home Front Morale and the Ministry of Information in World War II* (London, 1979); P. Addison, *The Road to 1945* (London, 1975); A. M. Winkler, *The Politics of Propaganda: the Office of War Information, 1942–1945* (New Haven, Conn., 1978).

a rash of articles on such topics as 'The Social Types of War' (Spier), 'The Social Function of War' (Park), 'An Anthropological Analysis of War' (Malinowski) and the influencing and measuring of morale.[74]

However this may be, for today's student there could scarcely be a richer field for investigating the interplay of the domestic and the international across a hugely diverse collection of societies: societies in which long-standing imperial relationships were being subjected to new levels of strain and questioning, and in which (in China and Yugoslavia, for example, and in parts of Indo-China and Korea) social and political revolutions were in the making; in which international conflict was prompting more radical and urgent responses to pre-war domestic crises (including, it is argued elsewhere, 'crises of conceptualization')[75] regarding technological change and economic interdependence; in which many were being confronted for the first time with a 'One World' perspective (to employ the title of Wendell Willkie's 1943 book, which sold in its millions in numerous languages),[76] even if the translation of perspective into sustained practical policy was to prove another matter altogether.

It is a conflict whose origins have for the most part been studied in terms of the policies of particular states and the nature of the regimes involved, some historians adding to this the question of the structure and properties of the international system as a whole during the inter-war years and even earlier.[77] Should we also view the approach of war, however, in relation to social structures and dynamics, not simply in terms of individual states (as Fukutake and Maruyama have done for Japan, and Grunberger, for example, for Nazi Germany),[78] but within a perspective that transcends the political boundaries of the time and even (as Wolf, for one, urges) the commonly accepted division between West and non-West?[79] It is worth recalling that during the period in question Norbert Elias was writing:

It is [structural] forces . . . it is tensions and entanglements of this kind, which at present constantly expose the individual to fear and anxiety . . . One can see the

74 For example, *American Journal of Sociology*, vol. 46, no. 4, 1941 and vol. 47, no. 3, 1941.
75 Thorne, *Issue of War*, ch. 3.
76 See E. Barnard, *Wendell Willkie: Fighter for Freedom* (Marquette, Mich. 1966); and R. A. Divine, *Second Chance. The Triumph of Internationalism in America During the World War II* (New York, 1967).
77 See, for example, A. W. DePorte, *Europe Between the Superpowers* (New Haven, Conn., 1979); and Thorne, *Issue of War*, pp. 41ff.
78 R. Grunberger, *A Social History of the Third Reich* (London, 1971); and see W. S. Allen, *The Nazi Seizure of Power. The Experience of a Single German Town, 1930–1935* (London, 1966); Fukutake, *The Japanese Social Structure*; Maruyama, *Thought and Behaviour in Modern Japanese Politics*.
79 See Thorne, *Issue of War*, ch. 3, for a preliminary and tentative essay in this direction.

first outlines of a world-wide system of tensions composed by alliances and supra-state units of various kinds, the prelude to struggles embracing the whole of the globe . . . The case is no different with economic struggles.[80]

We need, argued Margaret Mead in 1941, 'a critical re-evaluation of our culture in the light of changes resulting from the extraordinary advances in technology which have introduced so many discordances into our way of life and our value system', while three years later A. G. Fisher was reflecting in broadly similar fashion: that 'the whole development of modern mechanical industry has brought with it quite unintended changes in social structure, which are constantly presenting problems all the more difficult because their content and character are themselves constantly changing under our hands'.[81]

For all the endeavours of the New Deal, there remained around ten million unemployed in the United States on the eve of war; nor could a consensus be achieved among Americans regarding the appropriate relationships to adopt, in the face of rapid economic and technological change, between society, political processes and the state.[82] Meanwhile, profound social upheaval was being experienced in Japan (although 38 per cent of its population were living in towns by 1940, 80 per cent had been born and brought up in villages), in Korea (where the number of workers in the industrial sector doubled between 1932 and 1940), in the Philippines and Indo-China (in southern Vietnam, rural indebtedness had increased fourfold between 1900 and 1930), in the Dutch East Indies, and in Fiji (by 1933, Indians had come to number almost half of the total population and to dominate the main, sugar-cane, industry; 'Economic production and expansion are becoming increasingly vital questions for the Fijian', reported the District Commissioner for Lau in 1932, 'faced as he is by the clash of races and the power that belongs to money').[83] The warning uttered by Fung Yu-lan around the same time: 'Modern industrialism is destroying the traditional Chinese family system and thereby the

---

80   N. Elias, *The Civilizing Process*, vol. 2: *State Formation and Civilization*, trans. E. Jephcott (Oxford, 1982), pp. 331–2. And see Herf, *Reactionary Modernism*, and also, of lasting interest, K. Polanyi, *The Great Transformation* (1944; rev. ed. Boston, 1957).
81   Mead, *Anthropology: A Human Science*, p. 97; A. G. B. Fisher, *Economic Progress and Social Security* (London, 1946), pp. 40–1; and also *The Clash of Progress and Security* (London, 1935).
82   See B. D. Karl, *The Uneasy State. The United States from 1915 to 1945* (Chicago, 1983). And note, for example, the findings of Robert and Helen Lynd on their return to 'Middletown' in the mid-1930s (*Middletown in Transition*, New York, 1937): 'One thing everybody in Middletown has in common: insecurity in the face of a complicated world. . . . So great is the individual human being's need for security that it may be that most people are incapable of tolerating change and uncertainty in all sectors of life at once.'
83   Quoted in D. Scarr (ed.), *Fiji: The Three-Legged Stool: Selected Writings of Ratu Sir Lala Sukuna* (London, 1984), p. 131.

traditional Chinese society', was being echoed, *mutatis mutandis*, by various
'double patriots' in Japan. (Tokyo, wrote one, had become 'nothing but a
branch shop of London'.)[84] Meanwhile in Spain, civil and international
conflict was already raging as the outcome in part, as recent historians have
seen it, of 'a process of social evolution that had been gaining momentum
since the Great War', of 'a social system out of phase with its political
structure', of 'a level of structural complexity that resulted in concurrent
industrial and agrarian peasant crises, made much more acute by recent
growth and new interrelated dependencies'.[85]

The turmoil and structural shifts are plain enough. But there remains, of
course, the question that was posed above in relation to Mayer's thesis
regarding the origins of the 1914 conflict: to what extent can one argue –
and demonstrate – that it was these socioeconomic circumstances and
processes that brought about war, and not essentially, say, the idiosyncratic
characteristics of Adolf Hitler? Did the interrelated structural crises simply
create the preconditions in which Nazis and Japanese militarists were more
likely to come to power and, given their political predilections, to launch
their wars? Or did those structures and processes *themselves* make
international, as well as civil, conflict on a massive scale 'inevitable' within
a certain span of time, so that the peculiarities of a Hitler or the faction-
struggles in Tokyo are to be seen as being of less than primary
significance?[86]

The question of time, too, must preoccupy historian and sociologist alike
when they contemplate the gestation of such an event as the coming of the
war. Again, the approach that has been adopted by many students of the
subject would be described by members of the *Annales* school as *l'histoire
événementielle*, 'dating back' the origins of the conflict in the Far East, as
Professor Marder among others has done, no further than the Manchurian
crisis of 1931, or of the war in Europe to the arrival of the Nazis in power or
the Versailles peace treaty. But if, alternatively, we place the event within a
wider framework – within the perspectives proposed by Wolf or

84   Fung Yu-lan quoted in J. Stacey, *Patriarchy and Socialist Revolution in China* (Berkeley, Ca.,
1983), p. 71; Tachibana Kosaburo quoted in Maruyama, *Thought and Behaviour in Modern
Japanese Politics*, p. 42. And see M. Selden, *The Yenan Way in Revolutionary China* (Cambridge,
Mass., 1971); L. E. Eastman, *The Abortive Revolution: China Under Nationalist Rule, 1927–1937*
(Cambridge, Mass., 1974); and *Seeds of Destruction: Nationalist China in War and Revolution*
(Stanford, Ca., 1984); J. D. Spence, *The Gate of Heavenly Peace: The Chinese and their Revolution,
1895–1980* (London, 1982); G. R. Storry, *The Double Patriots* (London, 1957); S. N. Ogata,
Defiance in Manchuria (Berkeley, Ca, 1964); Jansen, *Changing Japanese Attitudes*.
85   P. Preston (ed.), *Revolution and War in Spain, 1931–1939* (London, 1984); and S. Payne's
review of this volume, *Times Literary Supplement*, 17 May 1985.
86   Not that even a highly idiosyncratic individual such as Hitler is to be viewed as somehow
standing outside sociological analysis. See, for example, Abrams, *Historical Sociology*, chs 8 and 9.

Wallerstein, say, or in a manner that would accommodate Eberhard's notion of 'world-time'[87] – then what criterion should determine exactly how long such a *longue durée* should be? Does one select the time-frame in order to accommodate a pre-determined theme, derived from an examination of the war itself, or establish it on other grounds and then find therein themes and causal chains that might not have been apparent within a different compass? (For example, the origins of the war in the Far East take on a much stronger racial aspect, if one chooses to cast back well before 1939 or even 1931.)[88] What of the implications of the various time-frames adopted by the historical actors themselves?[89] And – the question posed by James Joll and by Mills again – how to synthesize the patterns that emerge in the context of the *longue durée* with the detailed decisions, the selection of options, discernible within a smaller compass (assuming, that is, that one adopts an un-Tolstoyan view of the past: that one takes history to be 'not merely what happened', but also 'what happened in the context of what might have happened')?[90] How to combine, in terms of both observations to be explained and the explanations themselves, the 'macro' and the 'molecular'?[91] Can we achieve anything more than 'two-tier history' in explaining why so many millions were to die, why so drastic and widespread an upheaval was to occur for states, societies and individuals alike between 1939 (or 1937, from a Chinese point of view) and 1945?

The same question of what time-frame to adopt is again significant, of course, when we turn to consider the consequences of the war for both individual societies and social developments of a transnational kind. To take an obvious example, the nature, depth and width of the sociopolitical consequences of the conflict that enveloped China after 1937 can have, to some extent at least, a different look to them depending on whether we draw a *terminus ad quem* in 1945 or 1949 – and, perhaps, on whether the observer is looking back from a vantage point during the Cultural Revolution, say, or in the era of Deng Xiaoping's pragmatism. Or to be more specific still, one's judgement regarding the impact of the war with Japan on the position of women within Chinese society might vary in part

87   See Eberhard, *Conquerors and Rulers*, pp. 13ff; also Braudel, *On History*, passim; and Giddens, *Contemporary Critique*, pp. 19ff.
88   See C. Thorne, *Racial Aspects of the Far Eastern War of 1941–1945* (London, 1982).
89   See C. P. Fitzgerald, *The Chinese View of their Place in the World* (London, 1964).
90   H. R. Trevor-Roper, 'History and imagination', in H. Lloyd-Jones, V. Pearl and B. Worden (eds), *History and Imagination* (London, 1981). For an exploration of some of the problems involved, see J. Elster, *Logic and Society. Contradictions and Possible Worlds* (New York, 1978), particularly ch. 6.
91   Mills's own prescription in part, it will be recalled, was for a 'shuttle between two levels of abstraction *inside each phase* of our simplified two-step act of research' – that is, 'in instituting the problem *and* in explaining it'.

according to whether the point of measurement was the Japanese surrender, or the enactment of the 1950 Marriage Law, or the subsequent collectivization of agriculture.[92] Likewise, the social changes which the war engendered for women in the United States can appear less profound if viewed within a perspective that takes in the new (and, as D'Ann Campbell for one would argue, unrelated) feminist challenge of the 1970s and 1980s, rather than within one that stops short in the 1950s and 1960s, where 'the "suburban" ideal of companionate, child-centred marriages, with little scope for careerism, can be seen as a major result of the interaction between the values of the people and the disruption of the war'.[93]

Differences in time-frame could also be partly responsible for contrasting judgements regarding the effects of the war on the position of the black population of the United States, together with both black and white attitudes over the racial question. One notes, for example, that Lewis Coser was writing in the mid-1950s when he argued that 'one result of the war seems to have been an increase in Negro–white solidarity',[94] whereas it was in 1968 that Richard Dalfiume – quoting James Baldwin: 'a certain hope died, a certain respect for white America faded' – concluded that 'when the expected white acquiescence in a new racial order did not occur, the ground was prepared for the civil rights revolution of the 1950s and 1960s; the seeds were indeed sown in the World War II years'.[95] (Historical judgements concerning the consequences of the war for the entire international system and the distribution of power within it may equally be affected by the choice of cut-off point and the moments at which the judgements themselves are formulated.)[96]

Clearly, however, this matter of time-frame is not the only prior issue which confronts the student of the impact of the war. There is also the question, for example, of whether one can establish certain broad categories of consequence – certain 'modes', as Arthur Marwick has termed them – through which this or any war has affected the societies

92   See Stacey, *Patriarchy and Socialist Revolution*; M. J. Meijer, *Marriage Law and Policy in the Chinese People's Republic* (Hong Kong, 1971); E. Croll, *Feminism and Socialism in China* (London, 1978); B. Siu, *Women of China: Imperialism and Women's Resistance, 1910–1949* (London, 1982); Spence, *Gate of Heavenly Peace*.

93   D. A. Campbell, *Women at War with America. Private Lives in a Patriotic Era* (Cambridge, Mass., 1984). Cf. N. T. Dodge, *Women in the Soviet Economy: their Role in Economic, Scientific and Technical Development* (Baltimore, Md, 1966).

94   L. Coser, *The Functions of Social Conflict* (New York, 1964), p. 94.

95   R. Dalfiume, 'The forgotten years of the Negro revolution', *Journal of American History*, vol. 55, (1968). And see Thorne, *Issue of War*, pp. 274–5; A. R. Buchanan, *Black Americans in World War II* (Santa Barbara, Ca, 1977); M. P. Motley (ed.), *The Invisible Soldier: the Experience of the Black Soldier in World War II* (Detroit, 1975).

96   See the appendix to ch. 9 of Thorne, *Issue of War*.

involved.[97] Or again, if one wishes to ask whether the war on balance increased or diminished the cohesion of a particular society, what means of measurement both lie to hand and are valid for the purpose? The indictable crime rate, for instance (employed along with other criteria, by Arthur Stein for one);[98] the rate of divorce and/or of industrial disputes; patterns of debate and voting in a legislature; the 'utilization of violence for the maintenance of [a] political system' (in which regard Stohl, for example, finds a 'persistent pattern' within the United States)?[99] Does one need in such contexts to take cognizance of the Simmel/Coser concept of 'conflict as a form of socialization'; or of Durkheim's contention that 'great popular wars', by 'at least temporarily caus[ing] a stronger integration of society', diminish impulses towards 'voluntary death' (together with crimes other than homicide), whereas other 'disturbances of the collective order' foster 'anomic suicide'?[100] Can there be any validity in applying to markedly different societies hypotheses formulated primarily in regard to those of a Western-industrialized nature? ('Cohesion decreases during the course of war', submits Stein, 'as a function of mobilization, despite any positive effects the war may have in bringing a society together.')[101] Might it not be necessary, when seeking to make comparisons among a wide range of societies, to identify criteria of cohesion/fission for each, in order to allow for, *inter alia*, distinctive structures and value-systems (one thinks, for example, of the effects of the war on marriage, women and the family in the United States and Japan respectively),[102] and only then, when relativity has thus been applied, draw up the international comparisons in question?

Obviously, there are those aspects of the immediate consequences of the war whose measurement is comparatively straightforward: the expansion of larger firms at the expense of smaller ones in Japan, for instance, or the flattening of the pyramid of the distribution of national wealth among

---

97   Marwick, *Britain in the Century of Total War*, ch. 1; and *War and Social Change in the 20th Century* (London, 1977). And see the discussion in the introduction to K. L. Nelson (ed.), *The Impact of War on American Life: The Twentieth Century Experience* (New York, 1971).

98   A. A. Stein, *The Nation at War* (Baltimore, Md, 1980), pp. 47ff.

99   M. Stohl, *War and Domestic Political Violence. The American Capacity for Repression and Reaction* (London, 1976), p. 95.

100   Coser, *Functions of Social Conflict*; E. Durkheim, *Suicide. A Study in Sociology*, trans. J. Spaulding and G. Simpson (London, 1952), pp. 204–8, 246, 352.

101   Stein, *Nation at War*, p. 53. Cf. the hypotheses advanced by Stohl, *War and Domestic Political Violence*, p. 64.

102   See, for example, Campbell, *Women at War*, and Nelson, 'Social effects', in *Impact of War on American Life*; D. Robins-Mowry, *The Hidden Sun. Women of Modern Japan* (Boulder, Co, 1983); and T. R. Havens, *Valley of Darkness. The Japanese People and World War Two* (New York, 1978). For recent reflections on cultural relativism in regard to illness, see A. Kleinman, *Social Origins of Distress and Disease. Depression, Neurasthenia and Pain in Modern China* (New Haven, Conn. 1987).

Americans; the increased employment of women in Britain or the widening gap between the numbers of females and males in the Soviet Union; the widening of the gap, also, between the larger landlords and the remainder in China's villages and between landowners and peasantry in the Philippines; the sharpening of inter-communal tension and conflict in Burma and Fiji. But how is one to measure, for example, that seemingly important dimension which Pocock terms 'change in a society's self-awareness' – change which, he argues, when 'widely disseminated' (as one might suppose could well occur in time of total war), embodies change for the society itself?[103]

We also encounter, of course, the problem of deciding what will constitute, in this cohesion/fission context, an acceptable level of generalization. After all, depending on which criteria were given major emphasis, one could develop arguments on both sides of this balance in the cases of, say, the United States or Japan – or even, perhaps, of France, where, for all the Vichy/Resistance and Communist/Gaullist divides, there was taking place after 1940, in Stanley Hoffmann's words, 'a kind of rediscovery of France and the French by the French'.[104] Certainly, if we look at the question of the impact of the war in more limited contexts than that of overall cohesion or fission, it is often a set of contrasting patterns that emerge, as Francis Merrill emphasized – he was writing in terms of 'social problems' – not long after the end of the conflict with reference to American society in particular:

World War II . . . exerted a differential effect upon the social structure of the United States, intensifying some problems and temporarily reversing others. Certain trends long evident in peacetime were modified by introducing variables which changed the situation in wartime. Even these variables, however, were not something new under the sun, but evolved out of the general cultural situation. These wartime variables assumed three general forms [economic, psychological and familial], each with its effect upon social problems.[105]

Complexity is more apparent still, as one would expect, when we change our perspective to a transnational one – notwithstanding the emergence of certain patterns which (when cultural relativity has been allowed for) cut across the divisions marked by state boundaries.[106] Here, too, in terms of, say, the enhancing or diminution of cohesion, we encounter a considerable number of variables: the pre-war structure of each society, together with

103 J. G. Pocock, *Politics, Language and Time* (London, 1972), pp. 15ff, 239.
104 S. Hoffmann, *France: Change and Tradition* (London, 1963), p. 58.
105 F. Merrill, *Social Problems on the Home Front* (New York, 1948), as included in Nelson, *Impact of War on American Life*.
106 See Thorne, *Issue of War*, ch. 8.

the nature and extent of the divisions within it ('Untouchables' within Indian society and *burakumin* in Japan, for example, were from the outset less likely to be moved towards dissent by wartime circumstances than were blacks in the US),[107] the defining of the war (notably, the nature and degree of threat perceived in relation to the whole, or only part, of the society, and whether the threat was seen as being, in Stein's phrase, 'amenable to a cooperative solution'),[108] and the manner of initial involvement in it – the contrast between say, Britain and Burma in both these respects being evident; the nature, degree and length of involvement in the conflict subsequently (the significance of this factor in regard to changing attitudes and diminishing cohesion within the United States is well known in the context of two later wars, Korea and Vietnam);[109] the existence or otherwise of an alternative focus of identity and loyalty for a section of society (not simply a current focus, as provided by their suffering homeland for the expatriate Chinese of Malaya, but an envisaged one, as provided for many Muslims within India by a Pakistan option that became much more prominent during the war years);[110] wartime conditions as regards independent dissenting action (in China, for example, the more favourable circumstances provided for the Communists by the Japanese invasion of 1937 onwards – though Barrington Moore, following Chalmers Johnson, probably overstates the contribution that this external factor made to the creation of a revolutionary situation);[111] the evenness or otherwise of the effects of the war on cultural change[112] (the economic and social contrasts between the north and south of Korea, for example, were exacerbated as the Japanese, under the exigencies of their fight against superior powers, increased the forced industrialization of the former, yet reduced their extraction of Korean rice as alternative supplies became available to them from Indo-China).[113]

107 See, for example, Barrington Moore, *Injustice: The Social Bases of Obedience and Revolt* (London, 1978), pp. 55ff, 489ff.   108 Stein, *Nation at War*, p. 11.

109 Ibid., passim, and, for example, J. E. Mueller, *War, Presidents, and Public Opinion* (New York, 1973).

110 See V. Purcell, *The Chinese in Southeast Asia* (Oxford, 1965); B. N. Pandey, *The Break-Up of British India* (London, 1969); and, in general, A. D. Smith, *The Ethnic Revival in the Modern World* (Cambridge, 1981).

111 Cf. B. Moore, *Social Origins of Dictatorship and Democracy: Lord and Peasant in the Making of the Modern World* (London, 1967), p. 223; C. A. Johnson, *Peasant Nationalism and Communist Power: the Emergence of Revolutionary China, 1937–1945* (Stanford, Ca, 1963), pp. 69 and passim; W. Hinton, *Fanshen. A Documentary of Revolution in a Chinese Village* (New York, 1968); Selden, *The Yenan Way*; Eastman, *Seeds of Destruction*; Skocpol, *States and Social Revolutions*, ch. 7.

112 See Gellner, *Thought and Change*, p. 166; W. F. Ogburn, 'Cultural lag as theory', in *On Culture and Social Change* (Chicago, 1964).

113 See B. Cumings, *The Origins of the Korean War: Liberation and the Emergence of Separate Regimes, 1945–1947* (Princeton, NJ, 1981), pp. 26ff.

A further variable – of particular interest as a corrective to analyses that treat an individual society in purely intra-mural terms – is constituted by the extent and nature of the international contacts that were brought about by the war. One level on which to view such processes and experience is obviously that of the individual.[114] They could also involve, however, directly or indirectly, a particular section of a society. Thus, just as the experience during the First World War of encountering European societies while serving overseas had left its mark upon black American soldiers and, through them, black attitudes more generally in the years immediately following that conflict,[115] so the arrival of black GIs between 1941 and 1945 in countries where racism was less entrenched and institutionalized than in the United States contributed to an increased determination to challenge the status quo at home once the war was over. (So, too, did the incompatibility of that status quo with the proclaimed war aims of the Allies,[116] together with the more forceful racism of some whites when faced with a new level of socio-economic challenge on the part of blacks as a consequence of wartime developments.[117])

On a third level, however, the war in many instances brought about significant developments of a broader kind still, in what Giddens has termed 'the forms of contact – and often of interdependence – between different structural types of society', such contacts constituting, as he puts it, 'edges of potential or actual social transformation, the often unstable intersections between different modes of social organisation'.[118] Amidst the

---

114 See, for example, Thorne, *Issue of War*, p. 276.

115 See, E. D. Cronon, *Black Moses. Marcus Garvey and the Universal Negro Improvement Association* (Madison, Wis., 1969), ch. 2.

116 The subject of wartime propaganda and social change is one that could be pursued in its own right. See, for example, McLaine, *Ministry of Morale*; Winkler, *The Politics of Propaganda*; J. Hilvert, *Blue-Pencil Warriors: Censorship and Propaganda in World War Two* (St Lucia, Queensland, 1984); M: Anglo, *Service Newspapers of the Second World War* (London, 1977); R. Manvell, *Films and the Second World War* (London, 1974); A. Rhodes, *Propaganda: the Art of Persuasion: World War II* (London, 1976); K. R. M. Short (ed.), *Film and Radio Propaganda in World War II* (Knoxville, Tenn., 1983); L. W. Doob, *Public Opinion and Propaganda* (Hamden, Conn., 1966).

117 See Thorne, *Issue of War*, pp. 184, 274–5; essay number 12 below; S. A. Stouffer, E. A. Suchman, L. C. DeVinney, S. A. Star, R. M. Williams, *The American Soldier: Adjustment during Army Life* (Princeton, NJ, 1949), ch. 10; S. Terkel (ed.), *'The Good War', An Oral History of World War Two* (New York, 1984), pp. 264ff., 279, 343ff., 366ff.; Motley, *The Invisible Soldier*; Dalfiume, 'The forgotten years of the Negro revolution'. One particularly interesting perspective on the contact between black GIs and British civilians, as emphasized by the Executive Secretary of the National Association for the Advancement of Colored Peoples following a visit to the UK, involved comparative income levels and what the same Walter White termed 'an economic bond of sympathy'. See Thorne, *Issue of War*, p. 276.

118 Giddens, *Contemporary Critique*, p. 23.

geopolitical ferment engendered by the conflict, such contacts[119] (already in existence before the war, of course, within the frameworks of, *inter alia*, European, US and Japanese imperial rule) could involve the sudden juxtaposing of two extremes among societies, as when the modern US war machine, with all its attendant skills, assumptions and attitudes (these last recorded in somewhat roseate terms by Margaret Mead), descended upon the 14,000 or so inhabitants of the Admiralty Islands.[120] They could also entail what in some ways were a more complex set of repercussions within one 'Western' society as a consequence of wartime changes of relationship with another. Thus Australia, its own shift towards industrialization greatly accelerated by the international circumstances of the time, nevertheless found itself, in the words of the Association of Chambers of Commerce in Queensland, with the 'superior national economy [of the United States] being imposed upon [its own]'. Stimulated by the local threat from Japan and the diminished protection afforded by a distant Britain to see themselves as a separate and independent nation with distinctive interests of their own, Australians none the less found themselves having to rely upon US military assistance, while at the same time both their social mores and (it has been argued) their readiness after the war to accept immigrants of non-British stock were influenced by the (often friction-engendering) presence in their midst of large numbers of aliens who were products of the United States's proclaimed 'melting pot' and who had brought with them American attitudes to consumption, management and other aspects of 'modern' industrial and commercial existence.[121] Even the circumstances of the country's aboriginal population were soon to be viewed, by some Australians at least, in the light of external proclamations and expectations regarding the treatment of minorities and the underprivileged.[122]

It would be misleading, however, to conclude even a brief and highly selective survey of societies and the international during the Second World War with an emphasis upon change alone. Just as a new, wartime acquaint-

119 One could include under this heading contacts that for the time being, at least, remained in the realm of the mind only. Thus, for example, the achievements of the Red Army and of the Soviet Union generally during the war appear to have made a considerable impression on many of the young, in particular, in Southeast Asia at the time.

120 M. Mead, *New Lives for Old: Cultural Transformation: Manus, 1928–1953* (New York, 1961). Cf. E. Feldt, *The Coast Watchers* (London, 1967), p. 220. And see, regarding the growing intrusion of 'the modern' in Fiji, Scarr, *Fiji*, pp. 358ff.

121 See R. J. Bell, *Unequal Allies* (Melbourne, 1977), and 'Testing the open door thesis in Australia, 1941–1946', *Pacific Historical Review*, vol. 51, no. 3, 1982; J. H. Moore, *Over-Paid, Over-Sexed, and Over Here: Americans in Australia, 1941–1945* (St Lucia, Queensland, 1981); Thorne, Issue of War, chs 7 and 8; E. and A. Potts, *Yanks Down Under, 1941–5. The American Impact on Australia* (Melbourne, 1985).

122 S. N. Stone (ed.), *Aborigines in White Australia* (London, 1974), p. 191.

ance with other peoples often induced in those involved an insular rejection of the foreign and a reinforced adherence to existing domestic norms and aspirations,[123] so there were strong social continuities that, in the short run at least, defied the material and mental assaults that had accompanied total war. To say as much is not, of course, to deny the extent of change that was being precipitated during these years in, say, China and Yugoslavia. But to the non-specialized eye, at least, it is sometimes the tenacity of pre-war structures, hierarchies and mores (the membership, power and influence of the bureaucracy and the *zaibatsu* in the 'new', post-MacArthur Japan, for example, together with what Fukutake terms the 'familistic' basis of much of that country's social organization)[124] which is remarkable in retrospect, not least when set against massive upheavals in the international fortunes and position of the state concerned.

But then, again, such continuities, too, could owe something to developments of an international kind (for the Japanese, for instance, the onset of the Cold and Korean Wars in the Far East and the associated shifts in US occupation policies – developments accompanied by changes in the entire international system).[125] The conclusion must remain that if we wish, with Philip Abrams and Peter Burke, to see the further development of 'a social history or historical sociology . . . concerned both with understanding from within and explaining from without; with the general and with the particular'; of analyses that will 'combine the sociologist's acute sense of structure with the historian's equally sharp sense of change',[126] then we should at the same time foster the adoption of international perspectives among sociologists, as well as sociological perspectives (both transnational and national) among historians and theorists of international relations.

123 See Thorne, *Issue of War*, p. 276; I. de S. Pool, 'Effects of cross-national contact on national and international images', in H, C. Kelman (ed.), *International Behavior* (New York, 1966); M. Mead, 'The application of anthropological techniques to cross-national communication', in *Anthropology: A Human Science*.

124 Fukutake, *Japanese Social Structure*, pp. 84, 145, 153; C. Johnson, *MITI and the Japanese Miracle* (Stanford, Ca. 1982), pp. 172ff.

125 See, for example, M. Schaller, *The American Occupation of Japan. The Origins of the Cold War in Asia* (New York, 1985). For recent, brief examinations of current international issues from the perspective of societal change, see two Council on Foreign Relations publications: A. J. Pierre (ed.), *A Widening Atlantic? Domestic Change and Foreign Policy* (New York, 1986); A. D. Romberg (ed.), *The United States and Japan. Changing Societies in a Changing Relationship* (New York, 1987).

126 Burke, *Sociology and History*, p. 30; Abrams, *Historical Sociology*, p. 315 and passim. And see the appendix, 'Social science as public philosophy', to R. N. Bellah, R. Madsen, W. M. Sullivan, A. Swidler, S. M. Tipton, *Habits of the Heart. Individualism and Commitment in American Life* (Berkeley, Ca, 1985).

Part II

Conflict and Cooperation among the Western Democracies

A concern with certain sociological dimensions of international affairs, advanced in the preceding essay, is reflected again in the broad study of Anglo-American relations which follows. The elements in question, it seems to me, going well beyond expressions of 'public opinion' on this or that issue of the day,[1] have often contributed significantly to the course of inter-state dealings, where conflict and cooperation between proclaimed 'friends' – even allies – are frequently mingled.

To suggest as much, however, is not to minimize the importance of those immediate processes of foreign policy decision-making and of related exchanges between governments. And the group of essays in Part II is particularly concerned with this level of international history, incorporating as it does the responses of officials to what they perceived as 'public opinion', together with debates within what have been termed 'foreign policy communities', overlapping the official and the non-official worlds and illustrated here by the Royal Institute of International Affairs in London. The essays deal in particular with relations among those Western democracies (I include Australia in that designation) which came together between 1941 (some earlier) and 1945 in the face of German, Italian and Japanese aggression. The Anglo-American survey apart, the subjects taken are specific aspects of these intra-Western dealings, especially ones pertaining to questions of empire and to the shifting balances of power among the states concerned. In other words, the focus in each case is a restricted one, and the studies need to be set alongside others of a broader kind: those surveying this or that bilateral relationship in its entirety, for

1 For suggestions regarding one particular, socio-political element in the shaping of US post-war foreign relations, see my *American Political Culture and the Asian Frontier, 1943–1973* (London, 1988).

example,[2] and those that adopt a wider perspective still, involving changes in international structures, domestic societies and currents of ideas which surrounded, influenced and in return were influenced by developments among the Western states themselves.[3]

2 For example, H. G. Nicholas, *The United States and Britain* (Chicago, 1975); D. C. Watt, *Succeeding John Bull: America in Britain's Place, 1900–1975* (Cambridge, 1984); C. Thorne, *Allies of a Kind. The United States, Britain, and the War Against Japan, 1941–1945* (London, 1978); R. J. Bell, *Unequal Allies* (Melbourne, 1977); J. B. Hurstfield, *America and the French Nation, 1939–1945* (Chapel Hill, 1986).

3 For example, H. Bull and A. Watson (eds), *The Expansion of International Society* (London, 1984); A. DePorte, *Europe Between the Superpowers* (New Haven, Conn., 1979); C. Thorne, *The Issue of War, States, Societies and the Far Eastern Conflict of 1941–1945* (London, 1985); P. Calvocoressi and G. Wint, *Total War* (London, 1972); G. Wright, *The Ordeal of Total War, 1939–1945* (New York, 1968); H. Tinker, *Race, Conflict and the International Order* (London, 1977); H. Grimal, *La Decolonisation, 1919–1963* (Paris, 1965); W. R. Louis, *Imperialism At Bay* (Oxford, 1977).

4

The Near and the Far: Aspects of Anglo-American Relations, 1919–1945

At the heart of Winston Churchill's famous 'Iron Curtain' speech at Fulton, Missouri, 40 years ago lay his conception of what he called 'the fraternal association of the English-speaking peoples': his conviction as to what the essential nature of that 'special relationship' had been in the past, and his vision of what it could and should constitute in the future. It was a conception that, in broad terms, had been shared by others over a lengthy period, of course: by those who had founded The Pilgrims at the beginning of the century, for example; by those, such as Sir Evelyn Wrench, who had nurtured the English-Speaking Union; by Henry Stimson, for one, in the United States, for all his reservations about British approaches to international politics.[1] 'The long future and safety and happiness of both America and Great Britain', wrote the financier Thomas Lamont in 1917, 'are dependent upon these two great nations working in accord. The peace of the whole world is dependent upon the same thing. Both nations are, in the last analysis, animated by the same ideals, working for the same ends. . . . If it were geographically possible, the two nations ought almost to become one.'[2]

This essay was written for a conference held at Westminster College, Fulton, Missouri, in the spring of 1986 to mark the fortieth anniversary of the 'Iron Curtain' speech by Winston Churchill at the same institution.

1 See, for example, H. A. Allen, *A History of Anglo-American Relations* (London, 1954), ch. 5; J. E. Wrench, *Immortal Years, 1937–1944* (London, 1946); Stimson diary, entry for 11 May 1943, Henry L. Stimson Papers, Sterling Memorial Library, Yale University; C. Thorne, *The Limits of Foreign Policy. The West, the League and the Far Eastern Crisis of 1931–1933* (London and New York, 1972), passim; Thorne, *Allies of a Kind. The United States, Britain and the War against Japan, 1941–1945* (London and New York, 1978), e.g. p. 277; H. B. Ryan, *The Vision of Anglo-America* (Cambridge, 1987).

2 Lamont memo. for Lord Reading, n.d. (1917): 'Ways to bring about a closer union and to

There have been those historians, too, who have perceived Anglo-American relations in the twentieth century in essentially the same light. Indeed, one of them, Professor Harry Allen, writing in 1952, could envisage that Lamont's passing reflection might even become a reality: that 'it was by no means beyond the range of possibility that the deed of 1776 might in some sense be undone'.[3] And yet, of course, one has only to recall the strong and widespread reaction in the United States against Churchill's Fulton speech[4] to be reminded of how different was the approach of many other contemporaries to the transatlantic relationship, just as among subsequent historians, too, there have been many whose basic analyses stand in sharp contrast to the one put forward by Allen. Churchill's belief in a 'fraternal association', argues Correlli Barnett, was no more than a 'romantic British myth' which 'had already exercised so calamitous an effect on British policy in the past'; a myth which, in guiding the Prime Minister's war-time policies, enabled the United States, that 'lurking menace to British interests', to fulfil 'the long-cherished ambition . . . of humbling British world power'.[5] 'In the end', concludes Professor Donald Watt, 'the story of how America came to occupy "Britain's place" [in the world] is . . . a tragic one, a story of failures and missed opportunities, of misguided attitudes and misunderstandings, from which both nations have suffered.'[6] Even if we shift our focus to a more restricted sphere of Anglo-American relations since the First World War – to, say, the economic and financial dealings between the two countries in the years immediately following that conflict – there, too, there is a marked difference of historical emphasis between, for example, Michael Hogan, who is struck by the degree of collaboration that developed between London and Washington (or more often, London and New York), and his fellow-American Frank Costigliola, for whom it is rivalry and tension that stand to the fore.[7]

Such contrasting views among both contemporaries and historians constitute only one among many problems when it comes to drawing up

improve the relations between America and Great Britain', box 81 folder 12, Thomas W. Lamont Papers, Baker Library, Harvard Business School.

3 Allen, *Anglo-American Relations*, p. 128.

4 See, for example, R. M. Hathaway, *Ambiguous Partnership. Britain and America, 1944–1947* (New York, 1981), pp. 239–42. Also F. Harbutt, *The Iron Curtain, Churchill, America, and the Origins of the Cold War* (Oxford, 1987), and R. Edmonds, *Setting the Mould. The United States and Britain, 1945–50* (Oxford, 1986).

5 C. Barnett, *The Collapse of British Power* (London, 1972), p. 589.

6 D. C. Watt, *Succeeding John Bull. America in Britain's Place, 1900–1975* (Cambridge, 1984), p. 23.

7 M. J. Hogan, *Informal Entente. The Private Structure of Cooperation in Anglo-American Economic Diplomacy, 1918–1928* (Columbia, Missouri, 1977); F. Costigliola, 'Anglo-American financial rivalry in the 1920s', *Journal of Economic History*, vol. 37, 1977, and *Awkward Dominion. American Political, Economic and Cultural Relations with Europe, 1919–1933* (Ithaca, NY, 1984).

some kind of broad summary on the course and nature of Anglo-American relations between the end of the First World War and the end of the Second. Of course, there continues to be substance in the rueful observation made by Richard Heindel at the outset of his own study of American influences on Britain early in the present century: 'Nearly everyone will commit himself with startling authority to an opinion on Anglo-American affairs.'[8] Yet the more one learns and reflects on this rich and complex subject, the more unsatisfactory do most broad statements about it become. For this reason, and given the limited space available, the first part of this essay will seek to turn this difficulty to advantage by making the very problem itself the initial focus of attention: not in order to evoke sympathy for the student charged with the task of overcoming it, but rather as a way of drawing out some, at least, of the complexities of the historical Anglo-American relationship which is our concern.

Let us begin with the matter of periodization. This can often cause problems for the historian, of course, and certainly there is nothing particularly outlandish about taking as the outer limits of the present topic the endings of two major wars in which the British, the Americans and much of the world around them were involved. But the implications of those limits do need to be noted and alternative possibilities borne in mind. For example, if we were to decide that one significant aspect of Anglo-American relations has lain in the realm of ideas and assumptions current among the two peoples about their respective places in the world – about the opportunities and obligations facing each of them and the 'Anglo-Saxon' race in general; about empire and war, science and industry; about 'progress' and 'the modern' and the meaning and dynamics of history – then there could be much to be said for taking as our starting-point not 1919, but somewhere around the 1890s (not least, at the time of the Spanish-American war), when, as Robert Rydell's valuable study of the great international expositions that were held across the United States has shown us, the millions who crowded into those triumphant pavilions – in St Louis in 1904, for example – were imbibing or having confirmed for them notions that, *mutatis mutandis*, were very similar to the ones that were widely accepted in the Britain of Seeley, Kipling and the Imperial Jubilees.[9] Certainly, it is to this same initial period that we must look if we are concerned about, not only a new level of involvement on the international scene on the part of the United States, but more particularly the shaping in consequence (through difficulties over Venezuela, the Panama Canal and

8 R. H. Heindel, *The American Impact on Great Britain, 1898–1914* (New York, 1968), p. vii.
9 R. W. Rydell, *All The World's a Fair. Visions of Empire at American International Expositions, 1876–1916* (Chicago, 1984); and cf. for example M. Howard, 'Empire, race and war in pre-1914 Britain', in H. Lloyd-Jones et al. (eds), *History and Imagination* (London, 1981).

the Alaskan boundary, for instance) of a new *modus vivendi* between Washington and London, accompanied by a heightened mutual awareness, new associations, and evolving sets of images about each other's society. [10]

Yet if the period in Anglo-American relations that preceded the First World War – what Bradford Perkins chose to call 'the great rapprochment' – gives us one major thread which runs through to the vision expounded by Churchill in 1946, a thread blending the notion of 'kinship' with that of shared values, destinies and duties, it also provides evidence of a different kind. Even if the perceived conflicts of interest between the two states were not such after 1896 as those which had brought Lord Salisbury to observe in that year that war 'in the not distant future' had become 'something more than a possibility', [11] they existed none the less. And if a further thread that could be followed through to 1946 begins in the years before 1914 with the growing determination on the British side to avoid a confrontation over such differences (Churchill, it will be recalled, went so far in 1944 as to assure the Commonwealth Prime Ministers in private that the interests of Britain and the United States 'could not clash' [12]), yet another would link the outcry over the Fulton speech with, for example, the angry reaction among Americans in 1911 against the public assurance given in London by the commander of the US Navy's Atlantic Fleet that his country would stand by Britain to the last ship, man and dollar. [13]

One could argue, however, that there is another major theme to be traced in Anglo-American relations in the present century which, if deemed to be of greater significance than notions of either kinship or separateness, would lend itself to a point of departure, not in 1919, nor in the 1890s, but in 1916. That theme, of course, is the drastic and rapid shift in the balance of resources and power between the two countries, a shift dramatically accelerated by the Great War. 'If things go on as present', the Chancellor of the Exchequer warned the Cabinet in London in October 1916, 'I venture to say with certainty that by next June or earlier the President of the American Republic will be in a situation, if he wishes, to dictate his terms to us.' [14] (By this time, 40 per cent of Britain's war expenditure was being swallowed up by supplies from North America, and well before the actual entry of the United States into the conflict, Britain 'no longer had control over her external financial affairs', in Kathleen Burk's words, 'but

10 See Allen, *Anglo-American Relations*; A. E. Campbell, *Great Britain and the United States, 1895–1903* (London, 1960); Heindel, *American Impact*; B. Perkins, *The Great Rapprochement. England and the United States, 1895–1914* (London, 1969).
11 Quoted in Campbell, *Great Britain and the US*, p. 31.
12 See Thorne, *Allies*, p. 384.
13 Perkins, *The Great Rapprochement*, p. 294.
14 Quoted in K. Burk, *Britain, America, and the Sinews of War, 1914–1918* (London, 1985), p. 81.

was at the mercy of events and the American government'.[15]) And McKenna's summary of the new, underlying realities of the relationship was to be echoed only a shade less dramatically when the war itself had long passed, in 1928, by the Foreign Office's Robert Craigie, in a survey which is a cardinal document for our subject.[16] 'In the realm of finance', he wrote, 'good relations with the United States are for this country so valuable as to be almost essential', and he went on to summarize what he saw as 'a phenomenon for which there is no parallel in our modern history – a state twenty-five times as large, five times as wealthy, three times as populous, twice as ambitious, almost invulnerable, and at least our equal in prosperity, vital energy, technical equipment and industrial science'.

By 1944, other Foreign Office officials, like Keynes at the Treasury, were to be closer still to repeating McKenna's 1916 analysis of the situation. 'In order to preserve the good relations required [to secure vital post-war American financial assistance]', wrote the Head of the North American Department, 'we may well find ourselves forced to follow the United States in a line of policy with which we do not fundamentally agree.' 'Far from being the world's largest creditor', the Chancellor of the Exchequer now warned his colleagues, 'we shall have become at the end of the war the world's largest debtor.'[17] A mere 30 years, in other words, and the Anglo-American balance has been radically changed.

With this particular theme in mind, one could suggest alternatives, even, to the seemingly obvious choice of 1945 as a *terminus ad quem* for a study such as the present one: 1943, perhaps, when Britain attained the fullest extent of its mobilization for war, and when her junior status within the alliance began, to some at least, to become apparent;[18] or 1944, when, at the Second Quebec Conference, the consequences for the relationship of Britain's near-ruin, financially, made themselves felt to a new degree. (Much lay behind Churchill's resentful question to the President regarding aid during Stage II of the war: 'What do you want me to do? Get on my hind legs and beg like Fala?'[19]) And yet such an emphasis, and such a periodization in consequence, would itself not be immune to questioning. If we were to focus, rather, on the degree of collaboration between London and Washington, and on the notion of a 'world role' being, as it were, transferred from Britain to the United States, then arguably the period 1947–9 would provide a more suitable stopping-point than the surrender of

15 Ibid. p. 94.
16 *Documents on British Foreign Policy,* series 1A, vol. V (London, 1973), no. 490.
17 See Thorne, *Allies,* pp. 387, 503.
18 See, for example, Thorne, *Allies,* ch. 10 and W. F. Kimball, *Churchill and Roosevelt. The Complete Correspondence,* vol. II (Princeton, NJ, 1984), pp. 596ff.
19 See Thorne, *Allies,* ch. 17, and Kimball, *Churchill and Roosevelt,* vol. III, pp. 318ff.

Germany and Japan – bearing in mind the crucial role played by Ernest Bevin in the realization of the Marshall Plan and in the creation of NATO, the withdrawal, none the less, of Britain from Palestine as well as India, and from standing guard over Greece and Turkey, and the concurrent development in Washington of those attitudes and assumptions concerning international affairs that became embodied in what Daniel Yergin has termed 'the national security state'.[20]

This last reflection directs us towards a further problem for the student of Anglo-American relations, beyond, though linked to, that of theme and periodization: that is, the difficulties and, indeed, potential distortion, involved in maintaining an essentially bilateral perspective. On this complication – which deserves a paper to itself – three broad observations must suffice here. The first is that the fundamental alteration in the structure of the entire international system that took place between the turn of the century and the end of the Second World War – a complete 'system change', to adopt Robert Gilpin's terminology – was not simply a 'background' against which Anglo-American relations were played out, but was integral to the shifts and strains, even to some of the achievements, of that relationship itself.[21] We will return below to the related question of the consequences of this rapid and drastic change in terms of the often-uncertain perceptions of many of those responsible for US and British policies,[22] and of the dealings between them. Meanwhile, as examples of particular ingredients that contributed to that 'system change', we could refer to, say, scientific, technological and industrial developments – directly affecting Anglo-American relations in regard to the competition for oil supplies, for instance, as Dr Stoff for one has demonstrated;[23] or to the

20 See, for example, Hathaway, *Ambiguous Partnership*; A. Bullock, *Ernest Bevin: Foreign Secretary* (London, 1983); K. O. Morgan, *Labour in Power, 1945–1951* (Oxford, 1985), ch. 6; D. Yergin, *Shattered Peace. The Origins of the Cold War and the National Security State* (London, 1978). On these and other aspects which span the 1945 dividing line, see D. Reynolds, 'Roosevelt, Churchill, and the wartime Anglo-American alliance, 1939–1945: Towards a new synthesis', in W. R. Louis and H. Bull (eds), *The 'Special Relationship'. Anglo-American Relations since 1945* (Oxford, 1986).

21 See, for example, A. W. DePorte, *Europe Between the Superpowers* (New Haven, Conn., 1979); R. Gilpin, *War and Change in World Politics* (Cambridge, 1981); H. Bull and A. Watson (eds), *The Expansion of International S. .ty* (London, 1984).

22 On this topic in general, see, for example, J. Joll, 'The ideal and the real: Changing concepts of the international system, 1815–1982', *International Affairs*, spring 1982; C. Thorne, *The Issues of War. States, Societies, and the Far Eastern Conflict, 1941–1945* (London and New York, 1985), ch. 2; E. R. May, *'Lessons' of the Past* (London, 1975); D. C. Watt, 'Every war must end. War-time planning for post-war security in Britain and America in the Wars of 1914–18 and 1939–45', *Transactions of the Royal Historical Society*, 5th series, vol. 28, 1978.

23 M. B. Stoff, *Oil, War, and American Security* (New Haven, Conn., 1980).

consequences and repercussions of the Bolshevik revolution, a challenge flung down to Western liberals and conservatives alike, and so great a preoccupation in both Washington and London in the early 1920s, in relation to domestic, as well as international, stability;[24] or again, to changes associated with the upsurge of nationalisms outside the Western world, so copious a source of suspicion and tension between the British and the American publics and their respective governments.[25]

Secondly, the adoption of a strictly bilateral perspective for our subject could obscure the extent to which, for all its own refusal to acknowledge that it was essentially a European state, Britain in this period shared in certain dissatisfactions and resentments regarding the United States that had a wider, 'European' basis (or, to be more accurate, were common to several countries in Western Europe); and could obscure, too, the extent to which, in the reverse direction, American suspicion or resentment that encompassed Britain – as over the Lausanne Agreement of 1932, for example – could be directed essentially against a wider grouping of states and peoples whose political cultures and bases of identity stood in generic contrast to those of America and who went under the 'European' label.[26] (Many Britons at the time, suggests A. J. P. Taylor, 'never realized that even the most friendly Americans, including Wilson and House, looked on all Europeans as aboriginal savages – a mistake repeated by Winston Churchill in regard to F[ranklin] D. Roosevelt and Harry Hopkins during the Second World War . . . One set of savages might be a bit better than another; but all needed saving by the superior enlightenment of the New World.'[27])

Thirdly – and obviously – something more than a rigidly bilateral perspective is required if we are to appreciate the ways in which the course of the Anglo-American relationship was affected by specific third parties: by France, for example, between 1919 and 1933 in regard to such matters as disarmament, debts, reparations, and indeed the entire nature of the post-war international order;[28] by the Soviet Union and China among

24 See L. C. Gardner, *Safe for Democracy. The Anglo-American Response to Revolution, 1913–1923* (New York, 1984); also, for example, W. B. Fowler, *British-American Relations, 1917–1918. The Role of Sir William Wiseman* (Princeton, NJ, 1969), p. 284, and Costigliola, *Awkward Dominion*, pp. 41ff.

25 See, for example, Thorne, *Allies*; W. R. Louis, *Imperialism at Bay* (Oxford, 1977), and 'American anti-colonialism and the dissolution of the British Empire', *International Affairs*, summer 1985.

26 See, for example, S. P. Huntington, *American Politics: the Promise of Disharmony* (Cambridge, Mass., 1981), ch. 2, pp. 42ff. and 236–7; also, Thorne, *Limits*, pp. 308ff. and Burk, *Sinews of War*, p. 221.

27 A. J. P. Taylor, *The Troublemakers* (London, 1985), p. 157.

28 See, for example, M. P. Leffler, *The Elusive Quest. America's Pursuit of European Stability and French Security, 1919–1933* (Chapel Hill, NC, 1979), pp. 190–2; B. J. McKercher, *The Second*

others during the Second World War;[29] and, not least, throughout the period under review, by the Dominions.[30] The ways in which Irish issues, for instance, impinged upon the relationship – in 1922 and in the early stages of the Second World War – need no underlining. Over the abandonment of the Anglo-Japanese alliance, the return of Britain to the gold standard in 1925 and her tariff policies in the 1930s, London's dealings with Washington had a strong Commonwealth dimension to them. Canada, especially, was frequently seen in Whitehall as in danger of slipping or being pulled into America's orbit, while it was Churchill himself who, in 1922, warned that if Britain were to concede naval superiority to the United States it would indicate to the Dominions as a whole 'that a new centre had been created for the Anglo-Saxon world' – the kind of cry that was to be heard again, regarding Australia and New Zealand in particular, between 1942 and 1945. Conversely, however, it was also acknowledged in London that, as Craigie put it in his memorandum of 1928 that has already been cited, 'any policy of estrangement from the United States would put a great strain on inter-imperial ties'. What was needed, argued Walter Lippmann from the American side in 1942, was the development of a completely new 'philosophy and doctrine about the changing relationships between the United States, the British Commonwealth, and the British Empire', in the context of 'the mighty changes now going on in the world'.[31]

Like the choice of dominant theme, and hence of periodization, then, the need to bring to bear developments regarding the international system as a whole, mutual perceptions between the United States and Europe, and the influence of third parties must complicate any attempt to survey Anglo-American relations over a period spanning from somewhere around the First World War to somewhere around the conclusion of the Second. Moreover, even if we confine ourselves for the moment to the bilateral

Baldwin Government and the United States, 1924–1929 (Cambridge, 1984), p. 112; D. P. Silverman, *Reconstructing Europe after the Great War* (Cambridge, Mass., 1982), p. 41.

29 See, for example, Thorne, *Allies*, passim, and Kimball, *Churchill and Roosevelt*, vol. I, pp. 400ff., vol. II, pp. 596ff.

30 On this topic in general see, for example, R. F. Holland, *Britain and the Commonwealth Alliance, 1918–1939* (London, 1981), pp. 36, 208; N. Mansergh, *The Commonwealth Experience* (London, 1969); C. A. MacDonald, *The United States, Britain, and Appeasement, 1936–1939* (New York, 1981) pp. 22–5; Thorne, *Allies*, pp. 148–9; Costigliola, *Awkward Dominion*, pp. 128–30. On Britain, the US and Canada, see, for example, Watt, *Succeeding John Bull*, p. 43; Holland, *Britain and the Commonwealth Alliance*, pp. 72, 146–7; T. Jones, *A Diary with Letters, 1931–1950* (London, 1954), p. 50; McKercher, *Second Baldwin Government*, p. 169; R. Ovendale, *'Appeasement' and the English-Speaking World. Britain, the United States, the Dominions, and the Policy of 'Appeasement', 1937–1939* (Cardiff, 1975), pp. 29ff.

31 Quoted in Thorne, *Allies*, pp. 148–9.

relationship alone in the realm of 'high politics', we encounter sufficient sharp variations within our period to render once more an attempt at overall generalization hazardous. Consider, for example, the contrast between the situation in 1920 and the one that obtained between 1922 and 1925. In 1920 the debt question and other issues were prompting Lloyd George and Churchill in Cabinet, like Keynes among others, to refer to the United States as a major threat – perhaps now *the* major threat – to Britain, and as Craigie for one saw and later summarized it, 'the great mass of the [American] population was ill-disposed towards [the United Kingdom]'.[32] Yet a very different set of circumstances developed between 1922 and 1925, with debt repayments agreed, the Washington Conference treaties signed, and the Irish Free State in being. At the same time, what Hogan has termed a 'creditor entente' was emerging, involving the Federal Reserve Bank and the Bank of England as well as J. P. Morgan and Morgan Grenfell, in regard to reparations, Austrian and German stabilization schemes, and an American conception of the entire post-war international economic order that was sustained by Britain's return to the gold standard. And in this period, too, the Anglo-Persian and Jersey Standard oil companies, like Marconi and the Radio Corporation of America, were reaching a *modus vivendi* in overseas territories. ('Better Americans than Bolsheviks', wrote Eyre Crowe in the Foreign Office where the Persian oil carve-up was concerned.[33])

A further series of fairly rapid and drastic oscillations is apparent in this field of Anglo-American 'high politics' (embracing the press and public opinion in both countries) if we turn our attention to the period 1927 to 1932. There is no need to spell out in detail how strained transatlantic relations became in 1927–8 over the continuing issue of belligerent rights at sea, the breakdown of the Geneva naval negotiations and the achievement of an Anglo-French compromise on arms limitation. 'There are at present', wrote Craigie, 'all the factors which in the past have made for wars between States', and such a prospect – talked about by Hoover and the British ambassador, Esme Howard – was indeed examined at a detailed, practical level by Howard's staff. For Churchill (who even before the 1927 confrontations had been describing the Americans as 'sunk in selfishness', and who in turn had been labelled by the State Department's William Castle as 'always . . . violently anti-American'), the major lesson to be drawn was that Britain must 'do [its] utmost to keep a Navy which as a

32 See T. Jones, *Whitehall Diary*, vol. 1 (ed. K. Middlemas, London, 1969), p. 117; R. Skidelsky, *John Maynard Keynes*, vol. 1 (London, 1983), p. 345; Craigie memo., 1928, see n. 16 above.

33 See, for example, Hogan, *Informal Entente*, pp. 57ff and chs. 6–8; Jones, *Whitehall Diary*, vol. 1, p. 198.

whole is stronger and better than that of the United States'; and at
Chartwell, as a guest recorded it, he 'talked very freely' about the other
country as being 'arrogant, fundamentally hostile to us . . . and wish[ing]
to dominate world politics'. No longer were Benjamin Strong and Montagu
Norman collaborating in complete harmony; indeed, over financial matters
Paris was now closer to New York than was London. Less was heard now,
on either side of the Atlantic, of the kinship of the Anglo-Saxons, and in the
American press it was not only the Hearst chain and other 'Big Navy'
supporters, but the likes of Lippmann's *New York World* as well which
directed fierce criticism eastwards.[34]

Among the senior officers of the US Navy itself, there were those in
whom the belief that preparations should be made for a possible war with
Britain was still very much alive in 1932, a year in which bitterness in
Washington over the notorious (and in most instances, falsely recounted)
'Stimson–Simon' exchanges regarding the Shanghai crisis was matched in
Whitehall and Westminster by the widespread (if private) expression of
equally bitter distrust and dislike of Americans, Austen and Neville
Chamberlain, Baldwin, and Sir Warren Fisher at the Treasury being
notable contributors.[35] And yet in between this episode and the 1927–8
confrontation, Hoover and Ramsay MacDonald, with the help of Charles
Dawes, Henry Stimson, Admiral William Pratt and Robert Craigie among
others, had achieved, not simply an easing of tensions over belligerent
rights and the delimiting of cruiser categories and tonnage, but a considerable renewal of fellow-feeling, the *New York Times*, for instance, being
able to describe MacDonald's 1929 visit to the United States as 'an over-
powering success'.[36]

Marked fluctuations of this kind, to give one final example, also stand
out in the period 1938–42. That last year alone, of course, witnessed a
considerable decline from that 'spirit of harmony and endeavour' which
Henry Stimson noted as 'pervading everybody' when the Service chiefs of
the two countries met at the Arcadia Conference in Washington in
December 1941.[37] And only three years before this, while Chamberlain's

34 See, for example, McKercher, *Second Baldwin Government*, pp. 83ff, 150ff; S. W. Roskill,
Naval Policy Between the Wars, vol. 1 (London, 1968), chs 12 and 14; Roskill, *Hankey, Man of
Secrets*, vol. II (London, 1972), pp. 439, 450ff; M. Gilbert, *Winston S. Churchill*, vol. V
(London, 1976), pp. 92, 301–8; Costigliola, *Awkward Dominion*, pp. 135, 204–5; Heindel,
American Impact, p. 131; A. Boyle, *Montague Norman* (London, 1967), pp. 225, 236; Jones,
Whitehall Diary, vol. II, pp. 147–51.
35 See Thorne, *Limits*, pp. 75–6, 122–3, 316–20, and passim.
36 See, for example, McKercher, *Second Baldwin Government*, p. 193; Roskill, *Naval Policy
Between the Wars*, vol. II (London, 1976), chs 1 and 2; D. Carlton, *MacDonald Versus Henderson*
(London, 1970), chs 5 and 6; D. Marquand, *Ramsay MacDonald* (London, 1977), p. 508.
37 Thorne, *Allies*, p. 134.

manoeuvrings *vis-à-vis* Germany had, in Dorothy Thompson's phrase of May 1938, 'brought British stock to an all time low' in the United States, there was little diminution of that distrust of Roosevelt in London which, not least as a consequence of the economic nationalism of the New Deal, had already come to overshadow the admiration which he had engendered at the outset of his Presidency. Indeed, as David Reynolds has observed, amid the mounting perils of 1938–9 'neither government *wanted* a close relationship' with the other – inclinations which carried over into the early part of 1940.[38]

Yet even if we were to plot such fluctuations as these with much greater precision, the result would again, of course, in some ways be misleading. For one thing, this would tend to conceal the importance of longer-term, underlying attitudes and assumptions about the relationship, and the very great differences that existed in this regard within each of the two countries. Consider, for example, the sharp contrasts that are to be found in this respect among the senior officers of the US Navy: between on the one hand the predilections of two officers already mentioned, Commodore Sims and Admiral Pratt, together with those of, say, Admiral Harold Stark, and on the other the Anglophobia of Admiral Ernest King, whose war-time distrust and dislike of his allies can be placed alongside those of the Army's General Albert Wedemeyer or General Joe Stilwell.[39] Or again, on the American side, one could point to the differing approaches to be found among financiers and businessmen in the 1920s: differences, as Joan Hoff Wilson has summarized them, attributable to occupation, geography, politics, dimensions of business and organizational structure; differences as between bankers and manufacturers, importers and exporters; differences wherein many prominent individuals and groups urged in 1922 that Washington should cancel or defer at least part of those inter-allied debt repayments that others were demanding, and wherein the National City Bank of New York and its collaborators called for the creation of a new and entirely American institutional structure for world finance and trade, as opposed to the collaborative, Anglo-American framework envisaged by the Chase National Bank and J. P. Morgan among others.[40]

---

38 D. Reynolds, *The Creation of the Anglo-American Alliance, 1937–1941* (London, 1981), pp. 286–7; and see, for example, Watt, *Succeeding John Bull*, pp. 65–6, 83–4; E. A. Rosen, *Hoover, Roosevelt and the Brains Trust. From Depression to New Deal* (New York, 1977), pp. 345ff; Ovendale, *'Appeasement'*, p. 137; Jones, *Diary with Letters*, pp. 432ff.

39 See the comment by Kimball, *Churchill and Roosevelt*, vol. II, p. 479.

40 See, for example, Leffler, *The Elusive Quest*, pp. 67–8; C. P. Parrini, *Heir to Empire. United States Economic Diplomacy, 1916–1923* (Pittsburgh, 1969), pp. 65, 191, 222; Silverman, *Reconstructing Europe*, pp. 19, 38, 157; J. H. Wilson, *American Business and Foreign Policy, 1920–1931* (Lexington, Kentucky, 1971), pp. xi–xii, 7–8, 15, 26, 124ff.

As for the British side of the relationship, a particularly interesting example of such complexities is provided by the political Left. Even before the First World War, many of those who would fall within this broad category had moved a long way from the enthusiasm that their predecessors had demonstrated at the time of the Civil War for the United States as, in A. J. P. Taylor's words, 'the symbol of advanced democracy'. Indeed, in the inter-war years anti-Americanism became, to quote Herbert Nicholas, 'almost a hallmark of . . . the Left' in Britain, an attitude only partially moderated by the coming of the New Deal, and still clearly in evidence in 1945, when, as Kenneth Morgan has put it, 'Pavlovian anti-Americanism was widespread on the Labour benches . . . with echoes of it in the pronouncements of Labour ministers such as [Aneurin] Bevan and even Dalton'. And yet, as a warning against the easy generalization, there stand, for example, those liberals and radicals who looked to Woodrow Wilson in particular to create a League of Nations and an international order beyond 'power politics' that would reflect the highest ideals of both countries; and from among them, Ramsay MacDonald in particular, delighting in his visits to the mid-West, continuing to see in the United States, in his biographer's words, 'a symbol of hope – . . . the land of democracy and social equality, where his values were more fully realized than in his own country'; convinced, even amidst the bitter exchanges of 1927–8, that there were 'no two peoples in [sic] the face of the earth that ought to be on terms of more friendly cooperation than America and ourselves' – a 'friendly cooperation' that was also to lie at the centre of Ernest Bevin's conception of the Labour Government's foreign policy after 1945.[41]

Whether it is broad political groupings or business and political elites that are under examination in the two countries, there are obviously changes over time to be borne in mind, and in this connection Professor Donald Watt in particular has provided us with helpful reflections on the significance for Anglo-American relations of generational change as well as of the socioeconomic backgrounds of the elites in question.[42] At the same time, a complete study of the relationship would require the pursuit of these themes beyond the realm of the elites themselves. Indeed, it could be argued that it is here that one encounters the most challenging of those

41 Taylor, *The Troublemakers*, p. 65; H. G. Nicholas, *The United States and Britain* (Chicago, 1975), p. 77; Campbell, *Great Britain and the US*, pp. 9–10; Heindel, *American Impact*, pp. 356, 416; E. R. May, *The World War and American Isolation, 1914–1917* (Cambridge, Mass., 1959), p. 6; Morgan, *Labour in Power*, p. 262; L. W. Martin, *Peace Without Victory* (New Haven, Conn., 1958); S. P. Tillman, *Anglo-American Relations at the Paris Peace Conference of 1919* (Princeton, NJ, 1961); Marquand, *Ramsay Macdonald*, p. 472; Bullock, *Ernest Bevin*, passim.
42 See Watt, *Succeeding John Bull*, e.g. pp. 13, 41–2, 49–50, and Watt, *Personalities and Policies* (London, 1965), pp. 41–2, 48–9; also e.g. P. Abrams, *Historical Sociology* (Shepton Mallet, 1982), ch. 8; R. Wohl, *The Generation of 1914* (London, 1980); and May, *'Lessons' of the Past*.

problems which have provided the focus of this essay so far. For what is all too often ignored, in the concentration upon the 'high politics' of the subject, is that ultimately we have to look at a series of relationships, not simply between two sets of governments and elites, but between two changing societies.

True, it is not difficult to see that certain of the features of each society during the period under review should be linked – however complex the actual causal connections themselves may turn out to be – to the course of the inter-state relationship. (The focus here is upon domestic developments influencing external patterns; but this is not to suggest, of course, that such developments were not themselves influenced by movements and pressures of an international kind.[43]) For example, some of the consequences for the relationship of the much greater growth of wealth in American than in British society have already been touched upon – even though it must be added that contemporaries often failed to appreciate the extent of what was taking place. (As Professor Kimball has suggested, Roosevelt was only one of many Americans who, in the midst of the Second World War, continued to accept 'the myth of British opulence'.) A transformation had already come over relations between the two countries between 1895 and 1918, argues Kathleen Burk, as a result in large part of 'Britain's relative economic decline'. Between 1913 and 1929, in which period the US share of world exports increased from 12.4 per cent to 16 per cent, those of Britain declined from 15.4 to 11.8 per cent, while for all the huge number of unemployed in the United States shortly before the Second World War, average per capita income there stood at US$525 as against a British figure of $425, a contrast which was to grow even greater during the war itself, of course.[44]

The potential relevance to the Anglo-American relationship is also clear enough in the case of changes in the ethnic composition of American society, with the number of English-born as a percentage of all foreign-born dropping from 9.8 to 5.7 per cent between 1890 and 1930, and with inhabitants of primarily British descent declining to around 50 per cent of the whole by 1950. Indeed, while on the one hand the concept of, and campaigning for, 'Americanization' (which, as Philip Gleason reminds us in the *Harvard Encyclopedia of American Ethnic Groups*, gathered strength around the time of the First World War, not least in the context of growing

43 See 'Societies, sociology and the international', essay number 3 above; and, for example, A. Giddens, *The Nation-State and Violence* (Cambridge, 1985).
44 Kimball, *Churchill and Roosevelt*, vol. III, p. 318; Burk, *Sinews of War*, pp. 1ff, 224; Costigliola, *Awkward Dominion*, p. 142; Allen, *Anglo-American Relations*, p. 32. For an epitomizing item in the war-time Churchill–Roosevelt correspondence, see Kimball, vol. I, pp. 648ff; also Thorne, *Allies*, pp. 384ff and 536–7.

fears of social revolution) came to arouse strong antipathy in part because
of its very association with that Anglo-Saxon racism that was referred to
above in relation to the world fairs, on the other hand any notion of
'kinship' with the English or British was also diminished by the awareness
of a distinctive 'Americanism' that was strengthening none the less; an
'Americanism' that was accompanied, in Gleason's words, by an 'ideological basis of American identity', by the renewed relevance of 'the
American Dream', and by the notion that it was the immigrant, not the
original settler, who was 'the archetypal American'. As Huntington
observes:

In the 1830s, Tocqueville could still inaccurately refer to Americans generally as
'Anglo-Americans'. A century later, the emergence of the term 'WASP' marked the
final phase in the demotion of the Anglo-American to the status of one ethnic group
among many and the end of any effort to define American national character in
ethnic rather than political terms.[45]

Already, however, we have moved into an area that, while of profound
importance for our subject, encompasses considerations that are far from
easy to pin down in causal terms as regards Anglo-American relations in
their totality. For we are dealing here with not merely the composition and
the domestic politics of the two societies, but also their respective cultures
and political cultures, and the developments that took place over 30 to 40
years in these respects: the perceptions of self and of the other; the myths as
well as the realities of the time. In other words, we would need to explore,
were space and time to permit and in terms of their possible consequences
for our particular international relationship, for example the differing
responses of the two societies in this period to the problems and challenges
presented by the advance of 'the modern': of rapidly increasing industrialization and new technology; of associated developments in the extent,
degree and complexity of international economic interrelationships; of
associated questions concerning the role of government.[46]

45 D. Snowman, *Kissing Cousins. An Interpretation of British and American Culture, 1945–1975*
(London, 1977), p. 25; S. Thernstrom (ed.), *Harvard Encyclopedia of American Ethnic Groups*
(Cambridge, Mass., 1980), pp. 31ff, 335; Huntington, *American Politics*, p. 27. By 1979, while
22.3 per cent of the US population traced their ancestry in an English (as distinct from
British) direction, 24.4 per cent were of Irish descent and 28.8 per cent of German: W. Issel,
Social Change in the United States, 1945–1983 (London, 1985), p. 9.
46 See, for example, Thorne, *Issue*, chs 2 and 3; Bull and Watson (eds), *The Expansion of
International Society*. Cf. however, the recent argument by David Reynolds ('A "special
relationship"? America, Britain and the international order since the Second World War',
International Affairs, winter 1985/6) that, since 1945 at least, 'domestic factors . . . have rarely
made a decisive difference to Anglo-American relations'. For a stimulating essay on
transatlantic cultural contrasts in regard to the entire process of industrialization, see M. J.

Thus, to take an obvious example, if it is agreed that the Anglo-American relationship was not unaffected by the coinciding of a major war-time shift to the left in British politics (culminating in the Labour landslide of 1945) with a strong 'rightward' trend in American politics – for all that the consequences of this coincidence were not always as great as many expected at the time – then the causes need to be traced both outwards and back, so to speak: traced to contrasts of experience, perception and aspiration regarding the Second World War itself, of course ('If British planners were anticipating a wave of radicalism at the war's end', as Professor Karl puts it, 'American planners were learning to anticipate exactly the opposite'[47]); but also beyond this: on the American side, not only to the formulation and modification of the New Deal, but to what happened, and why, to progressivism (itself an essentially backward-looking movement) around the time of the First World War, and to the underlying reasons why, in Huntington's words, 'change and reform in America can go only so far and no further'.[48] For this earlier war, Karl suggests, had been perceived as 'foreign, hence alien to the American experience', and thus as bearing in its dreadful course no message for Americans concerning a wider 'threat to traditional democracy in the logic of science or in the complex demands of technological advance'.[49] In contrast, there had emerged from that same war, as Keith Middlemas, for one, sees it, the beginnings within British society of 'a new form of political activity, as yet only half understood, but radically different from the pre-war system'; a form which, for all the magnitude of the changes that were to take place between 1940 and 1945 in terms of 'social relations between classes' and expectations of the state as 'the real guarantor of reform and reconstruction', was to carry through, in essence, until the 1960s.[50]

The analyses of Karl and Middlemas, of course, will by no means be universally accepted as having demonstrated the essence of the politics of

---

Wiener, *English Culture and the Decline of the Industrial Spirit, 1850–1980* (Cambridge, 1981). For an enquiry into ways in which societal differences have come to affect relations between the U.S. and Western Europe as a whole since World War Two, see A. J. Pierre (ed.), *A Widening Atlantic? Domestic Change and Foreign Policy* (New York, 1986).

47 B. D. Karl, *The Uneasy State. The United States from 1915 to 1945* (Chicago, 1983), p. 215. And see, for example, J. M. Blum, *V was for Victory. Politics and American Culture during World War II* (New York, 1976); R. Polenberg, *War and Society. The United States, 1941–1945* (Philadelphia, 1972); Morgan, *Labour in Power*, pp. 41, 44, 86, 156; P. Addison, *The Road to 1945* (London, 1975); Thorne, *Issue*, chs 8 and 9.

48 See Karl, *The Uneasy State*, pp. 160ff; Rosen, *Hoover, Roosevelt . . .*, p. 327 and passim; Huntington, *American Politics*, pp. 90, 107, 226; M. Davis, *Prisoners of the American Dream. Politics and Economy in the History of the US Working Class* (London, 1986).

49 Karl, *The Uneasy State*, p. 33; and, for example, Costigliola, *Awkward Dominion*, pp. 17–18; Nicholas, *the US and Britain*, p. 77.

50 K. Middlemas, *Politics in Industrial Society. The Experience of the British System Since 1911* (London, 1979), pp. 18, 150, 273–4.

'mass society' in each case. They are cited here simply in order to drive home the evident differences between the United States and Britain in this respect, and to suggest that such differences (together with any similarities that may be descried) should be thought of as relevant in an international relations, and not only in a 'comparative sociology', context. Nor is there space in this essay to explore further the numerous facets of the comparison itself: for example, what could be seen as something of a paradox in which a greater acceptance on the British side of 'collective' solutions to some of the most pressing problems of modern industrial society (solutions widely rejected among Americans in the name of 'rugged individualism') coexisted with a much greater pressure, in some respects, of the collective upon the individual within the United States. (In this regard, as ardent a British admirer of the Republic as Professor Allen refers to its society's 'emphasis on individualism yet lack of individuality', which has an echo, of course, of de Tocqueville's observations on 'so little true independence of mind' and 'the despotism of the majority'. Among the French clerisy in the 1920s the characteristic tended to be referred to as 'le Babbitisation' – which was perhaps a little unfair on George F. Babbit himself, who did at least give the traces a shake.[51])

This particular perceived contrast, whether accurate or not, was itself of some relevance to Anglo-American relations in our period. For the 'high politics' of their development cannot be divorced entirely from the conviction that was growing on both sides of the Atlantic in the 1920s especially (and here is one theme in which Britain in turn cannot be divorced from other parts of Europe) that in 'Americanization' – the growth of mass society, American style – lay the essential pattern of the future. 'The New Age that is America', Bertrand Russell called it in 1927, as Hollywood and the likes of F. W. Woolworth, J. Walter Thompson, Coca-Cola and Kodak made their presence increasingly felt in Western Europe.[52] And among the British, as among the French, there were those who embraced this vision with eagerness. Others were appalled by it, for reasons, perhaps, of class privilege, or from a dismay at what Lewis Mumford termed 'purposeless materialism'; not least, from a belief that along with the growth of efficient and 'scientific' production, high-pressure salesmanship and a wider disbursement of wealth would cause a diminution of 'individuality'; and from the resentful fear that the 'cultural imperi-

51 Allen, *Anglo-American Relations*, p. 155; A. de Tocqueville, *Democracy in America* (trans. H. Reeve, London, 1946), pp. 192ff; D. Strauss, *Menace in the West. The Rise of French Anti-Americanism in Modern Times* (Westport, Conn., 1978), p. 281. And see, for example, Thorne, *Issue*, p. 240.
52 See, for example, Costigliola, *Awkward Dominion*, and Heindel, *American Impact*, chs 7, 8, 14, 15.

alism' epitomized by Hollywood represented a threat to the very soul of one's own nation and society.

Meanwhile, in the reverse direction there existed, of course, contrasts of attitude in this area every bit as great: between, say, on the one hand the conviction of the *Chicago Tribune* and its like that Britain epitomized those class-ridden, stuffed-shirt, backward-looking and reactionary societies that were the very antithesis of that free, egalitarian and ever-progressive American one whose principles, as Jefferson had proclaimed long before, were 'radically different', and on the other the cultural Anglophilia of sections of the East-coast clerisy in particular. 'The truth is', wrote the first director of Princeton's Institute for Advanced Study to a Welsh friend in 1932, explaining a longing for Oxford in particular, 'that when you really do educate an American, you educate him beyond the society in which he has to live, for you don't really know how barren this country is . . . We have grown far more rapidly in wealth than in culture. There are times when I would be more lonely in New York than I would be in the Sahara Desert if it were not for a very few precious souls in my family'.[53]

Indeed, if we may say that Dr Abraham Flexner and Colonel Robert McCormick was each, in his fashion, representative of a significant strain in American society in our period, then together they can serve in the present context as a concluding epitome of the difficulties that stand in the way of any broad, swift summary of relations between their own country and the one which the latter's main paper described as the home of 'fancy titles' and 'brutal [imperial] burocracies'; a country whose 'dirty game of European power politics' 'never varied'; a society to which, in essence, 'the members of the [American] seabord set', led by Franklin and Eleanor Roosevelt, were 'determined to return' in the status of colonial sycophants, 'so that, from the bottom rung of the British social ladder they may look down on the fellow-Americans whom they hold in contempt'.[54]

The submission thus far, then, is that the subject of Anglo-American relations during, roughly, the first half of the twentieth century is one which is particularly unsuited to summary treatment within a precisely defined time-frame suggested by this or that feature of the international scene. Nevertheless, an attempt to draw out a few broad conclusions is not to be avoided on an occasion such as the one for which the present paper is being written, and at least may perhaps serve, like the difficulties

53 Dr Abraham Flexner to Tom Jones, 17 March 1932, quoted in T. Jones, *A Diary with Letters, 1931–1950* (London, 1954), p. 34.
54 *Chicago Tribune*, 3 December 1942, 4 February 1943, 2 August 1943, 1 April 1945.

enumerated above, as a point of departure for more lengthy and refined analyses by others.

There are strong reasons for beginning such a summary by emphasizing that the relationship in our period was in several respects, both quantitatively and qualitatively, different from most bilateral dealings among states. Indeed, some of the difficulties surrounding it sprang in part from the very sense that dealings with the other party across the Atlantic were somehow *sui generis*; that different standards of behaviour, different kinds of responses, could be expected – even demanded – of the other government and people. Moreover, if the qualification, different from '*most* bilateral dealings', is required in the light of, say, aspects of relations between the United States and Canada, or between Britain and Australia or New Zealand, then surely no such hedging is necessary regarding the conclusion that the alliance that was achieved between the two states between 1941 and 1945 was unparalleled among major powers for its closeness and its effectiveness in organizing resistance to a common foe. As for the longer term, the importance of numerous ties, both tangible and intangible, has already been alluded to in passing: in terms of finance and trade, for example, wherein in 1928, as Craigie emphasized in his survey of the relationship, the United States was Britain's major customer for direct exports, and Britain second only to Canada from the US point of view.

Such ties were not, of course, symmetrical, either absolutely or in terms of their valuation, when examined at each of their two ends. The overall preservation and strengthening of good relations, for example, tended to be accorded a higher priority in London than in Washington over this period, not least as a consequence of the desire to harness American power to Britain's international policies.[55] (Even amid the strained circumstances of 1938, the Head of the Foreign Office's Economic Relations section was ready to endorse the view being propounded in a current stage play, that the two most important things in the world were 'love – and Anglo-American relations'.)[56] Or again, it is on the British side, as several students of the subject have remarked, that one encounters more of an emphasis upon the 'kinship' of the two peoples.[57] Such contrasts, however, were far from absolute. Ernest May has demonstrated, for instance, the extent to which the preservation of a working relationship between the two countries amid the difficult circumstances that obtained between 1914 and 1917 derived from the belief on both sides that the two peoples shared

55 See Burk, *Sinews of War*, p. 224.
56 Ovendale, *'Appeasement'*, p. 39. And see, for example, L. S. Amery as quoted in Fowler, *British–American Relations*, p. 232.
57 For example, Campbell, *Great Britain and the US*, p. 195; Barnett, *Collapse of British Power*, pp. 258ff; Reynolds, *Creation of the Anglo-American Alliance*, pp. 292–3.

values and ideals of which the world as a whole was in need.[58] Even within the ambiguous and ambivalent position adopted by the United States *vis-à-vis* international relations between the two world wars, Britain held a central place in the foreign affairs considerations that continued to preoccupy Washington and New York. And again in 1940-1, in addition to acute fears about the fate of the Royal Navy in particular,[59] Washington's concern over the consequences for Britain in her struggle against Germany were Japan to advance further into Southeast Asia played a major part – a greater one than, say, the immediate situation in China – in bringing the United States into confrontation with the Tojo government in Tokyo.[60]

Nor, of course, did the existence of strained relations between the two governments, even when accompanied by animadversions directed against certain supposed characteristics of the other nation as a whole, diminish that network of transatlantic connections between individuals and institutions that, jibes notwithstanding, was facilitated by the sharing of language. (It will be recalled that those in London who were critical of what they saw as undue deference to the wishes of the United States on the part of the British government were wont to blame the domestic pusillanimity of those politicians and senior diplomats – Lindsay, Vansittart and Craigie, for instance – who had followed the likes of Joseph Chamberlain and Lord Randolph Churchill in taking American wives.[61]) At bottom, it was the existence of such a network that made it not unthinkable that Britain's Acting Foreign Secretary should cable Colonel House in 1917 to ask not only what form British war-time representation in the United States should take but which people were thought best for the job; or that, in the reverse direction, William Wiseman should draft a cable that would go out to the US Army's General Bliss over the signature of Robert Lansing as Secretary of State.[62] In this same context, it is worth recalling the exasperated observation made to Thomas Jones by André Siegfried in 1930:

A Frenchman in the States is always made to feel that he is not one of the family. No Frenchman is given a position of trust in the USA. To be head of a university or to occupy any similar post you have to be, if not [of] British, of Nordic stock . . . Nor

58 May, *The World War and American Isolation*, pp. 434 and passim.
59 See Reynolds, *Creation of the Anglo-American Alliance*, passim, and J. R. Leutze, *Bargaining For Supremacy. Anglo-American Naval Collaboration, 1937-1941* (Chapel Hill, NC, 1977).
60 See, for example, Roosevelt to Sayre, 31 December 1940 (not 1941, as printed in error), in Thorne, *Issue*, p. 22.
61 See, for example, Allen, pp. 111ff; J. R. M. Butler, *Lord Lothian* (London, 1960), pp. 59 and passim; Heindel, *American Impact*, e.g. pp. 30-1; McKercher, *Second Baldwin Government*, pp. 18ff; Watt, *Personalities and Policies*, pp. 41-2, and *Succeeding John Bull*, pp. 20, 69, 98-9.
62 Fowler, *British-American Relations*, pp. 69-70, 169.

must the Frenchman say anything against the British [, although] the Americans may do so.[63]

As we have already noted, the Americans did indeed 'do so' over a number of 'high political' issues, both between the wars and during the second of those conflicts. Even in this sphere, however, it can be argued that in retrospect the overseas position and the foreign policies of the two countries had more in common over more aspects of international relations than was often recognized or publicly acknowledged at the time. In the Far East, for example, for all the widespread assumption in the United States that they were 'miles apart' where that part of the world was concerned, their interests in the face of Japanese expansionism and Chinese nationalism alike were, if not identical, essentially complementary, and the present writer has sought to demonstrate at length elsewhere that in the matter of actual policy towards China in particular, London's line in the 1930s and 1940s was far closer to Washington's than US policy-makers or their public would allow.[64] And if, within this limited space, we can employ the crude term 'appeasement' in its more pejorative sense, that is to describe a backing away from confrontation with another state or states whose actions and policies were not merely distasteful but implicitly or potentially threatening to one's own interests, then (passing over sharp divisions among policy-makers and legislators on both sides of the water, as well as differences of circumstance and shifts of emphasis over time), in relation to both the European dictators and Japan in the late 1930s, that label may be said to fit the basic stance of the United States and Britain alike. Indeed, where Japan was concerned between 1937 and 1939, it could be argued that such a description, crude as it is, would be more appropriate for the policies and actions of the United States, bearing in mind her continuing supply of vital strategic supplies to Japan during the crucial early stage of the latter's assault upon China.[65]

Further broad parallels may be observed when we step back further still and examine the underlying approaches of the two states to international affairs in general in our period. Professor Nicholas has remarked on the degree of similarity between Britain's pre-1914 determination to retain freedom of manoeuvre *vis-à-vis* continental developments and the United

63 Jones, *Whitehall Diary*, vol. II, p. 268.
64 Thorne, *Limits* and *Allies*; passim; and see, for example, Gardner, *Safe for Democracy*, p. 172.
65 See, for example, A. A. Offner, *American Appeasement. United States Foreign Policy and Germany, 1933–1938* (Cambridge, Mass., 1969); MacDonald, *The United States, Britain . . .*; Thorne, *Issue*, p. 17; Butler, *Lord Lothian*, p. 277; W. I. Cohen, *America's Response to China* (New York, 1971), pp. 142ff, and 'The role of private groups in the United States', in D. Borg and S. Okamoto (eds), *Pearl Harbour as History* (New York, 1973).

States's refusal to accept binding political obligations in the 1920s – what Joan Hoff Wilson has termed her 'independent internationalism'.[66] And indeed, if during the inter-war years London simply could not afford to adopt the ostensibly detached and distant stance towards international affairs frequently taken up by Washington ('the ideological extravagance of isolation', as Professor Gardner calls it[67]), nevertheless British aversion to becoming embroiled in continental European affairs – above all at a politico-military level[68] – remained profound. 'Isolationist' instincts were far from absent in Britain between the wars, while, notwithstanding her membership of the League of Nations, 'independent internationalism' would by no means be wholly inappropriate as a description of the approach many of her policy-makers would have liked to maintain. And yet at the same time we can observe in both countries an idealism, a desire to see the international environment and the practices of international relations substantially changed: a desire noted above with regard to the creation of the League, and epitomized thereafter by bodies like the League of Nations Union in Britain and the Women's International League for Peace and Freedom in the United States; a desire which, contrary to popular belief, was by no means absent from the corridors of Whitehall, any more than it was from those of Washington.

In both countries and among both sets of 'foreign policy communities', indeed, and in the context of those only partially perceived, underlying changes in the entire international system noted earlier, the inter-war years witnessed much confusion and a jumble of contending instincts and prescriptions regarding external affairs. In both, pragmatism and the pursuit of immediate self-interest failed to obscure a distrust of the pre-1914 'rules of the game' – not least the building-up of national armaments – which, it was widely believed, had brought about that appalling conflict. In both, the desire to see a higher standard of 'rules' adopted and adhered to by the nations of the world coexisted with the determination to reserve from the application of such rules areas like the Panama and Suez Canals deemed to be 'of special and vital [national] interest', to use the phrase employed by London in regard to Suez when negotiating over the Kellogg–Briand Pact.[69] In both, strong beliefs in the wider benefits of free trade and 'open doors' struggled with (and in the 1930s succumbed to) the instincts of economic nationalism; with arguments of the kind that brought about the Fordney–McCumber, Hawley–Smoot and Ottawa tariffs; and with the

66 Nicholas, *The US and Britain*, p. 61; Wilson, *American Business*, pp. xvi and passim.
67 Gardner, *Safe for Democracy*, p. 270.
68 See, for example, M. Howard, *The Continental Commitment. The Dilemma of British Defence Policy in the Era of the Two World Wars* (London, 1972).
69 See McKercher, *Second Baldwin Government*, p. 117.

double-standards that enabled Washington to grant its 'tacit approval', in Joan Hoff Wilson's words, for US businessmen when they were able 'to pursue a Closed Door policy . . . with impunity'.[70]

Such ambivalence, such contradictions and uncertainties, are not to be wondered at. Both as regards the traditional 'high politics' of international relations and in the sphere of international economics – still, significantly, often viewed as an entirely distinct and 'lower' set of dealings – they reflected in part what Dan Silverman has termed in respect of the economic field in particular 'the poverty of traditional . . . theory' within a rapidly changing environment.[71] As for Anglo-American relations themselves in this connection, three points are worth making here. The first is that this conceptual confusion played its part in shaping that basis of 'competitive cooperation' upon which much of the dealings of the two countries with one another took place, in both peace and war. (It is interesting to note the similarity between this phrase, employed by David Reynolds to describe the essence of the relationship between 1937 and 1941, and the term 'cooperative competition' used by Michael Hogan with reference to the philosophy which Hoover expounded for domestic and international politics alike during the years of Republican ascendancy.[72])

Second is the reflection offered elsewhere by the present writer in relation to the notorious Stimson–Simon exchanges of 1932 in particular:[73] the reflection that the perceived need, in the age of Covenant and Kellogg Pact, for governments of Western, liberal-democratic states to present their policies (inevitably, in a confusing and shifting world, pragmatic and self-interested) as being fully in accord with freshly proclaimed ideals and norms of international behaviour could create additional difficulties, mis-perceptions and tensions between London and Washington, and between the two peoples. And third is the relevance of these conceptual gropings as to the shape, nature and direction of international affairs as a whole when it came to thinking about the transatlantic relationship for the long-term future.

In this last connection, there were of course those on both sides of the water who thought and spoke – if only in private – of some form of joint Anglo-American 'policing' of a changing and turbulent world. Woodrow Wilson was one who could be heard musing aloud in this fashion at the end of 1918,[74] and the idea was still current during the Second World War. At

70 Wilson, *American Business*, p. 9.
71 Silverman, *Reconstructing Europe*, p. 298; and see, for example, Wilson, *American Business*, p. xiv; Hogan, *Informal Entente*, p. 209; Thorne, *Issue*, chs 2 and 3.
72 Reynolds, *Creation of the Anglo-American Alliance*; Hogan, *Informal Entente*, p. 40.
73 Thorne, *Limits*, pp. 411ff. See also Huntington, *American Politics*, p. 83.
74 Gardner, *Safe for Democracy*, p. 7.

the same time, however, the circumstances of that war gave much greater impetus to an alternative vision, which had itself been around well before this (Stimson had entertained it during the Manchurian crisis, for example):[75] that international affairs could be restored to order only if and when the United States alone assumed a beneficently hegemonic role. 'The world must accept [America's] moral leadership', wrote the Chief of the State Department's West European Division in his diary in 1922, 'because back of that leadership is power', and the notion of an 'American century' was being voiced well before Henry Luce's famous article on that subject appeared in 1941.[76]

On this last occasion, Luce wrote that 'in any sort of partnership' designed to create 'a vital international economy and . . . an international moral order', Britain would be 'perfectly willing that the USA should assume the role of senior partner'. And indeed there were those in Britain who, not least when the limits of their country's resources were being brought home amid the perils of 1940–2, not only envisaged but welcomed such a prospect.[77] Moreover, the concept of 'America in Britain's place' was of course to exercise considerable influence in the post-war era, particularly over the shaping of the North Atlantic alliance.[78] Also, it has been much used subsequently by historians seeking to describe the major international changes in the first half of the century – although it can be suggested in passing that in such a context the phrase carries with it misleading implications both as to what Britain had been in the nineteenth century and as to what the United States could and was to be in the very different circumstances that obtained after 1945.

However, for all that there were those in Britain who were resigned to or even welcomed the emergence of an American hegemonic role at the end of our period, there were others, not least in official circles, who viewed such a process as a threat to be resented and resisted. And in return there were many Americans – again, they were prominent in Washington – for whom Britain represented not so much a natural partner in the process of reordering

75 Thorne, *Limits*, p. 57.
76 William R. Castle diary, 20 November 1922, quoted in Costigliola, *Awkward Dominion*, p. 60; also, for example, ibid, p. 263, and Thorne, *Allies*, p. 107. And for longer-term perspectives, see e.g. E. M. Burns, *The American Idea of Mission. Concepts of National Purpose and Destiny* (New Brunswick, 1957); F. Merk, *Manifest Destiny and Mission in American History* (New York, 1963); E. L. Tuveson, *Redeemer Nation. The Idea of America's Millennial Role* (Chicago, 1968), and M. H. Hunt, *Ideology and U.S. Foreign Policy* (New Haven, 1987).
77 See, for example, the reflections of Stafford Cripps, quoted in Thorne, *Allies*, p. 104.
78 See, for example, D. P. Callen, 'Early American views of NATO: Then and now', in L. Freedman (ed.), *The Troubled Alliance: Atlantic Relations in the 1980s* (London, 1983). For David Reynold's argument against exaggerating the speed and extent of Britain's decline in this context, see his 'Roosevelt, Churchill and the wartime Anglo-American alliance'.

international affairs but a major obstacle to such an achievement: an obstacle because of its imperialism, its selfish commercial practices and its attachment to that anachronistic, conflict-engendering 'balance-of-power' and 'power politics' approach to international relations generally on which we have already heard the views of the *Chicago Tribune*. This, too, is a major thread running through our period. 'There is little evidence', writes Fowler, 'to indicate that [Woodrow] Wilson veered from his December 1916 opinion that Britain's ambitions were as objectionable as Germany's.' 'We will have more trouble with Great Britain after the war than we are having with Germany now', was Roosevelt's way of putting it in private in 1942.[79]

There is no need to rehearse here the extent to which, even during the partnership of 1941–5, some officials on each side of the water were ready to think and talk of the other country 'almost as an enemy'.[80] Nor do we need to adduce further detailed evidence from our period as a whole to support the obvious conclusion that, for all their ties, overlapping interests and shared inclinations, these were two states greatly differing from one another in their resources, their situations and their 'trajectories', so to speak, on the international scene; differing, too, in many aspects of their societies and political cultures; inevitably differing, for all the common ground, in their interests and goals (even the relative size of their trade links with each other was diminishing over these years[81]), in their mental 'maps' of the past,[82] their aspirations for the future, and their perceptions of the present. In this last respect, one vivid illustration is provided by the Gallup polls that were taken in both countries in the early summer of 1942, asking in each case which member of the anti-Axis coalition had up till then made the greatest contribution towards winning the war. The American sample placed their own country first (55 per cent), followed by the Soviet Union (32 per cent), Britain (9 per cent) and China (4 per cent); their British counterparts gave pride of place to the Soviet Union (50 per cent), followed by Britain itself (42 per cent), China (5 per cent), with finally a mere 3 per cent nominating the United States.[83]

79 Fowler, *British-American Relations*, p. 6; also, e.g., pp. 195 and 214; Thorne, *Allies*, p. 121 and ch. 3. See also, e.g., Gardner, *Safe for Democracy*, passim, and Kimball, *Churchill and Roosevelt*, vol. III, p. 535.
80 See Thorne, *Issue*, pp. 235–6 for a summary.
81 Allen (*Anglo-American Relations*, p. 66) gives the following figures for their trade in merchandise as percentages of their total imports and exports. US imports from the UK – 1913, 15.17, 1949, 3.4. US exports to the UK – 1913, 23.78, 1949, 5.8. UK imports from the US – 1913, 18.43, 1949, 9.8. UK exports to the US – 1913, 9.37, 1949, 3.4.
82 On this see, for example, Watt, *Succeeding John Bull*, pp. 72–3, and Huntington, *American Politics*, ch. 2.
83 Thorne, *Allies*, p. 145.

Moreover, as our sampling of periods of particular tension within the relationship has already suggested, alongside feelings of fundamental friendship and understanding there existed, on both sides, a significant degree of distrust and dislike. Among Americans, not only was the notion of 'kinship' with the British severely limited and diminishing, but fundamentally anti-British sentiments were judged in a survey by the Office of War Information in 1942 to be entertained by 40 per cent of the country's city dwellers and by 48 per cent of population of the rural mid-West – these figures exceeding those for the anti-Russian standpoint.[84] 'Beyond [a] small group of soft-voiced moderates . . . and friendly but troubled Washington officials', the British Embassy reported to London in December 1944, '. . . we seem to have little visible support in any camp'.[85] Among the British themselves, meanwhile, besides those prominent individuals who, like Baldwin, found Americans to be 'impossible people',[86] the public at large, if the primitive survey techniques of the time are to be trusted, were ready after the fall of Mussolini to speak more favourably of Italians than of their allies from across the water – this, even though a high proportion of American troops who passed through the European theatre between 1943 and 1945 expressed either 'fairly favour-able' or 'very favourable' views of 'the English' [sic].[87] Certainly, one can say that those 'ambiguous' and 'schizophrenic' attitudes towards the United States among the British, which David Watt has recently depicted for the period from the end of the war to the present day,[88] were strongly in evidence in our period also.

In no small degree, as some appreciated at the time, such mutual distrust and criticism was accompanied by much ignorance and misperception. 'Misunderstanding exists on both sides', wrote Thomas Lamont in the private survey of 1917 that was quoted earlier, 'and the greater part of the misunderstanding is due, on either side of the water, to ignorance.' As he saw it at the time, the want of understanding was greater within his own Republic; but among the British, too, as Professor Heindel has observed, neither a 'spasmodic fascination' for the United States, nor the multiplying products of Hollywood, nor even the founding of university chairs of American studies between the wars, generated real knowledge or a

84 Ibid., p. 146.
85 H. G. Nicholas (ed.), *Washington Despatches, 1941–45. Weekly Political Reports from the British Embassy* (London, 1981), p. 482.
86 Jones, *Whitehall Diary*, vol. II, 156.
87 A. Calder, *The People's War* (London, 1969), p. 309; A. Stouffer et al., *The American Soldier: Combat and its Aftermath* (Princeton, NJ, 1949), p. 576.
88 D. Watt, 'Perceptions of the United States in Europe, 1945–83', in Freedman, *The Troubled Alliance*.

concern to know.[89] Nor had the 'associated-power' relationship of 1917–18 created a lasting sense of shared suffering and identity of interest. There was lacking, wrote the Anglophile Felix Frankfurter amid the recriminations of 1942, 'a continuing consciousness of comradeship between the two peoples', with his fellow-Americans being unaware, as he saw it, of 'the actual make-up of the English people [and] the reality of their democracy'.[90] And though many examples of just such a sense of 'comradeship' were forthcoming, none the less, during the Second World War, so, too, were numerous illustrations of the extent to which, within as well as outside official circles, there was a lack of understanding and 'feel' for the politics, political culture and social complexities of the other state. (In this context, the present writer has already been joined by Professor Kimball, for one, in believing that the popular notion that Churchill, at least, was possessed of 'expertise' over American politics and society does not stand up to close examination.[91])

Perhaps it was inevitable that matters should have been thus, just as the conflicts of national interest were inescapable. There were indeed 'special connections' between the two societies, but these could not by themselves create a lasting 'special relationship' between the two states within the international arena. The Anglo-American partnership during the First World War had been at bottom, in Fowler's phrase, 'an embrace of necessity'.[92] That between 1941 and 1945 rested, in Professor Kimball's words, on the 'mutual self-interest' of the time, 'the same stuff as other alliances', and in the light of the preceding relations between the two, David Reynolds is justified in arguing, not only that such an alliance was not 'inevitable', but that there was 'something artificial about [its] closeness'.[93] It is legitimate, indeed, within such a perspective, to speculate on what might have been the nature and course of the transatlantic relationship after 1945 had there not appeared almost at once a shared perception of a major threat from a new quarter, to the east of that 'iron curtain' of which Churchill spoke at Fulton in 1946.

To argue in this fashion is not to ignore or belittle those 'special connections' and similarities that have been emphasized above. Nor is it to subscribe to historical interpretations of the Correlli Barnett variety, whereby the United States played a crucial role in thrusting Britain upon its

89 Heindel, *American Impact*, chs X and XI, and p. 412; and see Silverman, *Reconstructing Europe*, p. 152.
90 Thorne, *Allies*, p. 98.
91 See Kimball, *Churchill and Roosevelt*, vol. II, p. 108, and Thorne, *Allies*, p. 122.
92 Fowler, *British-American Relations*, p. 8; and see Nicholas, *The United States and Britain*, p. 66; Campbell, *Great Britain and the US*, pp. 207–8; May, *The World War*, pp. 5, 427.
93 Kimball, *Churchill and Roosevelt*, vol. I, p. 19; Reynolds, *Creation of the Anglo-American Alliance*, pp. 290ff and, for example, MacDonald, *The United States, Britain . . .*, p. 179.

downward path in terms of power and standing in the international arena. Such a decline would have taken place during the hundred years or so after 1870 whatever policies were adopted in Washington. Indeed, one could argue that without the substantial assistance Britain received from the United States between 1940 and 1945, it would have developed more precipitously still during the closing phase of our period. True, the United States did not always perceive and act upon the extent to which its own interests and those of Britain were complementary. But to suggest or imply that Washington and Americans generally could and should have aligned themselves more closely with Britain during the first half of the twentieth century would be to posit a potential relationship considerably more 'special' than the actual, historical one which is de-bunked as decidedly and inherently 'un-special' by some of the very same students who deplore America's independent and sometimes anti-British manoeuvrings.

'Special connections' linked the two countries, and their contrasting trajectories are not to be seen in terms of the endeavours of the one to supplant the other. None the less, all things being considered, what is perhaps remarkable is not so much that the Anglo-American relationship during the years under review was beset with many strains and conflicts, but that it culminated in a degree of understanding and effectiveness that did so much to check the advance of tyranny.

5

Indo-China and Anglo-American Relations, 1942–1945

Within the space of a single article, it is impossible to do justice to all the factors which, at various times during the Second World War, affected the particular issue of Indo-China between Britain and the United States. At the outset, therefore, the most one can do is to recall some of the main contextual elements which were involved. There was, for example, the shifting overall relationship between Britain and the United States, in which, from a position of morally, if not materially, equal partnership around 1941–2, Britain declined to junior status from about the time of the Cairo Conference onwards. Thus, for example, soon after that conference, the US Secretary of the Treasury, Henry Morgenthau, Jr could observe (and President Franklin D. Roosevelt, who read what he had written, did not contradict him) that 'the Roosevelt–Stalin axis is gaining strength and the Roosevelt–Churchill axis is losing strength in about equal ratio';[1] thus a State Department bureaucrat like Stanley Hornbeck could see his country as being 'in a position to get from the British agreement to and cooperation in any reasonable course of action upon which we may choose to insist';[2] thus, by the end of 1944, the

This essay is based on a paper read to the Southern California Japan Society; it is reproduced here from *Pacific Historical Review*, 45 (1976), pp. 73-96. While this paper was in press, Walter LaFeber published one on a similar subject entitled 'Roosevelt, Churchill, and Indochina: 1942-45,' *American Historical Review*, vol. 80, 1975, pp. 1277-1295. It will be seen that, while agreeing with LaFeber in several respects, the present article (making use of papers of Foreign Office departments other than the Far Eastern one, and, for example, of the SEAC War Diary) offers a differing emphasis on such matters as the setting up of South East Asia Command and the complexity of Churchill's policies in 1945. I also disagree with LaFeber's interpretation of British policy towards China, on which see the writer's *Allies of a Kind* (London, 1978).

1 Morgenthau, Presidential Diaries, vol. 5, Morgenthau Papers, Franklin D. Roosevelt Library, Hyde Park, NY.
2 Hornbeck to Cordell Hull, January 3, 1944, box 180, Hornbeck Papers, Hoover Institution, Stanford University.

head of the Foreign Office's North American Department would even feel bound to acknowledge that in order to secure essential postwar financial aid from the United States, 'we may well find ourselves forced to follow [her] in a line of policy with which we do not fundamentally agree'.[3]

The position of France and of Charles de Gaulle between both Britain and the United States is another obviously relevant factor, with various local episodes not only sharpening the hostility expressed towards the General in Washington, but also making Winston Churchill – as opposed to the Foreign Office – far more inclined to adopt the stance of Cordell Hull, William Leahy and Roosevelt. As one example, trouble over the Levant and the Val d'Aosta in 1945 diminished the likelihood that the Prime Minister would enter the fray there and then on behalf of France over Indo-China.[4] At the same time, two developments were taking place which also affected that issue, although they are too well-known to require further elaboration: the mounting evidence of ineptitude and declining authority on the part of the Chiang Kai-shek regime in China, and the growing stresses in Soviet–American relations, as perceived in Washington. Both these last-named factors, of course, worked to the benefit of France where Indo-China was concerned.

Other international issues becoming entwined in our subject included designs for the post-war political and security system in the Far East, trusteeships, access to markets and raw materials, and the fear, especially among certain US officials, that, even whilst losing the war, Japan might successfully create a fundamental division along racial and colour lines between Asia and the West.[5] For the moment, however, this sketch of the background requires a concluding emphasis upon certain aspects of the Anglo-American relationship as it evolved in Southeast Asia and the Far East. First, there is the fact that nowhere was American preponderance more evident than in the war against Japan: most surveys in official circles in Washington took the line that the United States was conducting that particular conflict virtually single-handedly, and the British effort within the South East Asia Command ('Save England's Asiatic Colonies', as it was known by Americans on the spot[6]) was regarded as not only small, but too often fainthearted. 'The British', wrote George C. Marshall in a draft note to the President in October 1944, 'have never been in accord with [Joseph

---

3 UE 615/169/53, FO 371 (all Foreign Office, Cabinet and Premier papers, Public Record Office, London).
4 For example, UE 2711/2/G, FO 371.
5 See, for example, US Dept of State, *Foreign Relations of the United States, 1942: China* (Washington, DC, 1956), p. 71.
6 See, for example, E. Taylor, *Richer by Asia* (London, 1948), and *Awakening from History* (London, 1971).

Stilwell's] aggressive policy.'[7] Moreover, within SEAC and neighbouring areas, the prevailing view in Washington was that US and British policies were very far apart. It was wrongly assumed (and trumpeted from the spot by that buffoon among ambassadors, Patrick Hurley[8]) that Britain was working for a divided China; in late 1944 it was passed on to the President by the Office of Strategic Services (OSS), the State Department, and again Hurley, that Britain, France and the Netherlands had closely coordinated their policies in Southeast Asia in the interest of rampant imperialism,[9] and while there was no foundation for this belief, there was more reason for American watchfulness over Siam, where Britain was rightly suspected ('Churchill' would be more accurate than 'Britain') of wanting some special arrangement by which the Kra Isthmus could be fortified to help prevent a repetition of the 1941-2 attack on Singapore.[10]

Thus, in Washington, it was believed, in the words of the Assistant Secretary of State, Adolf Berle, that Britain and the United States were 'miles apart in Asia'.[11] And on the spot, whilst Stilwell's Ledo Road strategy and personal bitterness toward the British ('pig-fuckers', he called them in his diary[12]) helped to sour relations between the China–Burma–India command and SEAC, the general's political adviser, John Davies, warned of wider dangers:

In so far as we participate in SEAC operations, we become involved in the politically explosive colonial problems of the British, Dutch and possibly French. In doing so, we compromise ourselves not only with the colonial peoples of Asia but also the free peoples of Asia, including the Chinese. Domestically, our Government lays itself open to public criticisms – 'Why should American boys die to recreate the colonial empires of the British and their Dutch and French satellites?' Finally, more Anglo-American misunderstanding and friction is likely to arise out of our participation in SEAC than out of any other theatre. Therefore we should concentrate our Asiatic efforts on operations in and from China.[13]

7 Draft of October 4, 1944, Exec. file 10, item 60, Army Operational Plans Division files, (hereafter cited as Army OPD files), National Archives, Washington, DC.
8 See Hurley's messages to Roosevelt, Map Room, box 11, Roosevelt Papers, Franklin D. Roosevelt Presidential Library, Hyde Park, NY.
9 See, for example, Hull to Roosevelt, September 8, 1944, Map Room, box 166; and Edward Stettinius to Roosevelt, November 2, 1944, President's Secretary's file, box 53, Roosevelt Papers.
10 See, for example, material marked 1–945 and 1–1045 in file 892.01, Dept of State Papers, National Archives.
11 Berle to Roosevelt, October 2, 1943, file 740.001 P.W./3499a, ibid.
12 Stilwell Diary, August 8, 1944, Hoover Institution.
13 US Dept of State, *Foreign Relations of the United States, 1943: China* (Washington, DC., 1957), p. 188.

Within SEAC, then, it seemed in General R. A. Wheeler's words that 'American interest points north to [China and] Japan, British interest south to Singapore'.[14] And two other features concerning this theatre were to become important as far as Indo-China was concerned: its command structure and its boundaries. Before the Quebec conference in August 1943 at which SEAC was set up, Churchill and the British chiefs of staff had wanted to secure a Douglas MacArthur-like status for a British supreme commander, answerable to them alone;[15] however, although General Marshall privately acknowledged that the British had not been kept adequately informed of developments within MacArthur's South West Pacific Area, the importance of SEAC for supply routes to China led the American side to insist upon and obtain a Dwight Eisenhower-type command.[16] This meant that while immediate operational matters were dealt with by London, the Joint Chiefs in Washington, through the Combined Chiefs of Staff, were equally responsible for overall strategy.

As for the boundaries of SEAC, as initially drafted on the American as well as on the British side, they included not only Burma and Malaya but also Siam and Indo-China. Belatedly, however, it was realized that for reasons of 'face' Chiang Kai-shek, within whose China theatre these two last named territories had been placed in 1941–2, would be unlikely to welcome such an arrangement. There seems little reason to believe that at this stage long-term political considerations predominated in this matter; what was to prove unfortunate, however, was the blurred nature of the arrangements which were arrived at thereafter.[17] (On into 1945, for example, one can find much confusion within both Whitehall and official Washington as to whether Siam was or was not in SEAC.) Briefly, what happened was that when the new supreme commander of SEAC, Admiral Lord Louis Mountbatten, visited Chunking with the American General Brehon Somervell in October 1943, the Generalissimo, according to Somervell's notes, confirmed that he

14 Wheeler to George C. Marshall, March 24, 1945, Army OPD files, Exec. file 17, item 26.
15 Material in PREM 3,147/2,4; Chiefs of Staff minutes, November 22, 1943, CAB 99/25.
16 Joint Chiefs of Staff minutes, August 16, 1943, Record Group 218, National Archives.
17 See, for example, the draft of June 22, 1943, by Marshall that proposed 'unity of command for Southeast Asia, that is, for operations against Burma, Indochina, Thailand, Malaya and Sumatra' (Map Room, box 3, Roosevelt Papers). See also Leahy's observations at Quadrant, August 23, 1943, CAB 99/23; Joint Chiefs of Staff minutes, August 29, 1944; Churchill directive for Louis Mountbatten, October 21, 1943, PREM 3,147/4; US Dept of State, *Foreign Relations of the United States, 1943: Cairo and Tehran* (Washington, DC, 1961), p. 391 US Dept of War to Dept of State, November 1, 1943, file 740.001 P.W./3575, Dept of State Papers; Churchill to Roosevelt, June 28, 1943, and Roosevelt to Churchill, June 30, 1943, PREM 3,471, in which the President originally accepted Indo-China as within SEAC.

felt that the inclusion of Thailand and Indochina in the Southeast Asia theater would not be practicable . . . [because] of the effect which a change of boundary would have on the Chinese people, on Chinese troops, on the people of Thailand and Indochina, and on the Japanese . . . [but] as the war develops, the scope of operations of the . . . Southeast Asia theater . . . may involve Thailand and Indochina, . . . [when] the boundaries between the two theaters are to be decided at the time in accordance with the progress of advances the respective [Chinese and SEAC] forces make.

This so-called 'Gentleman's Agreement' was accepted by the President and Joint Chiefs of Staff. It was not, however, formalized by the Combined Chiefs of Staff. Nor did it spell out that Chiang Kai-shek had also assured Mountbatten that, in the latter's words, 'I should have the right to send in any agents or carry out any subversive activities that are required for a campaign in Siam or Indochina'. Somervell's record did not contain this last point, which, as we shall see, was to be the focus of much controversy between Mountbatten and General Albert Wedemeyer in China in 1945. It is worth noting, therefore, that this point was recorded by Mountbatten at the time; moreover, despite later American denials of any knowledge of the agreement, evidence of its existence can be found in the files of the War Department's Operational Plans Division in Washington.[18] Meanwhile, in the rearrangement of the purely US military commands which took place in October 1944, following the recall of Stilwell from China, Siam was placed by the Joint Chiefs of Staff in General Daniel Sultan's India–Burma sphere, while Indo-China remained in the China sphere under Wedemeyer.

If this background of command arrangements and boundaries was confused, so, too, was the development of political policies over Indo-China within both US and British official circles, and between the two. The principal agitator among those concerned was, of course, Roosevelt. From May 1942 onwards, he let it be known to representatives of other Allied nations, mainly through the medium of the Pacific War Council in Washington, that he did not consider France worthy, in the light of her colonial record, of receiving back Indo-China after the war.[19] To Chiang Kai-shek at Cairo

18 Somervell memoranda, Exec. file 1, item 23, Army OPD files; Mountbatten to Chiefs of Staff, November 9, 1943, Exec. file 10, item 66, ibid; Mountbatten to Churchill, November 26, 1943, Exec. file 5, item 15, ibid., Mountbatten memo, November 25, 1943, and Chiefs of Staff to Mountbatten, November 29, 1943, CAB 99/25; SEAC War Diary, November 8, 1943, January 4, April 19, September 9 and 14, 1944, January 18, 1945, Federal Archives, Suitland, Md.; material in file 35968, FO 371.

19 See, for example, Lord Halifax to Anthony Eden, May 20, 1942, F 3825/1417/61, FO 371; Halifax to Eden, December 17, 1942, F 6656/1422/61, ibid.; Halifax to Eden, January 14, 1944, F 285/285/61 and F 360/66/61, ibid.; US Dept of State, *Foreign Relations, 1943: Cairo and Tehran*, pp. 322, 482; US Dept of State, *Foreign Relations of the United States, 1945: Malta and Yalta* (Washington, DC, 1955), p. 766.

and to Stalin at Tehran and Yalta he expressed the same thought, obtaining in return a broad assent; to de Gaulle himself, in January 1943, he developed the accompanying idea, that France in her present state was like a 'child' in need of trustees – not that assent was forthcoming on this occasion. As for his own officials, the President was likewise giving them, on into the beginning of 1945, a strong, if somewhat confused, negative line. To the Joint Chiefs of Staff, for example, he emphasized that no binding promises had been or could be made over Indo-China, while to the State Department he chose to assert, in November 1943, for example, that Indo-China posed 'entirely a military problem', and then, in January 1945, that the Indo-China question should not be touched until after the war.[20]

For all the subsequent modifying which Roosevelt's line was to undergo (as we shall see later), there can be little doubt that he did seriously hope to see France deprived of her main Far Eastern colony. His broad anti-imperialism had attached itself to this particular issue as to no other (except, perhaps, to the cause of greater self-rule for India in 1942). His disappointment with the French showing during the early stages of the war may well have been partly responsible – the Vichy government, in return, listed all its fruitless appeals for United States assistance in resisting Japanese pressure in Indo-China[21] – while his antipathy towards de Gaulle, encouraged by Hull, Leahy and others, certainly made it easier to think in these terms. It is also worth noting that Roosevelt was by no means alone in adopting such a stance in 1942. Within the State Department's Advisory Committee on Post-War Foreign Policy, for example, there was a widespread feeling that French surrenders to Japanese demands in the Far East justified an over-riding of French wishes as to the future. 'It was not felt', recorded the subcommittee on political problems in August 1942, 'that France had any claim to regain Indochina.'[22] Stanley Hornbeck was to supply similar arguments.[23]

Moreover, the President's own wishes were made sufficiently known to affect US wartime policies in various respects. The French Committee of National Liberation was denied the place it sought on the Washington

20 See, for example, Joint Chiefs of Staff minutes, January 7, 1943; US Dept of State, *Foreign Relations, 1943: China*, p. 886; Roosevelt to Hull, October 16, 1944, file 851G.00/10–1644, Dept of State Papers; Roosevelt to Hull, November 3, 1944, and Roosevelt to Stettinius, January 1, 1945, President's Secretary's file, box 53, Roosevelt Papers; US Dept of State, *Foreign Relations of the United States: Conferences at Washington and Casablanca* (Washington, DC, 1968), p. 694; Charles de Gaulle, *War Memoirs, 1942–1944* (London, 1960), p. 83.
21 Henry-Haye to Hull, March 5, 1942, file D2 E118 (18), Netherlands Foreign Ministry Archives.
22 See Harley Notter files, box 55, Dept of State Papers.
23 For example, Hornbeck to Hull, April 3, 1944, box 173, Hornbeck Papers.

Pacific War Council;[24] the assumption put to Roosevelt by Edward Stettinius in February 1944, that French troops would be used in the liberation of Indo-China and French officials employed there in an interim military administration, was drastically revised;[25] approval for a French military mission to go to SEAC in the summer of 1944 was vetoed by the President;[26] a French request for a civil affairs agreement over Indo-China was turned down by the State Department in April 1945;[27] the Office of War Information received 'quite rigid' orders from the highest quarters that it was to play down French resistance to the Japanese in Indo-China when it finally emerged in March 1945;[28] and in Chunking, General Wedemeyer felt obliged at first not to allow supplies to be flown in by US planes to aid that resistance.[29]

Yet the President's anti-French observations and occasional instructions did not amount to a clear and coherent policy, and both civil and military branches of the government were often moved to bemoan their lack of a comprehensive directive on the subject. In October 1943, for example, the Assistant Secretary of State Adolph Berle was emphasizing the need for a presidential policy decision on the entire question of Western colonial empires.[30] Hornbeck, as political adviser, was asking in December of the same year what was going on (the State Department did not receive minutes of the Pacific War Council);[31] and Robert Stewart, responsible for relations with British Commonwealth countries, was trying in vain to get an answer to the same question in the following year when the Australian Minister for External Affairs, Herbert Evatt, referring to Roosevelt's musings at the council table, took up the cause of France in a sharp exchange with Hull.[32] In September 1944 John Paton Davies, back from China, asked Harry Hopkins about Indo-China, but was told that the President was more interested in European matters at the time.[33] The US Army's representative on the State–War–Navy Coordinating Committee was still observing in April 1945 that 'the lack of a policy is a source of serious

24 Dept of State to Roosevelt, October 29, 1943, file 740.0011. P.W./3648, Dept of State Papers.
25 See file 851G.01/46, ibid.
26 Joint Chiefs of Staff minutes, August 29, 1944; Henry Stimson to Roosevelt, November 24, 1944, and Roosevelt to Stettinius, November 24, 1944, President's Secretary's file, box 53, Roosevelt Papers.
27 See file 740.0011. P.W./3–2645, Dept of State Papers.
28 File 851G.00/3–2145, ibid.
29 File 740.0011, P.W./3–1245, ibid.; SEAC War Diary, March 11, 1945.
30 US Dept of State, *Foreign Relations, 1943: China*, p. 883.
31 Hornbeck to James Dunn, December 18, 1943, box 172, Hornbeck Papers.
32 Stewart to Hornbeck, April 3, 1944, box 262, ibid.
33 Davies memo, September 4, 1944, box 15, Stilwell Papers.

embarrassment to the military,'[34] whilst on the spot the OSS were eventually ordered by Wedemeyer to give arms both to the French and to Annamite resistance groups, with instructions to the latter not to use them against the former. (As is well known, some OSS members did in fact aid the rebels.)[35] It was not, in all, a helpful picture, and in a way it anticipated the situation in post-war years when Sir Robert Thompson, British special adviser on counterinsurgency in Vietnam, found no two Americans in Washington agreed on what their country was seeking to do in that part of the world.[36]

Meanwhile, estimates of the Indo-Chinese situation and proposals as to its future varied considerably among US officials between 1941 and 1945. There was at least general agreement in 1942, when the question first arose, and afterward that if strategic needs were met, there was no objection to the Chinese invading Indo-China.[37] (Both Vichy and Gaullist French regimes were loud in their warnings against such a move.) From 1942 onwards it was also generally accepted that the 'politically conscious' Annamites were anti-French,[38] and indeed Joseph Ballantine, who became chief of the Far Eastern Division of the State Department, had in the 1930s gone to Indo-China and studied the history of the Vietnamese people and their enduring sense of national identity.[39] But judgements as to the current strength and capabilities of the nationalist movements were usually extremely tentative: in October 1945, a survey by the Research and Analysis branch of the OSS would still find it impossible to give a firm opinion.[40] True, an earlier OSS survey, in March 1942, had gone so far as to pronounce that 'the Annamites have proved themselves capable of self-government',[41] and a Far Eastern Division memorandum supplied similar testimony in July of the same year. Yet the advice received from US diplomats in China was mainly to the effect that the Indo Chinese nationalists who had found shelter in that country were being used by Chiang Kai-shek's regime for its own opportunist ends. The consul general in Kunming, who fiercely criticized the French colonial record, nevertheless judged in August 1944 in a highly praised despatch that

34 State–War–Navy Coordinating Committee minutes, April 13, 1945, National Archives.
35 China Command, Wedemeyer files, box 1, Federal Archives, Suitland, Md; see also file 851G.00/6–445, Dept of State Papers; P. Kemp, *Alms for Oblivion* (London, 1961), p. 46; R. H. Smith, *O.S.S.* (Berkeley, Ca, 1972), p. 330.
36 Robert Thompson, *No Exit from Vietnam* (London, 1969), p. 112.
37 See, for example, files 740.0011. P.W./1956, 1957, and 1877, Dept of State Papers.
38 See, for example, file 851G.00/75 and 76, ibid.
39 Ballantine, Diary, ch. 7, Ballantine Papers, Hoover Institution.
40 OSS Research and Analysis Study no. 3336 (October 1945), National Archives.
41 OSS Research and Analysis Study no. 719 (March 1942), ibid.

the Annamites are not yet materially or politically prepared for independence or
capable of resisting aggression from neighbours. Nor would they be able alone to
hold back the peaceful but none the less racially annihilating, smothering
penetration of Chinese immigration. Therefore . . . independence at this time
would be doing the Annamite people no real kindness . . . [and] a further period of
dependence and protection seems to be the only logical proposition . . . As to which
power should exercise this temporary dominion, obviously [it] must be France for
practical reasons.[42]

The US ambassador to China, Clarence Gauss, took a similar line in
September 1944: 'It appears to this Embassy that the Indochina Independence League is of Chinese origin, has little or no basis of support in Indo-
china, and is unlikely to influence further developments in Indochina.'[43]
Within the State Department itself, meanwhile, no agreement could be
reached on whether France should be allowed to return. The Inter-
Divisional Area Committee on the Far East confessed itself in February
1944 'perplexed' over the matter: 'about half the Committee favored
international trusteeship as the best preparation for self-government or
independence, and half favored a continuation of French administration
under some form of international accountability.'[44] In particular, there was
a considerable difference of opinion between the European and Far Eastern
offices. In April 1945, when a reexamination of policy was being prepared
for presentation to the new President, this disagreement would still be in
evidence, this time over how specific should be the pledges and reforms
obtained from France before she was allowed to resume control of Indo-
China.[45]

One aspect of the situation which troubled the State Department during
these debates was the number of clear assurances which had been given to
the French by US officials during the early stages of the war, stating, as
Sumner Welles put it to the French ambassador in April 1942, that 'the
government of the United States recognizes the sovereign jurisdiction of the
people of France over the territory of France and over French possessions
overseas'. Such pledges did not appear to trouble Roosevelt, but they
helped to increase the bewilderment and exasperation over US policy which
was felt in London. Within the Foreign Office it was even suggested that
the President was beginning to show signs of that megalomania which had
marked Woodrow Wilson in 1919.[46] 'I find it very difficult', wrote the head

42 William Langdon to Dept of State, August 3, 1944, file 851G.00/8-344, Dept of State
Papers.
43 Gauss to Dept of State, September 30, 1944, file 851G.00/9-944 and 9-3044, ibid.
44 Box 118, Notter files.
45 See file 851G.00/4-2045, 4-2145, and 4-2345, Dept of State Papers.
46 F 6656/1422/61, FO 371.

of the Far Eastern Department in January 1944, 'to comment seriously on this flow of eloquence which from anyone but the President of the USA would not command the attention of anyone.'[47] Reasons were sought which went beyond simple anticolonialism. Perhaps it was part of a plan to keep SEAC out of Indo-China and Siam, and to minimize the British role generally against Japan, a tendency for which there was sufficient evidence for a new head of the Far Eastern Department to write in May 1945: 'The Americans are virtually conducting political warfare against us in the Far East.'[48]

The Foreign Office's own interpretation of the French record in Indo-China was that on the whole it was a good one, holding together an area which otherwise would be fragmented and chaotic.[49] In contrast to the Washington scene, there was little disagreement in the Foreign Office over either the present or the future: the Annamite revolutionaries had been stirred up by the Chinese for their own ends, and this should not prevent a continuation of French sovereignty. (Only Sir Maurice Peterson, an assistant under secretary of state, disagreed over this last point, and then because he thought France would be too weak to undertake all her former commitments, and had best concentrate on her recovery in Europe and the Mediterranean.)[50] It was believed that Britain and France had common interests in Southeast Asia: a desire to resist Chinese territorial ambitions, to prevent trouble from expatriate Chinese communities,[51] and to re-establish pre-war sovereignties. (The communique originally proposed by the Americans for the Cairo conference was disliked because it made no mention of this restoration of European-owned territories.) 'In view of the well-known American attitude towards the restoration of colonies generally,' wrote Sir Alexander Cadogan, permanent under secretary at the Foreign Office, to Churchill in November 1944, 'there is much to be said for the colonial powers sticking together in the Far East.'[52] A common interest was also discerned in their being producers of such raw materials as rubber, a commodity which had long been a source of tension with the United States, a major consumer. (London sought in vain to obtain Washington's consent to French representation on the newly formed International Rubber Committee.)[53] On the spot in SEAC, Mountbatten from early 1944 onwards strongly expressed the view 'that French help was

47 F 285/285/61, ibid.
48 See, for example, F 184/52/61 and F 2873/69/23, ibid.
49 See, for example, F 6656/1422/61 and F 6582/6582/61, ibid.; and PREM 3, 180/7.
50 See F 1784/779/61; F 4646/1422/61; F 6441 and 6808/4023/61; F 3812/58/61, all in FO 371.
51 F 242/71/61 and F 5964/74/10, ibid.
52 See PREM 3,180/7; and F 6583/6583/61 and F4028/9/61, FO 371.
53 See, for example, UE 2435/2/53 and F 5868/168/61, FO 371.

essential in the re-conquest of Indo-China.'[54] And although one general in the War Office did foresee 'that the inhabitants . . . will be more than anxious to throw off French rule',[55] care was taken that, in conducting political warfare in the region, Britain 'refrained from taking a line with the native population which could undermine French sovereignty.'[56] In addition, both the Australian government, as has been mentioned, and the government of India – for obvious reasons – supported the sustaining of that same sovereignty.[57]

Leaving aside the vicissitudes of Anglo-Gaullist relations, therefore, the only reason for hesitation on the British side was the desire to avoid a confrontation over this issue with one's dominant partner, the United States. It was for this reason, no doubt, that Eden, visiting Washington in the spring of 1943, did not speak out bluntly when the President aired his ideas once more. (Some US officials, indeed, read the record as indicating that the Foreign Secretary had expressed his agreement on the matter; but as others pointed out, the wording was ambiguous, and it seems likely that the agreement referred to another matter covered in the same paragraph.)[58] But although, in August 1943, a Foreign Office minute concluded that Britain could not afford to break with the United States over Indo-China,[59] even this was eventually to change, so that the briefing prepared for the delegation to the United Nations Conference at San Francisco warned: 'We might find ourselves forced to side against the United States' if the question should come to a head.[60]

In short, as far as the Foreign Office was concerned, Britain urgently needed a strong, friendly France after the war, both for reasons of European defence and as a counterweight to the growing predominance in world affairs of the United States and the Soviet Union. And a strong and friendly France meant supporting the continuation of her rule in Indo-China.[61] As expressed in a Post Hostilities Planning Committee/Foreign Office paper, approved by the Cabinet in February 1944:

54 SEAC War Diary, February 3, 1944.
55 SEAC War Diary, April 19, 1944.
56 F 242/71/61, FO 371.
57 US Dept of State, *Foreign Relations of the United States, 1944* (Washington, DC 1965), III, p. 185; Australian Dept of External Affairs Papers, files A 981, War/France/13; A981/New Caledonia/7; A989/43/735/310/2; A989/43/735/302, Commonwealth Archives, Canberra; and F 6353/11/61 and F 4220/4220/10, FO 371.
58 US Dept of State, *Foreign Relations of the United States, 1943* (Washington, DC, 1963), III, p. 36; Hornbeck to Dunn, December 18, 1943, box 172, Hornbeck Papers.
59 F 4646/1422/61, FO 371.
60 F 2431/11/61, ibid.
61 See, for example, Z 605/60/17, Z 4105/77/17, F 1269/11/6, and F 2010/2/61, all in FO 371.

The menace of a rearmed Germany being greater than the menace of a rearmed Japan, a friendly and prosperous France is a strategic necessity to the Empire and Commonwealth as a whole . . . To deprive her of her economic stake in French Indochina would weaken her seriously . . . and would be passionately resented.[62]

At the same time, a stable Indo-China was also seen by the committee as a vital 'anchor' for the defensive chain of bases (stretching through Formosa, the Philippines, Marshalls and Carolines) which would be needed after the war. (Needed against whom was another matter. For the Foreign Office, a resurgent Japan was the only likely threat; in the British armed services in 1944–5, there was a tendency to see the Soviet Union as the greater menace. Happily, the services were able to argue that a defence line ostensibly drawn up against Japan would also serve against the Soviet Union.[63]) Yet France alone might not be strong enough to make Indo-China fully secure. It was held, therefore, in the words of the paper endorsed by the Cabinet, that 'it is important to the future security of India, Burma, Malaya and the British Commonwealth and Empire in the South Pacific that the United States should be directly involved in the event of an attack on Indochina'. France should agree to include the territory, as Britain would agree to include her territories, within an international security system, and to accept in those areas the establishment of international bases 'under US control or otherwise'.

If this policy position seemed clear enough, however, there was much frustration in London, as in Washington, over a lack of leadership and clarity at the top. For Churchill, like Roosevelt, declined to bring the matter of Indo-China to a head. The reason was not that he doubted the wisdom of the conclusions reached by the Foreign Office and Cabinet; indeed, he regarded the President's notions as almost too absurd to be worthy of discussion between the two of them.[64] But the Prime Minister was always inclined to put consideration of post-war issues well below immediate business, and took little sustained interest in Southeast Asia generally. (In March 1945, when the French troops in Indo-China clashed with the Japanese, he had to ask his aide, General 'Pug' Ismay, how the French had got there in the first place.[65]) Moreover, he was too often angered by de Gaulle and, above all, too anxious to preserve his relationship with the President – 'My whole system', he wrote, 'is based on partnership with Roosevelt' – to take up the French cause when so many other and bigger issues were pending.

62 W.P. (44) 111, CAB 66/47; Cabinet Minutes, February 24, 1944, CAB 65/41.
63 See, for example, U 36/36/G, U 3390/36/G, U 4024/36/G, and U 4757/36/G, all in FO 371.
64 F 6808/4023/61, ibid.
65 F 1648/11/81, ibid.

Thus, in November 1943, Churchill merely observed that the whole matter could 'certainly wait'.[66] In the following January he told the Foreign Office to take up the subject with the State Department, but in March and May 1944, he found various reasons why things should be left for the time being: the election was pending in America; the French would only make trouble within SEAC to ease their pride; it was only a bee in the President's bonnet.[67] Although a brief on Indo-China was prepared for the Prime Minister to use in talks at Hyde Park after the second Quebec conference, he chose not to raise the subject, and again in November 1944 observed: 'This can certainly wait', and 'Nothing doing while de Gaulle is master'.[68] He again avoided the issue at Yalta, and it was only on 11 April, 1945, the day before Roosevelt's death, that he finally sent a message to the White House, urging that every assistance be given to the French forces which were now fighting the Japanese in Indo-China.[69] Even then, this soon became a small matter by comparison with, for example, worsening relations with the Soviet Union and the uncertainty over lend–lease supplies to Britain during Phase Two (the war against Japan alone).[70] When the ambassador in Paris, Duff Cooper, remonstrated in June over Britain's failure to support the French on Indo-China, Churchill – already angered by de Gaulle over Syria and the Val d'Aosta – snapped back: 'We have reached a point where any decisive taking up of position by the United States should, in nearly all cases, be supported by us, and we should not drag our feet in matters of passing importance.'[71]

The key to the mounting impatience of both the Foreign Office and service chiefs in the matter in 1944–5, and to the eventual British proposal that Indo-China should come within the area of SEAC, lay in the tangled history of command boundaries which, for this reason, was sketched earlier in this essay. During 1944, the idea of ultimately increasing SEAC's territory was always in Mountbatten's mind. 'If SEAC was to play a part in the final thrust against Japan,' he told his staff in January, 'it was essential that the boundary should be extended further eastwards to cover part of the South China Sea, and if possible ports on the China coast. He felt that Hong Kong should be included.'[72] Siam and Indo-China were a matter of particular concern to SEAC because, in the words of Mountbatten's political adviser, 'through them lies the enemy land and air reinforcement

66 F 5608/1422/61, ibid.
67 PREM 3, 178/2, 180/7.
68 PREM 3, 180/7.
69 F 986/11/61 and F 1829/11/61, FO 371; cf. PREM 3, 178/3.
70 See, for example, the messages in PREM 3,473.
71 UE 2588/2/53, FO 371.
72 SEAC War Diary, January 4, 1944.

route to Burma and Malaya'.[73] By the late summer of 1944 it was considered a matter of urgency to clarify the question of boundaries and jurisdiction, not in order to undertake a full-scale attack in the near future, but
to build up clandestine operations which could provide intelligence on the
situation in Indo-China and Siam and make it possible to cut vital
communications to assist major SEAC thrusts elsewhere.[74]

Meanwhile, the French were themselves urging that a mission under
General R. C. Blaizot be allowed to go to SEAC, that there should follow
a body of troops ready to go into Indo-China (the Corps Léger
d'Intervention), and that they should have a share in the planning of
operations.[75] Their case was strengthened in that their battleship *Richelieu*
had already been working for some time in the area, as part of the Eastern
Fleet. Mountbatten, too, supported them, warning London that if the
French were rebuffed, they might seek entry into Indo-China via China
and in collaboration with the Americans there (there was already a Gaullist
mission in Chungking). He also urged that the French staff and troops be
allowed quietly to filter into his command, thus eventually presenting
Washington with a *fait accompli*.[76] Such tactics seemed necessary because of
the attitude of the President. The Chiefs of Staff in London had, in August
1944, supported the proposal for the Blaizot mission and the Corps Léger,
the Joint Chiefs in Washington had agreed, but Roosevelt had thereupon
revoked that agreement. London, therefore, allowed Blaizot to proceed
'temporarily' to Mountbatten's headquarters – a move which provoked
loud warnings to the State Department from the US consul-general in
Colombo, Max Bishop, who was keeping an eye on SEAC affairs.[77]

It was an unsatisfactory situation all round, and was worsened by three
new developments. First, there was the sudden increase in the pace of
SEAC's advance towards Rangoon, which brought nearer the possibility of
action in Indo-China and Siam. Second, there arose between Mountbatten
and his former deputy, Wedemeyer, now commander of US forces in
China and chief of staff to Chiang Kai-shek, a major dispute over the
control of clandestine operations in those two territories. The details
need not concern us, but, briefly, Mountbatten stood upon his 1943
'Gentleman's Agreement' with the Generalissimo, while Wedemeyer
insisted that the latter's approval must be obtained for any activities which
SEAC wished to carry on in Indo-China. Eventually, in the spring of 1945,

73 SEAC War Diary, September 9, 1944.
74 See, for example, SEAC War Diary, September 14, 1944.
75 See, for example, F 4870/1422/61; F 3017/100/23; F 9/9/61; and F 4028/9/61, all in
FO 371.
76 See F 19111/9/61; F 2703/9/61; F 3948/9/61; F 4495/9/61; and F 3404/69/23, ibid.
77 F 4930/9/61, ibid.; files 740.0011, P.W./10–2444 and 10–2844, Dept of State Papers.

the Chiefs of Staff in London got Churchill to raise the matter, first with Roosevelt and then with Harry Truman. A solution based on an exchange of information was patched up, and there was agreement on the spot when Wedemeyer visited Mountbatten's headquarters in April; it broke down, however, because, in Mountbatten's words, Wedemeyer continued 'to take unto himself the right to evaluate my operations and oppose them as he wishes even though they do not conflict in any way with his own operations in French Indochina'.[78]

It was this continuing friction which prompted the Chiefs of Staff in London to proffer a still more drastic solution. In April, as the US attack upon Japan drew nearer to her home islands, the US Joint Chiefs had proposed that, in order to relieve MacArthur of some of his responsibilities, the British and Australians should take over his South West Pacific Area, excluding the Philippines and Hainan.[79] Now, in June, the British Chiefs of Staff suggested in turn that Indo-China, too, should go to SEAC, a change which was finally agreed to in July at Potsdam, although, with the Generalissimo's *amour propre* in mind, the area north of the 16th parallel was left in the China theatre.[80] Meanwhile, in March 1945, there had occurred the third development which heightened the whole problem: the outbreak of fighting between the Japanese and the French forces within Indo-China, resulting in insistent calls for help from the Provisional Government in Paris to London and Washington. Mountbatten, with the limited resources at his disposal, sent in what aid he could to the beleaguered French troops. The dilemma, however, was above all an American one. What now of Roosevelt's anti-French line? Should Claire Chennault's 14th Air Force be allowed to fly in supplies from China?[81]

In fact, unknown to his civil and military officials, the President had already begun to shift his ground. In January, told by Halifax that Mountbatten considered the need to employ Frenchmen for clandestine operations in Indo-China to be urgent, he had replied in the ambassador's words, 'that if we felt it was important we had better tell Mountbatten to do it and ask no questions'.[82] (When Mountbatten did go ahead, he was formally opposed by his American deputy, General Wheeler, and by General Sultan of the Burma–India theatre, whom London felt unable to

78 See the material in files 46305, 46306, and 46307, FO 371; PREM 3, 178/3 and 473; SEAC War Diary, February–May 1945, passim.
79 PREM 3, 159/7.
80 Chiefs of Staff minutes, April 26, 1945, CAB 79/32; May 30 and June 11, 1945, CAB 79/34; June 21 and 26, 1945, CAB 79/35; July 17 and 20, 1945, CAB 99/39; Combined Chiefs of Staff minutes, July 24, 1945, CAB 88/4.
81 See, for example, file 740.0011. P.W./3-1245, Dept of State Papers; SEAC War Diary, March 20, 1945.
82 F 190/11/61, FO 371.

tell of the President's strictly confidential approval. This was a typically Rooseveltian episode.[83]) In March, the President went further. To his adviser, Charles Taussig, on the 15th he conceded that France could, after all, have Indo-China back following the war, provided that she accepted the obligations of a trustee, including the eventual granting of independence.[84] And on the 19th, he authorized Chennault's planes to fly in aid to the French in Indo-China itself, so long as this did not interfere with other operations already planned.[85] The limitations on what he could do were closing in upon the ailing President. As he had wearily written in January to his friend Harold Laski, who had urged on him the necessity for creating a revolutionary peace: 'Our goal is, as you say, identical for the long range objectives, but there are so many new problems arising that I still must remember that the war is yet to be won.'[86]

Yet Roosevelt's own shift was only part of a series of developments within Washington official circles which, in the latter part of 1944 and in early 1945, made it increasingly unlikely that a radical American line on Indo-China would be forthcoming. For one thing, there was an admission on the part of the United States of the increasing status of France and of the Gaullist movement. In October 1944, after much delay and sourness, the French Committee of National Liberation was given official recognition as the provisional government of the country; thereafter, the briefing papers prepared by the State Department for the conferences at Yalta and Potsdam emphasized the rapid strides France had taken towards regaining her position as an ally of substance – a status eventually recognized by the award of her own occupation zone in Germany.[87] On his visit to Paris in January 1945, Harry Hopkins was accommodating and friendly in a manner very different from the American approach to de Gaulle in earlier years.[88] The General himself, despite his continuing prickliness, had for some time been ready to flatter American susceptibilities. (To James Forrestal, in August 1944, he even observed that 'the United States and France are the only two major powers with no imperialist ambitions'.[89])

83 Wheeler to Marshall, March 22, 1945, Exec. file 17, item 26, Army OPD files; file F 163/11/61, FO 371; B. Sweet-Escott, *Baker Street Irregular* (London, 1965), p. 238.
84 Taussig memo, March 15, 1945, box 49, Taussig Papers, Roosevelt Library; US Dept of State, *Foreign Relations of the United States, 1945* (Washington, DC, 1967), I, p. 121.
85 Files 740.0011. P.W./3–1945; 851G.00/3–1945, Dept of State Papers.
86 Roosevelt to Laski, Jan. 16, 1945, box 75, Felix Frankfurter Papers, Library of Congress.
87 See, for example, US Dept of State, *Foreign Relations, 1945: Malta and Yalta,* 300; US Dept. of State, *Foreign Relations of the United States; Conference of Berlin* (Washington, DC 1960), 1, p. 251.
88 Caffery to State Dept, January 28 and 30, 1945, box 337, Harry Hopkins Papers, Roosevelt Library.
89 James V. Forrestal, Diary, August 18, 1944, Princeton University Library, NJ.

For good measure, the Gaullists were emphasising their reformist – though in fact by no means radical – colonial policies at the Brazzaville Conference of January – February 1944. Their views about Indo-China in particular were proclaimed in a declaration in March 1945, in which an Indo-Chinese Federation was promised a degree of administrative autonomy within a French Union.[90]

At the same time, the emphasis of US policies over colonial and trusteeship issues was moving away from the brave days of 1942–3, when Washington's insistence on the word 'independence' and on specific dates being given for the achievement of that status had prevented agreement being reached with London on a joint declaration of colonial principles.[91] The shift can be traced, for example, in the discussions of the State Department's Advisory Committee on Post-War Foreign Policy. In 1942, there had been a strong feeling in that body that all colonies, and not simply former League of Nations mandates, should become trusteeships under an international organization: 'the United States must take a stand on its principles at the end of the war, since the imperial powers might desire to return to the status quo ante'. By March 1943, however, the changed mood was reflected in Summer Welles's remark that 'perhaps the most that can be hoped for is that the administration of colonies [belonging to the United Nations] will be kept in harmony with the principles of trusteeship by the pressure of international public opinion'.[92] By the summer of 1944, when Isaiah Bowman of Johns Hopkins University visited London as part of the Stettinius mission, he confided that the American approach to these matters would be 'entirely realistic',[93] and at Yalta Washington's proposal was indeed a modest one: that trusteeship status should be given only to ex-League mandates, ex-enemy territories and any colonies voluntarily placed in that category by the sovereign power concerned. This line was further pursued at the San Francisco Conference, where Harold Stassen, speaking for the United States, joined Britain and France in opposing the wishes of the Soviet Union and China to enshrine in the UN Charter a universal obligation for colonies to be led towards 'independence'.[94]

90 See D. B. Marshall, *The French Colonial Myth and Constitution-Making in the Fourth Republic* (New Haven, Conn., 1973), pp. 102ff, 133ff; US Dept of State, *Foreign Relations of the United States; 1945* (Washington, DC, 1969), VI, p. 295.
91 See, for example, files 31526 and 35311, FO 371; box 120, Notter files, Dept of State Papers.
92 Minutes of Subcommittee on Political Problems, March 13, 1943, box 55, Notter files, Dept of State Papers.
93 Record of Bowman talks with Foreign Office officials, April 14, 1944, U 3386/3386/74, FO 371.
94 See, for example, US Dept of State, *Foreign Relations, 1945*, I, pp. 790 ff, 954.

Britain's own stubborn refusal to consider surrendering supreme administrative powers over her colonies had contributed to the change in the US position after 1942. So, too, had the embarrassing question of US possessions in the Western Hemisphere.[95] Another major factor, of course, was the well-known desire of the US Navy and War departments to lay their hands for all time on the Japanese mandated islands in the Pacific, and the compromise which was reached with the State Department before the San Francisco conference whereby their wishes could be fulfilled without going so far as to proclaim American sovereignty over the islands in question.[96]

Meanwhile, similar changes of emphasis had been taking place over the specific colony of Indo-China. Since at least late 1943, Isaiah Bowman, as special adviser on such matters, had been advocating leaving France in control there (although with the understanding that she would be obliged to permit international inspection), lest independence should lead to 'division within the country and social and political disintegration'. Sumner Welles had put the same line to Halifax and Eden even earlier, in March 1943.[97] In September 1944, two of the more powerful men within the State Department, Joseph Grew and James Dunn, drew up for the President their own suggested solution for the whole Southeast Asian region. They stressed that American interests there might best be served by limited, rather than total, forms of independence:

These areas are sources of products essential to both our wartime and peacetime economy. They are potentially important markets for American exports. They lie athwart the Southwestern approaches to the Pacific Ocean and have an important bearing on our security and the security of the Philippines. Their economy and political stability will be an important factor in the maintenance of peace in Asia. Emergence of these regions as self-governing countries would appear desirable as soon as they are capable of self-rule, either as independent nations or in close voluntary association with Western powers, for example as dominions. Such association might indeed lend them political and economic strength (the weakness of Asiatic powers has long been a cause of war) and help prevent further cleavage along regional or racial lines.[98]

95 See, for example, the minutes of the Committee on Political Problems of the Post War Advisory Committee, April 10, 1943, box 55, Notter files, Dept of State Papers.

96 Edward Stettinius, Diary, April 1945, Dept of State Papers; James Forrestal, Diary, March–April 1945; Henry Stimson, Diary, January–April 1945, Sterling Memorial Library, Yale University; box 49, Taussig Papers; US Navy, General Board Studies No. 450, USN Operational Archives.

97 Bowman memorandum, October 24, 1943, box 70, Notter files, Dept of State Papers; Halifax memorandum, March 25, 1943, F 1851/877/61, FO 371.

98 Grew and Dunn to Roosevelt, September 8, 1944, file 851G.01/9–844, Dept of State Papers.

A need for an even more drastic revision of the President's ideas was put
forward by Harry Hopkins at a meeting on January 3, 1945, with the
Secretary of War, Stimson, the Secretary of the Navy, Forrestal and the
Secretary of State, Stettinius. As Stettinius recorded it,

Mr Hopkins suggested that there was need for a complete review not only of the
Indochina situation but of our entire French approach. In this connection he
referred to instances in the past where we had held back on certain French matters,
but on which we had finally, because of British pressure and other reasons, changed
our position. He expressed the opinion that this had resulted in the French feeling
that we were opposed to their regrowth.

The feeling seemed to be that with the British position what it is our policy of
deferring a decision on Indochina until some general peace settlement would
probably be doomed to failure. [99]

Allied diplomats were also hearing similar opinions expressed to them
privately by US officials. Grew observed in January to the Australian
minister, Sir Frederick Eggleston, that he believed Indo-China would stay
French, and Dr George Blakeslee, special assistant to the chief of the Far
Eastern Division, voiced the same opinion a month later. [100] Back in 1944,
the French ambassador to China, General Ziaovi Pechkoff, had told a
British official that while he was in Washington both General Marshall and
the Assistant Secretary of War, John J. McCloy, had spoken to him in
favor of a restoration of the French empire. [101] Now in March 1945, following a highly confidential conversation with Admiral Ernest J. King, the
head of the British naval mission in Washington, Admiral Sir James
Somerville, wrote to Mountbatten: 'It seems quite clear to me that the US
Chiefs of Staff are by no means in favour of the President's policy of
keeping the French out of Indochina.' [102]

Within the State Department, the difference of opinion between Far
Eastern and European officials clearly inclined in favour of the latter. 'We
have no right to dictate to France', wrote the Assistant Secretary, Dunn,
'nor to take away her territory'. [103] For President Truman, a list of reforms
which the United States would like to see undertaken in Indo-China was
drawn up for use in discussions with General de Gaulle. [104] But the fundamental issue of sovereignty was no longer in doubt. At the San Francisco

99 Stettinius memorandum, January 4, 1945, file 851G.00/1–445, ibid.
100 File A1066/P45/153/2, Australian Dept of External Affairs Papers, Canberra.
101 John Keswick memo, March 20, 1944, F 1450/100/23, FO 371.
102 Somerville to Mountbatten, March 27, 1945, file 9/2, Somerville Papers, Churchill
College, Cambridge University.
103 Dunn to Grew, April 23, 1945, file 851G.00/4–2345, Dept of State Papers.
104 Grew to Hurley, June 7, 1945, file 851G.00/6–745, ibid.

Conference, indeed, Stettinius assured the French foreign minister, Georges Bidault, that there had been no official US statement which 'even by implication' called for the removal of that territory. When Madame Chiang Kai-shek visited Truman in August, he swept aside all notion of a trusteeship.[105] Everywhere – with the exception of a few anticolonial stalwarts like Charles Taussig – there had been a retreat from Roosevelt's more extreme utterances, a retreat in which the late President himself had taken part. As John Hickerson of the State Department's European Office put it to a British colleague,

the American proposal at Yalta in connection with trusteeship had been partly phrased by the State Department in order to permit a climbdown from the position that President Roosevelt had taken in conversation as regards Indochina . . . He made it clear that the State Department felt that President Roosevelt had gone too far and that Category C [the voluntary placement of colonies under trusteeship] was a useful face-saver.[106]

These changes of emphasis arose partly from the recovery of France and from the increasing likelihood that confusion and weakness, rather than great-power stability, would characterize China's contributions to East and Southeast Asia immediately after the war. There was also the significant fact that major military operations against the Japanese were passing Indo-China by. In addition, however, increasing tension between the United States and the Soviet Union was making its influence felt. De Gaulle himself stressed the Soviet threat to Europe and asked whether the United States, in antagonizing France, wanted to play into the hands of the Communists.[107] The State Department, for its part, was drawing up briefing papers which emphasized that the process of moving towards colonial self-government should not 'undermine the influence of the West',[108] while a memorandum from the OSS, prepared just before Roosevelt's death, went farther still: 'The United States should realize its interest in the maintenance of the British, French and Dutch colonial empires. We should encourage liberalization of the colonial regimes in order the better to maintain them, and to check Soviet influence in the stimulation of colonial revolt.'[109] The same thought was expressed during

105 US Dept of State, *Foreign Relations, 1945,* VI, p. 312, VII, p. 540; cf. Truman–Grew conversation, May 19, 1945, Joseph C. Grew Papers, vol. 7, Houghton Library, Harvard University.
106 Nevile Butler memo, July 10, 1945, F 4240/11/61, FO 371.
107 US Dept of State, *Foreign Relations, 1945,* VI, p. 300.
108 Ibid., 556ff.
109 OSS memo, April 2, 1945, Harry S. Truman Papers, Harry S. Truman Presidential Library, Independence, Mo.

the private discussions of the US delegation to the San Francisco conference – discussions which frequently took on an aggressively nationalistic tone. 'When perhaps the inevitable struggle came between Russia and ourselves', observed Isaiah Bowman, 'the question would be, who are our friends . . . [?] Would we have the support of Great Britain if we had undermined her [colonial] position?' As Representative Charles Eaton put it: 'The basic problem was who was going to be masters of the world.'[110]

As they had for Britain throughout the period, European questions thus came back to affect US policy on Indo-China. Even without the Cold War aspect, however, it is unlikely that Roosevelt's early desires would have been fulfilled. It was one of a good many foreign policy issues for which, at his death, he had provided little solution beyond brave talk and bonhommie. In the meantime, the question had remained in a curiously suspended and inarticulate state between the United States and Britain. Churchill was ready at times to have it discussed at a Foreign Office–State Department level, but would not talk it through with the President; the latter was ready to air his personal views, but not to allow officials to negotiate on the matter. The result was virtual non-communication, coupled with a certain amount of bewilderment and suspicion. For this, Roosevelt may have been the chief culprit. But at least he had divined and supported more than most the direction of the nationalist tide which was beginning to flow strongly in Southeast Asia. And had his early wishes been fulfilled, France herself – perhaps the United States as well – would have been spared much agony.

110 US Dept of State, *Foreign Relations, 1945,* I, pp. 790ff.

6

Britain, Australia and the Netherlands East Indies, 1941–1945

In the autumn of 1945, developments in the East Indies suddenly became an extremely sensitive issue in Anglo-Dutch relations. And there are those in the Netherlands today who continue to feel strongly that there was something devious about British policy towards Soekarno and the Indonesian nationalists, or at least that London could have done far more to assist in the restoration of Dutch rule. In order to understand the reasoning behind that British policy, however, together with its Australian counterpart, it is necessary to go back into the entire period of the war against Japan.

It is worth recalling at the outset that when one talks of 'British policy' or 'Australian policy', one is in fact using a convenient, shorthand term for numerous strands of thought and action, not all of which may fit comfortably together. One is also concealing what may have been considerable differences of emphasis among those in official circles. The war-time policies of the Netherlands themselves furnish examples of this, for example over the broad issue of whether Great Britain or the United States should be looked to as the main agent for securing the return of the East Indies. The Prime Minister of the Netherlands, Dr Gerbrandy, clearly inclined in a British direction. 'My Queen and I', he told one of Churchill's assistants in March 1945, 'would prefer to do whatever is to be done in the Far East in partnership with the British rather than . . . with the Americans. I have no doubts about the British attitude towards the Dutch possessions in the Pacific. I am not happy about the American attitude in that region.' In June 1945, he also suggested that the London inter-Allied Pacific War Council should be revived as a counter to the domination being exercised

This essay was originally published as 'Engeland, Australië en Nederlands Indië, 1941–1945', in *International Spectator* (The Hague), August 1975. The writer's thanks are due to Dr Albert Kersten, who provided indispensable assistance in Dutch archives and made the translations that appear in what follows.

by Washington.[1] The Netherlands' ambassador in the United States, Dr Loudon, shared Gerbrandy's unease over American intentions, and at times in 1942–3 Dr van Kleffens, as Minister for Foreign Affairs, expressed similar sentiments.[2] The ambassador in Chungking, Dr Lovink, was particularly concerned at what he saw as the enthusiasm of the United States for the China of Chiang Kai-shek, and believed that Washington might use the latter as an agent against the European colonial powers; in the armed forces, Admiral Helfrich talked to British officers of his frustration at the dominance of the US Navy in the Southwest Pacific, and of what he saw as 'American pretentions' in the East Indies region.[3]

There was indeed some reason for such apprehensions. The Dutch, together with the British and French, were at times the targets for anti-colonialist ideas within the US administration. Roosevelt himself told the British minister in Washington in August 1942 that it was unlikely that the Dutch, 'the poor dears', could have the East Indies back to themselves, and that they might have to be only one of several trustees for that territory. And at the end of 1944, he ordered a special watch to be kept on the activities of the three main European colonial powers in Southeast Asia, following (false) reports by the State Department and Office of Strategic Services that those powers had formed a 'confederacy' to shape the future of the region regardless of US wishes. In the summer of 1945 there was little urgency, and indeed some opposition, in Washington over the matter of conveying Dutch and French forces to the Far East to fight for their colonial possessions.[4]

On the other hand, Roosevelt did usually make a clear distinction between the colonial record of the Dutch and that of the French in Indo-China, which he considered disgraceful. He also took a special (some thought it snobbish) pride in his friendship with the Dutch Queen, whose broadcast of December 1942 on colonial policy – designed with the United

1 Foreign Office files, series FO 371: F2413/52/61 and F3340/3340/61; Pacific War Council, 12 March 1942, CAB 99/26. All British official documents (FO, CAB, PREM) are from the Public Record Office, London.
2 For example, Loudon to van Kleffens, 21 September 1944, Loudon bundel Amerika, Netherlands Colonial Ministry archives, The Hague; minutes of the Netherlands Cabinet, 9 July 1943, Algemeen Rijksarchief, The Hague; FO 371, A2492/60/45. For the debates on these and related issues within the Netherlands Government and Foreign Ministry during the war, see A. Kersten, *Buitenlandse Zaken in ballingschap* (Alphen, 1981).
3 For example, Lovink to van Kleffens, 6 February 1945, Political Reports, Chungking 20, Netherlands Foreign Ministry archives, Algemeen Rijksarchief; Admiral Somerville diary, 4 July 1944, Churchill College, Cambridge; Hillgarth report, PREM 3, 159/10.
4 Campbell to Cadogan, 6 August 1942, PREM 4, 42/9; materal in Roosevelt papers, Map Room files 11 and 166 and President's Secretary's file 53, Roosevelt Library, Hyde Park, New York; FO 371, F5868/168/61; State-War-Navy Coordination Committee, 13 June 1945, National Archives, Washington, DC.

States in mind – he called 'a remarkable example of statemanship'.[5] To van Kleffens in July 1942 he had already observed that 'the Netherlands Indies should stay without any discussion as part of the Netherlands Kingdom'.[6] In his manner of being all things to all men, Roosevelt also scornfully spoke to a Dutch official of Britain's 'old-fashioned ideas', while in Australia in 1944 General MacArthur alarmed Dutch representatives by referring to 'annexationist desires' regarding the East Indies in certain Australian circles, and to the disadvantages that would follow if Britain were given strategic responsibility for the area, which at that time (excluding Sumatra) was under his command.[7] In a letter to Gerbrandy of June 1944, generally approved by van Kleffens, Dr van Mook himself, as Lieutenant Governor of the Indies, emphasized these dangers:

It is a fact that cooperation with Great Britain in SEAC is more difficult than are our relations with the Americans in the S.W.P.A. The British have no designs upon Netherlands Indies territory, but in Australia there undoubtedly exists an annexationist group . . . [and] I question how far London is opposing such designs; the Government in London might be appeasing the Australians by letting them go ahead with such unwise expansionist designs, in order to maintain imperial harmony . . . We should avoid giving the impression . . . which undoubtedly exists in American circles   that in our military contribution and colonial policy we are merely playing second fiddle to London . . . [and] we should for our own sake choose to maintain the present [command boundaries] and avoid a change in favour of SEAC.[8]

How real was this threat from Australia, which van Kleffens was again emphasizing to the Netherlands Cabinet on 18 June 1945? In brief, one may suggest that very general ideas did exist in some Australian circles for an extension of influence to the north and west and in an area which included the East Indies, but that these ideas did not reach the stage of becoming a clear and accepted policy. Australia was concerned both for the welfare of dependent peoples and for her own safety in the event of a future Japanese drive to the south, the two being connected in her eyes in that good colonial regimes which possessed the loyalty of contented native populations were expected to be a better military shield for Australia than had been the case in 1941–2. Even then, the introduction of outside

5 For example, Eggleston papers, 423/10/838, National Library of Australia, Canberra; Loudon to van Kleffens, 22 July 1943, Brandkast 1a2, Netherlands Foreign Ministry; Joint Chiefs of Staff, 19 November 1943, National Archives, Washington, DC.
6 Loudon report, 15 July 1942, GA D2D31a, Londens archief, Netherlands Foreign Ministry.
7 van der Plas reports, August 1944, Brandkast 1a13, Londens archief, NFM.
8 van Mook to Gerbrandy, 29 June 1944, ibid.

influence might be necessary. Thus, in January 1944 for example, the Australian Government let Britain know that it wanted a share in policing the East Indies area after the war, while the Australian Prime Minister, John Curtin, told the Commonwealth Prime Ministers' Conference in London in the following May that 'he would welcome the intrusion of US influence between [Australia] and Japan . . . [not] at the expense of British territory but at the expense of the Japanese and if need be the Dutch and the French'.

British representatives in Australia had heard of even more radical notions. One reported in November 1942 'a childlike faith that Australia can and should dominate the post-war situation throughout the Southwest Pacific, politically and economically, especially in the Netherlands East Indies and Malaya'. In December 1942 the High Commissioner, Sir Ronald Cross, reported similar 'grandiose ideas', for example of the East Indies under an Australian-led condominium, adding that the Australian propaganda and information departments were being unofficially encouraged by the Australian Attorney-General and Minister of External Affairs, Dr Herbert Evatt, to think in such terms. Evatt himself admitted to Cross in January 1943 that

he was anxious that we should not tie our hands much at this stage . . . and in particular he had in mind relinquishment of sovereignty . . . He said for one thing he had the Netherlands East Indies in mind. He agreed . . . that he was thinking of an economic and political participation in these territories . . . He was seeking time, feeling that something more favourable for Australia might be obtainable later on.

In this same spirit Evatt made fierce efforts late in 1943 and early 1944 to prevent van Mook coming out to Australia as Lieutenant Governor of the Indies, a move which he described as 'most embarrassing' at a time when he had in mind, for example, a long lease for Australia of Dutch New Guinea and Dutch Timor. Evatt failed on this occasion and van Mook duly arrived in Australia; but later on, there was great procrastination following Australia's agreement 'in principle' to allow 30,000 Dutch troops and administrators to come out for training in Australia in order to be on hand when the East Indies were freed, and the agreement was finally withdrawn in June 1945. Meanwhile, a close adviser of Evatt's had envisaged a reactionary Dutch regime returning to Batavia, but one whose fears of 'a second Asiatic conquest' could be taken advantage of by Australia, while she herself would 'follow no policy which would offend Indonesian aspirations or compromise our long-term aims'.[9]

9 For example, FO 371, F7601/2000/16 and U1909/828/70; PREM 4, 50/2 and 42/5; Australian Ministry of External Affairs, file A989/44/600/5/1/5, and Australian Department of Defence, file A816/19/305/114, Commonwealth Archives, Canberra.

Those long-term Australian aims included a system whereby colonies generally would become trusteeships, with the administering state being highly accountable to in international organization. On this, the British Government steadily opposed Canberra's policy, despite attempts to paper over the differences between them before the United Nations San Francisco Conference in 1945. For Britain, only if a colonial power volunteered this course (League of Nations Mandates apart) should a trusteeship come into operation; otherwise international accountability should be at only the most general level. London never considered the idea of an international trusteeship for the Netherlands East Indies, and when Curtin talked of a US presence at the expense of the Dutch if necessary, Churchill openly disagreed. Within the Foreign Office, Evatt's ideas were considered 'wild and potentially dangerous', while the Prime Minister was obviously genuine when he told the Dutch Ambassador, Michiels, in May 1944, 'that the Netherlands should not cede one inch of its territory in consequence of this war'. To Eden in June 1945, referring this time to US anti-colonialism, Churchill minuted: 'I will not lend myself to any trickery to deprive the Dutch of their territories'.[10]

The ambivalent Australian attitude over the Netherlands Indies was not to exercise much influence on Britain during the crisis of the autumn of 1945, however – and in any case it was to be offset then in Commonwealth circles by the support of Smuts and South Africa for the Dutch cause. It also counted less than the important consideration of relations within Europe, where Britain anxiously sought friends. Sir Orme Sargent of the Foreign Office, observing in July 1945 the growing tendency of the United States and the Soviet Union to regard Britain as a second-rate power, warned that

We must do something about organising our side or we shall find our friends gradually drifting away from us. It is essential that we should increase our strength not only in the diplomatic but also the economic and military spheres. This clearly can best be done by enrolling France and the lesser Western European powers . . . as collaborators with us in this tripartite system.[11]

There was an added incentive for this search for friends in Europe in the shape of US anti-colonialism, prompting Sargent to suggest that in the Far East Britain should 'organise under [her] leadership the lesser colonial

10 On Britain and Evatt generally, see the present writer's articles in the Melbourne *Age*, 31 May and 1 June 1974, his *Allies of a Kind* (London, 1978), and, for example, material in PREM 4, 50/12. For Churchill's remarks, see FO 371, F3340/3340/61, and minutes of the Netherlands Cabinet of 5 May 1944.
11 FO 371, U5471/5471/G.

powers'. The very origins of the independent United States made it natural for Americans to assume the worst about British imperialism in particular, and to decry it accordingly. In 1942 there had been an especially strong outcry against Britain's refusal to grant immediate Dominion status to India (even though the sending out to Delhi of Stafford Cripps with certain lesser concessions to offer the Indians had created a more favourable impression). Incidents such as this, together with the continuing anti-colonial speeches and writings of prominent Americans like Wendell Willkie, made the Foreign Office in London anxious to find means of bridging this particular gap. An inter-departmental committee on American opinion and the British Empire was set up for this purpose, and in 1942–3 great efforts were made to find a formula for a declaration of colonial principles which Britain and the United States could sign and issue jointly. (This last project, which had been initiated somewhat casually by the US Secretary of State, Cordell Hull, foundered on the American insistence that the word 'independence' should receive prominence in the declaration, and that dates should be set in advance, as had been done for the Philippines, when that independence would be granted. Unlike the United States, the Foreign Office also wished to consult the Netherlands and other colonial powers on the matter.[12])

Similarly, in terms of the Far East as a whole, Britain was aware of American suspicions – for example, that she did not desire to see a strong and united China. Yet although Churchill in particular was, indeed, scornful of Roosevelt's conception of China as one of the Big Four, and although there was much resentment in Whitehall at what were described as 'American intentions to keep the conduct of the war in the Pacific in their own hands, to relegate us to a purely subordinate role, and to misrepresent the objects of our efforts in the Far Eastern war', even so it was thought essential to try to keep in step with Washington.[13] One of the reasons for this stance is an important factor to bear in mind when viewing Britain's subsequent role in the affairs of the East Indies in 1945: by 1944, if not earlier, Britain was increasingly becoming the junior partner in the Anglo-American relationship. As the material might of the United States became more powerfully harnessed to the war effort, so Britain's resources were stretched to their fullest extent, with no reserves left to call upon. While Roosevelt increased London's apprehensions over the future by stressing that he must bring all US troops back from Europe after the war 'as rapidly as transportation problems will permit', he was also cooling somewhat in his relationship with Churchill and tending to side with Stalin at the conferences of the Big Three. Even when Roosevelt was

12 See in general FO 371, files 31517, 31521, 31526.
13 For example, FO 371, F3243/602/61, F214/127/61, F1955 & 2873/69/23; Far East Committee minutes, 15 November 1944, CAB 96/5.

dead and US-Soviet relations were beginning to be severely strained, Lord Halifax, the British Ambassador in Washington, noted that the US administration now expected Britain to fall dutifully into line as a loyal but junior partner.[14]

Lack of money was one of Britain's biggest handicaps by the summer of 1945. As early as July 1944, the Chancellor of the Exchequer had warned his Cabinet colleagues that 'from being the world's largest creditor we shall have become by the end of the war the world's largest debtor'. Liabilities at the end of the war with Japan were foreseen as being of the order of £4,500 million, against gold and dollar reserves of around £400 million; in May 1945, Keynes was forecasting for the Cabinet an annual deficit on the country's overseas account of £1,400 million. Then, in August, came the shock of the sudden cutting off of lend–lease after the surrender of Japan, and the need, as the Chancellor of the Exchequer put it to the Cabinet in the middle of August, of financial assistance from the United States to the tune of about £1,250 million.

Indebtedness could have wider implications: already, at the end of 1944, the Foreign Office had foreseen the possibility that, in order to obtain the required loans, 'we may find ourselves forced to follow the United States in a line of policy with which we do not fundamentally agree'.[15] The same pressures could be felt in the sphere of military supplies, where, even by the autumn of 1942, Britain had already become dependent upon the United States for 99 per cent of her landing-force ships, 88 per cent of her landing craft, 77 per cent of her escort vessels, nearly 100 per cent of her transport aircraft, 100 per cent of her large trucks and tank transporters, 100 per cent of her synthetic rubber, and so on.[16] Thus, for example, Britain had had to ask for the loan of US ships when a serious shortage of grain arose in India in 1943–4, while South East Asia Command operations in 1945 were to a significant extent dependent on US transport and other equipment. Moreover, after the defeat of Germany the agreement which Roosevelt and Churchill had reached in the autumn of 1944 on lend–lease supplies to Britain during Phase Two (i.e. the war against Japan alone) was increasingly disregarded by the US armed services, who were eager to lay their own hands on as many supplies as possible.[17] At the same time, Britain's manpower shortage (she had reached the peak of her mobilization in the autumn of 1943) became increasingly serious, with the demands of

14 FO 371, AN2560/22/45.
15 WP(44)419 in CAB 66/53; WP(45)24, CAB 66/60; WP(45)301, CAB 66/65; material in FO 371, files 40952, 45852, 45854.
16 WP(42)486, CAB 66/30.
17 For example, Committee on Indian Food Grain Requirements, CAB 91/6; material in PREM 3, 149/2, 8, 11.

reconstruction and export industries, on top of munitions factories and the armed services. Occupation troops had to be found for Germany; demobilization, it was felt, had to begin for those who had served longest in the Far East; new incentives had to be found for those required to fight on against Japan.[18] It was in this context that Admiral Mountbatten found himself so dependent on Indian troops for his operations in the East Indies and elsewhere in SEAC in the summer and autumn of 1945.

If these material constraints upon British policy in Southeast Asia in 1945 were inherent in the size of her resources, there were other handicaps which were less unavoidable. One was what the Foreign Office termed 'the comparative lack of interest and understanding in this country of our position and responsibilities in the Far East'. Even in Whitehall itself, Sir Orme Sargent felt that 'we tend to be apathetic on the subject and to underestimate the importance of the Far East on our future policy'.[19] More serious still was the long delay in producing Cabinet-endorsed policies for medium- and long-term issues involving British Far Eastern imperial territories and neighbouring areas such as Siam. There were, of course, considerable differences of opinion and approach on these matters within the Government and among the various ministries. Yet in general there was a substantial shift of outlook between 1939 and 1943, and there were many who were impatient for new policy pronouncements: the Governor of Burma, for example, was seeking from 1942 onwards a public pledge of independence for that country within a fixed time limit.[20] Some proposals were belatedly formulated – for instance in the White Paper on Burma in May 1945, and over Malaya and North Borneo. But it was generally too late and too little, and there was much impatience within the Foreign Office at the encouragement given thereby to American suspicions. 'Our apparent lack of frankness', ran one typical minute, 'is often accounted for by the fact that we have not yet got agreement in the War Cabinet on a policy'; and again: 'We must formulate [policies]. This is a formidable task . . ., but long term issues must be tackled some day'. 'I hope', wrote Mountbatten's political adviser, Esler Dening early in 1945, 'that some day in the not too distant future it will be possible to make some pronouncement [on Burma] which is not open to the suspicion that we do not mean what we say . . .'[21]

18 For example, WP(44)173, CAB 66/48; WP(44)379, 380, 381, CAB 66/52; WP(44)722, CAB 66/59; Earl Mountbatten, *Report to the Combined Chiefs of Staff* (London, 1951), p. 167.
19 FO 371, F6966/16/61 and U5471/5471/G.
20 For example, material in Dorman-Smith papers, E215/3, 17, 19, India Office Library, London; Cabinet's India Committee, CAB 91/3 and 4; Malay and Borneo Committee CAB 98/4; Armistice and Postwar Committee, CAB 87/69; Cabinets of 4 and 14 May 1943, CAB 65/50; of 1 June 1945, CAB 65/53.
21 For example, FO 371, F2469/993/61 and F129/129/61.

The main cause of these delays and frustrations was Churchill himself. Whilst the war was being fought he devoted little attention to post-war planning, and he had little sustained interest in the Far East. Over imperial affairs, moreover, in the words of his Secretary of State for India, Leo Amery (himself no radical), 'he has instinctive hatred of self-government in any shape or form and dislikes any country or people who want such a thing or for whom such a thing is contemplated'. (For one, lengthy example, see the problems encountered by Wavell in India, as reflected in the journal he kept as Viceroy.[22]) Churchill was also chiefly responsible for the long delay in 1944 over deciding where Britain's main military effort should be made against Japan. The Chiefs of Staff wanted it to be in the Pacific, against the home islands of the enemy; the Prime Minister doggedly kept his eyes on a possible landing in Sumatra, and on a forceful recovery of Singapore that would remove the disgrace of 1942. While Mountbatten and Dening urgently appealed for long-term guidance, Churchill delayed. 'Our troubles are largely due', wrote a Foreign Office official, 'to our not having made up our minds as to what we desire our Far Eastern strategy to be . . . If the Prime Minister had not repeatedly postposed any decision in this matter because of the strength of the opposition to operation "Culverin" [a landing in Sumatra] we should be far better off.' Churchill's military aide, General Ismay, felt that the whole business would be 'one of the black spots in the record of the British higher direction of the war'.[23]

A strategic policy had been arrived at, of course, by the time the East Indies issue arose in the summer of 1945, but there remained a breathlessness and lack of clear direction about Britain's intentions in Southeast Asia. Meanwhile, a difference of emphasis over one particular issue, which had arisen between SEAC and London, was significant for what was to come in Java. The question was whether, in Burma, to welcome the aid of the guerrilla Burma National Army, led by Aung San, who had earlier collaborated with the Japanese before turning against them. To the Governor of Burma, Sir Reginald Dorman-Smith, as to Churchill and Eden, this would be a perilous policy which threatened to undermine the rule of law (Aung San had confessed to the Governor the murder of an Indian headman) and to dishearten those Burmese who had remained loyal to the British cause. To Mountbatten, on the other hand, military necessity pointed to accepting Aung San's help; the alternative, he believed, would be to run up against 'a formation of up to 10,000 armed Burmese . . . This would be tantamount to proclaiming that we were prepared to engage in civil war

22 Dorman-Smith papers, E215/3; P. Moon (ed.), *Wavell: the Viceroy's Journal* (London, 1973).
23 PREM 3, 149/7, 8, and 160/3, 5, 6, 7; CAB 69/6 and 79/89; FO 371, files 41795, 41797, 41798, 42677, 46432; Ismay papers, IV/Pow/4/2, King's College, London.

against forces we had announced were on our side . . . and who are known to have killed some 700 Japanese'. Another, political argument was put forward by the Head of the Political Warfare Section of Force 136, the Special Operations Executive units operating behind the Japanese lines. To use Aung San, he wrote,

would be a crushing reply to one of the most prevalent slanders against British rule in the East [i.e. that native populations were hostile]. In fact one might almost say that if the Burmese resistance movement did not exist it would be justifiable to invent it.

Mountbatten had his way, and it is important to note that the underlying restraint in dealing with native nationalist movements was to remain in force after Japan had surrendered. Mountbatten visited the Governor of Burma, for example, in January 1946, and warned him, in the latter's words, 'that in the event of Aung San raising the flag of "Freedom" and starting an armed rising such as the Indonesians had staged against the Dutch, under no circumstances would I be allowed to use Indian troops to suppress the rising.' This left the Governor with little military support. (Although he still wished to arrest Aung San, he was prevented from doing so by London, and removed from office.) In short, restrictions that Britain was to observe in the East Indies were also being applied within her own territories.[24]

Within this framework we may now turn more specifically to Anglo-Dutch relations concerning Southeast Asia. It can be said at the outset that the official records in London bear testimony to a general warmth of feeling towards the Netherlands. General Pownall, for example, Mountbatten's Chief of Staff, wrote in May 1944: 'Of all our allies in this war, the Dutch are the most cooperative and reliable.' 'Hear hear!', someone in the Foreign Office added in the margin. Before the Pacific War, in 1941, the Foreign Office had pressed for a guarantee to be given of British assistance in the event of a Japanese attack on the East Indies – a proposal which the Admiralty and Churchill had resisted until Britain in turn had received a pledge of US armed support. Once the war had begun, the lesson drawn by the Foreign Office was summarized by the Head of the Far Eastern Department in December 1943:

24 For example, Cabinet's India Committee, CAB 91/3 and 4; PREM 3, 149/5; Dorman-Smith papers, E215/2 and 29; FO 371, file 46334A. See also P. Ziegler, *Mountbatten* (London, 1985); H. Tinker (ed.), *Burma: the Struggle for Independence, 1944–48*, vol. 1 (London, 1983), and, on British overseas policies generally, A. Bullock, *Ernest Bevin, Foreign Secretary* (London, 1983).

Before the Pacific War broke out the Foreign Office failed to convince His Majesty's Government that our natural allies in Southeast Asia were the Dutch. I suggest we profit by the lessons which events have afforded. This would entail not only close contact on all planning for the future of our colonial territories, but also the exercising of our influence to ensure that whatever Dutch territory is occupied, civil affairs shall at once be put into the hands of the Dutch.

It was in this spirit that – despite US opposition – British officials secretly showed their Dutch colleagues drafts of the treaties being negotiated with China in 1942–3 for the surrender of extraterritorial privileges in that country. '[The Dutch] are an important Far Eastern ally', it was noted in justification, 'whose cooperation later on will be indispensable.'[25] Likewise, it was taken as axiomatic that the British and Dutch shared a common interest as producers of rubber and tin in Southeast Asia, and that they should keep in close touch in the face of US opposition (as a major consumer) to production and pricing agreements, and of the rapid rise of the synthetic rubber industry in the United States. The two countries were also believed to have a common interest in keeping an eye on the activities of the expatriate Chinese communities in the region, and in resisting the more radical US schemes for international supervision of colonies. 'In view of the well-known American attitude . . .', wrote Sir Alexander Cadogan, Permanent Under-Secretary at the Foreign Office, 'there is much to be said for the colonial powers sticking together in the Far East', although drastic action in this direction was prevented by Churchill's desire not to do anything that would diminish his crucial relationship with Roosevelt, as well as by his irritation and at times anger against General de Gaulle. In all Britain's own schemes for regional colonial bodies and for security in Southeast Asia, the Dutch figured as a basic element.[26]

As for the handing over of Netherlands' territories after their capture by SEAC, no problems were anticipated on the British side, and the civil affairs agreement, signed on 24 August 1945, went through smoothly enough. By this agreement, of course, Britain was obliged to allow the Dutch to resume effective control of their possessions as soon as the situation *vis à vis the enemy* permitted. In other words, the contingency of the need for action *against the native population* was not covered. In British – as indeed in Dutch – official circles, there was no awareness of the strength of the Indonesian nationalist movement which was to be encountered. (Churchill, in fact, has been particularly pleased in September 1942 when

25 For example, FO 371, F2741/100/23, F6673/260/61, U58/14/70.
26 For example, material in PREM 3, 180/7; PREM 4, 31/4; CAB 79/28 and 36; FO 371, files 31490, 35253, 40461, 40740, 40943, 41625, 41627, 41727, 42678, 45651, 45655, 46280, 46417, 50774, 50775.

Dr Gerbrandy reported to the Pacific War Council that, in the former's words, 'the natives [of the East Indies] were looking to Europeans for their future and were not making common cause with their fellow Asiatics'.[27])

As for the movement of Dutch officials and troops out to the Far East ready to enter the East Indies, there was the major problem of shipping, over which the American Joint Chiefs of Staff insisted on being consulted even if the proposed move would have only an indirect effect on the prosecution of the war against Japan. And there were limits beyond which Churchill and the British Chiefs of Staff would not go in pressing such matters on the Americans, at a time when larger issues were at stake and relations as a whole were somewhat tense. There was also the time factor: in May 1945 the British Chiefs of Staff were not expecting to capture Singapore until March 1946, and in July – when it was decided that Java would become a British strategic responsibility – the earliest estimate was still no better than the end of 1945; only at the Potsdam Conference was Mountbatten told of the atomic bomb and warned that developments might be considerably speeded up. Moreover, there was no economic or strategic reason to give the East Indies high priority, whatever the timetable: their rubber and oil were by now not needed, whereas Siamese rice supplies were, while Saigon had the attraction of being the command centre for Japanese forces in the entire area. Thus, on 13 August 1945, the Chiefs of Staff in London fixed as an order of priority after the taking of Singapore: Indo-China, Siam, Java, Sumatra.[28]

Within the limits of Allied strategy and the overriding relationship with the United States, however, it is clear that the British authorities, both military and civil, were anxious to see Dutch (and French) forces sent out to Southeast Asia as soon as possible. In October 1944 the Chiefs of Staff approved the idea of 15 Dutch battalions going to Australia to complete their training, and in April 1945 they agreed with Churchill that if transport permitted (and the Joint Planners pointed out that the Dutch were themselves making a substantial contribution to the Allied pool of shipping) there should be a speeding up of such movements by the European allies. The Chiefs of Staff expressed their anxiety to maintain 'close and cordial contact with the Dutch, both in Europe and in the Far East', and wanted the Prime Minister to take the matter up with the President; Churchill, however, preferred that the case should be made by the Foreign Office, where the Far Eastern Department again expressed

27 FO 371, U4968/3386/74, F1705/2/61. F12362/6398/61; Pacific War Council, 21 October 1942, CAB 99/26; interviews with Dr J. E. van Hoogstraten and Mr J. G. Kist.
28 For example, Chiefs of Staff minutes, 21 April 1945, CAB 79/32; 30 May 1945, CAB 79/34; 21 June 1945, CAB 79/35; 4 July 1945, CAB 79/36; 8, 10, and 13 August 1945, CAB 79/37.

themselves in June as being 'all in favour of helping the Dutch to secure a greater degree of participation in the Far Eastern war'. In July the British planners were still pressing in the same direction, and at Potsdam – despite the inability of senior Netherlands politicians to get a hearing – the Chiefs of Staff tried to secure a more welcoming response by their US colleagues to French and Dutch requests. Although the shipping bottleneck and the relative lack of interest displayed by the Americans remained decisive for the time being, the Chiefs of Staff were still emphasizing the same conclusion as the war against Japan came to an end: French and Dutch forces should be shipped out to take over their own territories as soon as possible.[29]

By this time, Java, as well as Sumatra, had become a British responsibility. Contrary to ideas still accepted in some Dutch quarters, however, this transfer of Java from MacArthur's Southwest Pacific Area to SEAC had been a US, and not a British, initiative. The confusion has arisen through a failure to separate developments in 1945 from those a year earlier. In the summer of 1944, as part of the confused debate over British strategy which has been noted above, there had indeed been a proposal from London to obtain a role within MacArthur's area. This project – a compromise 'middle course' between the emphasis of the Chiefs of Staff on Japan itself and Churchill's on Sumatra – had been for a Commonwealth land, sea and air force to operate on MacArthur's left flank and under his supreme command. General Blamey of Australia was also in favour of the idea as his own relations with MacArthur were becoming more strained, while in London there was the additional hope that the supreme commander could eventually be made answerable not simply to the US Joint Chiefs of Staff alone, but to the Anglo-American Combined Chiefs of Staff. When General Marshall (the US Chief of Staff) and Admiral King (US Chief of Naval Operations) were in London in June 1944, they unofficially gave their support to this idea of a force on MacArthur's flank; King, however, when passing on the notion to MacArthur, chose to give him the impression that the British intended to take away his Area altogether, and the Prime Minister of Australia, Curtin, did the same. MacArthur thereupon raised a storm with Roosevelt (he cited the prestige and commercial opportunities which the United States derived from his command) and sought to enlist the support of the Dutch, but he was assured by Churchill that there was no intention to deprive him of his Area. In any case, *the whole project was withdrawn by Britain at the Second Quebec Conference in September 1944*, when Roosevelt – despite King's opposition – accepted a major contribution by

29 For example, Chiefs of Staff, 10 April 1945, CAB 79/31; 11 July 1945, CAB 79/36; 16 July 1945, CAB 99/39; Combined Chiefs of Staff, 18 July 1945, CAB 88/4; material in FO 371, files 41742, 46321, 46322, 46323, 46370.

the Royal Navy for Pacific operations against Japan; Britain's main land effort in Southeast Asia thereupon reverted to being the capture of Rangoon and Singapore.[30]

Quite separate from this fracas was the sudden proposal by the US Joint Chiefs of Staff on 13 April 1945 that the Southwest Pacific area, minus the Philippines and Hainan, should be taken over by SEAC or a separate British/Australian command, thus relieving MacArthur (despite his own reluctance) of responsibility in order that he could concentrate on the main drive against Japan to the north. Only after much consideration did the planners in London decide that the advantages of such a move might outweigh the disadvantages – one factor being the ability to preserve close relations with the Dutch. Obvious difficulties still existed, however, not least the US intention, conveyed to London in June, to withdraw their supplies from the area at the same time. The British Chiefs of Staff were thus anxious to postpone the transfer beyond the date of 15 August, which their US colleagues now proposed, but at Potsdam reluctantly accepted that in the rapidly changing circumstances of the time it would have to take place 'as soon as possible'.

Subsequently, 15 August became the date of transfer, but this did not mean that British troops could move into Java immediately. Not only was that area rated below Singapore, Saigon and Siam, but MacArthur ordered that the acceptance of local Japanese surrenders must wait until after the main capitulation ceremony in Tokyo bay. It was therefore 3 September before SEAC operations could move forward again, which they did on 5 September against Singapore. (It must be remembered that this had to be on a full military basis, since it was not known whether local Japanese commanders would obey the surrender order or choose to continue resistance.) It was for these reasons that it was not until 15 September that HMS *Cumberland* arrived off the East Indies, and 29 September that the first main body of SEAC troops came into Java. Meanwhile, of course, on 17 August, an Indonesian Republic had been proclaimed by the nationalists, and an entirely new and unforeseen situation awaited the British commanders and their Government.[31]

30 Material in PREM 3, 159/4 and 14, 160/4, 5, 6, and 7; Combined Chiefs of Staff, 11 June 1944 and 14 September 1944, CAB 88/4; Churchill-Curtin-MacArthur correspondence, CAB 69/6; MacArthur to Marshall, 27 August 1944 and Marshall to MacArthur, 21 August 1944, RG 4 and 10 respectively MacArthur papers, MacArthur Library, Norfolk, Virginia; King to MacArthur, 21 July 1944, King papers, box 4, US Navy Operational Archives, Washington, DC.
31 Marshall to MacArthur, 2 January 1945, RG 4, MacArthur papers; material in PREM 3, 159/7; Chiefs of Staff minutes, 26 April and 1 May 1945, CAB 79/32; of 8 June 1945, CAB 79/34; of 17 July 1945, CAB 99/39; of 8 August 1945, CAB 79/37; FO 371, F9991/6398/61; J. Ehrman, *Grand Strategy*, vol. VI (London, 1956), pp. 228–32, 253.

At the time of writing, official records in London – and then only for certain ministries – are not open beyond the end of 1945. Enough are available, however, to outline a number of features of British policy over the East Indies during the period September–December of that year.[32] The first is that, rightly or wrongly, both London and South East Asia Command firmly believed that there was insufficient military force at their disposal to impose a solution upon the nationalists. 'The overriding factors', wrote a Foreign Office official at the end of September, 'are the very limited number of troops . . . and the very limited shipping.' The Chiefs of Staff agreed: the most that could be done, they reported early in October, was to occupy key areas required for the release of prisoners of war and internees (and the dilemma of these hostages to the nationalists remained acute), and for the disarming of the Japanese. 'There was no military solution to this problem', declared the Vice Chief of the Imperial General Staff, pointing out that the terrain of Java was admirably suited to guerrilla tactics. The Prime Minister, Clement Attlee, endorsed this judgement: SEAC could not hope to do more than disarm the Japanese, release the prisoners and 'progressively hand over key points to the Dutch'. If a full military solution *were* to be sought, London estimated it would require at least four divisions, Mountbatten (who at the end of November put the number of armed Indonesians at 100,000) estimated six divisions. Nothing like these forces were available, and in addition there was the political problem, explained below, that of Mountbatten's eventual 30 battalions, all but four were of Indian troops. Fifteen Dutch battalions were thought to be available, but not all of these were due to arrive until February 1946, and it was uncertain whether they would be adequate to maintain law and order. (On 10 October, the Cabinet's Defence Committee authorized transportation for an additional four Dutch battalions in October–November, on top of the eight already planned for those months. 'At no time', reported the VCIGS, 'had we refused to provide the ships when Dutch troops had been available to put into them.') When forceful operations to restore order were finally undertaken in Batavia and Western Java on 28 December, the Chiefs of Staff emphasized that only now was this possible, as a result of increased British numbers.

This enforced delay was seen by Esler Dening as having been decisive. He wrote at the end of December: 'Had we had the shipping lift available and the mines swept in time, and had we thus been able to land [two divisions] simultaneously and in full strength in Java and Sumatra, I feel certain that the present situation would not have arisen because the

32 The following material on British views and decisions from August to December 1945 is all taken from FO 371, files 46392–46409. See also F.S.V. Donnison, *British Military Administration in the Far East, 1943–46* (London, 1956), ch. 22.

Soekarno administration would not have had time to gain control and to feel its strength.' Dening himself, it is quite clear from his reports, wished to see the Dutch regain control, however much he deplored the behaviour of some of their officials and soldiers on the spot. Within the Foreign Office in London, however, pro-Dutch sentiments were stronger still, and it was felt that SEAC were too ready to be critical of their allies, and too ready 'to justify everything that the Indonesians do'. The Head of the Far Eastern Department wrote on 9 October:

The whole Republican movement looks like a political time-bomb planted by the Japanese, and I think we must guard against being unduly impressed by it. In advocating that we should press the Dutch to grant some form of independence, I think that the Supreme Allied Commander [Mountbatten] is going too far to one extreme, just as the Dutch Government are going too far to the other by their proposed negative proclamation [of the illegality of the Republican movement].

In this same spirit, the Foreign Office welcomed the proposals for a settlement which were eventually put forward by The Hague, and wished to defer any active part in the issue being taken by the United States, for fear it would encourage the Indonesians to increase their demands. The general Foreign Office line, in fact, was reflected in a minute written at the end of September: 'The Dutch stood by us in 1940–41 when things were very black in the Far East, and were we now by inactivity to favour the schemes of these people who have been collaborating with the Japanese we should do great harm to Anglo-Dutch relations.'

It is important to note, in addition, that both Ernest Bevin, the Foreign Secretary, and Attlee himself, were working in this period within a basic assumption of respect for Dutch sovereignty over the East Indies. 'From the political angle', Bevin wrote to Dening at the beginning of October, 'the arguments in favour of non-intervention . . . must be balanced against the very harmful effect on Anglo-Dutch relations which may be produced . . . Our action must be conditioned by the forces available. But I feel that no recognition should be given to any authorities not approved by the Netherlands Government.' Attlee, for his part, was quick to question his Secretary of State for War, J. J. Lawson, when the latter was reported in the press as saying in Singapore that Britain would not intervene. (Lawson denied having said this, but a question was arranged in the House of Commons so that the refutation could be made public.) To the Australian Prime Minister, who had urged that the issue called for international intervention, Attlee replied on 5 November:

Further concessions might only encourage the extremists to open their mouths wider still . . . [and] we have need for good relations with our neighbour in Europe. It would be wrong for us to take advantage of the accident that war has placed us in temporary military control of Java to go any further in the direction of intervening in the domestic affairs of our Ally than is strictly necessary. We should indeed be most reluctant to do anything to suggest that sovereignty is a factor which can be lightly set aside . . . Our attitude to the introduction of further Dutch forces into Java must be guided by the necessity of maintaining law and order . . . But we have to be careful to do nothing which could be construed as an attempt to impede the resumption of Dutch control.

In harmony with such sentiments was an increasing exasperation on the British side with the nationalist extremists in Java. This was particularly evident from the time of their murder of Brigadier Mallaby, with the Chiefs of Staff concluding on 5 November that 'Soekarno had lost control of the extremist element, who had now turned anti-British'. Even earlier, on 31 October, Dening had judged that 'an exhibition of the lethal capacity of our weapons is probably the only thing which will bring the extremists to their senses'; on 12 November he was writing that 'there is no body of Indonesians capable of ruling the country adequately and to its benefit at present', while by the end of the month he was even further disenchanted: 'The fact is that the Indonesian leaders are . . . incapable of exerting their authority. In such circumstances talking to them is just a waste of breath as far as practical results are concerned.'

Yet Dening himself had also been stressing that, whatever its short-comings, the nationalist movement was a substantial phenomenon which had to be treated with care. In a report of 11 October which Attlee regarded as 'most important . . ., the first time that we have had a really authoritative view on the position in Indonesia', he had warned:

Sympathetically handled, the Indonesian independence movement might well be absorbed. But occupying as it does key positions, it can create a very serious situation if driven to do so by unsympathetic handling . . . There seems little doubt that nobody in Indonesia wants the old gang back, and one report which I would regard as dependable states that this view is [also] held by the majority of the 140,000 odd Dutch and Eurasians who have been interned in Java. It is the arrival of van Mook and van der Plas (who is since believed to have changed his views) and members of the old gang which has rendered the population suspicious.

Dening's source of information on this last point was Laurens van der Post, a Dutch-speaking South African who had himself been interned in Java, and who quoted Jkr van Karnebeek, 'the most outstanding young Dutch civilian figure on the island', as saying: 'Give us a military dictatorship [preferably all-British] for six months, and keep the old gang out. That is what we need most of all'. Van der Post's own opinion of Soekarno and his fellow leaders was that they were 'rather pathetic figures . . . If they are only seen and spoken to and tactfully handled, in three or four months' time they will be ignominious and forgotten figures in the life of the country'. He was flown back to England to give these views to Attlee himself, and then sent on to The Hague, where, late in October, he urged flexibility on Professors Schermerhorn and Logemann and Dr van Kleffens, suggesting that van Mook should be allowed to talk to Soekarno and be given as free a hand as possible.

Mountbatten himself reported in more grave terms about the nationalists, whom he saw by 11 October as being 'the de facto government of the country'; they had the merit in his eyes of being 'strongly anti-Japanese', while 'moderate elements of the independence movement appeared prepared to accept a further period of European tutelage before attaining complete independence'. It followed for the Supreme Commander, as it had in the Burmese situation, that flexibility was essential, and he had begun to push van Mook in this direction as early as 28 September. 'A conciliatory policy', he telegraphed on 9 October, 'of readiness to meet and negotiate with Soekarno, and a declaration of Dutch intentions to grant some form of Indonesian independence would probably remove the danger of resistance by force.'

Attlee in his turn, while not committing himself so far on the matter of independence, urged the Dutch Government at least to negotiate. In general, however, London found the administration in The Hague 'weak and inexperienced', regretting its repudiation of van der Plas's well-known conciliatory broadcast and its initial refusal to allow van Mook to talk with Soekarno, while taking little account of its domestic political difficulties over these matters. Much greater impatience, however, was expressed by SEAC officers and officials with their Dutch counterparts on the spot in Java. 'Unfortunately', wrote Dening on 11 October, 'there is far too much evidence of a die-hard and uncompromising spirit among the Dutch officers and officials who are destined to go back.' A month later he was describing a 'total lack of initiative and leadership' locally; van Mook he thought the best man present, but he too 'lacked tact and discretion' and was alarmingly ready to commit his Government without prior approval. Netherlands Army officers were thought to be far too prone to try to 'shoot their way in', and it was this belief, that the presence of more Dutch troops would only provoke an uglier situation which could not be contained, that led to a halt being called to such arrivals. General Christison, himself the object of much Dutch resentment, reported that he had no confidence in General van Oyen.

Meanwhile, domestic pressure was increasing upon the Government in

London. The *Manchester Guardian*, for example, which on 15 October had declared:

Order must be restored in Java and the Dutch must go back. They understand the country and its people and we are in no danger of setting Imperialists back on their throne . . . As France and Holland renew their strength we shall depend upon their friendship in the West, and to earn it we must now perform the office of a friend in the East.

had become greatly impatient by 22 November:

We cannot go on reinforcing troops and allow ourselves to be dragged into a minor war to subdue rebels . . . We have enough troubles of our own on our hands in the East . . . And we get no support, indeed something perilously like abuse, from our American and Russian friends, to whom this miserable involvement is only fresh evidence of our 'Imperialist' habits.

Fenner Brockway and other members of the left wing of the Labour Party were also urging Attlee not to betray socialist principles over Indo-China and Indonesia, even though he resisted their arguments ('Not every movement that claims to be democratic', he wrote to Brockway, 'can be accepted as such on its own statement.'[33]) More ominously, the United States was showing signs of being ready to leave Britain in an isolated position on the issue. On 15 October she instructed that all lend–lease markings must be removed from vehicles etc. being used in the East Indies, and on 11 December Mountbatten was told that in future United States ships could not be employed to move SEAC troops to Java. The American press was also becoming increasingly critical of what it tended to see as a European imperialist conspiracy in Southeast Asia. Perhaps most important of all, the Government of India, faced with fierce criticism from the Congress Party over the use of Indian troops to suppress Asian nationalist movements, was insisting that no more Indian reinforcements should be sent (the Indian 5th Division was the only one readily available), and on 25 November declared that a time limit must be set on the presence of troops already in the East Indies: 'The sooner they can be sent back the better for our chances of preventing widespread disorder in India and preserving the morale of the Indian Army.' Mountbatten reported that indeed the morale of all his troops, British and Indian, was beginning to suffer. 'Both by the press and by letters from home', he cabled on 3 December, 'the British troops are being made to believe that the imposition of Dutch authority by force of British arms is a wrong cause . . . The Indian troops are subject to Indonesian propaganda which is insidious and well directed.'

33 Attlee papers, boxes 4 and 9, University College, Oxford.

In these circumstances, London at the end of the year was still trying to balance the various obligations, pressures and desiderata. The possible solution now winning support was a 'middle course' of withdrawing to West Java alone, and by force establishing there a strong Dutch base from which negotiations could proceed. Already, however, a fresh dilemma was apparent, of whether one could leave to their fate loyalist elements in Sourabaya; Mountbatten wanted to allow fresh Dutch troops to proceed there, but London instructed that they be sent to West Java instead. Meanwhile, as leading Dutch Ministers arrived in London to reveal their new constitutional proposals, the idea began to be canvassed of a Netherlands–Indonesian conference under British chairmanship. First, however, firm military action would be taken in Batavia.

In conclusion, one may suggest that it was well-nigh inevitable that, shaped as it was within severe constraints, British policy would satisfy no one. It can also be said, however, that in general it was well intentioned, and, while critical of some aspects of Dutch policy and actions, by no means inimical to the Netherlands. Indeed, given the tenacity and strength of the Indonesian nationalist movement and the wider currents of international relations at the time, London's insistence that the Dutch should be flexible and negotiate with those who had set up the Republic can be seen in retrospect as having considerable merit, even though it had failed to bring about a solution to the impasse in the Indies by the time the British withdrew from the territory, to be replaced, in effect, as the uncomfortable third party in the anti-colonial struggle by the United States.[34]

34 For an excellent survey of American post-war policies towards the Indonesian struggle for independence and the Netherlands, with reflections also on Britain's role in 1945–46, see R. J. McMahon, *Colonialism and Cold War. The United States and the Struggle for Indonesian Independence, 1945–49* (Ithaca, NY, 1981).

7

MacArthur, Australia and the British, 1942–1943: The Secret Journal of MacArthur's British Liaison Officer

Colonel Gerald Hugh Wilkinson, CBE, was one of those civilians who found themselves 'instant-officers' as a result of the Second World War. When Japan struck at Pearl Harbor in December 1941, he had for some years been living in the Philippines as the manager there of a Hawaian-based British firm dealing in sugar and other commodities. In addition to his normal work, however, he had also since 1940 been sending intelligence reports to London, presumably on Japanese shipping and similar matters. It was not entirely surprising, therefore, that when war came to the Far East he found himself a major overnight – later colonel – and given the quasi-official post of British Liaison Officer with the American commander in the Philippines, the redoubtable General Douglas MacArthur.

As the Japanese invaders of the Philippines closed in, Wilkinson accompanied MacArthur to the island of Corregidor where the Americans were to make their final stand.[1] Before the end came, however, he was sent

Reproduced from *Australian Outlook*, 29 (1975), pp. 53–67, 197–210. The writer is grateful to Professor Bruce Miller of the Australian National University for making helpful comments on a preliminary draft of this essay and above all to the family of the late Colonel Wilkinson for generously allowing access to his papers.

1 Wilkinson went to Corregidor on MacArthur's orders. At the Pearl Harbor hearings in 1946, the General's G2, General C. A. Willoughby, sneered that Wilkinson had left his wife and children 'to fend for themselves'; he also accused Wilkinson of 'duplicity' as a British agent in his dealings with the Americans. Willoughby's grotesque assertions (prompted by the embarrassing revelation that Wilkinson on 2 December 1941 had sent a warning to the Americans at Honolulu that Japanese action against Britain and the United States appeared imminent) were easily and devastatingly rebutted by Wilkinson, who also obtained a grudging but full retraction from Willoughby. *San Francisco Examiner*, 14 February 1946; *Honolulu Advertiser*, 15 February 1946; Wilkinson Papers.

to make contact in Java with General Wavell, whose hastily constructed and ill-fated inter-Allied ABDA (American, British, Dutch, Australian) Command was trying to hold the Japanese in the Dutch East Indies and neighbouring areas. Wilkinson first attempted this journey by plane, which crashed; he then succeeded in reaching Java by submarine. From there he went to Australia, then via Washington to London, gathering material with which to offset MacArthur's conspiracy theory, that Churchill alone was leading America to neglect her Pacific interests for the sake of the European theatre.[2] In June 1942, Wilkinson had an interview with Churchill himself, at which it was agreed that the former would continue to be the Prime Minister's link with MacArthur, reporting through the Head of the Secret Intelligence Service, Sir Stewart Menzies, known as 'C'. (Later messages from London indicated to Wilkinson that 'Churchill seems to have remembered myself and my small ideas more strongly than I had hoped.'[3]) The Prime Minister also emphasized his current belief that 'the place to strike the octopus [Japan] was the centre, not the tentacles, [adding]: "There is much to be learned from simple nursery tales: Lady Bird, Lady Bird, fly away home, your house is aburning, your children are gone" – i.e. that this will be the effect of an attack upon Japan proper upon her forces in her outposts'.[4]

Meanwhile, MacArthur, by order of President Roosevelt, had been smuggled out of Corregidor and away to Australia. There, in the late summer of 1942, Wilkinson rejoined him, 'free and alive', in his own words, 'by a miracle – or rather a steady chain of most fortunate incidents, preservations and opportunities'. His wife and two children, however, remained behind in the Philippines, interned by the victorious Japanese.

In Australia, Wilkinson, now aged 33, began to keep a journal which has remained in the possession of his family. Of great interest in its own right, this personal record can now be placed in a setting based partly on newly available official British documents for the period. For around the time when Wilkinson was writing, relations between Britain, Australia and the United States were in a fluid and in some ways critical condition. And it was in this situation that the newly fledged Colonel recorded, day by day, his talks with MacArthur, with various leading Australians, and with British officials like the Governor-General, High Commissioner and State Governors. Above all, he was preoccupied with the task of retaining MacArthur's confidence and nurturing the slender contacts between that proud and suspicious man and London. As he wrote in a letter after his

2 Wilkinson Papers. These are now available to researchers in the Archives Centre of Churchill College, Cambridge.
3 Wilkinson Journal, 7 January 1943.
4 Ibid., 30 March 1943.

subsequent return to Britain and reversion to the rank of major), 'Trying to play the role of honest broker between this Government and a great personality and to develop recognition and sympathy between the two parties during the past 17 months has not been an altogether easy role to play unofficially.'[5]

MacArthur in 1942 was already something of a legend. Theatrical in manner and acutely sensitive about his personal position, he was nevertheless widely recognized as possessing great military ability (Field Marshal Lord Alanbrooke was later to rate him 'the greatest general and best strategist that the war produced').[6] MacArthur had long been convinced, as he was to write in his memoirs, that 'the future and, indeed, the very existence of America was irrevocably entwined with Asia and its island outposts, . . . Western civilization's last frontier'.[7] Now his defeat in the Philippines (during which he had been proved over-confidently fallible and had even, in a despairing moment, supported a proposal that the Filipinos should sever their American connection and seek peace with the Japanese)[8] had to be avenged with all speed. Only thus could he keep faith with himself and with his vision of America's destiny.

By the end of February 1942, Wavell's ABDA Command had fallen apart under the assaults of the Japanese. There followed a global reallocation of strategic areas and command responsibilities, as agreed between Roosevelt and Churchill. Australia, together with the Philippines, most of the Dutch East Indies, New Guinea and other islands, now came within a new South West Pacific Area to be commanded by MacArthur; for operational strategy (grand strategy remaining the prerogative of the Anglo-American Combined Chiefs of Staff) he would be answerable to General George Marshall and the American Joint Chiefs of Staff in Washington.[9]

A defender was what Australia was looking for, and when MacArthur arrived in March 1942 he was received as St George come to save the maiden from the advancing dragon. With his headquarters first in Melbourne and then in Brisbane, and in close touch with the Australian Prime Minister, John Curtin, either directly or through F. G. (later Sir

5 Wilkinson to Dewing, 4 June 1943, Wilkinson Papers.
6 A. Bryant, *Triumph in the West* (London, 1959), p. 513.
7 D. MacArthur, *Reminiscences* (London, 1964), p. 32.
8 See, for example, D. C. Jones, *The Years of MacArthur*, vol. 1 (London, 1970), p. 583, and H. L. Stimson and M. Bundy. *On Active Service in Peace and War* (New York, 1948), p. 398. Also W. Manchester, *American Caesar. Douglas MacArthur, 1880–1964* (London, 1979), and C. M. Petillo, *Douglas MacArthur: the Philippine Years* (Bloomington, Indiana, 1981).
9 See, for example, J. R. M. Butler, *Grand Strategy*, vol. III, part II (London, 1964), pp. 470ff; M. Matloff and E. M. Snell, *Strategic Planning for Coalition Warfare, 1941–42* (Washington, DC, 1953), pp. 169ff.

Frederick) Shedden, Secretary of the War Cabinet, he at once became a towering figure in the country. At the same time he was potentially a force in US politics also, as a focus for those 'Pacific-First' sentiments which were especially strong among some sections of Roosevelt's domestic opponents. Indeed, the idea of 'MacArthur for President' had already received an airing by the time Wilkinson began his journal in September.

Wilkinson was not blind to MacArthur's shortcomings. After a long talk with him on 3 November, for example, he noted the General's 'fantastically sensitive suspicions of hostility' and his 'peculiarly feminine streak of intuitive personal sensitivity'. His wider judgement, however, was set out in an interview on 24 October with the Governor-General of Australia, Lord Gowrie, VC (a British former guards officer who held that office from 1936 to 1944):

I told Gowrie that my own opinion of MacA was that, especially to any English person of good sense, the first 5 minutes might give an impression of 'phoneyness', theatricality and of possibly a meretricious person – but that, after that, I had become more and more of the opinion that MacA had real mental distinction, width of view . . . and exceptional political acumen . . . That any extravagance of speech was not accompanied by extravagance of decision and that in large matters he had in fact shown considerable conservatism, e.g. . . . his handling of Australian authorities. That he also was a most able handler of press and public relations and that surely the combination of these qualities – plus the defects in the present administration of the Pacific War – would enable him to 'stage a come back' at the time that he would think it right.

Meanwhile, as Wilkinson had explained on 22 September to the Governor of Queensland, Sir Leslie Wilson (a former British army officer and Conservative MP), MacArthur's policy was

to lie low, (a) to reduce the malicious opportunities of jealous Washington, (b) to encourage the officer class of Australia to come forward more – i.e. permeation of leadership, not one-man show.

Wilkinson, however, was thinking more of MacArthur's 'come back' and what this could mean for Britain 'even if he isn't President'. His idea, as he put it to the General himself on 19 October, was to visit Washington in order to suggest to senior British officials there

that it would be in the long-term interests of Great Britain to take a leading hand in urging the simplification of the Pacific Commands and the promotion of one [MacArthur] who could do far more for post-war Anglo-American influence in the Far East than any single US Admiral – quite apart from his obvious and immediate meritings [sic] of a higher command. M's answer to this was that anyone who could get to Washington and hammer a little strategic sense into their heads would be doing a good job.

To Gowrie on 24 October, Wilkinson explained further what he had in mind:

HMG would be wise to take the initiative in simplifying things and . . . the promotion of MacArthur . . . And if such influence was exerted, MacA should be made unofficially aware of it so that we might hope for his friendship and understanding in future Anglo-American matters such as Pacific and Asiatic post-war settlements.

Gowrie appeared receptive to these ideas, thinking it advisable to 'ignore completely [but] not contradict' MacArthur's presidential ambitions. The Governor-General, who was, in Wilkinson's view, 'wise, quiet and trusted', also revealed himself to be 'surprisingly well informed on US affairs and obviously in full knowledge of local affairs'. At this interview on 24 October, he observed to Wilkinson

that he too had had his doubts about MacA – as possibly a showman – during the first five minutes of their meeting, but that he had been increasingly favourably impressed by him – that the showmanship was a good thing in Australia and quite possibly consciously put on. He ended by saying that he too felt MacA to be a person of unusual stature – and greater potentialities than a usual C in C. [At an earlier meeting, on 4 October, Gowrie had also remarked] 'that MacA has handled his relations here extremely well . . . Curtin is an excellent man and MacArthur's relations with him are very good and deservedly so'.

Britain's High Commissioner, Sir Ronald Cross, had spoken to Wilkinson in a similar sense on the previous day: 'He considers MacArthur has handled the Australian Government – and all his local political relations – with perfect ability and judgment and MacA obviously impresses [him] as potentially far larger than a general.' On 26 January 1943, Sir Campbell Stuart, former Managing Director of *The Times* and Chairman of the Imperial Communications Committee (who also had connections with the Secret Service and propaganda in enemy territories)[10] was clearer still:

Whether extravagant or not, right or wrong, MacA is a really great man and an attractive one – the one man who, in Stuart's opinion, would be capable of, and has the line of talk to upset the President. In fact, that M will be the next Republican

10 On Stuart, see B. Sweet-Escott, *Baker Street Irregular* (London, 1965), p. 29.

nomination for President of the US . . . Stuart [therefore] emphasizes the importance of my staying here and keeping close to this man.

However, substantial reservations concerning the new hero had been expressed to Wilkinson in an interview on 29 October with the former Australian Prime Minister, R. G. (later Sir Robert) Menzies, whose high reputation in London and Washington Wilkinson privately contrasted with 'his fellow-countrymen's recognition of his abilities [but their] dislike and almost distrust of his leadership':

Menzies a large, genial fellow . . ., grey-white hair, pink healthy complexion, blue eyes – the manner of a successful, self-confident and humorous barrister . . . [He said that] MacArthur infuriated him at [a summer] meeting of Australian War Cabinet [in fact it was the Advisory War Council] by his exaggerated praise of present Government's leadership and war effort and improvement in Australia's position compared with 5½ months earlier when Australia stood (according to MacA) 'naked and defenceless against the invader'. Menzies felt that as he had bumped up Aussie defence expenditure from £14 million to £200 million p.a. during his incumbency as PM, MacA's remarks showed little understanding of facts and that he (Menzies) had told [Major General Richard] Sutherland [MacArthur's Chief of Staff] after the meeting that he would like to 'throttle MacA'. (This must have entertained the hard-boiled little Sutherland.) . . . Menzies said that he thought MacA was *not* clear in his mind on the actual merits and facts of things and people, and he made a reference to people who mistake their emotions for their principles.

He agreed that . . . the credit side of MacArthur's record was considerable, i.e. stiffening of morale, acquisition of equipment, etc, [and said] that there had been real ugly fear over prospect of invasion among many of the Australian Government leaders around February/March until MacA came along – men turning 'nasty colour' etc. He entirely agreed with the 'beat Germany first' decision in Allied strategy, but did not think this 'island-to-island' plan of beating Japan would work. Burma-to-China-to-Japan preferable.

Menzies' remarks concerning Australian fears of invasion earlier in 1942 have to be seen partly in their international political context. Once installed in Australia, MacArthur had become more than a military commander and potential force in American politics. In 1942–3 especially, he was also a focal point in the shifting relationships within the Australian–British–American triangle.

Even before Japan had launched her attack in the Pacific, new strains had appeared between London and Canberra – over military operations in the Middle East and Mediterranean, for example, and over the vain attempt by Menzies, then Prime Minister, to persuade Churchill to set up an Imperial War Cabinet where Australia and others could make their voices heard more clearly and systematically. [11] At the same time the actual and potential significance of the United States (where the first Australian Minister, R. G. Casey, was installed in 1940) was daily more apparent – although this did not mean that politicians and officials, embroiled in the business of the war, had yet developed an adequate new perspective within which to view developments. Walter Lippmann, for example, was soon to complain to Maynard Keynes that none of the British representatives in Washington 'had any philosophy and doctrine about the changing relationships between the United States, the British Commonwealth and the British Empire. There is almost a complete intellectual vacuum on the subject . . . The whole approach . . . is ad hoc on details of this and that arising from the conduct of the war itself.' [12]

The early disasters of the Pacific War at once created a new level of tension, even bitterness, in Anglo-Australian relations. The sinking of the *Prince of Wales* and *Repulse* and the swift surrender of Singapore not only stunned Australians but led many of them to feel that Britain had let them down. Nor did they lack grounds for such sentiments. As late as 1939 London had assured the Australian Government of a degree of naval protection which Britain was not in fact in a position to provide in the event of global war. Churchill himself had long and grievously miscalculated over the danger of a Japanese attack – 'possible but unlikely', as he assured the Cabinet and Sir Earle Page of Australia on 12 November 1941 – just as he clung too late to the notion of Singapore as a fortress and misjudged the deterrent effect of sending out – over Admiralty protests – the two ill-fated capital ships. [13]

In this situation John Curtin's Labor Government, in power in Canberra since October 1941, were prepared to give freer expression to their resentment than Menzies would have done. In the Melbourne *Herald*

11 See, for example, A. Watt, *The Evolution of Australian Foreign Policy* (Cambridge, 1967), pp. 29ff; J. M. A. Gwyer, *Grand Strategy*, vol. III, part I (London, 1964), pp. 223ff; W. S. Churchill, *The Second World War*, vol. III (London, 1950), p. 365; and in general, C. H. Grattan, *The United States and the South West Pacific* (Cambridge, Mass., 1961); R. J. Bell, *Unequal Allies* (Melbourne, 1977) and 'Testing the Open Door Thesis in Australia 1941–1946', *Pacific Historical Review*, vol. 51, no. 3, 1982; D. M. Horner, *High Command: Australia and Allied Strategy, 1939–1945* (Canberra, 1982).

12 Lippmann to Keynes, 2 April 1942, in FO 371/30655, A4574/60/45. Public Record Office, London, as with all subsequent references to Foreign Office files (FO), Prime Minister's files (PREM), Cabinet minutes, memoranda, committees, Chiefs of Staff, etc. (CAB). Extracts from Crown Copyright records appear by permission of the Controller of HM Stationery Office.

13 See, for example, Cabinets of 27 October and 12 November 1941, in CAB 65/23 and 24; Churchill to Chamberlain, 25 March 1939 (in which he dismissed the idea of a Japanese attack on Singapore), PREM 1/345; British naval assurances to Australia in 1938 and 1939 in PREM 1/309.

of 27 December, Curtin let it be known 'without inhibitions of any kind' that his country 'looks to America, free of any pangs as to our traditional links or kinship with the United Kingdom'.[14] Churchill's bitter private reactions, recorded by Lord Moran,[15] were modified in the replies which he sent back to further demands by the Australian Prime Minister, but at the end of January the series of private premier-to-premier telegrams was suspended by Churchill 'in view of Mr Curtin's tone'.[16] Cool and now well-known exchanges continued on a formal level, however, over Canberra's demands for the return home of Australian divisions then fighting in the Middle East and its refusal to allow the diversion of some of these troops to Rangoon; over its desire to see an Anglo-American naval striking force rapidly built up in the Pacific, to receive greater military supplies, and to encourage the Soviet Union to come into the war against Japan. In addition Curtin demanded regular representation for Australia within the Cabinet in London, and a share in the management of the Pacific War in direct contact with the US, not simply through Britain (an emphasis and issue on which New Zealand joined Australia and which Churchill was to gloss over in his own published account).[17] The Australian Government also publicly revealed its anger when Churchill appointed their Minister in Washington, Casey, to be Britain's Minister of State in the Middle East with a seat in the Cabinet.[18]

The seriousness of this rapid decline in relations made a deep impression in at least some quarters of Whitehall. Indeed, at a Cabinet meeting towards the end of January, one of those present even went so far as to scribble on a piece of paper preserved by the First Lord of the Admiralty that 'Australia is the most dangerous obstacle in the path of this Government'.[19] More thoughtfully, the Dominions Secretary, Lord Cranborne, warned his colleagues that it would be 'a great and possibly disastrous mistake' to underestimate the strength of Australian feeling, and that with 'centrifugal tendencies' already present in South Africa and elsewhere, 'a rot which started in Australia might easily spread to other Dominions'.[20]

14 See P. Hasluck, *The Government and the People, 1942-1945* (Canberra, 1970), p. 39.

15 Lord Moran, *Winston Churchill: The Struggle for Survival* (London, 1966), p. 21.

16 Churchill minute, 30 January 1942, PREM 4,50/7.

17 Cf. Churchill. *The Second World War*, vol. 4 (London, 1951), p. 17, and, for example, the documents in WP (42) 38, CAB 66/21, and PREM 3, 145/3 and 5. The New Zealand Premier warned Churchill on 26 January 1942: 'Your proposals as explained do not meet the requirement of direct contact with the Americans . . . If we were obliged to choose between a Council as contemplated in London without fully adequate American representation, and a similar Council established in Washington . . . then we would be forced to prefer the second alternative.' See further New Zealand messages in PREM 3,145/4.

18 See Lord Casey, *Personal Experience*, 1939-46 (London, 1962), p. 93.

19 A. V. Alexander Papers (Churchill College, Cambridge), box 5/6.

20 Cranborne memo., 21 January 1942. WP (42) 29 in CAB 66/21.

The King, too, conveyed to Churchill his 'genuine alarm at the feeling which appears to be growing in Australia and may well be aggravated by further reverses in the Far East'.[21] And from Australia itself, a former Prime Minister, Billy Hughes, sent a private message to Churchill to emphasize that while Curtin was a moderate, 'some of his Ministers [are] extremists and anti-British. All must bow to leagues and unions . . . Curtin is at best cool towards Britain. Under influence of caucus and leagues [he] may plump for America as against Britain. The press, almost solidly behind Government, feeds people daily with insidious pro-American propaganda . . . The Empire needs a victory'.[22] At the same time Britain's High Commissioner telegraphed to warn that the greatest individual influence in the Australian Cabinet was Dr Herbert Evatt, Attorney-General and Minister for External Affairs, and that his strong desire for personal advancement was channelled in 'nationalistic or possibly secessionist' directions.[23] (In Sir Campbell Stuart's opinion, Evatt had his eyes on the office of Prime Minister, and was 'looking around for other possible associates or political alliances than with Curtin'.[24])

In the event, Australia kept her 'accredited representative' on the War Cabinet in London, Evatt himself filling that role briefly during a visit in May 1942, and being succeeded by the High Commissioner and former Prime Minister, Stanley Bruce (later Viscount Bruce). But although Churchill went out of his way to soothe Evatt, sending some Spitfire squadrons to Australia and assuring him that Britain still felt bound to come to her aid if she were attacked in force,[25] he continued to pay only passing attention to Commonwealth views – save where Smuts was concerned. Bruce (who was not in Evatt's confidence either)[26] soon found his War Cabinet role a hollow one. 'I am given so little information and consulted so little', he

21 Hardinge to Churchill, 22 January 1942, PREM 3,167/1.
22 Hughes to Churchill, 30 May 1942, PREM 4,50/6. Churchill soon afterwards explored the possibility of sending an aircraft carrier to Australia, minuting: 'We have to consider our permanent relations with Australia, and it seems very detrimental to the future of the Empire for us not to be represented in any way with their defence.' Churchill to Pound, 17 May 1942, PREM 3,151/4.   23 Cross to Dominions Office, 27 March 1942, PREM 4,50/6.
24 Wilkinson Journal, 11 January 1943.
25 Cabinets of 4 and 21 May 1942, CAB 65/26. Cf. PREM 4,50/8 for Churchill's invitation early in 1943 to Curtin to visit Britain. In view of the Middle East crisis, Churchill in June 1942 had to delay sending the bulk of the promised Spitfires. Curtin was at first inclined to accept this, but Evatt – 'utterly disgusted', as he cabled to Brendan Bracken –prompted his Prime Minister to register a strong protest. Attlee wrote to Churchill: 'It looks as if Evatt is trying to undermine Curtin's position.' PREM 3,150/7. At the end of 1943, MacArthur was to complain to a party of visiting British newspaper executives that the Spitfires had been antiquated, their pilots raw, and their results poor. None of these statements was true, as the Chief of Air Staff was able to demonstrate to Churchill. PREM, 3,159/2.
26 See C. Edwards, *Bruce of Melbourne* (London, 1965), pp. 337ff.

protested to Churchill in September 1942; and indeed, as Cranborne pointed out to the Prime Minister a year later, the High Commissioner was not even being allowed to attend all those Cabinet meetings at which questions affecting Australia were discussed, contrary to the assumption of his Government in Canberra. '[Bruce] had not disabused them of this impression, as he had been anxious to avoid friction between them and the United Kingdom.' Churchill was persuaded by the Dominions Office to tone down most of his written responses to Bruce to an adequately courteous level, but he was nettled by the latter's suggestion that he, Churchill, was treating the British Cabinet as a whole with indifference (a view for which Bruce found warm support from Lord Hankey among others). Early in 1943 the Prime Minister was writing to Attlee that the High Commissioner 'should be brought up with a round turn', reasoning in a manner which casts some light on his own general view of the Japanese war and his limited sympathy for Australia: 'The position of Mr Bruce is highly anomalous. The Australians have now moved their last troops away from the general war zone [i.e. the Middle East] to their own affairs. Why should Australia be represented on the War Cabinet when Canada, which has five Divisions, and New Zealand and South Africa, which each have one, are not similarly represented?'[27] (The insistence of Mackenzie King's Canada that existing Commonwealth consultative arrangements were entirely adequate was in fact one of the handicaps encountered by Australia throughout the war.)

Apart from Cranborne and Attlee as successive Dominions Secretaries, few ministers and senior officials in London appear to have been ready to go far out of their way to make allowances for Australian fears and resentment. Sir Alexander Cadogan, Permanent Under-Secretary at the Foreign Office, was usually scornful when referring in his diary to the Dominions in general or emissaries like Menzies and Bruce in particular ('what irresponsible rubbish these Antipodeans talk!').[28] The Chiefs of Staff for their part, who (rightly as we know now) refused to accept Australian estimates of the dangers of a major Japanese invasion, were to make it clear to the Prime Minister that they were opposed to staff officers from that country being 'let into all our secrets', and thought that Dominion premiers should receive only the same kind of periodical summaries of the strategic situation that Churchill sent to Stalin.[29]

Nor were relations greatly helped by the gesture of sending out as

27 Bruce–Churchill, Churchill–Attlee and Churchill–Cranborne correspondence in PREM 4,50/1; Edwards, *Bruce of Melbourne*, pp. 351, 367, 381. Cf. Hasluck, *Government and People*, p. 229, and R. G. Menzies, *Afternoon Light* (London, 1967), p. 92. Also Hankey Diary, 4 June 1941 and 31 August 1942 (Churchill College, Cambridge), and Bruce Papers, Commonwealth Archives, Canberra.
28 D. Dilks (ed.), *The Diaries of Sir Alexander Cadogan* (London, 1971), pp. 359, 394, 429.
29 Ismay to Churchill, 9 May 1943, PREM 4,50/8. Cf. Bryant, *Turn of the Tide* (London, 1957), pp. 364–5.

Britain's High Commissioner the Unionist MP and unremarkable member of the Government (Minister of Economic Warfare, and then of Shipping), Sir Ronald Cross. During the storms of January 1942, for example, when he was satisfied that a virulent anti-British campaign in Australia was being 'inspired and conducted by ministers' (though not Curtin, whom he respected), Cross's advice to London was that if Canberra continued 'to ignore the obligations of the spirit of Imperial partnership', Britain should refuse to meet Australian desires on economic and financial questions. 'The time has come', he telegraphed, 'to collect all our weapons and to fight for British prestige in Australia'; not surprisingly, however, his particular selection from the armoury was rejected by Cranborne as certain to make matters a great deal worse.[30]

Meanwhile, in Washington, Australia obtained her place on the Pacific War Council which met there for the first time at the beginning of April 1942. But despite this, and despite Roosevelt's understanding reassurances over the despatch of adequate reinforcements to the area,[31] it was soon evident that Australian influence over United States strategy and policies was no greater than it was over Britain's. The Pacific War Council was, in Halifax's phrase, 'merely a facade'.[32] Its meetings were not attended by the American Chiefs of Staff, but were taken up by Roosevelt, in his own words, 'telling stories and doing most of the talking'.[33]

Although in the United States generally, as Halifax, the British Ambassador, reported to London, public clashes between Britain and Australia were being taken as further evidence that the Commonwealth and Empire were falling apart,[34] Roosevelt himself was embarrassed by these episodes, urging that they should be cleared up and preferring to deal with London as agent for the Commonwealth as a whole. It was not the President, but the British Chiefs of Staff who belatedly, in May, revealed to Evatt that as the basis of Allied strategy it had been agreed at the beginning of the year that priority should be given to the defeat of Germany. (This was apparently the first Evatt had heard of the decision. On the other hand it had been referred to directly by Churchill at a meeting of the British Defence Committee (Operations) on 21 January, when Sir Earle Page of Australia was present.)[35] Roosevelt was also quick to placate Churchill

30 Cranborne memo., 22 January 1942, WP (42) 33, in CAB 66/21; Cross to Cranborne, 9 January and 5 February 1942, PREM 4,50/7.

31 See e.g. Matloff and Snell, *Strategic Planning*, p. 131; cf. Menzies, *Afternoon Light*, p. 135.

32 Halifax to Eden, 22 June 1942, FO 371/30659, A6050G.

33 Roosevelt to Winant, 17 June 1942, in E. Roosevelt, *F.D.R.: His Personal Letters, 1928–45* (New York, 1950).

34 For example, Halifax to Eden, 26 March 1942, FO 371/30652, A2963/31/45.

35 CAB 69/4. I have not been able to find material on this matter in the Earle Page papers. See J. Robertson, 'Australia and the "Beat Hitler First" Strategy, 1941–42', *Journal of Imperial and Commonwealth History*, vol. xi no. 3, May 1983.

when the latter queried MacArthur's role in supplying Curtin direct with estimates of military requirements, estimates which Curtin in turn had used when pressing his demands on London.[36] The President also rejected Australian requests in the spring of 1942 for 100,000 US troops and 1,000 planes to be stationed there,[37] while the talented but blustering Evatt overplayed his hand during his visit to Washington.[38]

Essentially, the United States military presence in Australia was part of an independently conceived strategy – first as a supply route to the Philippines, then as a fall-back position and base for eventual advance. Moreover, by closely identifying themselves with MacArthur, the Australian Government were backing only one of the US Army and Navy factions which in 1942 were already in fierce contention for the shaping of future strategy in the Pacific and globally.[39] Yet for all these disappointments and limitations, there remained every reason for Australia to look for help in 1942, not to a desperately over-extended Britain but to the rapidly growing power of the United States.

MacArthur's own version of how matters had stood on his arrival in Australia was given to Wilkinson in a lengthy conversation of 19 October:

He commented on the fact that when he had reached [this country] in March, Curtin had indicated to him that Australia was ready to shift over to the US away from the British Empire, but that he (MacA) had refused to listen to any such talk and had discouraged any contemplation of a change in the 'status quo', defining his duties as essentially a C. in C. owing allegiance now to the several governments of the area under his command, etc. He added that he had, in fact, been a pretty good friend to British interests.

His quotation of Curtin's remark is probably extravagant, but he – MacA – *has* previously told me that Curtin and Co. more or less offered him the country on a platter when he arrived from the Philippines. My own conclusion is that Curtin was badly panicked at the time – and that MacA's steadfast adherence to his duties of C.

36 PREM 3,151/1; Matloff and Snell, *Strategic Planning*, pp. 215–6; Butler, *Grand Strategy*, pp. 492–8; R. E. Sherwood, *Roosevelt and Hopkins: An Intimate History* (New York, 1948), p. 508; Roosevelt to Churchill, 23 March 1942, in which he conveyed deep disquiet over the Casey affair's publicity and the growing sense of Anglo-Australian tension. PREM 3,470.
37 Matloff and Snell, *Strategic Planning*, pp. 217–21.
38 F. C. Pogue, *George C. Marshall, Ordeal and Hope, 1939–1942* (New York, 1966), p. 372. For Justice Felix Frankfurter's 'sponsorship' of Evatt, see M. Freedman (ed.), *Roosevelt and Frankfurter* (London, 1967), pp. 650, 654. In May 1942, Roosevelt obtained Churchill's blessing for an invitation to Curtin to visit Washington. 'From all I hear', cabled the President, 'he is thoroughly honest and sincere person but has had little opportunity to appreciate the world situation outside his own sphere. There are also matters regarding command and operational problems on which I should like to try my hand at indoctrination.' PREM 3,470. On Evatt in general, see A. Watt, *Australian Diplomat* (Sydney, 1972), pp. 45, 49. See also my articles in the Melbourne *Age*, 31 May and 1 June, 1974.
39 See, for example, Matloff and Snell, *Strategic Planning*, pp. 259–64, 368ff.

in C. was due, not primarily to his love of the British Empire, but to his shrewd common-sense informing him that any impropriety in his Australian relationship would give his Washington enemies a lovely opportunity to cut his throat.

MacArthur had also formed some very definite views on various British officials in Australia, finding Lord Gowrie 'sound, experienced and trusted by the Australians; a professional soldier and a good man'. Sir Leslie Wilson, Governor of Queensland, was also 'energetic and keen; very well liked by the people', whereas Lord Wakehurst, Governor of New South Wales, was 'ambitious, [possibly having] wanted to be Governor-General when the war stopped the appointment of the Duke of Kent; clever and not entirely to be trusted' (19 September). As for the High Commissioner, Cross, MacArthur was ready to agree with Wilkinson's own estimate:

Peter Lubbock, brother in law of Lord Wakehurst, . . . thinks that Ronnie Cross is not making the grade at all . . . (and) has missed the bus by being far too grand and Old Etonian. I fear he's right and that poor Cross, nice, honest and intelligent, just lacks the sheer earthy nous to establish working relations with Aussie politicos. But one must also recognise that the post – halfway between Ambassador and Consul-General and more suspect than either – is a very tricky one' (19 November).

Called on Cross and had ¾ hour or so chat . . . He contributed little of consequence and, from his comments and questions, struck me as behind hand in time, and detached in touch, from what is really happening in Australia' (22 December). Sir Campbell Stuart 'said Cross no good and indiscreet in his own and his staff's unfavourable comments on Australia. He agrees that Cross will eventually have to go' (11 January).[40]

Meanwhile, although Britain had readily agreed to operational control over the South West Pacific Area being exercised by the United States Joint Chiefs of Staff, she retained an interest in developments there and in the South Pacific from the point of view of her own projected, though long-delayed, advance into Southeast Asia from India. Yet London found itself largely ignorant of what was taking place under both MacArthur and Nimitz.[41] In the summer of 1942, therefore, London proposed to send out to Australia a small mission which became known as the UK Army and Air Force Liaison Staff, led by Major-General R. H. Dewing, who had served as Chief of Staff in the Far East earlier in the war, and then on a mission to Washington. This new Liaison Staff was obviously intended to supply a

40 In the spring of 1944, the Chief Intelligence Officer of Britain's Eastern Fleet, after a long series of interviews in Australia, likewise concluded that 'neither Cross nor his staff cut much ice'. Hillgarth report, PREM 3,159/10.
41 J.I.C. (42) 421 in Chiefs of Staff 300th meeting, 1942. 26 October, CAB 79/23; JP (43) 92 in Chiefs of Staff 62nd meeting, 1943, 11 March, CAB 79/26.

degree of military expertise which Wilkinson could not and did not claim, but he, too, was to join its ranks. Even so, he was aware that the arrival of Dewing was viewed with suspicion and hostility in many quarters:

[19 September] Talk with MacArthur . . . He told me much of previous negotiations between London and Canberra about a Mission . . . to the Australian Forces etc. Curtin and Co. obviously fearful of Whitehall usurping control of some of their Dominion powers, through medium of Mission which they had energetically opposed. M says they regard Cross as wanting to use Mission to increase his own power. MacA, rightly or not, is clearly influenced by this opposition to and distrust of Cross and thinks he conspires with Menzies and flirts with the opposition in general. I should have thought it more probable that the very able Menzies utilizes the lesser but agreeable Cross. MacA agrees.

On 3 October, Wilkinson talked to Cross himself about the position. The High Commissioner 'expressed himself as chagrined' at the Curtin–MacArthur suspicions, emphasizing that the proposal for a Mission had originated entirely from London, and that 'its primary function is liaison – not direction or control of anything'.

Cross considers his former membership of Cabinet a point of suspicion to Dominion-complex Aussies. He came out when Menzies was PM, as Menzies' personal friend and at M's request. After 10 weeks in Australia, M's cabinet was out of power – no fault of Cross's. He naturally could not drop Menzies cold . . . – in addition to which he frankly does enjoy Menzies, who is head and shoulders in ability above present Govt.

A week later, on his return from Canberra to Brisbane, Wilkinson reported to MacArthur

that in the case of Cross we were dealing with a second-rate intellect and lightweight – a very straight, decent, friendly fellow, but not by any means a powerful schemer, and that Curtin had perhaps made rather a mountain out of a molehill . . . about the Mission . . . MacA seemed . . . prepared to accept my view.

It soon became evident, however, that MacArthur and his American staff officers continued to be highly suspicious of the planned Mission. When General Marshall telegraphed from Washington to say that its Head, Major-General Dewing (whose status was to be that of 'military attaché or observer' at MacArthur's Headquarters) had worked well with Eisenhower, matters were only made worse:

Major-General R. Sutherland [MacArthur's Chief of Staff] stated that MacA proposed to . . . confine the Mission's relations with GHQ rigidly to that of Attaché or Observer and not an inch more – also that the selection of an officer who had been with Eisenhower seemed to MacA a hostile appointment (2 November). [On the following day, despite Wilkinson's strong arguments to the contrary, MacArthur himself] insisted on applying the word 'sinister' to the appointment of Dewing, as a man steeped in the hostile atmosphere of Washington and recently associated with his particular critic, Eisenhower . . . He yielded [so far as to say] that he would certainly see D on arrival and would keep an open mind . . . But he suggested that D might be coming for *critical* investigation and for certain purposes which would not be disclosed to me . . . I regard this supposition as altogether too intricate and said so clearly . . .

Dewing himself, on arrival early in the New Year, confirmed to Wilkinson that although his instructions were 'scanty' his purpose was simply 'to obtain fuller knowledge of operations and conditions in this theatre' and 'to secure better coordination between Wavell [operating from India] and MacA so that the timing of their future offensive strokes may . . . help each other' (7 January, 1943). Dewing also confirmed that Wilkinson's own liaison with MacArthur was not to be disturbed, and that he had been informed that Churchill insisted upon this. Dewing, however, found General Blamey, the Australian Commander in Chief, particularly hostile.[42] And at a dinner in Melbourne on 9 January, given in Dewing's honour by the Chief of the Australian General Staff, Lt General Northcott, Curtin delivered a speech

with a complete absence . . . of any reference to the guest of honour [or] to the UK Mission . . . I thought this a grave and crude discourtesy, savouring more of a suspicious peasant than the elected leader of a great Dominion. The atmosphere thereafter, especially in the upper circles of Curtin, Shedden and Northcott, seemed to me thick with reservations.

The storms over the Military Mission served as a reminder – if one were needed – that MacArthur was the last person to permit outside interference in the mysteries and conduct of his command. He was also far from being an Anglophile. Nevertheless he was less bristling towards the British than was Admiral King at the head of the US Navy, and less concerned than he to keep Britain from playing any major role in the Pacific. He always judged possible links with London in the light of the repercussions they might have in turn on his tense dealings with Washington – which will be enlarged upon below. But the existence of such links remained a matter of some concern to him, and during the winter of 1942–3 the subject gave rise to yet more flurries.

42 General Dewing, letter to the writer, 25 November 1973.

One of those involved was Sir Keith Murdoch, chairman and managing director of the Melbourne *Herald* and other newspapers. Murdoch had been Australia's Director-General of Information for a time in 1940; he also became a leading figure in the Australian–American Cooperation Movement, and was to argue publicly in the spring of 1943 that United States interest in the area after the war (leading, he hoped, to an alliance with Australia) could be sustained by giving Australian citizenship to American soldiers who fought there.[43] On 10 October 1942, Wilkinson noted:

Interview with MacArthur 5 pm to 6.10 pm . . . Keith Murdoch has told [him] recently that British War Cabinet is hostile to [him] – in conspiracy with New Deal. I told MacA that I thought he had more friends in London than in Washington and that SW Pacific Area occupied too small a place in thoughts at present of Europe-occupied people to warrant a story that was probably sensational. MacA agrees.

The present writer has found nothing in official or private British records to invalidate Wilkinson's verdict. However on 23 October MacArthur returned to the subject:

He started straight in – looking rather grave and sounding hurt – by telling me that an attack on himself was being made by spreading the story that he is anti-British. I asked him who he thought was responsible. He replied that he thinks it is Eisenhower. In view of the reported friction between E and MacA when E was M's Chief of Staff in Manila, and remembering the tone of the questions E asked me about MacA and Bataan [i.e. the final stages of MacArthur's fight against the Japanese in the Philippines] in the War Department [in Washington] in April 1942, I'm inclined to think MacA is right.

As noted here, Eisenhower had served under MacArthur in the Philippines in the late 1930s. His own star was now rapidly ascending, however – in association with a European and North African strategy which MacArthur deplored. The 'Torch' landings in North Africa in November 1942 not only turned the spotlight upon this new American hero, but helped deprive MacArthur further of those large reinforcements for which he was calling in order swiftly to fulfil his pledge to return to the Philippines.

1 November. MacA [said that Eisenhower was] the ablest officer he has ever known at absorbing 30 minutes detailed description of an idea or plan . . . and getting the whole thing out on paper – orders, arrangements, etc. – in 10 minutes; a brilliant executive of someone else's original thought but *not* . . . in any way an original

43 See WP (43) 170, in CAB 66/36.

mind, and no fighting experience. Ambitious, clever, hard-working . . . MacA thinks E will command the North African . . . landings . . . and thinks (and possibly almost hopes?) that commanding fighting British officers will show up E's true propositions . . . [He said] E was jealous of Sutherland's direct access to him [in the Philippines] . . . and when MacA was having his difficulties with Filipino politicos E tended to side with latter and build up a strong personal position with them . . . MacA feels E was not wholly loyal in fact . . . He thinks E spotting White House jealousy of himself (MacA), has enhanced his own position by feeding the White House with anti-MacA data.

Meanwhile Wilkinson on 24 October had reported to the Governor-General, Lord Gowrie, MacArthur's concern at what Murdoch had told him.

[Gowrie said] that Murdoch was a clever business-man, not over-scrupulous, who was quite capable of using one thing to achieve another; that he had given great trouble at Gallipoli by smuggling 'that story' out when there was an understanding not to do so. [During the First World War, as a correspondent attached to Australian forces, Murdoch had visited Gallipoli on a mission for the Australian Government, and had subsequently submitted to the British Prime Minister, Asquith, a report on the situation there which was highly critical of the British generals. Murdoch's various reports were later publicly castigated by the commanding officer at the Dardanelles at the time, Sir Ian Hamilton, as containing falsehoods and having been in contravention of their author's undertaking on field-censorship.] [See volume 2 of Hamilton's *Gallipoli Diary*.]

I asked Lord Gowrie if he thought Murdoch capable of reporting fabricated stories to MacA in the guise of helping MacA, with the real object of maintaining contact to help his own newspapers, editorials, etc. Gowrie replied: 'Yes – that sort of thing.' . . . He thought I should inform London of the incident . . . and [said I could] inform MacA unofficially that every report to London from [himself] and Cross that referred to MacA was favourable to [him].

Two days later Wilkinson also discussed the matter with Lord Wakehurst, Governor of New South Wales, who 'felt that Sir Keith Murdoch is patriotic and able and therefore probably useful in war effort – but that he and all newspaper kings are unscrupulous and that I should advise MacA to weigh carefully any private report from Murdoch'. Wakehurst also lent Wilkinson a copy of Ian Hamilton's *Gallipoli Diary;* he in turn handed it to MacArthur when he next saw him, the General 'reading with interest' the passages relating to Sir Keith.

MacArthur, as will be seen below, continued to display a desire to remain in touch with Churchill. Always, however, there was the complicating factor of the relations of each of them with Roosevelt.[44] And

44 See Jones, *MacArthur*, pp. 4,354.

Roosevelt himself was stepping warily where MacArthur was concerned, despite his private exasperation at the latter's 'constant playing to the grandstand'.[45] The General was publicly declaring that he had no political ambitions, but this was far from putting an end to the possibility of his becoming a presidential candidate in 1944. In fact Senator Arthur Vandenberg and other prominent Republicans continued to think along these lines, receiving encouragement both from senior members of MacArthur's staff when they visited the United States in 1943 and from the man himself, who was to write in the spring of that year seeking Vandenberg's 'experienced and wise mentorship'.[46] The balloon finally burst in the spring of 1944 (when a Republican Congressman clumsily published a letter from the General praising his attacks on the New Deal), but the tension between the White House and South West Pacific headquarters had been substantial. Nor had the atmosphere been improved earlier, during the period when Wilkinson was writing, by the proposal (later abandoned) to replace the career diplomat, Nelson T. Johnson, as US Minister to Australia by a professional Democrat politician from Roosevelt's entourage, Edward J. Flynn.[47]

MacArthur talked at some length to Wilkinson about these matters. On 1 November 1942, for example, he suggested

that in view of his recent declaration in the press that he has no political ambitions . . . I should *not* go to Washington and London at the present time on the subject of Pacific Commands and strategy; that the whole question is developing fast of its own volition, and that in any case it would be most dangerous for me to discuss his advancement even with British Ambassador and British Staff Mission in Washington – as 'Roosevelt has his spies right down to the kitchen sink . . . Your outstanding loyalty to me is too well known, Gerry; they'd seek you out and destroy you. Halifax would be asked by Roosevelt to remove your credentials.' Therefore if I go it should be direct to Churchill – but that the time wasn't now. He then covered his position by emphasising that he could enter into no subterfuge of private communication with Churchill, although he realized that Churchill would probably be fully willing and ready to protect him with privacy and discretion . . . He thinks [however] that if Roosevelt gains strength politically, it is quite possible that he will find some pretext to relieve MacA altogether of his command . . . and thinks that R might well pull it off on grounds of 'no confidence'.

MacArthur was also sensitive to the degree of recognition accorded him in

45 William D. Hassett, *Off the Record With F.D.R.* (New Brunswick, 1958), p. 88.
46 Arthur H. Vandenberg (ed.), *The Private Papers of Senator Vandenberg* (London, 1953) pp. 76ff.
47 Flynn later accompanied Roosevelt to Yalta. On Johnson's views, see the writer's article in the Melbourne *Age*, 8 and 9 January 1975.

London. Fortunately Wilkinson (having prompted his superiors) was able to begin an interview on February 13

by telling MacA that Churchill's recent mention of his brilliant leadership had roused the House [of Commons].[48] MacA hadn't noticed this in Press and was most interested and pleased. He said that the English (or British) had a most basic sense of fair play . . . and that Americans were different – anything to get victory but not the same sportsmanship . . . I reminded him that I had always told him that London was his friend – [and] that that was why I had had Murdoch 'bitched' by reporting him home for his untrue story to MacA that British Cabinet was conspiring with US New Deal against him etc. etc. . . . He [later] referred again to the jealousy of Washington and of the US Navy – Churchill his only ally, and if Churchill should ever want his advice or should ever feel the desirability of getting MacA's views direct to him he would be glad to . . . send such help – *to him alone* . . . It is evident that MacA feels that he can . . . justify communication with Churchill, if caught at it, by the fact that, as an Allied C. in C., he owes allegiance not only to the US but also to Curtin, Queen Wilhelmina [of the Netherlands] and Churchill . . . This whole conversation and the messages he is giving me constitute a considerable advance, and are very different from what Sutherland describes as proper . . .

These relations of MacArthur's with London and Washington have to be seen in part in the context of his immediate problems and of the military and political situation in Australia at the time. Although the Japanese had in fact decided against an invasion of Australia, intending, rather, to cut her off from the north,[49] their threat from the Dutch East Indies, the Bismarcks, Solomons and New Guinea hung heavily over the country for much of 1942. In February Darwin was bombed, and at the end of May midget submarines attacked Sydney Harbour. Despite the setback inflicted on the enemy at the battle of the Coral Sea in May and the decisive defeat of Midway in June, and despite also MacArthur's assessment in June that the defence of Australia was now assured, Curtin was still proclaiming that the country 'could be lost'.[50] This emphasis tended to overshadow his accompanying one, that 'our minds are set on attack',[51] and indeed Australia's official historian has commented that 'the Curtin Government consistently acted as though it expected Australians to be scared'.[52] Some

48 Churchill, having been informed of Wilkinson's report, had also cabled MacArthur direct. PREM 3,158/7.
49 Butler, *Grand Strategy*, p. 470. Ikeda Kiyoshi, 'Japanese Strategy and the Pacific War, 1941–5', in I. Nish (ed.), *Anglo-Japanese Alienation, 1919–1952* (Cambridge, 1982); on later Australian demands and scepticism in London, see M. Howard, *Grand Strategy*, vol. IV (London, 1972), pp. 79–80.
50 Hasluck, *Government and People*, p. 172.
51 Ibid, p. 157.
52 Ibid, p. 128.

US officials were commenting on what they saw as an isolationist and defensive attitude.[53] Sir Ronald Cross, too, wrote to Churchill: 'It is too much to hope that Australia will prove able to put forth a full war effort; the general mental approach still leaves a good deal to be desired, and the country is too much obsessed with conceptions of the rights and liberties of labour. MacArthur observes this, but says that the margin of loss . . . is not enough in so small a people to affect the outcome of the fight.'[54]

Images of Australia such as this were fostered in part by the statutory maintenance (despite its blurring in practice) of the long-standing distinction between the volunteer Australian Imperial Force, which could be called upon to serve anywhere in the world, and the Australian or Citizen Military Forces, which could be used only in Australian territory. Curtin – who had himself campaigned against conscription during the First World War – did in fact tackle this explosive issue within the Labor Party during the period covered by Wilkinson's journal. (According to MacArthur in June 1943, Curtin had actually promised him when he arrived in Australia 'that Australian troops should fight wherever he needed them in SWPA'.)[55] The ensuing Defence Act of February 1943, however, was to do no more than extend the area in which the AMF could serve to a 'South West Pacific Zone' – still less than the extent of MacArthur's command and covering only a part of territories such as Celebes and Borneo. In going merely this far, the Prime Minister, it has been suggested, was not only manoeuvring cautiously within the minefields of his party, but was also displaying his readiness to see the bulk of Australian forces engaged in areas nearer home rather than pushing up to the Philippines and beyond with their American allies.[56]

Meanwhile the 6th and 7th Divisions of the Australian Imperial Force had at Curtin's insistence arrived back in Australia from the Middle East, some via a stay in Ceylon; by September 1942 (when 48,000 Australians were still serving overseas) many of these forces had joined those already facing the Japanese in New Guinea. In addition, following further exchanges between Curtin, Churchill and Roosevelt, the 9th Division of the AIF was to return from its desert triumphs to Australia in February 1943.[57]

The Commander in Chief of these and all Australian Army forces since March 1942 was the blunt and controversial General (later Field Marshal) Sir Thomas Blamey, who also served as MacArthur's commander of Allied

---

53 Ibid, p. 155. Cf. E. King and W. Whitehill, *Fleet Admiral King* (London, 1953), p. 161, and my Melbourne *Age* article of December, 1974.
54 Cross to Churchill, 26 June 1942, PREM 4, 50/7.
55 Dewing report, 29 June 1943, PREM 3, 158/5.
56 Hasluck, *Government and People*, pp. 326ff.
57 Ibid, pp. 190ff.

land forces in the South West Pacific Area. Some, in and out of the Army, believed that there were more suitable candidates for his post within the ranks of his senior colleagues, while his arrival in New Guinea in September 1942 to take over operational command from Major-General S. F. (later Sir Sydney) Rowell led to a clash between the two men which had long and unpleasant echoes.[58] But Blamey retained the confidence of Curtin, despite the great differences between them, and he also admired the military ability of MacArthur.[59]

Under his command, of course, Blamey had American as well as Australian troops. The first of these had arrived in Australia in December 1941, their numbers reaching 98,000 by the following September when the US 32nd Division crossed to New Guinea to join in the battles there, and 160,000 by the end of April 1943.[60] In the fighting area, relations between the two allies were usually reported to be good; but this was by no means always the case further back and in Australia itself, where there were complaints of the kind to be heard in New Zealand, Britain and elsewhere, of boastful and overpaid GIs muscling in on the local girls.

The relative merits of the Australian and American fighting man in New Guinea were also a matter of some dispute, not least because of the tendency of MacArthur and sycophantic American staff officers to keep the spotlight focused on the Supreme Commander and the American contribution generally. 'I am convinced', wrote the Head of the British Services Mission to Wilkinson in February 1943, 'that MacArthur is working steadily to exclude the Australians from any effective hand in the control of land or air operations or credit in them, except as a minor element in a US show'.[61] In fact, by the end of January 1944 there was to be a total of 10,470 Australian casualties in New Guinea and the adjoining islands, as against 8,032 for the Americans.[62] British observers for their part were describing the local US soldiers as 'very poor indeed' as compared to Australian 'first-class fighting men'.[63] MacArthur , as will be seen, thought differently.

Wilkinson's own opinion of the tone of Australia's leadership in this period was close to that of Cross and other observers, and led at times to

58 See J. Hetherington, *Blamey* (Melbourne, 1954), pp. 157–8, and Hasluck, *Government and People*, p. 572.
59 See ibid, pp. 144–5.
60 See, for example, S. W. Kirby, *The War Against Japan*, vol. 2 (London, 1958), passim.
61 Dewing to Wilkinson, 10 February 1943, Wilkinson Papers.
62 Hasluck, *Government and People*, p. 418.
63 Somerville Diary, 31 December 1943, Somerville Papers (Churchill College, Cambridge); Somerville to Ismay, 19 January 1943, Ismay Papers (King's College, London). And see C. Thorne, *The Issue of War* (London, 1985; p.b. edn re-titled *The Far Eastern War. States and Societies, 1941–45*, London, 1986), ch. 7.

exasperated reflections. For example, after the dinner in honour of General
Dewing referred to earlier, he noted:

Curtin spoke for about 15 minutes, quite straightforwardly and sincerely, I thought,
but without any demonstration of ability. Theme was almost entirely praise and
appreciation of Australian Staff officers and their contribution to national safety –
note again the *defensive* note; he even said that their good work had been probably
largely responsible for the enemy not having bombed any of the Aust. cities – which
(he said) might have gravely harmed the war production. I hoped he would be
humorous about this but no, the man really must fail to realize that a little
bombing of the big centres might have done Australia's soul, and her war effort, a
power of good.

Shortly afterwards, on 20 January, Wilkinson had his diagnosis endorsed
by the Governor of Queensland, Sir Leslie Wilson:

He agrees that there is not much offensive spirit against Japan, and thinks that
removal of threat to Australia itself will cause a reduction in war effort. Obviously
feels Australia is rather a spoilt child – interesting and sad news from a popular
Governor who has had his term of office thrice extended.

Similarly, Group Captain Harold Gatty, Tasmanian-born and Director of
Air Transport in Australia, who before the war had worked for Pan
American Airways and become famous for a round-the-world flight, maintained 'that Australian forces, in general, think in terms of defence of
Australia and will not have their heart in going northwards towards Japan
– not interested in offensive' (18 October). On the following day, therefore, Wilkinson put the question to MacArthur himself:

I then asked him whether, even if major offensive operations were authorised along
his proposed route, the Australian forces could be expected to have their heart in
fighting outside Australia, through the islands towards Japan. He is obviously
doubtful about this and said, rather sweepingly, 'Gerry, I tell you, these Australians
won't fight'. (This was the most downright statement I've ever heard him make on
Australian morale.) He went on to say that he has 40,000 troops in Port Moresby
but that when the September 'flap' was on (over the Jap. advance through the
Owen Stanley Range) he told Curtin that 140,000 men would be no good unless
they'd fight. He added that the Jap. attempt to advance on Moresby over the Range
was the wildest, most over-confident and senseless action possible. I suggested to
him that it was inspired not only by over-confidence but possibly by Jap. contempt
for white morale (for 'Aussie morale' would have been better).

Later, in February, when Wilkinson raised the related question of the very
restricted A.M.F. Zoning Bill which Curtin was pushing through,

MacArthur said that 'it really didn't matter except that it looks bad on paper for the Aussie Govt. but that the bulk of the AMF will anyway be required as garrison troops for communication and supplies and for rear areas' (13th February).

MacArthur's opinion of Australian troops in general does not appear to have been very high. On 19 October, for example, he told Wilkinson that 'his best troops in this command are not the AIF but his American divisions, although he does not rate *them* higher than fairly good'.[64]

Perhaps the greatest degree of controversy, however, surrounded some of the leading Australian generals of the period. One of those involved, Major General Rowell, talked to Wilkinson on 7 October:

Rowell says he is just back from New Guinea and is out of a job having been relieved of his command after a personal row with Blamey; that he has obtained 3 weeks leave from the PM and proposes to go home and do some gardening; that he is a young 47 and thinks some work will turn up soon. [After returning briefly to the Middle East, Rowell was to become Director of Tactical Investigation at the War Office in London, and Chief of the Australian General Staff from 1950 to 1954.] I told him I felt sure it would . . . He strikes me as a *very* decent fellow . . . He thinks that Port Moresby cannot be taken except by naval action and that 1 division must therefore be kept at Moresby as garrison in case of any sudden naval disaster . . . In response to a question from me he agreed that he had really borne the burden and heat of the day – that he had cleared up a muddle inherited with his command; that the alarm over Port Moresby was entirely unnecessary and that Blamey rushing up had put him (R) in impossible position. That he had always got on best with B when they stayed 300 miles apart.

Others less qualified were also ready with strong opinions about Blamey. Sir Alfred Davidson, for example, Managing Director of the Bank of New South Wales, 'talked voluminously and unnecessarily about weakness of Blamey and present Australian Government, fishing out of his private files a list of Australian generals who "might do", as better than Blamey, for all the world like a race fan drawing up a lunch-time list of hot tips for the 3 o'clock. I . . . beat a cordial retreat' (26 October).

Wilkinson had already been told by the Governor of Queensland, Sir Leslie Wilson, that Lt General Sir John Lavarack (Chief of the Australian General Staff 1935–9, Acting C. in C. of the Australian Army in March 1942 while Blamey's return from the Middle East was awaited, and Commander of the 1st Australian Army, AIF, thereafter) 'is scheming against Blamey and that there is much political intrigue to get Blamey out'. On the same day, 22 September, MacArthur

64 See the corroborating evidence published by the writer in the Melbourne *Age*, 1 June 1974, e.g. from the diary of the American Secretary of War, Henry Stimson.

says Wilson is right about Lavarack . . . [and that he is] intelligent and ambitious but Blamey thinks he is *not* a fighter and MacA inclines to agree . . . MacArthur considers Blamey [to be] sensual, slothful and doubtful moral character but a tough commander likely to shine like a power-light in emergency. The best of the local bunch . . . [On 19 October MacArthur added that 'it would *not* do to leave Blamey in supreme command.'] MacArthur thinks whole senior officer class in Australia too complacent and easily pleased with work half done; live off but not up to the name of Anzac . . . Gordon Bennett he considers a capable, energetic fellow, worth a division anywhere, but a cantankerous crab – low Australian type; second to Blamey in ability but not as a possibility.' [Lt General Gordon Bennett, who had commanded the 8th Division of the AIF in Malaya, was under a cloud thereafter for having left shortly before the fall of Singapore; there was to be a Court of Enquiry into this after the war, by which time he had resigned from the Army, criticising Blamey for not giving him an active command.][65] 'MacA agrees that post-Malaya publicity – much of it of Gordon Bennett's own making – has further reduced his eligibility for High Command. MacA thinks G-B may have received money (from publicity concerns presumably) for this.'

MacArthur had gone on to refer to the beginnings of the Blamey–Rowell affair, describing the latter as a 'sound staff officer – Blamey's ace – but doubts if he is a fighter; disappointing in improvisation in New Guinea lately'. (Sir Sydney Rowell's own version of these and other episodes is now available in his book, *Full Circle.*) In the event, the Japanese forces which had landed near Buna, in the north of New Guinea, in July and August and had crossed the Owen Stanley mountains to within 32 miles of Port Moresby, were forced back. Blamey's troops advanced in turn towards Buna under appalling conditions of rain, mud, thick jungle and disease, while part of the US 32nd Division moved along the northern coast of New Guinea towards the same destination. Both advances had reached the Japanese defence perimeter round Buna and Sanananda before the end of November; after bitter fighting, the last enemy resistance was overcome on 21 January 1943. Australian casualties in the campaign had been twice those of the Americans.[66]

MacArthur's own estimate, given to Wilkinson on 1 November, had been that he would 'take Buna on November 15 (here he touched a wooden table with a humorous gesture)'. His later summary, on 13 February, was that

in September after the Japs came over the Range and Aussie troops looked over their shoulder – Sid Rowell and Co. being down in the mouth – he (MacA) had got

65 See, for example, Hetherington, *Blamey*, pp. 208–11; also D. M. Horner, *Crisis of Command: Australian Generalship and the Japanese Threat, 1941–1943* (Canberra, 1978).
66 Kirby, *The War Against Japan*, pp. 286ff.

the senior officers together and told them that they were going right back, the hard way, over the Range to take Buna, and that when they ultimately succeeded all the glory would be theirs – and that they had responded splendidly . . . Part of the huge sickness figure among Aussies [however] was due to their lack of discipline [over] taking quinine treatment.

In this campaign naval forces had played little part, in marked contrast to the fierce struggle which had been waged at the same time for the island of Guadalcanal in the British Solomons Protectorate, following landings there by US Marines in August under the Navy's command.[67] MacArthur's opinion, as recorded by Wilkinson on 10 October, was that 'the smart thing for the Japs to do now would be to swing suddenly up to Midway' although they were 'capable of serious SW Pacific assault . . . to divide US Fleet from Australia and New Zealand'. What he most feared over Guadalcanal, he observed nine days later, was that 'the US Navy, perhaps failing to engage the enemy adequately and efficiently, [might then] withdraw, leaving the ground troops in another Bataan'. He himself had warned that to land in Guadalcanal would be 'a reckless gamble', but had been 'presumptuously overruled' by Washington.[68]

By early February 1943, however, victory had been gained in Guadalcanal as well as at Buna, and the way thus cleared for the two-pronged advance envisaged by the American Chiefs of Staff, through the Solomons and along the coast of New Guinea to take the New Britain–New Guinea–New Ireland area and break the Japanese barrier in the Bismarck Islands.[69] Even so, MacArthur's feud with the US Navy continued – several scornful references by the General to American admirals appear in the journal. At the same time, Admiral Nimitz's planned drive across the Central Pacific[70] might well come to overshadow MacArthur's advance towards the Philippines, despite the spectacular techniques now evolving in the General's mind for combined operations to cut behind many of the enemy's island garrisons:

MacA asked me [on 13 February] to tell the Prime Minister [i.e. Churchill] but *not* the Chiefs of Staff that he had a plan for striking Japs on a major scale – details not advisable to mention at this stage. No one knew, not even Blamey [MacArthur had, however, written to Curtin in January outlining his new tactical ideas],[71] but the whole method of Japanese defence has been unique and 'I think I have the key' – a new dimension in war; a combination of surprise and use of the air. 'I am

67 See King and Whitehill, *Fleet Admiral King*, p. 220.
68 Ibid, p. 179.
69 Kirby, *The War Against Japan*, p. 270.
70 See e.g. King and Whitehill, *Fleet Admiral King*, p. 225; F. C. Pogue, *George C. Marshall: Organizer of Victory, 1943–1945* (New York, 1973), ch. 8.
71 Hasluck, *Government and People*, p. 205.

organizing guerrillas and secret concealed airfields [in Mindanao][72] and when the time comes I will fly a whole division in there at one clip – I will by-pass the Netherlands East Indies and firm my new position with air power and supporting sea [power]. I will cut the Jap sea lanes to Malaya and Burma – and help Wavell.'

MacArthur's hopes may have been raised at this time by the increase to well above the planned total in the number of US forces committed in the Pacific theatres. (At the end of 1942, partly in consequence of the desperate fight for Guadalcanal, there were 346,000 US troops in the Pacific, roughly equal to those in North Africa and the United Kingdom combined, and 150,000 more than projected.[73]) In September the British Joint Staff Mission in Washington had warned London of a 'swing-over taking place in the highest quarters towards Pacific strategy'.[74] And indeed, in the previous July General Marshall and his colleagues had proposed to Roosevelt (on Marshall's part, though not on King's, there had been an element of bluff in this) that if Britain persisted in favouring the Mediterranean and going slow on a cross-Channel assault, the United States should turn away from the Eastern Atlantic and seek 'decisive action against Japan in the Pacific'.[75]

Nevertheless, the President had insisted on adhering to the grand strategy agreed with Churchill of 'Germany first', and had pressed ahead with the North African campaign. Moreover, at the Casablanca conference in January 1943 (when it was again made plain to the British Chiefs of Staff that they had no standing in the matter of the Pacific war) it was reaffirmed that efforts within the commands of MacArthur and Nimitz should not jeopardize the main intention of bringing a maximum effort to bear against Germany in the hope of knocking her out that year.[76] MacArthur viewed these developments with exasperation. On 14th January, for example, he observed to Wilkinson

---

72 Wilkinson left blank the name of MacArthur's target, but from his later talks on the subject the General clearly was referring to Mindanao in the Philippines.

73 Matloff and Snell, *Strategic Planning*, ch. 16.

74 Howard, *Grand Strategy*, ch. 11. Cf. Bryant, *The Turn of the Tide* (London, 1957), pp. 358, 389.

75 See e.g. Matloff and Snell, *Strategic Planning*, pp. 268–70; Stimson and Bundy, *On Active Service*, pp. 424–5; Pogue, *Marshall: Ordeal and Hope*, pp. 340–1.

76 See, for example, Howard, *Grand Strategy*, Appendix III D. Curtin had again tried to influence these decisions, cabling Churchill and Roosevelt on 19 January to convey the essence of MacArthur's new ideas for attack and appealing for an additional 1,500 combat planes and 500 transport planes for this purpose. Having received no reply, Curtin repeated his cable to Churchill in March. Churchill then admitted that he had been shown the original by Roosevelt at Casablanca, but reiterated that supplies were short and the defeat of Germany must have priority. PREM 3, 142/7.

that the recent North West African campaign was a real blunder and would bog down in a mess from which it would be very difficult to go forward or backwards; that he was aware that Marshall and Eisenhower had been against it and that he considered the thing inspired by Roosevelt, with Churchill's assistance, primarily to save Roosevelt from growing feeling against him . . . Germany was operating on interior lines and could hold us. The directors of Allied war strategy were just plain wrong.

Again, on 26 January, MacArthur forecast to Sir Campbell Stuart (who then gave Wilkinson a full account of his talk with the General) that the African campaign 'would be the greatest disgrace ever suffered by American arms', contrasting Eisenhower's lack of qualifications with the 'magnificent' Montgomery and his 8th Army. The same views were given directly to Wilkinson by MacArthur on the 13 February, to pass on to Churchill:

'I regard the solution of the African command as 100% wrong. It does the greatest credit to Churchill's magnanimity of heart but from a military standpoint was wrong. From Alexander to Montgomery we had a great team [which] should not be debased . . . What can the troops think . . .?' The solution that the Prime Minister may yet have to come to is to put those 2 men in charge of all military affairs in North Africa and the Foreign Office to run political matters; the US to furnish help but to get out of control . . . MacA [also] asked me to stress to PM that if British Eastern fleet was ever free, he would strongly favour basing it upon West coast of Australia at same time basing a US fleet upon East coast of Australia. He added that he was preparing for such an eventuality (!?).

For all his friendly messages to Churchill, however, MacArthur, like his staff, blamed the Prime Minister and Roosevelt alike for the error, as they saw it, of concentrating against Germany. The General's chief of intelligence, for example, Brigadier General Charles Willoughby, preached to a sceptical Wilkinson 'the same old line about . . . Allies real war is with Japs, war against Germans being merely (!) an ideological matter; our right tactics should now be to hold them in Europe – let Naziism mellow or rot itself out, let Germans and Russians kill each other off, and concentrate on the most formidable foe – Japan'. Campbell Stuart reported a similar diatribe by MacArthur, in which his suspicions and incipient megalomania once more showed through:

[He said] that Japan, not Germany, is our main enemy. Germany can now never do in the UK – and even if she won a partial victory or only half lost the peace, life under a civilized race, or with a civilized people, would be tolerable. But Japan is a real menace to civilization; and life under her would be impossible. MacA does *not* want the war against Germany to stop or be compromised, but wants a modest diversion of Allied strength to this theatre, so that he can do his stuff before Japan gets too strong . . . That, if all this goes wrong, as he (MacA) seems always to infer that it must, these two men, Roosevelt and Churchill, may yet have to answer to the Anglo-American people. That there is another element, the fighting services, whose voice may one day have to be expressed (M did not say by whom). That Roosevelt's ambition and plan is to let Churchill have his way over the war so that he (R) can have his way over the peace and thereby a fourth term as US President, plus becoming head of the British Empire [as well as] US (Stuart thinks M not too far off the mark about this.)

With MacArthur's various messages and prophecies fresh in his ears, Wilkinson left Australia on 16 February 1943 and reported in person to Churchill in London. He told the Prime Minister over lunch at 10 Downing Street that

whatever his failings and meretricious qualities I felt MacArthur to be a man of real calibre . . ., that I regarded him as essentially a political general, a sort of 21st Century Smuts à la American; not in the sense of a General desiring political office, but of a man who, a General first and foremost, definitely not desiring to enter politics, had nevertheless a considerable understanding of personalities and political development. During this the Prime Minister had interjected that there was no reason under our democratic system of government why any man should not honourably have political ambitions . . . At my reference to Australian political waverings [towards the USA] last year . . . Churchill chuckled rather grimly and asked me if I knew what Washington's reply had been. I said that I did, to which the PM replied: 'Yes, they told them [the Australian Government] they would not have them.'[77]

Wilkinson's views may have carried all the more weight in that he had brought with him a letter from Lord Gowrie to the Head of the Secret Intelligence Service, applauding his 'very accurate and well-balanced view as to men and things in this part of the world' and 'very much hoping that he may come back to these parts . . . where he has done excellent work'.[78] In addition, Wilkinson was soon to receive the American Legion of Merit 'for exceptionally meritorious conduct in the performance of outstanding service in the Philippines'. He was not to return to MacArthur's side, however, and for this the General himself was responsible. His real reason was probably the one which he gave in his first talk with – or rather at – General Dewing. He had a great affection for Wilkinson personally, he said, but he disliked his connections with the British Secret Service, and there would be added trouble if ever Curtin's Government found out about those links. Therefore he could not give Wilkinson full access to his head-quarters.[79]

77 Wilkinson Journal, 15 March 1943.
78 Gowrie to 'C', 9 February 1943, Wilkinson Papers.
79 General Dewing, letter to the author, 25 November 1973.

Churchill, however, was unaware of these views of MacArthur's, and was all for sending Wilkinson back 'as my personal representative'. The Secret Service, the Foreign Office and the Dominions Office were all in favour of this, and eventually the Prime Minister telegraphed to MacArthur to propose that Wilkinson should now 'be posted to your staff as your British Military Assistant'.[80] MacArthur replied on 12 April:

come under Allied, and not simply British, over-all direction. Curtin I personally would be honoured to have Colonel Wilkinson attached to me, and especially because of my real affection for him. My specific instructions from Washington, however, render it impossible for me to utilize him as a channel of communication between us. Those orders definitely limit me to official communication to the Joint Chiefs of Staff . . . I am permitted direct discussion with the Prime Minister of Australia because of the inclusion of the bulk of the Australian military forces in this command, and because of his own predominant responsibilities in this area. I have, however, been sharply reminded by direct order that my prescribed channels shall not be violated.[81]

Prompted by his chief military aide, General 'Pug' Ismay, Churchill made one further attempt, this time to secure a place for Wilkinson on Lord Gowrie's staff, from where he could visit MacArthur from time to time and report back to 10 Downing Street. But the Governor General, while praising Wilkinson, felt that his return in this new capacity would arouse Australian suspicions, and that prior approval would have to be obtained from Curtin. Churchill therefore, by now somewhat exasperated by the whole business, agreed to let it drop and to await General Dewing's return to report in June.[82] Meanwhile Wilkinson went on to the United States to join the British Security Coordination team there,[83] working with the Americans on Far Eastern intelligence matters.

As for the task of maintaining contact with MacArthur, by the end of 1943 it had passed to Lt General Sir Herbert Lumsden (believed by Brooke to have gained the General's 'entire confidence')[84] and then, following Lumsden's death in action on board the US battleship *New Mexico*, to Lt General Charles Gairdner. This new arrangement of having a General as liaison officer at South West Pacific HQ was negotiated by Churchill with Roosevelt and Marshall as something of a *quid pro quo* for his own acceptance that Mountbatten's new South East Asia Command should

80 Minutes, memos and telegrams, March 1943, PREM 3, 158/5.
81 MacArthur to Churchill, 12 April 1943, PREM 3, 158/3.
82 Churchill to Gowrie, 26 April; Gowrie to Churchill, 3 May; Churchill to Ismay, 4 May 1943, PREM 3, 158/5.
83 On British Security Coordination, see H. Montgomery Hyde, *The Quiet Canadian* (London, 1962).
84 Bryant, *Triumph in the West*, p. 148; MacArthur, *Reminiscences*, pp. 240–1, 257.

agreed to Lumsden's coming, although in private he described the appointment as 'somewhat abnormal and unconstitutional'.[85]

Meanwhile the British Empire's gratitude to MacArthur had been signalled by the award of a GCB – though not until he had indignantly refused to contemplate the original notion of a (lesser) KCB.[86] His political prospects were also watched from time to time by the Foreign Office until all chance of the 1944 Republican nomination had passed him by. In the light of his 'Pacific-first' appeal with the American public and his resentment at not receiving greater reinforcements, it was felt in the Foreign Office towards the end of 1943 that the General was 'not without certain dangerous possibilities'. (A Gallup poll taken at the time in the United States, on a hypothetical Roosevelt versus MacArthur election fight, gave the latter 42 per cent of the votes.)[87] Wilkinson himself was consulted again on the subject for the benefit of the newly appointed Lumsden. The written summary of his views was deemed to be 'a very dangerous document in improper hands', and after being seen by Cadogan and a few other senior officials it was destroyed.[88] A copy survives among Wilkinson's papers, however, and suggests that by then he had come to a rather harsher judgement of MacArthur than when he had been at the latter's side:

He is shrewd, selfish, proud, remote, highly-strung and vastly vain. He has imagination, self-confidence, physical courage and charm, but no humour about himself, no regard for truth, and is unaware of these defects. He mistakes his emotions and ambitions for principles. With moral depth he would be a great man; as it is he is a near miss, which may be worse than a mile . . . His main ambition would be to end the war as Pan-American hero in the form of generalissimo of all Pacific theatres . . . He hates Roosevelt and dislikes Winston's control of Roosevelt's strategy . . . (He) is not basically anti-British, just pro-MacArthur . . . Curtin will be uneasy if he knows of your [Lumsden's] connection with Winston, for an inferiority complex vis-à-vis Whitehall permeates Australian labour politics. But it will help you with MacArthur if you could become persona grata with Curtin.

85 Churchill to Curtin, 24 August 1943, PREM 3, 158/5; Lumsden to Churchill, 19 November 1943, PREM 3, 158/7.   86 Hetherington, *Blamey*, pp. 191–2.
87 Pogue, *Marshall, Organizer of Victory*, p. 282.
88 FO 371/34163, A 10502/G; cf. FO 371/34181, A 3993/361/45 and Somerville Diary, 11 March 1944. On 30 March 1943 Brendan Bracken observed to Wilkinson (journal) 'that MacArthur was one of the most important figures in the international picture today . . . because as a successful general and a great public figure he was a potential threat to the conduct of the war as a whole if he should ever exert his full influence to rock the boat of Allied strategy, i.e. to join up with the Chinese lobby in Washington, with the Pacific-minded elements of the US Navy, and with any Republican and isolationist groups that might from inherent opposition to participation in the war against Germany prefer to prosecute as America's first task the war against Japan'.

It is clear that by this time MacArthur was regarded quite widely in Whitehall as egocentric and not altogether reliable in his judgements. But it seems that Churchill had a genuinely high regard for him, and was not merely flattering him for political reasons. The Prime Minister might cock an eyebrow when MacArthur, through Dewing and others, privately urged as late as March 1944 that the correct and only safe way to attack Germany was not via Italy or across the Channel, but for Britain and the United States to take over a section of the Russian front – the Foreign Office, not the State Department, to undertake to convince Stalin of the wisdom of this course, since US diplomats were 'too clumsy and lacked the English skill'. ('The General's ideas', noted Churchill, 'are singularly untroubled by considerations of transport and distance.'[89]) But when Cross, for example, suggested that MacArthur was 'absorbed by the business of being a great man', he did not carry the Prime Minister with him.[90]

In Churchill's eyes, there were good reasons for being especially grateful to this particular US commander. Did not Lumsden and Gairdner endorse the General's claim that 'it always had been and was his firm wish to see a strong British Empire'?[91] Did not MacArthur look forward to working with the Royal Navy ('it would be a great thing', he remarked to Cross, 'that an American general should sail into Manila under the British flag')?[92] Did he not share the British view that the efforts of General Stilwell (not exactly a supporter of the Empire) to reopen the Burma Road in order to get supplies to China were 'nonsense',[93] and were not his plans for advancing against Japan superior, in Churchill's view, to those of Admiral King, who, in his campaign against the Marshall Islands, was 'taking a steam hammer to crush a nut' and who, 'although a most agreeable person, is the evil genius of this war'?[94] Did not MacArthur privately suggest that, in its own interests at the peace table, the British Empire should provide garrison troops to take over its Pacific territories once they had been wrested from the Japanese, since 'possession is nine-tenths of the law',[95] and that

89 Dewing to Churchill, 25 June; Churchill to Chiefs of Staff, 5 July 1943, PREM 3 158/5; Hillgarth report of interview with MacArthur in March 1944, PREM 3, 159/10.

90 Cross to Churchill, 30 August 1944, PREM 3, 159/4.

91 Lumsden memo. of interview of 22 August 1944; Lumsden to Ismay, 13 July 1944, PREM 3, 159/4; Gairdner to Ismay, 13 and 30 May 1945, PREM 3, 159/14.

92 Cross to Churchill, 30 August 1944, PREM 3, 159/4. Gairdner's views in 1945 strongly echo those of Wilkinson in 1942: 'I think that it would pay a very good dividend to back [MacArthur] whenever it is possible without imperilling paramount interest.' Hillgarth report, PREM 3, 159/10.

93 Hillgarth report, PREM 3, 159/10.

94 Churchill to Chiefs of Staff, 13 February 1944, PREM 3, 159/14, and 14 February 1944, PREM 3, 160/7. Churchill saw MacArthur's strategy as complementary to his own pet scheme for a landing in Sumatra by Mountbatten's forces.

95 Lumsden to Ismay, 24 April 1944, PREM 3, 159/14.

Imperial forces, not American or Chinese, must recapture Hong Kong and Singapore?[96] When Churchill several times cabled his thanks to MacArthur for 'your admirable conduct of our joint affairs', he meant it.[97]

As the General completed his triumphant return to the Philippines, the South West Pacific Area diminished in significance. By the last months of the war, at Washington's suggestion, it was about to be handed over to the Australians and Mountbatten, while MacArthur pressed on with the preparations for the assault on Japan itself.[98] Yet in the intervening period – before this final stage in the summer of 1945 and after Wilkinson had ceased to observe affairs early in 1943 – there had been further ructions involving the General, the Australians and the British which require at least a brief mention if one is to obtain a complete perspective when reading the secret journal itself.

For example, there was the sudden storm in the late summer of 1944 which arose when London aired the possibility of a major British naval force, and possibly a Commonwealth land force, being assembled to operate on MacArthur's flank and under his command. Admiral King in Washington chose to arouse the General's anger and strong private protests ('the American people would never forgive Mr Churchill and would never forgive England') by informing him that what the British Chiefs of Staff were in fact proposing was to take away from him altogether his whole area except for the Philippines. As General Marshall apparently recognised and the London records prove, there was no foundation for 'this mischievous tale', as Churchill called it. Possibly King was deliberately creating a diversion to assist in his own manoeuvrings against MacArthur and the US Army.[99]

96 Lumsden notes, 4 October 1944, PREM 3, 159/5.
97 For example, Churchill to MacArthur, 14 September 1944, PREM 3, 159/4, and 12 March 1944, PREM 3, 159/14.
98 Even then, MacArthur was reluctant to see the SWPA change hands. Gairdner to Churchill, 12 May 1945, PREM 3, 159/7.
99 According to MacArthur, Marshall acknowledged that his own interpretation of the British proposal differed from King's. Curtin to Churchill, 3, 16 September; Churchill to MacArthur, 4 September; MacArthur to Churchill, 6 September 1944, CAB 69/6; minutes, reports and telegrams in PREM 3, 159/4; Combined Chiefs of Staff minutes, 14 June and 14 September 1944, CAB 88/4; Pogue, *Marshall, Organizer of Victory*, p. 452. According to the British Chiefs of Staff, Marshall and King, during their visit to London in June, expressed 'off the record' agreement with the idea of Australian troops eventually moving from MacArthur's direct control to form part of a Commonwealth force. Hollis to Churchill, 30 June 1944, PREM 3, 160/5. It should also be added that the British Chiefs of Staff *had* thought, earlier in 1944, of an eventual Commonwealth build-up in the South West Pacific Area after the defeat of Germany, which would lead to a preponderant role in the area, and hence justify not only overall control moving to the Combined Chiefs of Staff, but also a British Supreme Commander. Chiefs of Staff to Churchill, 8 March 1944, PREM 3, 160/7.

At the same time, there was considerable controversy in Australia over what seemed to some to be the secondary role being allocated to their country's forces. Australia's great problems over manpower resources complicated matters, as did the desirability of having her mandated territories liberated by her own troops.[100] The issue also created strains between MacArthur and Curtin on the one hand and General Blamey on the other. Blamey had visited London in the early summer of 1944, and according to General Lumsden's report (seen by Churchill) 'had returned full of admiration and loyalty towards all things British'. Moreover, he was now less keen on merging the Australian Army's advance with that of the Americans, and questioned MacArthur's plans for using the AIF in the Philippines assault. Lumsden wrote:

General Blamey has undoubtedly changed his outlook since he left this country and is not now on as good terms as formerly with General MacArthur . . . Now he appears to favour the operation of Imperial forces under an independent command and on an axis separate from that of the American forces . . . Mr. Curtin . . . fully appreciates the change which has come over General Blamey. He is, however, still firmly allied to General MacArthur. As a result, General Blamey is, I am told, not at all popular with Mr Curtin, who feels that his loyalty is more than doubtful and that . . . unless he watches his step another may take his place. General MacArthur now says that he considers General Blamey to be so unreliable that . . . Mr Curtin would be well advised to make a change . . . [Even so] General Blamey rules his own roost with a rod of iron and has assiduously eliminated all those who might approach too close to his throne. (15 July 1944.)[101]

This new tension between MacArthur and Blamey was to continue till the end of the war. In May 1945, for example, General Gairdner, after talking to MacArthur and senior Australian officers, reported trouble between the two men over such matters as the offensive tactics being employed by Blamey against by-passed Japanese units in New Guinea and elsewhere. (MacArthur, like Churchill when Blamey's plans had first been developed, held such action to be unnecessarily costly.[102]) Blamey was also resisting MacArthur's proposal that once Australian troops were ashore in

---

Churchill himself at one time envisaged operations on MacArthur's left flank being so distinct from the General's main forces, that they should come under South East Asia Command. Churchill to Ismay, 20 June 1944, PREM 3, 160/5.

100 Hasluck, *Government and People*, pp. 566ff.

101 Lumsden to Ismay, 15 July 1944, PREM 3, 159/4.

102 On 23 September 1944 Churchill minuted: 'I do not think much of General Blamey's idea of stirring up the by-passed Japanese in Rabaul etc.'. PREM 3, 159/14. For Blamey's views, as he developed them in the summer of 1945, see Hasluck, *Government and People*, p. 577.

Japan itself they should adopt American weapons and ammunition in order to facilitate a single line of communication from the United States. Suggesting that 'General Blamey wants to be Supreme Commander', MacArthur observed

that he found that General Blamey's dual position was an intolerable situation. On the one hand General Blamey was under his orders, on the other he was quite independent, [and] unless General Blamey was assigned to him entirely, he would not be prepared to take him as Commander of the Australian forces for any further operations which might arise . . . General MacArthur feels very acutely the loss of Mr. Curtin as Prime Minister, as he knew and trusted him. Mr Chifly [Curtin's deputy], he feels, is very ignorant of military matters and is completely dominated by General Blamey whom he [MacArthur] does not trust. He advised me that if I had any interviews with General Blamey, to insist on having a third officer present![103]

American–Australian differences such as these were more than a matter of personalities. Curtin himself, up till his illness in 1945 (he died in July of that year), had continued to insist to Churchill that nothing should be done to disturb his own special and direct links with MacArthur. But although Curtin's admiration for the General remained undiminished,[104] he too was not unaffected by a certain disenchantment with America and Americans which was developing in Australia. According to hopeful reports reaching London from 1943 onwards, this trend was accompanied by 'a noticeable swing in Australian feelings from anti- to pro-British',[105] while even earlier Churchill had been able to fasten with delight upon a *Sydney Morning Herald* leading article which roundly answered those Americans like Wendell Willkie who were declaring that they were not fighting for the British Empire: 'Well we are, and we fight because we believe in the Empire and its civilising mission.'[106] Or again, in the summer of 1942, Attlee had reported to the Prime Minister that all the Dominions' High Commissioners were 'considerably exercised in their minds as to the habit of prominent Americans, including members of the Administration, talking as if the British Empire was in the process of dissolution'. They were also disturbed, added Attlee, 'by the economic imperialism of the

103 Gairdner to Ismay, 30 May 1945, PREM 3, 159/14.
104 See, for example, Curtin's remarks at the Commonwealth Prime Ministers' Conference in London, 3 May 1944, PREM 4, 42/5.
105 FO 371/34089, A 3970 and 4359/3/45; Lumsden to Churchill, 19 November 1943, PREM 3, 158/7; Sir Walter Layton report, PREM 3, 159/2; Somerville Diary, 23 December 1943. See in general T. R. Reese, *Australia, New Zealand and the United States* (London, 1969).
106 PREM 4, 27/1.

American business interests [like Pan American] which are quite active under the cloak of a benevolent and avuncular internationalism.'[107] (By the end of 1943, even MacArthur would be admitting to General Lumsden that there was 'an awakening imperialist feeling in the USA and that it was possibly on the increase'.[108])

By 1944 Curtin himself was urging Britain to make haste to play a larger role in the Pacific war in view of the growing American tendency to regard it as their private preserve 'even though they seek maximum aid, hoping to keep the publicity regarding the British forces limited'. 'I am deeply concerned', he wrote to Churchill in August of that year, 'at the position that would arise in our Far Eastern Empire if any considerable American opinion were to hold that America fought a war on principle in the Far East and won it relatively unaided while the other Allies including ourselves did very little towards recovering our lost property.'[109] At the Commonwealth Prime Ministers' conference in London that May, Curtin had already urged the need for improved machinery to facilitate closer and more regular consultation – and had been privately exasperated by the cool response from the British as well as the Canadians, particularly when Churchill did not even attend the session specially devoted to the subject.[110]

Even so, the possible ways in which the Dominions could be associated with Britain in world affairs after the war did receive considerable attention in Whitehall. It was also clear that where Australia was concerned Britain would have to accept a continuation of that new degree of independent assertiveness which had come with the war. If there had remained any doubts on that score, they were removed in January 1944 when, without consulting London, senior members of the Australian and New Zealand Governments conferred and publicly proclaimed their views on the future course of affairs in the Pacific.[111] True, Evatt privately indicated that the main motive behind this move had been anxiety over US infiltration and influence in Pacific islands south of the equator, over 'similar tendencies in Australia and New Zealand', and over Britain's inclination 'to concede too easily proposals made by the United States [as at the Cairo Conference] in relation to the Pacific'.[112] It was also true that on these subjects, together with others such as the surrender and occupation of Japan, acerbic Australian–American exchanges lay ahead.[113] Yet at the same time there

107 Attlee to Churchill, 16 June 1942, PREM 4, 42/9.
108 Lumsden to Churchill, 19 November 1943, see n. 105.
109 Curtin to Churchill, 12 August 1944, DO (44) 13, CAB 69/6.
110 Commonwealth Prime Ministers' meeting, 15 May 1944, PREM 4, 42/5; Hankey Diary, 25 May 1944.
111 See, for example, Reese, *Australia . . .*, pp. 32ff.
112 Cranborne memo., 2 February 1944, WP (44) 70, PREM 4, 50/12.
113 See, for example, Reese, *Australia . . .*, pp. 50-2.

was little inclination on the part of Australia to gloss over differences with Britain concerning, for example, the degree of accountability of colonial powers to a new international organization,[114] or the role of states other than Great Powers within that organization. From the United Nations Conference at San Francisco, Eden reported to Churchill in April 1945 that of the Commonwealth delegates 'Evatt is the most tiresome and Fraser [Prime Minister of New Zealand] the most woolly'; at least, however, 'between them they are making clear to the Americans and all concerned that we do not control their votes'.[115]

The future pattern of relationships between Britain and the Dominions was still far from clear, however. For example, while Attlee for one argued privately that 'if we fail . . . to maintain ourselves as an Empire and a Commonwealth . . . we cannot exist as a world power',[116] others in London held, conversely, that 'the moment we cease to be a World Power the Commonwealth automatically dissolves because the Dominions (with the possible exception of Australia and New Zealand) have no strong political affinities between themselves'.[117] Not everyone in the Government – certainly not Leopold Amery at the India Office, for example – accepted that the commercial ties of Imperial Preference should be weakened or abandoned at the behest of the United States. Nor would everyone have accepted the Foreign Office's assertion, that 'In their habits and ways of living, people of the Dominions, with the exception of French Canadians and possibly South Africans, are in many respects more akin to Americans than to ourselves.' By the end of the war, however, few could dispute the conclusion which accompanied this last statement, that 'the United States as a factor in Dominion affairs have come to stay'.[118] In this development, MacArthur's period in Australia – pointing ahead as it did to the ANZUS Pact of 1951 – had been a significant episode.

114 For example, Attlee to Churchill, 5 March 1945, PREM 4, 31/4.
115 Eden to Churchill, 30 April 1945, PREM 4, 31/7.
116 Attlee memo., 28 January 1943, WP (43) 44, CAB 66/33.
117 Foreign Office circular, 'The British Commonwealth', 11 December 1943, W 12262/5467/68 in FO 371/38522. Cf. Foreign Office and Dominions Office surveys in July and August 1945 in FO 371/50912.
118 FO circular, supra.

8

Chatham House, Whitehall, and Far Eastern Issues, 1941–1945

In one of its aspects, the essay that follows is a brief exploration of a little-known side of reactions within Britain to the war against Japan between 1941 and 1945, and to Anglo-American relations in the context of that conflict. At the same time, however, it seeks to raise certain questions concerning the degree of independence that the Royal Institute of International Affairs was able to preserve within the special circumstances of the war years, and to ask whether, with particular regard to the Far East, the Institute can be said to have had any significant influence on the policies of the British government. Finally, it is hoped that, in the process of pursuing both these lines of inquiry, some indication will emerge of ways in which documentary material existing in the archives of Chatham House (especially when used in conjunction with papers in the Public Record Office in London and in official and private collections abroad) provides an insight into various ideas about aspects of international affairs that were being discussed at some time in the past among members of the 'attentive' and 'opinion-forming' publics,[1] both within and outside Britain.

Reproduced from *International Affairs*, January 1978, pp. 1–29. The preparation of this article was greatly facilitated by a grant given to the Royal Institute of International Affairs by the Leverhulme Trust, which enabled the Institute to put its archives in an order more readily accessible to researchers. With the exception of papers dealing with the internal affairs of the Institute, those archives more than thirty years old are now open to bona fide research workers. The writer would like to express his own thanks to the archivist involved in that project, Stephen Brooks. He is especially grateful to Miss Dorothy Hamerton (Librarian and Archivist), Miss Elisabeth Campbell (former Press Librarian), and A. S. Olver (who in 1943 became Assistant to the Secretary of Chatham House and secretary to, *inter alia*, its Pacific Affairs Committee) who all provided him with valuable background information and read the article in draft, though the responsibility for its contents remains, of course, his alone.

1 See, for example, J. N. Rosenau, *Public Opinion and Foreign Policy* (New York, 1961, chs 4 and 5). Some of what follows is also of interest in connection with what Rosenau has termed 'linkage groups'. See his *Linkage Politics* (New York, 1969)

From the founding of the British Institute of International Affairs in 1920 (it became the Royal Institute six years later) great emphasis was placed upon its status as 'an unofficial and non-political body', and upon its refusal, spelt out in the preliminaries of all the books published under its aegis, to express a collective opinion on any international issue. As set out in its Royal Charter, the object of the Institute was rather to 'advance the sciences of international politics, economics and jurisprudence', to 'provide and maintain means of information upon international questions', and to 'promote the study and investigation of [such] questions . . .'

Not surprisingly, however, the Institute did not escape criticism for its policies – or what were alleged to be its policies – both before and after the Second World War.[2] In 1925, for example, the charge was made that it had become a vehicle for foreign propaganda; yet it was the contrary notion that was probably more widespread: that is, that its connections with individuals in Westminster and Whitehall gave the Institute some kind of quasi-official standing – rather as the *Times* was assumed by a good many people outside Britain to be the mouthpiece of the government of the day.[3] This was not, in fact, the case, although politicians and officials did come to Chatham House to speak or to take part in discussions, thus, incidentally, underlining the need for such occasions to remain private. (In the first year of the Institute's existence, for example, Sir Maurice Hankey, the Secretary of the Cabinet and the Committee of Imperial Defence, was asked to read a paper on 'Diplomacy by Conference', with Arthur Balfour being invited to preside over the meeting.[4]) Even an episode – it appears to have been a rare occurrence – when someone in an official position sought to exert influence over one of the Institute's publications serves in retrospect to emphasize the independence possessed by those who were working in St James's Square. For although, when Elizabeth Wiskemann was preparing her timely history of *Czechs and Germans* in 1937–8, Arnold Toynbee, as Director of Studies at the Institute, did endeavour, on his own private admission, 'to correct [its] pro-Czech leaning' (he believed he had succeeded in doing so 'very substantially'), he nevertheless declined to delay the publication of the book when that course was suggested to him by a member of the Foreign Office, who feared that the appearance of the volume in the summer of 1938 would mean 'a set-back to the very real effort . . . which is being made to bring M. Benes to a sense of the

2 Material on Criticisms of Chatham House Policy, Chatham House archives (hereafter, 'CHA'), sections 2 and 8.
3 It can of course be argued that in 1938 *The Times* under Dawson did, indeed, compromise its independence where foreign policy was concerned. See, e.g., K. Middlemas, *Diplomacy of Illusion* (London, 1972), pp. 102, 289, 323.
4 Council minutes, CHA/1, vol. 1.

"realities" of the situation and so to direct negotiations with Henlein [the leader of the Sudeten German extremists]'[5]

It is not to be wondered at that the special circumstances of the wartime years between 1939 and 1945 did, however, blur the dividing line between Chatham House and the official world. Even so, the evidence now available suggests that in certain respects this process went much further than many realized at the time – far enough, indeed, for the very independence of the Institute to be compromised at least in one specific connection, even if that independence was to be re-established once peace had returned. The aspect of Chatham House's work that was involved was its role as the body representing Britain within the Institute of Pacific Relations, but this can usefully be set alongside other ways in which the Institute was concerned with Far Eastern issues during the war. At this point, obviously, the wider context of international, and particularly Anglo-American, relations regarding that part of the world also becomes relevant. Given the size of that subject, however, the most that can be done here is to refer readers who wish to examine the intergovernmental side of things to a more lengthy and forthcoming study by the present writer.[6]

Between 1939 and 1945, as will emerge below, the staff of Chatham House tended to find themselves engaged in new duties. However, many of the normal activities of the Institute continued during these war years, under the guidance of a small band of administrators (notably Miss Margaret Cleeve) who had not become involved in government work. Various study

5 Hadow to Toynbee, May 16, 1938; Toynbee to Macadam, May 17, 1938; Toynbee to Hadow, May 19, 1938, CHA/16/23. It is interesting to read Toynbee's strong personal views on various international issues during the 1930s, especially in the light of what was appearing from his pen or under his guidance in the annual *Survey of International Affairs* at the time. Thus, for example, he wrote privately from his home in York to Miss Margaret Cleeve at Chatham House on July 18, 1931: 'I sit here considering the philosophy of history and then the paper comes and I start boiling over at the latest enormity of the French. I suppose my feelings against them go back to the peace conference. They are now at white heat! It looks as if we were assisting now at the grand dénouement of the last dozen years. Do you think the next chapter – beginning after the Disarmament Conference – will end in another war, with France playing Germany's part this time? In my antigallicism I am almost in danger of becoming patriotic.' CHA/4/Toynbee.

In 1942, however, on his return from a visit to the United States, where he had been struck by the far greater margin of security enjoyed by that country than by Britain, he was to confess to a Chatham House audience: 'Again and again when I was in America I said to myself: Now I know how the French have felt and how very good it is for me to know that. Now I understand what they could never make me and my fellow-countrymen understand until it was too late.' Address of December 7, 1942, CHA/4/Toynbee.

6 *Allies of a Kind. The United States, Britain and the War Against Japan, 1941–1945* (London, 1978). On wartime issues surrounding a comparable body in the USA, see R. D. Schulzinger, *The Wise Men of Foreign Affairs. The History of the Council on Foreign Relations* (New York, 1984).

groups went on meeting, for example, and among them was one that devoted its attention to Far Eastern affairs. Its members included Sir Frederick Whyte, a former Liberal Member of Parliament who had also been President of the Indian Legislative Assembly and Political Adviser to the Chinese government, and had written books on *Asia in the Twentieth Century* and *The Future of East and West*; Sir Andrew McFadyean, a former Treasury official and President of the Liberal Party, and at the time a director of the British North Borneo Company; and Sir John Pratt, a retired senior official of the Consular Service in China who, while on attachment to the Foreign Office during the 1930s, had played a significant part in helping to shape Britain's Far Eastern policies.[7]

It is not proposed to examine in detail the proceedings of the Far Eastern Group, but it is worth noting a few of the speakers and topics that were involved, together with some of the more interesting ideas that emerged.[8] Certain visitors, for example, raised the question of whether China, for the time being Britain's ally, might not make trouble for it after the war. Sir Muhammed Zafrullah Khan for one, who had for a short while been India's Agent General in Chungking, suggested at a meeting of the Group early in 1943 that China's desire to recover what it regarded as integral parts of its historic territory might well extend beyond Manchuria and Tibet to include parts of Indo-China and upper Burma as well. A sharp disagreement over this same issue arose during a session later in the same year when the speaker was Sir Olaf Caroe, the Indian government's Secretary for External Affairs, who emphasized that 'history had shown there was such a thing as Chinese imperialism', and that therefore care must be taken to maintain a number of buffer states between China and India. To this, Sir John Pratt fiercely retorted that 'there was no danger to India from China', and that Britain itself 'had called Chinese imperialism into existence by [its] own follies – as in the case of Tibet'. Britain's true interest in the Far East, he asserted, was 'always identical to that of China', with the 'real danger' being represented by Japan and with the Soviet Union also being likely to extend its influence in the area.

Meanwhile on a number of occasions the Group had also discussed the related topic of likely post-war political developments within China. Several visiting speakers referred, for example, to the growing strength of the Communists in Yenan and to what a former Financial Counsellor of the British Embassy in Chungking described as their 'popular appeal';

---

7 For material on Pratt's role during the Far Eastern crisis of 1931–3, and his subsequent public criticisms of the version of the crisis put forward in book form by Henry Stimson, who had been the American Secretary of State at the time, see C. Thorne, *The Limits of Foreign Policy* (London, 1972), passim. Pratt was an Anglo-Indian.

8 Far Eastern Group proceedings, CHA/8, passim.

Zafrullah Khan, too, suggested that, although inferior in numbers to the armies of the Kuomintang, 'the Communists might be a more efficient fighting force'. A speaker with a rather different background, Victor Farmer, who was a director of ICI (China) and who in 1944 had recently returned from a visit to the Far East, offered for his part a misunderstanding that was already fairly widespread in both London and Washington at the time:[9]

I have met some [Chinese] Communists and their ideas are not as Communistic as one would imagine. In fact they are very open-minded. If you could get rid of this ultra-nationalistic clique in the saddle at present in Chungking, and many Government officials [there] are extremely broad-minded, I think that the way would be open for a compromise with the Communists; and an effective compromise.

In addition to the Far Eastern Group, there also existed at Chatham House, from 1942 onwards, a private members' study group on War Strategy, which was set up by Lt Colonel Oliver Garsia[10] and contained among its members Lord Hankey (as he had become) and Major-General F. S. G. Piggott, Military Attaché in Tokyo in the later 1930s, whose strong views on the ease with which Britain could avoid clashing with Japan had set him apart from officials in London.[11] Indeed, Piggott, even after Pearl Harbor, maintained this line of argument (together with his reputation for being somewhat bizarre) during the meetings of the War Strategy Group, submitting in September 1942, for example, that 'it was a fact that at the outbreak of war with Germany, Japan was more pro-British than pro-Germany'.[12] At the same time – and in this he was in accord with the official view adamantly held in Washington – he agreed with other members, such as Field Marshal Lord Milne (a former Chief of the Imperial General Staff), that if Japan were ever to be defeated, greater attention would have to be paid to the vital contribution that China could make.

One of the last papers submitted to the War Strategy Group came in June 1945 from Sir Josiah Crosby, formerly Britain's Minister in Bangkok,

9 On Western misperceptions of the nature of the Chinese Communist Party before 1945, see, for example, Tang Tsou, *America's Failure in China 1941–50* (Chicago, 1963), and K. E. Shewmaker, *Americans and Chinese Communists, 1927–1945* (Ithaca, NY, 1971).

10 War Strategy Group papers, CHA/9.

11 See, for example, B. A. Lee, *Britain and the Sino-Japanese War, 1937–1939* (London, 1973), p. 115.

12 The large degree of oversimplification involved in this assertion is revealed in, for example, D. Borg and S. Okamoto, eds, *Pearl Harbor as History* (New York, 1973), and J. Morley, ed., *Deterrent Diplomacy: Japan, Germany and the USSR, 1935–1940* (New York, 1976).

under the heading of 'The Shape of Things to Come in the Far East'. Sir Josiah described Chinese immigration and economic penetration into Southeast Asia as 'alarming', and attacked suggestions that the European colonial powers in the area should hand over their territories to an international body; he recognized, nevertheless, that Japan's dramatic military victories in 1941–2 had put an end to what had remained of the prestige of the white man in the Far East, and argued that the only future for Western people there lay in returning 'as friends and mentors bent upon showing [Orientals] the road to progress and to government by themselves within the shortest possible space of time'.

Even this modified, paternalist approach was of course by then quite unacceptable to some of the rapidly developing nationalist movements in Southeast Asia.[13] And in this connection, a lecture which Crosby had delivered at Chatham House earlier, in 1943, had given rise to some disquiet within the Foreign Office, for not only had the speaker proposed that Siam – already an independent state – might require a period of Western tutelage after the war, but in the opinion of a member of the Foreign Office's Far Eastern Department, the whole tone of the ensuing discussion had been 'very reactionary'. The Head of the Department, Ashley (later Sir Ashley) Clarke, agreed that any mention of what had been said at the meeting 'should be suppressed', and that an article which Crosby proposed to write for *International Affairs* ought to be postponed lest its tone should offend the Chinese.[14] In the event, an essay by Crosby was published in *International Affairs* in July 1944, whereupon his reference to a possible period of tutelage for Siam was taken by US officials as clear evidence of sinister intentions on the part of the British government towards that country in particular and Southeast Asia generally. There was some irony in this, in that Crosby's private view, as expressed in conversation with former colleagues in the Foreign Office, was that tutelage over Siam should be exercised, not by Britain, but by the United States.[15] Regardless of the facts of the case, however, the episode remains of interest as an example of how discussions and publications centred upon Chatham

13 Nevertheless, A. S. Olver's comment on Crosby's remarks is important. The latter, he recalls, 'was an amusingly old-fashioned character from an age when the British Minister in Bangkok was indeed a power in the land. The quotation from him therefore suggests a striking change in attitude in Britain to the future of South-east Asia since before the war, when the prospect of self-government was hardly considered as compared with the discussions which went on about India'. (Letter to the author, October 16, 1977.) On the extent of the change that took place during the war years, see, for example, V. Purcell, *The Chinese in Southeast Asia*, 2nd edn (London, 1965), p. 551.
14 FO 371, F6050/1953/61 (35927), Public Record Office, London.
15 Ibid., F606/169/40 (35977) and F696/222/40 (35979); R. Harris Smith, *OSS* (Berkeley, 1972), p. 303.

House, especially where officials or former officials were involved, could have repercussions in the wider field of international relations at the time.

While an examination of Far Eastern issues continued to take place at Chatham House during the war years, various individuals connected with the Institute were contributing to a similar process in an official capacity of one kind or another. In some cases, the person concerned had been in the service of the government before the war. Sir George Sansom, a member of the Institute from 1931 onwards (though not closely involved in its work), was an outstanding example in a Far Eastern context. Having long been recognized as a leading scholar in the field of Japanese studies, he was also Commercial Counsellor in the Embassy in Tokyo before 1941. After Pearl Harbor, he eventually took up a senior post in the Washington Embassy with special responsibility for Far Eastern affairs, also contributing to discussions within the Foreign Office – on such issues as the future of the Throne in Japan – views that were accorded great weight.[16] For other individuals, meanwhile, entry into the world of officialdom had come about only recently, as a consequence of the special circumstances created by the war. Thus G. E. Hubbard, who had been the coordinator of Far Eastern research at Chatham House, was seconded in 1939 to the Political Intelligence Department of the Foreign Office, where he developed the argument, for example, that in 1942 'nothing in the Far East mattered so much as keeping China in the war'.[17] Not surprisingly, when, as we shall see below, he returned to his post at Chatham House in 1943, Hubbard kept in fairly close touch with his former colleagues in Whitehall.[18]

At the same time, the Institute also found itself involved during the war in a more wholesale new relationship with the official world when, with the aid of a government grant and under Toynbee's direction, it set up the Foreign Research and Press Service at Oxford in 1939, and even more so in 1943 when the FRPS was transformed, still under Toynbee, into the Foreign Office Research Department. The work undertaken by the FRPS

16 Interview with Sir Ashley Clarke. For examples of Sansom's contribution to official policy discussions, see FO 371, F4052/584/61 (46346) and F3768/364/23 (46447). Sansom had a poor opinion of the Foreign Office, however, suggesting privately in 1945 that it needed 'the most drastic overhaul, physically and morally', and that 'the whole machine is slow, cumbrous and obsolete, [with] still too much of the annointment with holy oil. . . .' K. Sansom, *Sir George Sansom and Japan: A Memoir* (Tallahassee, Fa, 1972), p. 145.

17 FO 371, F2754/289/61 (31760). Some of Hubbard's personal correspondence was, alas, among the archive material that was 'weeded out' before the survey and re-ordering of the Chatham House archives.

18 For example, FO 371, F4767 and 5163/1935/61 (35927).

for a large number of government agencies (17 of them used the press-cuttings library) deserves an article to itself, but it can be summarized here as having involved studying the foreign press, responding to inquiries from government departments and carrying out research initiated from within. [19] Two points of wider interest need to be emphasized as well, however, in connection with the establishment of the FRPS/FORD. The first is that the employment of the Institute's resources in an official capacity of this kind was not undertaken on the initiative of Whitehall alone and against the wishes of those responsible for the conduct of its affairs. Toynbee had been envisaging some such development a year before war broke out, writing to a member of the staff in St James's Square as the Czech crisis of 1938 approached its climax: 'We shall have to put in some strenuous work persuading HMG to *use Chatham House* instead of breaking us up.'[20]

Nevertheless – and this is the second aspect of general interest – the ensuing establishment of the FRPS did raise substantial questions concerning the status of Chatham House and of its staff (even though many non-Institute people also became involved in the work of the new organization), as well as the general issue of relations between government and intellectuals in wartime. [21] There is not room in this article to examine the discussions that went on before members of the staff of the Institute were transformed in 1943 into temporary civil servants under the aegis of

19 FRPS Committee papers, CHA/2. One example of a specific contribution by a member of the FRPS outside Far Eastern matters involved Professor Charles Webster, who was not averse to intervening in Whitehall debates in magisterial fashion when the opportunity arose. On this occasion, in May and June 1944, an argument on paper had developed between the Head of the Foreign Office's Reconstruction Department, Gladwyn Jebb, and the Head of the North American Department, Nevile Butler, following comments by Jebb on statements made by Walter Lippmann about the need for realism in American post-war foreign policy. Emphasizing the importance of a continuing 'balancing of power', Jebb had observed: 'all this talk of morals in international politics is beside the point. . . .' This shocked Butler, who responded that the question of morals was 'really the whole point', adding that when Hitler's Germany had become aggressive 'we pursued a Police policy [and] did not intentionally seek anything as precarious or nicely calculated as a Balance of Power.' Webster, invited to comment, thereupon dismissed Lippmann as a slovenly and confused thinker and suggested that both Jebb and Butler were oversimplifying their own views. The balance of power, he asserted, had never been the *object* of British policy. The object, rather, had been to prevent an aggressive power dominating Europe and threatening British interests; if a dominant power were peacefully inclined, as Germany had been for the most part between 1871 and 1890, then Britain was ready to accept the situation. FO 371, AN2320/34/45 (38556).

20 Toynbee to Cleeve, September 6, 1938, CHA/4/Toynbee. Emphasis added. See material on plans for Chatham House in wartime, CHA/2.

21 Toynbee memo., March 30, 1942, and Council minutes, November 18, 1942, CHA/1. There is probably room for a study of the contribution made to British wartime diplomacy and foreign policy making by the 'outsiders', who included Isaiah Berlin, R. H. Tawney and Professor T. N. Whitehead.

the Foreign Office. It can be suggested, however, that while the long-term independence of Chatham House was not compromised, its new role, though temporary, probably helped to reinforce the belief held by some foreign observers that it was in any case some kind of quasi-official organization. Indeed, in 1942 Lord Hailey was already asking his fellow members of the Institute's Committee 'whether any action could be taken to dispose of the confusion which existed in the minds of a number of people, government officials and others, that Chatham House and the FRPS were one and that accordingly Chatham House was now an official body.'[22]

Meanwhile the contribution to policy debates on Far Eastern affairs that was made by the FRPS and later the FORD consisted in the main in the provision of raw material in the form of historical background studies and surveys of factors that might come to play a part in the future. For example, the Foreign Office was presented with memoranda dealing with Chinese attitudes to the status of Tibet, with those aspects of the Chinese scene likely to affect the fate of Manchuria and Korea (special FORD committees, their members including Toynbee and Professor C. K. Webster, were set up to study the future of these last two territories), and with the circumstances Britain itself was likely to encounter in that part of the world after Japan had been defeated.[23] That is not to say, of course, that such material was or

22 Council minutes, May 13, 1942, CHA/1, vol. 21. It is interesting to note that in 1942, when the Foreign Office proposed to bring the FRPS under its direct control, many members of the Committee of Chatham House were extremely unhappy at the prospect, a subcommittee reporting that it was 'not convinced that an organisation which owes its acknowledged success to the fact that its members were recruited from outside the Civil Service is not more likely to prove effective if its management is left to those who in normal times were directly and primarily concerned with the conduct of research into International Affairs, namely the Council of the ... Institute'. The Foreign Office, for its part, emphasized the need to incorporate the FRPS now that work was beginning on possible aspects of the peace settlement, the way in which an official label would make the FRPS more readily trusted by other government departments, and, as Richard Law (Parliamentary Under-Secretary of State) put it to Lord Astor, that if the FRPS remained under Chatham House control, 'there might be criticism in Parliament of the Government's policy being dictated by what might be termed "long-haired" people.' Toynbee supported the Foreign Office argument, and threatened, within the Institute's Committee, that if he were not given this opportunity to watch the development of the peace settlement from within the official machine, he would not continue to write the Institute's annual *Survey* after the war. In this connection, A. S. Olver's recollection is of interest. 'I was always told', he writes, 'that Toynbee was amongst those who had wanted the rump of Chatham House, after FRPS had been formed, to be wound up, and that the chief resistance to this had come from Margaret Cleeve, who had a vision of the Institute as an essential source for un-officials, as well as officials, if they were to be able to develop informed views of international relations. Is it possible that Toynbee and Miss Cleeve saw "Chatham House" as two different things?' (Letter to the author, October 16, 1977.)
23 Respectively FO 371, F7546/2768/10 (31760); F2664/2426/10 (46271); F6012/102/23 (41801); F2330/1394/23 (46468); F5661 and 5742/623/61 (31774).

could be somehow selected and presented in a 'neutral' form, and indeed on some occasions Toynbee in particular put forward very definite views of his own that involved an interpretation of an aspect of the international scene – for instance, British public opinion regarding colonial issues.[24] The FORD also went on record in 1944 on the subject of Chinese domestic politics with two opinions that were by no means accepted throughout Whitehall: that Mao Tse-tung and his colleagues were, indeed, the Communists that they claimed to be, and that, despite hopes of a compromise arrangement being reached between them and the Chungking government of Chiang Kai-shek, anything more than a temporary 'papering over of the cracks' was improbable.[25]

Among the staff of the FRPS/FORD, two individuals in particular stand out in retrospect for the contributions they made to the study of Far Eastern affairs in Whitehall during the war. One was F. C. Jones, the author of such books as *Japan* and *Extraterritoriality in Japan*, formerly of Harvard and subsequently of Bristol University.[26]

Undoubtedly, however, the greatest single contribution on Far Eastern affairs made by a member of the FRPS was that of Geoffrey Hudson, whose book on *The Far East in World Politics* had been published in 1939 and remains of value to this day. It was not simply that Hudson was responsible for the Far Eastern section of the FRPS, but that the Far Eastern Department in the Foreign Office was ready to include him in the circulation of a growing number of official despatches and policy papers, and to give some weight to both his minutes and his memoranda. One consequence, of course, was that the Department was able to make use of Hudson's extensive knowledge of, say, the background to Sino-Soviet tension over Sinkiang, which manifested itself in fighting for a brief while.[27] But Hudson was no mere source of information: he was prepared to express his own views on current policy issues in a forceful manner, and in a direction that tended towards conservatism and *realpolitik*. Thus, where the future of Siam was concerned, he saw no reason why Britain should be 'timid' in claiming for itself after the war a base on the Kra Isthmus ('The Siamese', he wrote, 'ought to be made to feel so frightened at the prospect of retribution for what they have done in joining the Japs that the demands we have to make on them will come as a relief'[28]). As for President Roosevelt's notion of taking Indo-China away from France and placing it

24 Ibid., U947/191/70 (50807).
25 Ibid., F2375/159/10 (41613).
26 See, for example, ibid., file 31702; F4049/877/61 (35917); F399/34/10 (41579).
27 For example, ibid., F6732/11/10 (35710); F4681/62/10 (46187).
28 Ibid., F5550/1599/40 (41848).

under international trusteeship, it evoked Hudson's scorn,[29] while although, where the future of Hongkong was concerned, he believed that London should inform Chiang Kai-shek's government that it would be prepared to discuss the matter, his overriding aim was to find means of preventing China from presenting Britain with a fait accompli by taking over the colony from the Japanese.[30] In addition, he was at one with most of those in Whitehall who examined the subject in envisaging a vital role for a fully committed India in post-war imperial defence schemes, and especially where a counter to pressure from China was required.[31]

Hudson did not limit his advice to specific territorial issues, warning, for example, of the likelihood that 'the racial equality question will come up again in some form in the post-war settlements.'[32] His most substantial and important contributions, however, centred upon the interrelationship between likely political developments inside China and the positions and policies of the great powers in the Far East. In this connection he was blunt in his rejection of the notion, fashionable in the United States at the time and also quite widespread in Britain, that Chiang Kai-shek's regime was essentially democratic. 'It is possible', he wrote in 1943, 'that most of the Kuomintang leaders view the downfall of Italian Fascism with regret rather than with enthusiasm', and he described Chungking's promises of a transition to constitutional, democratic rule as virtually certain to prove 'a fake, mainly designed to impress Anglo-Saxon opinion'. All such talk, he repeated in the following year, was 'hocus-pocus'.[33] At the same time, however, Hudson was equally scornful of the idea put forward in parts of the American press in 1944 and 1945, especially, that Chungking, as distinct from Yenan, had contributed little or nothing to the fight against Japan, suggesting in April 1945 that it was 'surely about time that someone pointed out that Chiang Kai-shek did *not* capitulate in 1938 – or in 1942, that, apart from guerrilla activity, the only real fighting against the Japanese has been done by the Central Army troops, and that in 1939–40 the Chinese Communists duly denounced the "imperialist war" then being waged by Britain and France against Nazi Germany'.[34]

Indeed, as the prospect of widespread conflict between opposing parties in China increased, so Hudson's strongly anti-communist stance became

---

29 Ibid., F417/295/10 (41627). On the issue in general, see 'Indo-China and Anglo-American relations, 1942–1945', essay number 5 above, and on wider policy issues, the writer's *Allies of a Kind* and his essay 'Wartime British planning for the post-war Far East', in I. Nish (ed.), *Anglo-Japanese Alienation, 1919–1952* (Cambridge, 1982).
30 FO 371, F2172/1505/10 (41657).
31 Ibid., U4136/1970/70 (35445).
32 Ibid., F1106/91/61 (46324).
33 Ibid., F4480/10/10 (35689); F1441/159/10 (41611).
34 Ibid., F2251/35/10 (46167).

all the more evident. In one important respect he did supply a much-needed corrective within the Foreign Office to the opinions encouraged there by individuals like Sir Archibald Clark Kerr, Ambassador to China until 1942 and then to the Soviet Union, who repeatedly insisted that the men who ruled in Yenan represented no more than a 'mild radicalism'.[35] Mao Tse-tung's book, *The New Democracy*, Hudson emphasized in May 1943, made it clear that 'he at any rate regards Chinese Communism as part of a world proletarian revolution'. Hudson also pointed out on several occasions that 'the Communists do not, any more than the Kuomintang, think of "democracy" as a system which gives a chance to opposition parties', adding that 'what is really meant by the "democracy" of the Communists is that they are strongly supported by the poorer peasantry, who are the "masses" in rural China'.[36] As for the belief being put forward by certain US diplomats in the Far East at that time, such as John Paton Davies, that Mao Tse-tung and his colleagues might be drawn closer to the United States than to the Soviet Union,[37] that, too, was based in Hudson's eyes on a complete misreading of the nature of the Yenan regime. 'It is extremely unlikely', he argued in June 1945, 'that a Communist China would be any more pro-American than Tito's Yugoslavia is pro-British. The Moderator of the Church of Scotland *might* have more influence over the Catholic clergy than the Pope, but probably not.'[38]

In the same context, however, Hudson himself derived some comfort from a forecast based on a false reading on his part of the strengths and weaknesses of the two main contending parties in China. Unless they received more assistance from the Soviet Union than did the Kuomintang forces from the United States, 'the odds', he believed, 'would probably be heavily against the Communist troops . . ., in spite of [their] fervour and fighting quality in a renewed civil war'. Again making a comparison with Tito and Yugoslavia, he argued that in China circumstances were less favourable to the Communists, in that the areas over which they had already obtained control were accessible 'only through the Kuomintang territory', while Chungking, on the other hand, could utilize US-built airfields if it came to a showdown.[39] Nevertheless, he saw a great danger of 'a repetition of the Spanish Civil War, with the legal government on the right', should the Soviet Union step in to aid Yenan.[40] Moreover, this

35 For example, Clark Kerr to Eden, February 3, 1942, FO 800/300.

36 FO 371, F2315/1893/10 (35838); F1546/159/10 (41612).

37 For a convenient summary, see John P. Davies's own valuable book, *Dragon by the Tail* (New York, 1972; London, 1974), and J. W. Esherick (ed.), *Lost Chance in China: The World War II Despatches of John S. Service* (New York, 1975).

38 FO 371, F3065/36/10 (46170).

39 Ibid., F2431/254/10 (35799); F4023/159/10 (41613).

40 Ibid., F4852/74/10 (35778).

alarming prospect was linked, in his mind, with the belief that in Japan, too, 'Communism would probably thrive on the conditions [there] produced by defeat'.[41] Overall, indeed, he envisaged the possibility that so blatant would be 'Soviet . . . southward expansionism' that the United States might 'be driven to favour' a course whereby Japan, although deprived of its naval forces, would be 'allowed to retain military power on the mainland of Asia'. (He added that any suggestion of this kind would be 'political dynamite' and that 'in any case it should never be urged by Britain because Americans already have an ineradicable suspicion that we stand for a soft peace with Japan and are lukewarm about the Pacific War'.)[42]

Hudson thus acted as something of a gadfly, as well as an area expert, in wartime Foreign Office discussions about the Far East. Yet whether one's focus is upon the role after 1939 of an individual or on the indirect contribution made by the Institute itself in the shape of the FRPS/FORD, the involvement in the official world in each case was essentially a straightforward one; and if it could at times give rise to questions concerning the independent status of the Institute, the problem was at least there for all to see. In another field, however, there was developing meanwhile a threat to that independence which, even if again a temporary wartime one, was more shadowy and hence, perhaps, more dangerous – especially since it involved the direct relations between Chatham House and a number of foreign affairs organizations in other countries. This other threat arose from the position held by Chatham House as the British unit within an international body, the Institute of Pacific Relations.

The Institute of Pacific Relations, founded in 1925 at a gathering in Honolulu of various scholars, religious leaders and businessmen concerned with the affairs of East Asia and the Pacific, had not attracted widespread attention before the Second World War. In its attempts to create an awareness of the problems of the area in question, it had probably been preaching to the converted for the most part, and certainly the significance of its work and the size of its organization were far smaller than might have been imagined subsequently by those who read of the accusations brought against it after the war.[43]

41 Ibid., F8119/205/23 (31827): and see F459 and 931/94/23 (41793).
42 Ibid., F1334/127/61 (46325). Oddly enough Hudson, though long involved in the affairs of the RIIA, did not become a member until 1947.
43 For a useful, if not entirely satisfactory, history, see J. N. Thomas, *The Institute of Pacific Relations* (Seattle, 1974). The present writer is indebted to Dr Dorothy Borg of Columbia University's East Asian Institute, who was formerly a member of the IPR Secretariat, and

The IPR was a confederation made up from a number of national societies (there were separate councils in Australia, Canada, France, India, Japan, the Netherlands, New Zealand, the United Kingdom and the United States), being financed mainly by contributions from those national bodies and by grants from American foundations such as Rockefeller and Carnegie. Its governing board was known as the Pacific Council, the chairmen of which included at various times Ray Lyman Wilbur (a former US Secretary of the Interior), Newton D. Baker (a former Secretary of War) and, between 1939 and 1942, Philip C. Jessup, Professor of International Law at Columbia University. In addition to developing programmes of research and convening a number of international conferences composed of delegates from the constituent national councils, the IPR also produced books and journals, the best known of the latter being the quarterly *Pacific Affairs*, whose editor for most of the 1930s was Owen Lattimore. Meanwhile Chatham House, as the national council for Britain, set up its own IPR Committee,[44] whose members included Whyte and McFadyean, both mentioned above, and A. V. Alexander, the Labour Party politician who subsequently served in the wartime National government as First Lord of the Admiralty.

Later, in the early 1950s, during the McCarthy years in the United States, the IPR and some of its American members were of course to become the subject of fierce accusations to the effect that the organization had been one of the centres of a communist conspiracy aimed at thwarting America's true interests in the Far East, and in particular at bringing about a victory for Mao Tse-tung and his Party in China, thus causing that country to be 'lost' to the United States. A Senate Judiciary Subcommittee on Internal Security, under the chairmanship of Senator Pat McCarran, devoted a vast amount of time to investigating the IPR; the tenor and level of the subcommittee's proceedings, as well as their direction, were reflected in McCarran's own assertion that 'but for the machinations of a small group that controlled and activated the IPR, China today would be free . . .'.[45] Similar conclusions appeared subsequently in the writings of right-wing authors such as Anthony Kubek.[46]

who assisted him in finding a way through the files of IPR papers, still in the tangled state left by the rude hands of the McCarran Senate Judiciary Subcommittee on Internal Security. Professors Owen Lattimore and John K. Fairbank have also kindly discussed aspects of the IPR's history with the writer.

44 IPR committee files, CHA/6.

45 US Senate, Committee on the Judiciary, *Institute of Pacific Relations Hearings*, 15 vols (Washington, US Government Printing Office, 1951–52). See also the IPR's own *Commentary on the McCarran Report* (New York, 1953).

46 A. Kubek, *How the Far East was Lost* (Chicago, 1963), ch. 15.

This is not the place to examine such charges in any detail, for not only were they pungently dismissed by a number of commentators at the time, [47] but they have been well assessed by various recent historians. [48] It is worth noting in the context of the present article, however, that members of Chatham House, notwithstanding their past exasperation with some of the Americans involved in the IPR's activities, were prepared to write on behalf of that Institute when it came under attack. Thus McFadyean declared in a letter of 23 May 1952: 'The fact that I have criticised certain activities and certain officers of the [IPR] entitles me to say with greater emphasis, firstly that it would have been a useless body if it had not represented a wide variety of political views, and secondly that throughout my acquaintance with the Institute its governing body, while respecting the rights of free expression, has never encouraged or countenanced subversive views.' And Toynbee himself wrote in June 1952 to describe the IPR as 'an indispensable [and] impartial forum in which controversial questions . . . can be discussed objectively in a dispassionate atmosphere'. [49]

As we shall see below, the IPR's wartime conferences had in fact scarcely been notable for their 'dispassionate atmosphere', and there had been a good deal of resentment within Chatham House against what were seen as the unbalanced and unbridled attacks launched on British colonial policies by individuals serving in the IPR's New York headquarters and/or its American branch. Sansom, too, in his Washington post, found many of the IPR people in New York 'a smug lot', [50] while an article which appeared in the December 1942 issue of *Pacific Affairs*, in which W. L. Holland, the New Zealander serving as the IPR's International Research Secretary, attacked aspects of Britain's policies over China, aroused considerable anger in St James's Square (even though Holland was generally more favourably regarded than his New York colleagues). Members of the IPR from other European colonial powers were also tending to react in this way, a senior Dutch member of the Institute, for example, writing in 1945 that

47 Eric Sevareid of CBS described McCarran's assertion about China as 'Hollywood history in glorious technicolour; dime store history in who-done-it form, strongly similar to the methods of Stalin's commissars purging deviationist intellectuals; double-think redoubled'. The *Washington Post* (July 4, 1952) concluded: 'The McCarran subcommittee has given us not a report but a revision of history – a revision compounded out of McCarthian bigotry, McCarranesque spleen and MacArthurian legend. It is an attempt to perpetuate another fraud and hoax on the American people.'

48 See, for example, Shewmaker, *Americans and Chinese Communists*, ch. 18.

49 These and other letters are reprinted in the American IPR's *Commentary on the McCarran Report*, p. 34ff. Sansom's private opinion, on the other hand, expressed in a letter of December 14, 1957 to Ivison Macadam of Chatham House, was that, although the McCarran Committee's 'methods and purposes [had been] deplorable', he 'could not escape the conclusion that the American IPR had been used by subversive people . CHA/4/Sansom.

50 Sansom, *Sansom and Japan*, p. 135.

'the International Secretariat has developed its own principles of Far Eastern policy to pure American principles, and propagates them in the name of the IPR'.[51]

Strong anti-colonial inclinations, often coupled with a belief that British attitudes towards China were dangerously anachronistic and of a 'treaty-port' variety, were, indeed, to be found among members of the IPR's International and American Secretariats, which were housed side by side in a somewhat dilapidated building in New York. 'We cannot fight imperialism in the Pacific by tripping along behind and challenging every imperialist proposal', ran one fairly typical internal memorandum of 1943. 'We ought to be there first with our democratic proposals . . . as the carpet of Japanese occupation is rolled back.'[52] In addition, there were one or two people who had been involved in the IPR's affairs in the United States, such as the wealthy Frederick Vanderbilt Field, who may have been Communists at the time, but this was far from the case where the Institute's principal officers were concerned. Neither Holland (who became a naturalised US citizen in 1944) nor his Secretary-General, the patently ambitious Edward C. Carter, were anywhere near the left wing of the political spectrum, while among others who were prominent in the US branch were such non-conspiratorial individuals as Admiral Harry E. Yarnell, a former C.-in-C. of the US Asiatic Fleet, Henry Luce, publisher of *Time* and *Life* magazines, and Ralph Bunche, a subsequent winner of the Nobel Peace Prize and senior UN official. As for the role played by the American IPR during the war years, it did, it is true, become a substantially enlarged one, including, for example, the preparation of pamphlets on various Far Eastern subjects for officials distribution to members of the US armed forces. (Leading State Department officials, such as Sumner Welles and Joseph Grew, paid tribute to the value of this work.)[53] On the other hand, even the strongly anti-communist Stanley K. Hornbeck, Political Adviser in the State Department during the war, together with Joseph Ballantine, who had been Director of the Department's Office of Far Eastern Affairs, subsequently testified that in their experience the IPR had not sought to influence US policies over Asia.[54]

This brief indication of the controversy that came to surround the IPR in the United States is one necessary preliminary to an examination of the wartime association of Chatham House with that organization. Another is

---

51 Material on Holland article, 'War aims and peace aims in the Pacific', and Dr Boeke's letter of September 27, 1945, Pacific Council papers, CHA/6.
52 B. L(asker) to M. F(arley), March 14, 1943, IPR Papers, box 392 (Columbia University).
53 Welles to Carter, March 17, 1942, IPR Papers, box 376; Grew to Cabot, June 7, 1944, Grew papers, vol. 118 (Houghton Library, Harvard University).
54 Thomas, *Institute of Pacific Relations'*, pp. 83, 96.

the reminder of the extent to which the anti-colonial inclinations of the Institute's Secretariat, mentioned above, were only a local manifestation of a much wider movement of opinion, for herein lies the reason why, between 1941 and 1945, the involvement of Chatham House in the IPR's affairs suddenly took on an increased degree of significance and attracted the attention of the Foreign Office. In essence what occurred was that the international conferences convened by the IPR became a forum for the debating of Allied war aims in Asia, with representatives of several of the constituent national bodies showing themselves eager to attack the colonial record and policies of Britain in particular (France and the Netherlands were sometimes placed in the dock as well). And in doing so they had behind them a substantial body of public opinion in the United States, as well as in Asian countries.

For despite Churchill's refusal to accept that the Atlantic Charter, and in particular its third article (in which the Prime Minister and President declared that their countries respected 'the right of all peoples to choose the form of government under which they will live'), applied to Africa and Asia, and not simply to those European territories occupied by the Nazis, Roosevelt had massive support for his insistence that the document was of universal relevance. Books like Wendell Willkie's *One World* pushed home the same, anti-imperialist message, while in a poll conducted in June 1942, for example, 56 per cent of those Americans questioned agreed that the British could rightly be described as 'oppressors . . . because of the unfair advantage . . . they have taken of their colonial possessions'. In an open letter to the British people, Henry Luce's *Life* urged them to 'stop fighting for the British Empire and fight for victory', warning that 'if you cling to the Empire at the expense of a United Nations victory you will lose the war because you will lose us'. A sense of urgency over the need to prevent Britain from tarnishing the image of the West as a whole was also heightened in official circles in Washington by the evidence that was coming in of the extent to which the triumphant Japanese were fostering anti-white nationalist movements in the territories they had overrun, and by indications, such as the Great East Asia Conference held in Tokyo in 1943, that something in the nature of a pan-Asian movement might be developing.[55]

Here, then, is one reason why the two IPR wartime international conferences, the first at Mont Tremblant in Canada in December 1942 and the second at Hot Springs, Virginia, in January 1945, were of some significance at the time and remain of interest to the historian of Far Eastern

55 See, for example, W. H. Elsbree, *Japan's Role in Southeast Asian Nationalist Movements, 1940 to 1945* (Cambridge, Mass., 1953), and Ba Maw, *Breakthrough in Burma* (New Haven, Conn., 1968). Western fears of a wartime pan-Asian movement are explored in the present writer's *Allies of a Kind*, and his *Issue of War*, chs. 5 and 6.

aspects of the war years. In addition, these gatherings are all the more deserving of attention in that they were attended by officials from both sides of the Atlantic who, under their conference guise of private citizens, felt able to address one another with a forthrightness not usually indulged in within the confines of formal diplomacy. Moreover, both during the preparation of papers beforehand and at the conferences themselves, attention was paid to long-term issues and ideas were put forward in that respect to an extent that was unusual among those whose official positions subjected them in the ordinary course of events to the day-to-day demands of the war.

An idea of the subjects covered and ideas raised at Mont Tremblant and Hot Springs can be obtained from the two post-conference volumes that were published by the IPR. [56] What neither book conveys, however, is the atmosphere in which the debates were held. (Delegates were divided up into a number of 'round tables', each of which focused on a particular area or theme, making use of papers prepared beforehand by various national councils.) In this respect it is interesting to read the comments of some of those who were not usually in the front line of the exchanges – that is, who were attending on behalf of councils other than those of Britain and the United States. The Netherlands delegation for example, in its private report on the Mount Tremblant meeting, described the two main areas of controversy as having centred around American, Chinese and in some cases Dominion distrust of Britain's interpretation of the Atlantic Charter, and around British and Dutch criticisms of the United States for preaching to others while declining to assume its share of responsibility in the field of international affairs, leaving its degree of future involvement uncertain and ignoring its own domestic inter-racial failings. [57] 'British colonial rule was severely criticised', wrote an Australian observer (later to be his country's Governor General), while he himself questioned the assumptions that he felt had lain behind the views on this issue held by the majority of delegates, 'that all dependent peoples of Southeast Asia are capable of self-government at an early date, that Japan is the only possible Pacific aggressor now and for all time, . . . and that balanced economic development can be taken for granted'. [58]

Two years later, after the Hot Springs conference, another Australian

---

56 *War and Peace in the Pacific* (New York, London, 1943); *Security in the Pacific* (New York, London, 1945). Papers prepared in Chatham House in 1942 and 1944 will also be found in the files of the Anglo-American Pacific Study Group, the Pacific Collective Security Study Group (both CHA/9) and the Pacific Council (CHA/6).

57 Draft report, December 20, 1942, files of the Netherlands Embassy in Washington. PI 8/41.9, Netherlands Foreign Ministry Archives, The Hague.

58 Hasluck report, in Washington Legation to Canberra, December 22, 1942, Department of External Affairs files, A989/43/735/321, Australian National Archives, Canberra.

diplomat, the Counsellor of the Legation in Washington, Alan (later Sir Alan) Watt, was reporting that:

It was clear at once that the old feeling between the American and British delegations on the subject of Dependent Areas was still strong. The pattern was the same as usual. The Americans, who were often not very well informed of the facts, . . . were critical of British 'complacency' and failure to adopt a 'progressive policy' . . . , [while] showing much greater tolerance towards . . . French and Dutch dependent areas than towards the British [ones] . . . The United Kingdom representatives tended to be stiff and resentful of the American attitude . . . [59]

The Australian Minister himself, Sir George Eggleston, who was a keen student of Far Eastern affairs, likewise noted: 'There was much more controversy than Sir George Sansom admits',[60] while the Dutch representatives, who found their British colleagues 'solid and determined, . . . a team that knew what it was speaking about', observed that the 'unwieldy' American delegation was aided in its attacks on the European colonial powers by members of the IPR's International Secretariat who were helping to run the conference.[61]

One of the Americans who attended the Mont Tremblant meeting was an official who had long been the leading Far Eastern specialist within the State Department, the pedantic and often maladroit Stanley Hornbeck. And in his own post-conference report to the Secretary of State, Cordell Hull, he touched upon a background issue which points us towards the heart of the matter we are considering in relation to Chatham House. The proceedings at Mont Tremblant, wrote Hornbeck, had amounted in large part to 'Britain against the field'. (In saying this he was unwittingly echoing Roosevelt himself, who a fortnight earlier had remarked to his Vice President, Henry Wallace, that he supposed that at the conference 'the Britishers [had taken] their typical [imperialist] slant', and that their overall position among the Allies was that of the odd man out in a game of poker.)[62] Hornbeck added:

It needs to be kept in mind . . . that whereas, as a rule, the Groups from most countries, including the British countries, attend and function as 'delegations' (with a certain amount of guidance if not definite instructions from their Governments),

59 Watt to Hood, January 23, 1945, Australian Department of External Affairs, A1066/145/153/2, part I.
60 Washington notes, January 22, 1945, Eggleston Papers, Australian National Library, Canberra.
61 Report of March 31, 1945, Netherlands Foreign Ministry Archives, DZ/D12.
62 J. M. Blum (ed.), *The Price of Vision: The Diary of Henry A. Wallace, 1942–1946* (Boston, 1973), entry for December 16, 1942.

the members of the American Group attend and function as individuals (without express guidance and with no instructions from their Government). From this it results that the American Group listen to and participate in discussions with greater openness of mind, less inhibition, and more attention to the merits of questions under consideration.[63]

Now, Hornbeck's views, leaving aside their self-righteous naïvety as regards the American approach to Far Eastern issues, were not shared by all the non-British people present at the IPR conferences. For example, what struck Sir Frederick Eggleston at both Mont Tremblant and Hot Springs was the very extent to which delegates from London were more positive in their attitude towards the notion of an international organisation playing a significant part in the postwar affairs of dependent areas than was the British government at the time.[64] Moreover, although it was true that the American delegations did not receive prior instructions from Washington, the presence within them of, for example, Hornbeck himself at Mont Tremblant, and at Hot Springs a substantial number of men in official positions, resulted in an awareness of governmental attitudes and policies that could not somehow be suspended during the proceedings of the conferences. (The Hot Springs meeting was attended by, among other officials, Harry Dexter White of the Treasury; John Carter Vincent, Chief of the China Section of the State Department's Office of Far Eastern Affairs; Owen Lattimore, Director of Pacific Operations for the Office of War Information; Laughlin Currie, whose various functions had included that of special assistant to the President; and Major General Clayton Bissell, one of the Army's Assistant Chiefs of Staff.)[65] It is also worth noting that W. L. Holland himself, the IPR's Research Secretary, went to work for the Office of War Information and Office of Strategic Services in 1944, and between February and October 1945 was to be Acting Director of the OWI's China Division in Chungking.

Even so, there did exist within the International Secretariat and American headquarters of the IPR a considerable degree of suspicion regarding the composition of the British delegations to the two wartime conferences. Holland, for example, wrote to the Secretary-General, Carter, in August 1942: 'Perhaps someone ought to suggest tactfully to Chatham House that they include at least one person who would be a little more representative of the "lower classes" ', while Carter in turn was to observe in December 1944 that the British team setting out for Hot Springs contained 'several big-shot

63 Hornbeck to Hull, December 31, 1942, Hornbeck Papers, box 218 (Hoover Institution, Stanford University).
64 Washington diary, 423/10/1669, Eggleston Papers.
65 See the remarks of the chairman of the American delegation during a private, pre-conference meeting on October 28, 1944. IPR Papers, box 358.

business representatives', including McFadyean, Farmer of ICI and John Keswick of Jardine Matheson (who was attached to the British Embassy in Chungking at the time), besides government officials such as Sansom.[66] In 1942 the nature of the delegation from India, which in effect was chosen by the government in New Delhi, also led to its being dismissed in advance by Carter as likely to be 'more British than the British', despite his own endeavours to find within its ranks someone 'who would take an entirely different line from Lord Hailey and Sir Frederick Whyte'.[67] All in all, the evidence appeared to many of the Americans concerned to reinforce their existing belief that Churchill's government, having set its face against any radical developments in the field of imperial policies, was ensuring that, even at private gatherings such as those of the IPR, those who represented Britain would not stray from the line laid down in Whitehall.[68]

Leaving aside the question of whether or not colonial policies were, in fact, being re-thought within official circles in London – and a brief, simplified answer would be that, to a far larger extent than was realized at the time, such a process was taking place, but that those involved repeatedly ran into the reactionary stance adopted by the Prime Minister – what truth was there in the belief that the delegations from Chatham House which arrived at the two IPR conferences had in some sense been 'tampered with' by Whitehall?

The Foreign Office was aware, even before Mont Tremblant, of discussions that were taking place under the auspices of the American branch of the Institute, their informant being Sansom, who was welcomed at such gatherings as a scholar of world renown.[69] As for the preparations being

66 Holland to Carter, August 21, 1942, IPR Papers, box 62; Carter to Dennett, December 27, 1942, ibid., box 363. A. S. Olver comments: 'Curiously enough, Chatham House had a tradition of trying to achieve just what Holland had in mind for its groups for conferences. The classic example was sending Ernest Bevin to a Commonwealth Relations Conference before the war, which was sometimes claimed to be the origin of his interest in foreign affairs.' (Letter to the author, October 16, 1977.)

67 Carter to Jessup, November 17, 1942, ibid., box 379. The composition of delegations from India and the nature of the Indian Institute of International Affairs also troubled some members of Chatham House. See various references in the Council's minutes for 1944, CHA/1, vol. 25.

68 This belief also accorded with the widespread American assumption that, whilst their country was fighting only for the speediest possible victory over Germany and Japan, in an essentially 'a-political' manner, Britain on the other hand, steeped as it was in the evils of 'power-politics', was fighting a 'political' war, and was subordinating strategic considerations to selfish, political ones. The validity or otherwise of this belief is examined in detail in the writer's *Allies of a Kind*.

69 For example, Sansom to Clark, November 2, 1942, FO 371, F7827/3806/61 (31803).

made for the conference of December 1942, papers drafted by groups based
on Chatham House were shown to Ashley Clarke and other members of the
Foreign Office's Far Eastern Department by some of those involved, such
as Hudson and Victor Farmer, and were commented on in detail before
being returned.[70] The India Office, too, saw, for example, a Chatham
House briefing paper on 'A Post-war System for the Indian Ocean' that
had been drawn up by H. V. Hodson, finding its proposals (they included
encouraging, rather than resisting, China in its interest in Malaya and
Burma, thus obtaining its endorsement of an 'Indian Ocean system')
highly controversial, to say the least.[71]

   Like those responsible for directing the affairs of Chatham House itself,[72]
Foreign Office officials were convinced of the need for Britain to be
represented at Mont Tremblant lest the case for its colonial policies,
especially, went by default and lest the conferences became 'dominated by
Chinese and Sino-American influences to our great detriment', as Sir
Maurice Peterson put it. (He was the Assistant Under-Secretary of State
responsible for the Far Eastern Department.) The Colonial Office, too,
were in favour of sending a strong British team 'so that it may be made
plain in America and the rest of the world that we have faith in our future in
the Far East'.[73]

   There was thus already considerable interest in the forthcoming IPR
conference within government departments when a development took place
which substantially increased the extent to which those departments
became involved in the matter, and which, by the same token, diminished
the degree of independence remaining to Chatham House in terms of its
IPR activities. What occurred was that at the beginning of July 1942 Ivison
Macadam, the Secretary of Chatham House, dropped what Ashley Clarke
described as 'a bombshell' when, in conversation with the latter at the
Foreign Office, he revealed that the Institute did not have the funds to pay
for sending a delegation to Mont Tremblant. The surprise was all the
greater in that Richard Law, the Parliamentary Under-Secretary of State
(subsequently Minister of State) at the Foreign Office, had earlier received
from the already-nominated leader of the delegation, Lord Hailey, the
impression that Chatham House could find the money to cover six representatives. Law himself decided that, in the new circumstances, government finance would have to be supplied; he added the rider, however, that
since that was to be the case, the selection of members of the delegation

70 For example, ibid., F5874/3806/61 (31801); F6224, 6469 and 7190/3806/61 (31802).
71 Ibid., F8028/3806/61 (31803).
72 Council and IPR Committee material (especially IPR Committee report of May 11),
summer 1942. Council minutes, CHA/1, vol. 21 and CHA/6 respectively.
73 FO 371, F3814 and 4108/3806/61 (31801).

should not be left to the Institute and should include, for example, an invitation to someone from the Labour Party. 'The Foreign Office and the Treasury', the Council of Chatham House were told, 'would want to examine very carefully the precise qualifications of the Group whose expenses they would have to meet.' (In the event, the India Office and Colonial Office were also consulted.[74])

These conditions were accepted by the Institute's officials, it seems without demur or hesitation. Indeed, in its first response to the idea of such a conference, the Chatham House IPR Committee had itself clearly pointed the way towards close contact with the official world, suggesting that 'the full support of the Foreign Office, the Dominions Office, the Colonial Office and the India Office' would be essential in ensuring 'that the Group [from the Institute] was adequately informed on the subjects to be discussed'.[75] Macadam, who had been seconded to the Ministry of Information between 1939 and 1941, liked to keep close to the centres of power and influence, while an important linking role was played by Frank Ashton-Gwatkin, who sat on Chatham House's Council while still serving as an Assistant Under-Secretary at the Foreign Office. Hailey, too, a former Governor of the United Provinces in India, a member of the League of Nations Mandates Commission, author of *An African Survey* and a member of the Council of Chatham House, liked the idea of including someone from the Labour Party and welcomed Attlee's suggestion that it should be Arthur Creech-Jones, MP, who was to become Colonial Secretary after the war. (Significantly, Hailey remarked to Ashley Clarke that 'he thought he could keep him within bounds'.) Eventually a list was agreed which included, in addition to Hailey and Creech-Jones, Sir Frederick Whyte, Sir John Pratt and Ivison Macadam, together with various individuals such as Sansom who were already on the other side of the Atlantic, where they were serving in official capacities. At the same time the question arose of whether, and if so to what extent, the delegates should be given something in the way of guidance from Whitehall. For those involved on the official side of the fence, there was one major difficulty in this connection that can be given only a passing mention here: that is the lack of

---

74 Ibid., F5151, 5158 and 1559/3806/61 (31801); Council minutes, July 8, 1942, CHA/1, vol. 21. The financial arrangements ultimately arrived at involved a temporary alteration in the funding of the FRPS. Council minutes, July 29, 1942, CHA/1, vol. 22; Ashton-Gwatkin/Macadam telephone record, June 1, 1942, Mont Tremblant file, Pacific Council papers, CHA/6. On Law's reference to the need to involve a member of the Labour Party, A. S. Olver comments: 'This suggests a lack of knowledge of the Institute's policy of achieving a political balance within Chatham House itself and on delegations. In my time, Labour Members of Parliament seemed more active within the Institute than the Tories.' (Letter to the author, October 16, 1977.)
75 IPR Committee report, May 11, 1942, Council minutes, CHA/1, vol. 21.

anything approaching a clear Cabinet policy in respect of, say, the post-war treatment of Burma and other territories in Southeast Asia.[76] Nevertheless, Ashley Clarke made it plain through Hudson that 'guidance as to [Britain's] "aims" must come from HMG'.

This decision was qualified to some extent as the result of a letter written by Sansom from Washington, in which he advised that 'if the unofficial nature of the delegation were to be sustained' its members should not speak with a single voice at Mont Tremblant. It was therefore accepted within the Foreign Office that guidance should be 'given in an informal manner to Lord Hailey only . . . , leaving him to keep the delegation more or less within bounds'. Even so, Pratt, as well as Hailey, was shown relevant official documents, while a summary of Britain's post-war aims, prepared for the delegation's benefit by Hudson, was written only after its author had discussed the subject with Ashley Clarke. Finally, Clarke and his colleague Nevile Butler, Head of the North American Department, came to Chatham House on 17 November to meet and answer questions from the entire Mont Tremblant party.[77]

Thus, although it remained true that the British representatives at the December 1942 conference were not obliged to follow instructions laid down by Whitehall, the unofficial and independent nature of their utterances, like their Chatham House label, was not entirely what it seemed. Moreover, the violent and often ill-informed attacks on Britain's record at Mont Tremblant had the effect of reducing any divergencies that might otherwise have emerged, and of drawing together the members of the team (Creech-Jones included, for all his criticisms of government policies back at Westminster)[78] in a defence of their country's colonial achievements and intentions.

A similar process was to occur at Hot Springs in January 1945. Before the conference Macadam, on behalf of Chatham House, again sought government money to meet the cost of sending a delegation, as well as asking the Foreign Office to help obtain permission for a number of civilian officials and senior members of the armed services to attend. As in 1942, in other words, the quasi-official aspect of the group attending the IPR conference in the Institute's name was by no means forced by Whitehall upon a reluctant Chatham House.[79] The upshot was that of the 20 people who represented Britain at Hot Springs under the leadership of Sir Andrew McFadyean, over half were officials or serving officers. (They included

76 See, for example, the minute by Sir John Brenan in FO 371, F4369/3806/61 (31801).
77 Ibid., F5874/3806/61 (31801); F6584 and 7398/3806/61 (31802).
78 On Creech-Jones's angry defence of Britain's colonial record, see MacDougall to Sabine. December 22 and 30, 1942, FO 371, F457/186/61 (35905).
79 Material in FO 371, file 41769.

Sansom, Harold Butler, Hudson, Keswick, and from New Delhi Sir Frederick Puckle.) Indeed, to such an extent had the business of selection become a matter for arrangement between Macadam and McFadyean on the one hand and the Foreign, India and Colonial Offices on the other, that those within Chatham House who were charged with the conduct of the Institute's relations with the IPR were not even consulted.[80]

To the British delegations thus assembled, the proceedings at the two IPR conferences were scarcely a pleasant experience. Those who arrived at Mont Tremblant were met by what Macadam described as 'sustained criticisms of British policy . . . at practically all the Round Tables', with the Americans being joined in their onslaught not only by the Chinese but also, Macadam recorded, by the Australians and New Zealanders. In response, Hailey, whose own extensive studies in the field of colonial affairs fitted him for the task, presented a powerful defence of Britain's imperial record; in addition, as 'an answer to those who demanded some recognition of the principle of accountability in colonial administration', and also, as he put it later, 'because we felt that it had merits of its own', he suggested that after the war a Pacific Zone Council might be established in order to link the colonial administrations of individual territories to one another and to an international organisation. Meanwhile at the round table on China, Pratt, in the face of what he subsequently described as 'silly charges pressed not by the Chinese but by their rather ill-advised American friends, . . . a rather unpleasant clique of young, highbrow, left-wing intellectuals . . .', insisted that Britain's dealings with that country in modern times, culminating in its agreement to surrender its extraterritorial privileges there, were nothing to be ashamed of.[81]

So great, indeed, was the resentment among the British delegation against the tone and style of the proceedings at Mont Tremblant, and against the role played by the IPR Secretariat there, that some time later, in 1944, Hailey raised the question of whether Chatham House should withdraw from the IPR altogether. At the special meeting of the Council called to discuss the issue, however, A. V. Alexander, then First Lord of the Admiralty and a former chairman of the Institute's IPR committee,

80 Council minutes, December 13, 1944 and January 10, 1945, CHA/1, vol. 25.
81 Council minutes, February 10, and Macadam report, February 24, 1943, CHA/1, vol. 22; Whyte record of Anglo-Canadian meeting, Feb. 1943, CHA/4/Whyte; Pratt talk, March 3, 1943, Far Eastern Group, CHA/8; Hailey to Hubbard, March 16, 1944, IPR Committee papers, CHA/6. Unfortunately, files originally located in the Chatham House archives containing correspondence of Hailey's before 1949 were lost before the reorganization of the archive material.

urged that 'we must not think of withdrawing [as] . . . it would be greatly misunderstood in New Zealand and also in American circles'. Hailey himself then decided that, much as he disliked the way in which, 'either through conviction or expediency, [the IPR] had developed into an organization which was perpetually critical of Great Britain and her policy', Alexander's advice was probably correct in the long-term view. It was agreed, therefore, that Chatham House would continue to act as the British national council for the IPR, while at the same time 'vigorous and robust' efforts would be made 'to alter the present trend of much IPR activity so that it is objective, scholarly and informed in its approach to the study of Far Eastern affairs'.[82]

Even before this decision was taken – in fact, during the immediate aftermath of Mont Tremblant – various moves had been proposed with a view to correcting the IPR's wayward tendencies. It had been agreed that Chatham House's own work on Far Eastern questions should be increased, with E. M. Gull, for example, for many years the Secretary of the China Association, undertaking to explore China's likely postwar economic problems, and with Hubbard returning from Whitehall to the Institute in August 1943 in order to resume his work as Far Eastern Research Secretary. At the same time, and pending a permanent British appointment to the IPR's International Secretariat, a special eye was to be kept on the affairs of that body by Sansom. It was also suggested that it would be excellent if the editorship of *Pacific Affairs* could be obtained for Hugh Byas, a British journalist and the author of books on Japan such as *Government By Assassination*. Byas, who had been a member of the Mont Tremblant delegation, was well known in the United States for his articles in the *New York Times*, and was well thought of by Joseph Grew of the State Department among others. In the event, however, he was unable to become a candidate for the post.[83]

The Foreign Office, already informed by Sansom of what had transpired at Mont Tremblant,[84] was consulted about the above proposals, and gave its agreement to the moves involving Hubbard and Sansom. 'As Mr.

---

82 Council minutes, March 8 and 15, 1944, CHA/1, vol. 24.

83 Council minutes, February 10, 1943, CHA/1, vol. 23; Macadam to Sansom, March 16 and May 25, 1943, CHA/4/Sansom; Grew to Byas, October 16, 1943, Grew Papers, vol. 118. Byas became a member of Chatham House in 1943.

84 FO 371, F674/186/61 (35905). Sanson described the conference proceedings as having been 'a vicious circle [in which] the British said: "We can go ahead with a sudden and drastic change in the political status of British or other dependencies in the Pacific area . . . if we are confident that the United States will bind itself to an international policy." The Americans said: "The American people will not agree to an internationalist policy unless the British Government promises to go ahead" '. As for the troublemakers, it was, declared Sansom, 'the professors of International Relations and suchlike amorphous studies who displayed an irritating combination of ignorance and prejudice'.

Ashton-Gwatkin pointed out to me', minuted Ashley Clarke, 'there has always been fairly close liaison between Chatham House and the Foreign Office in Far Eastern affairs, and if the studies of Chatham House are really to serve a useful purpose, it is in our interest that they should be on the right lines.'[85] Members of the Foreign Office were all the more anxious to keep a hand on the wheel in that one or two individual members of the Mont Tremblant delegation, despite their informal briefing, had entertained ideas that could have proved embarrassing had they been publicized. In the case of Sansom there was no great problem, it is true, in that, as a serving official, he could be instructed as to what he could and could not reveal. And although it was decided that he should not publish his opinion that, despite its 'discreditable record . . . in many important respects', Japan would respond better after the war if it were 'invited to join the club and observe the rules instead of being blackballed', there was sympathy in London for the belief itself; the fear was simply that if it became known it would serve only to reinforce the widespread American conviction that Britain was 'soft' towards Japan.[86] More alarming was the way in which Pratt was fiercely arguing that in its own interest Britain should return Hongkong to China with all speed – thus leading Sir Maurice Peterson and the Permanent Under-Secretary, Sir Alexander Cadogan, to conclude that it had been a mistake to include him in the delegation in the first place.[87]

In a more positive vein, the Far Eastern Department of the Foreign Office reacted favourably to another consequence of the brawling at Mont Tremblant: the establishment of parallel study groups in Chatham House (under the chairmanship of Sir Frederick Whyte and including Pratt and Creech-Jones) and in Washington (where the convener was Professor William C. Johnstone of George Washington University) which were to exchange papers on various aspects of Far Eastern affairs.[88] Those involved in the project at the London end did not find the ensuing dialogue a particularly satisfactory one, largely because the Americans still seemed reluctant to explore in a precise way the nature of the disagreements between the two countries over, say, colonial policy. ('The issue as presented by them', commented Whyte privately, 'lies mainly in American feeling and not in the merits of the questions themselves.') Conversely,

---

85 FO 371, F3430 and 5059/186/61 (35907).

86 Ibid., F186/186/61 (35905).

87 Ibid., F232 and 233/186/61 (35905). Pratt developed his Hongkong argument at length to the Chatham House Far Eastern Group on March 3, 1943. CHA/8.

88 The papers from Chatham House were despatched to Washington via the Foreign Office and Sansom. FO 371, F4767 and 5163/1953/61 (35927). On the other hand the Foreign Office declined to allow Hudson to participate in the work of the London group.

although the Chatham House group was able to put forward detailed studies of a particular territory, such as Malaya, it was burdened, as was the Foreign Office itself, by the need to explain away the public remarks on imperial affairs made by Churchill. ('Neither the British Government nor we as a group', wrote Whyte to Johnstone, 'use the word "restoration" in any reactionary sense. It is limited to the resumption of British responsibility for territories temporarily wrested from us by the Japanese, which, when restored to their place in the British Empire, will continue at an accelerated pace towards the goal of real autonomy.' As an interpretation it was, indeed, accurate so far as not only Whyte and his colleagues but also many members of the British government and its departments were concerned. It was far removed, however, from the approach of the Prime Minister, who would certainly not have allowed that Chatham House members were in any position to speak for Britain on such matters.[89])

Nevertheless, the existence of the Anglo-American Pacific Study Groups, as they were called, seems to have helped create a somewhat warmer atmosphere when the time came for the national delegations of the IPR to assemble at Hot Springs in January 1945. McFadyean, making the opening speech for Britain, tried to improve matters further still by emphasising that the vast majority of his fellow countrymen stood by the Atlantic Charter as being universally applicable, and he even ventured to assure his listeners that some of the suggestions that had been put forward during the Mont Tremblant conference had 'certainly influenced British policy and [had] led to certain notable reforms and a certain reorientation of policy'. (Again, one would have liked to hear Churchill's reaction to such statements.) In turn, McFadyean was able to write back to Macadam in London to say that 'the general atmosphere here is very much better than it must have been at Mont Tremblant. . . . There is much less disposition to twist British tails just for the fun of seeing how the animal reacts.'

Yet a week later McFadyean was describing the tone of proceedings at Hot Springs as 'unpleasant', blaming this once more on the IPR's Secretariat and Secretary-General. 'It has been catch-as-catch-can, with no holds barred,' he declared in his closing speech, 'and occasionally, when the referee was not looking, I think there was some biting.' He added a defiant conclusion: 'The great ideals which animate the American people are shared by the British people . . . , but we shall not permit ourselves to be hustled out of evolution into revolution.' As for the reaction within the Foreign Office to these Hot Springs exchanges and their public reverber-

89 For a list of topics and papers, together with related correspondence, see the files of the Anglo-American Pacific Study Group, CHA/9.

ations,[90] the new Head of the Far Eastern Department, J. C. Sterndale Bennett, had by now come to 'doubt the wisdom of these conferences and of the participation in them of British officials'.[91]

It is not difficult in retrospect to see what had led to a disillusioned verdict being pronounced by officials in London on the international gatherings organized during the war by the IPR. Nor does a detailed examination of the development of Britain's colonial policies between 1942 and 1945 sustain McFadyean's assertion at Hot Springs that the debates at Mont Tremblant had led directly to changes in the relevant plans that were being prepared in Whitehall.[92] At the same time, as we have seen, the considerable degree to which both individual officials and government departments in London became involved in the Chatham House side of the IPR's affairs created a situation in which, while on the one hand even delegation leaders like Hailey and McFadyean could not say with any authority or certainty what Churchill and his Cabinet colleagues would decide, on the other, foreign assumptions about the limited extent of the Royal Institute's independence for once had some validity. Appearing to speak for Britain – and language of the kind used by McFadyean encouraged such an interpretation – and yet unable to speak for the British government (whose members in any case included Churchill as well as Bevin, and Beaverbrook as well as Cripps), the Chatham House delegations ended up in a thoroughly ambiguous position.

Even so, the IPR conferences did help to bring home to officials and influential members of the public on both sides of the Atlantic the extent of the mistrust and, in some degree, misunderstandings that surrounded such Far Eastern issues as the future of Southeast Asian colonial territories and the post-war international role of China. And although those two meetings did not lead directly to changes in London's attitude towards imperial affairs east of Suez, they did focus a general state of opinion on the subject

90 In particular, trouble had arisen over one of the papers provided for the conference by Chatham House (it had been drafted by a group under Sir Paul Butler), 'Japan in Defeat'. In this document, the suggestion was made that it would be found after the war that 'no alternative to a monarchical system under the present Emperor or some other member of his family will be likely to provide the focus of stability which will be essential if [Japan] is not to dissolve into chaos in the impending crises'. Similar views were held within the State Department by Grew among others; but when the columnist Drew Pearson got hold of and published the allegation that 'Britain' wanted to retain the Emperor, it produced an outcry among Americans whose suspicions of their Ally in a Far Eastern context were already high.
91 McFadyean speeches enclosed in Council minutes, CHA/1, vol. 25; Pacific Council papers and IPR Committee papers CHA/6; FO 371, F514, 676, 714 and 831/327/23 (46444).
92 On this aspect of Britain's wartime policies, see W. Roger Louis' *Imperialism at Bay* (Oxford, 1978) and the writer's *Allies of a Kind*.

that existed in the United States and elsewhere, that opinion being one factor (others included the pressure for change that was coming from various members of the British government, from officials like the Governor of Burma, Sir Reginald Dorman-Smith, from Members of Parliament and from writers such as Margery Perham) which helped to ensure that the reactionary attitude of Churchill was an increasingly isolated one. Conversely, the attempts made by Hailey, Whyte and others to make foreign members of the IPR aware of the difficulties inherent in, say, the plural societies to be found in a single territory like Malaya may have played some part in bringing about the less simplistic approach to colonial problems that obtained in leading circles in the United States by 1945, as compared to 1942.[93]

As for the role played by Chatham House within the wartime scene in London, it clearly made a useful contribution to the amount of information available to Foreign Office and other officials through the FRPS/FORD, where G. F. Hudson in particular took part to a significant extent in the discussions on Far Eastern affairs that were going on in Whitehall. In both respects, however, the qualification has to be added that, not only did the views of permanent officials remain of far greater weight overall, but even *their* policy submissions were often of little consequence, given the manner in which the Prime Minister conducted the nation's wartime business and the very limited extent to which post-war foreign policy questions received attention, let alone answers, from the hard-pressed men who made up the Cabinet. As one Foreign Office official commented in connection with a FORD paper on the future of Korea and the discussion of that subject on a transatlantic basis: 'That is another example of exchanging ideas with the Americans on a low level when we have not the remotest idea of the policy upon which Ministers will decide.'[94]

It would be wrong, therefore, to suggest that newly available material in the Chatham House archives throws an important light on the formulation of British policies – certainly where the Far East was concerned – during the Second World War. At a different level, however, involving the climate of opinion and specific attitudes to be found in those areas in both Britain and the United States where officialdom overlapped with prominent outsiders who had an interest in international affairs, that material is of considerable value.

93 See, for example, essay number 5 in this volume.
94 FO 371, F6012/102/23 (41801).

Part III

Individuals, Societies and the Challenges of International Change

It is now a historical truism to observe that in the 1930s and during the Second World War the structure of the international system as a whole, together with the structures of individual societies, economies and polities, was undergoing considerable and rapid change. Many contemporaries felt and/or perceived that the ground was shifting beneath their feet, however much their particular analyses and expectations may sometimes appear wayward in retrospect. Others clung all the more fiercely to existing certainties, or to the local and the short term, or to prescriptions for maintaining the status quo.[1]

The group of essays that follows does not exclude those official, foreign-policy-making bodies that provided the main focus for the immediately preceding pieces. It goes wider, however, in examining the ways in which a variety of individuals, groups and societies responded to international challenges and uncertainties during these years. Such challenges could centre upon the functioning and future of a particular institution, such as the League of Nations, or upon an immediate foreign policy decision, such as whether or not to sell arms in the Far East, or upon a practical problem within the domestic sphere, such as whether or not to adopt the segregationist policies of the US Army when making arrangements to receive American troops in war-time Britain. At the same time, however, these challenges also involved issues (sometimes perceived by contemporaries, sometimes not) of a deeper and wider kind: whether the objective and the subjective conditions necessary for the successful operation of a world-wide system of collective security could ever be achieved, and whether the dictates

---

1 See, for example, Thorne, *The Issue of War, States, Societies and the Far Eastern Conflict of 1941–1945*, and essay number 3 above.

of immediate national self-interest could or should be transcended in an increasingly interdependent system of states and peoples; whether the dictates of conscience and morality had a place in the conduct of international politics, and whether the individual ultimately owed a greater duty to such promptings than to the proclaimed policies of his or her government; whether a new set of values, norms and policies should or could be instituted in regard to race relations and to the imperial subjugation of one people by another; whether the assumptions, goals and procedures that were to direct the re-ordering of the entire post-war world could or should be derived from those adhered to in a single domestic society and its body politic.[2]

This last issue emerges in the context of the final essay of the collection, an exercise which contains a dimension lacking in those that precede it. In that the conference for which it was written sought to view developments during the Second World War in terms of 'the shaping of modern America', an invitation existed to draw out connections between this particular section of the past, the years 1941 to 1945, and the present day. It could be argued, of course, that such connections will never be entirely absent from the mind of the contemporary historian in particular, and that there are advantages in making them more explicit than is usually the case. And indeed, Carr among others has argued that it is 'the function of the historian . . . to master and understand [the past] as the key to the understanding of the present.[3] Yet the dangers for the historian of what Americans themselves term 'presentism' need to be acknowledged; and so, too, does the fallibility of historians when they turn to analyse the characteristics of their own age.

'What is it all about?' Never was it more incumbent upon each of us to pursue, as it pertains to current international affairs in particular, the question which Carl Becker echoed from his young students. Never have the complexities and the tumbling changes of our world so reinforced the likelihood that any 'answers' we formulate, together with our interpretations of contemporary history, will prove far from definitive. I would add, moreover, that as regards, in particular, the concluding reflection of

2 Clearly there are lines of inquiry which could be taken up here relating to the concept of hegemony. For stimulating essays on such perspectives in regard to international relations, see Robert W. Cox, 'Social forces, states, and world orders: Beyond international relations theory', *Millenium: Journal of International Studies* Summer, 1981, and 'Gramsci, hegemony and international relations: an essay in method', *Millennium: Journal of International Relations*, Summer, 1983. Also of relevance, in terms of the concept of 'public opinion' vis-à-vis foreign affairs and foreign policy is T. J. Jackson Lears, 'The Concept of Cultural Hegemony: Problems and Possibilities,' *American Historical Review*, vol. 90 No. 3 (June 1985).
3 E. H. Carr, *What is History?* (Harmondsworth, 1964), p. 26.

the final essay of this collection, I should indeed be glad to think that, 50 or so years on, others would be able to judge as unjustified those forebodings that have come to accompany my reading of certain aspects of our recent and so turbulent past.

9

Viscount Cecil, the Government and The Far Eastern Crisis of 1931

It is often suggested that the Far Eastern crisis of 1931–3 marked the beginning of the Second World War, that 'the road . . . is now clearly visible . . . from the railway tracks near Mukden to the operations of two bombers over Hiroshima and Nagasaki'.[1] In many eyes, too, this episode was also crucial for the League of Nations and the cause of collective security, an opportunity to vindicate the peace-keeping machinery of 1919 which, had it been taken, might have proved decisive in preventing the slide into international anarchy which followed.[2] 'This has been the vital test for the League,' Philip Noel-Baker wrote to Gilbert Murray at the time, 'and the greatest opportunity it has ever had, especially in view of USA cooperation'.[3] When Japan had triumphed nearly two years later, he saw the whole structure of organized international co-operation as being 'in grave danger', and the League as 'never having sunk to so low an ebb in influence and prestige'.[4]

The belief that the Manchurian episode not only preceded but led to the subsequent aggression of the 1930s may be thought to rest on questionable

Reproduced from the *Historical Journal*, 14 (1971), pp. 805–26. The writer is grateful to the Rt Hon. Philip Noel-Baker for permission to quote from his letters of the time, to Professor Ann Lambton for similar permission relating to material in the Cecil Papers, and to his colleague of the time Peter Calvocoressi, who made helpful comments on the first draft of the article.

1 Henry L. Stimson and McGeorge Bundy, *On Active Service in Peace and War* (Harper, NY, 1948), p. 221. For a full examination of this assertion and of Western policies during the crisis itself, see C. Thorne, *The Limits of Foreign Policy* (London, 1972).

2 See, for instance, F. P. Walters, *A History of the League of Nations* (Oxford, 1960), pp. 467 and 499; Lord Cecil, *A Great Experiment* (London, 1941), pp. 235–6.

3 Gilbert Murray Papers (Bodleian Library); letter of 11 October 1931.

4 Cecil of Chelwood Papers (British Museum), Add. 51108; Noel-Baker memorandum of 5 July 1933. Cf. G. P. Gooch, 'Some consequences of the Sino-Japanese dispute', in *The Problems of Peace* (London, 1933), and A. J. Toynbee, *Survey of International Affairs, 1933* (Oxford, 1934), pp. 517–8.

assumptions. The purpose of this article, however, is to focus on the early months of the 1931–3 crisis, and in particular on the views at the time of Viscount (formerly Lord Robert) Cecil. It will first be necessary to outline what can be termed the 'standard' view of Cecil's relations with the Government in this context; to suggest why a fresh look at the subject seems worthwhile; and to explain the emphasis on the brief period between the Mukden incident of 18 September 1931 and the end of the year. On the other hand, it scarcely seems necessary to explain why Cecil's views are of interest in the first place. As Japan's Kwantung Army pushed out from its railway zone and leased territory in September, eventually to take the whole of Manchuria,[5] the man who was Britain's principal delegate to the Assembly and on the Council at Geneva was also one of the outstanding architects and champions of the organization which was now being put to its severest test to date.

Although such a notion is bound to be somewhat crude, it appears reasonable to suggest that there exists a standard image of the views on Far Eastern events of Cecil on the one hand, and of predominant opinion in the Government and Foreign Office on the other. In these terms, the relationship between Cecil in Geneva and those to whom he was responsible in London could be summarized, from Cecil's side, as one of frustration and growing anger throughout the crisis. He was completely at odds with men who were unable to appreciate the wider significance of events in terms of the Covenant and world peace, and who were unwilling to give a clear lead at Geneva in the direction of firm action which would force the Japanese to back down.[6]

This kind of view was given public expression as early as 19 December 1931, in a *Spectator* article by William Martin, an outspoken champion of the League through the columns of the *Journal de Genève*. Suggesting that at the time of the London Naval Conference Britain and the United States

5 For accounts of the Japanese side of these events, see, for instance, J. B. Crowley, *Japan's Quest For Autonomy* (Princeton, NJ, 1966); Takehiko Yoshihashi, *Conspiracy at Mukden* (New Haven, Conn., 1963); and S. N. Ogata, *Defiance in Manchuria* (Berkeley, Ca, 1964). *The Report of the League of Nations Commission of Enquiry* (Washington, DC, 1932) remains of great value, as does the typescript 'Documents and Proceedings of the International Military Tribunal of the Far East', of which there is a set in the Imperial War Museum.

6 In *The Baldwin Age*, ed. John Raymond (London, 1960), p. 98, Mr Noel-Baker writes simply that 'Henderson often said that, if he had still been in office, he could have used the League to turn [the Japanese] out'. This is argument-by-implication, of a kind that avoids having to raise the formidable questions involved. The same writer argues in similar fashion in an obituary notice on Sir Alexander Cadogan (*The Times*, 15 July 1968): 'Cadogan *knew* that, with a Simon lead, and with Stimson's help from Washington, the League could stop the Japanese in Manchuria.'

had promised Japan a free hand in Manchuria in exchange for a reduction of the Japanese fleet, Martin added that

Lord Cecil, M. Briand and Mr Stimson have all three had to fight their officials, and it cannot be said that they have emerged victorious. That is one of the gravest factors of the whole affair, in view of the future. It proves that secret diplomacy is not dead, that its poison has not ceased to work.

Martin's article called forth a strong denial by the Foreign Office of any bargain with Japan. But before long, Cecil himself (from early February 1932 no longer an official representative of his country) was revealing his own dissatisfaction with government policy. By February Japanese aggression, including the indiscriminate bombing of civilian areas, had spread to Shanghai. On the 12th, the Executive Committee of the League of Nations Union, of which Cecil was joint President,[7] passed a resolution calling on the League to associate itself with Stimson's celebrated 'non-recognition' note of 7 January[8] and for the application of Article 16 against Japan. Cecil and others issued an accompanying statement which enlarged on the urgent need for 'collective pressure',[9] and a letter from Cecil and others to the same effect appeared in *The Times* on 18 February. Nine days later Cecil declared to an emergency meeting of the LNU Council that 'from February 3rd Japan . . . was, in the ordinary sense of the word, the aggressor',[10] while he assured a meeting of the LNU in the Albert Hall on 7 March that the Assembly of the League 'had ample power if it chose to exercise it'.[11] And although agitation died away for a time after the fighting at Shanghai had ceased, Cecil was still expressing his dissatisfaction in May 1933. (By then the Japanese had seized the whole of Manchuria and Jehol, as well as spilling south of the Great Wall.) In the face of events since September 1931, he told the House of Lords, 'the attitude of the Government appears to me to have been lacking in firmness and consistency'.[12]

7 The other President was Viscount Grey of Fallodon; Baldwin, Clynes and Lloyd George were Honorary Presidents, and Gilbert Murray was Chairman of an Executive Committee which included Norman Angel, Philip Noel-Baker, David Davies, the Earl of Lytton and Professor A. E. Zimmern. Sir Austen Chamberlain joined the Committee in February 1932, thereby increasing the amount of dissension within it.

8 This note declared that the United States would not recognize the legality of any situation or treaty between Japan and China which might impair United States treaty rights or which had been brought about by means contrary to the Pact of Paris. See R. Hecht, 'Great Britain and the Stimson Note of January 7, 1932' in *Pacific Historical Review*, May 1969.

9 *Manchester Guardian*, 13 February 1932.

10 *The Times*, 29 February 1932.   11 *Manchester Guardian*, 8 March 1932.

12 Hansard, *Parliamentary Debates*, House of Lords, LXXXVII, 875 (11 May 1933). In the *League Year Book, 1933* (London, 1933), Cecil described the behaviour of certain great powers over the Far East as 'poltroonery or worse'.

In other words there was enough contemporary evidence to make it easy to assume that Cecil's sharp disagreement with and alternative to official policy in 1932 and 1933 existed from the outset, but had of necessity been muted while he represented the country at Geneva. Moreover, anyone drawing this conclusion would find it reinforced on reading Cecil's own later account in *A Great Experiment*. For example, Cecil refers to a report on possible further steps against Japan, including diplomatic and economic sanctions, which he drew up after a meeting with Salvador de Madariaga, M. Colban and M. Massigli[13] on 18 October 1931. Lord Reading (then Foreign Secretary) was 'much disturbed', writes Cecil, 'and begged me to take no further action of that kind . . . To him and his colleagues it seemed a matter of relatively small moment what happened in Manchuria.'[14] Similarly with Sir John Simon (who replaced Reading), 'it quickly became apparent that he was not prepared to take any step to compel Japan to leave China', while Cecil found J. H. Thomas, when he deputized for Simon in the New Year, 'much more sympathetic than Sir John'.[15] So far as Cecil could ascertain, the Foreign Office, too, was quite inadequate in the attempts it made to find out if the United States would join in taking a stronger line against Japan,[16] and this in a situation where 'no honest man could doubt that Japan had "resorted to war" in breach of her undertakings under the Covenant, or that members of the League were bound to take action under Article 16 to assist China'.[17] (This last quotation needs to be read carefully in the context of its paragraph; Cecil is clearly referring to the Manchurian situation in the autumn, before the Lytton Commission was constituted.) In sum, Britain refused to risk anything in the cause of peace. 'Not only was force not used to restrain the aggressor, but the reason given for not using it reduced League action to fatuity or worse.'[18]

It is likely that the general picture which emerges from evidence such as this is still the one most commonly held, although a reappraisal of British opinions, including Cecil's, on the Far Eastern crisis was offered by Reginald Bassett in 1952.[19] Working towards his final judgement that no greater measure of success could have been achieved against Japan,[20]

13 Respectively Spanish and Norwegian representatives on the League Council, and a member of the French delegation to the League. The substance of this report will be examined below.

14 Cecil, *A Great Experiment*, pp. 225–6. Cf. below, p. 208, n. 66.

15 Ibid., pp. 227 and 232.

16 Ibid., p. 228.

17 Ibid., p. 231.

18 Ibid., p. 332. The 'reason given', Cecil suggests, was that British interests were not at stake.

19 *Democracy and Foreign Policy* (London, 1952). This books deals more satisfactorily with the press and Parliament than with public opinion as a whole.

20 Ibid., p. 624.

Bassett emphasized the limited nature of the opposition to the Government's policy in the early months of the crisis,[21] the small number of those who advocated sanctions,[22] and the limited nature of those measures which Cecil himself came to advocate in public.[23] Since 1952, of course, a great deal of new material has become available to the historian, and to suggest some further revision of the standard view does not entail an acceptance of the whole of Bassett's thesis – his rather fulsome praise of Simon, for instance,[24] or his defence of the latter's notorious December 1932 speech at Geneva,[25] or his denial that Britain helped to weaken the League.[26] Similarly, to question parts of Cecil's record of events does not necessitate disagreement with every one of his judgements on British policy and on Simon's performances at Geneva.[27] Although these wider aspects of the crisis must be developed elsewhere, it is perhaps worth citing the view of another leading figure at Geneva, the Secretary General of the League, Sir Eric Drummond. What had 'really damaged the League', he wrote to Cecil on 29 December 1931, were the limits placed on its actions, above all by Britain: 'I can no longer confidently affirm to foreigners that a British Government will always scrupulously carry out all its engagements under the Covenant at whatever cost.'[28] In retrospect, one may say that if Drummond had really believed up to then that Britain would uphold the Covenant 'at whatever cost', then he had been deceiving himself. But what mattered what that he, and many other supporters of the League, *thought* that the Far Eastern crisis marked a change in British policy and reliability.

21 Ibid., pp. 20-8. The *Manchester Guardian* was particularly (and excessively) critical of the moderation of the League of Nations Union in this period. See, for example, the editorial of 8 December.

22 Ibid., pp. 43-57.

23 For example, ibid., p. 198.

24 Ibid., pp. 624-5. It is worth noting that Austen Chamberlain – who found the LNU Executive Committee contained 'some of the worst cranks I have ever known', and who thought Cecil's methods 'nearly always wrong and his judgement wholly unreliable' – was privately extremely critical of Simon's handling of British policy. Though he supported Simon over the Far East in the House of Commons in March 1932, he was writing in September that he doubted whether the latter 'has any policy beyond drifting', and found the British delegation at Geneva in October 'ill at ease and floundering, lacking any sure aim or certain guidance'. (Austen Chamberlain Papers, Birmingham University: references respectively: AC 40/5-9, letter to Lord Tyrrell of 13 February 1933; AC 6/1/902-1062, letter to Lady Chamberlain of 22 March 1933; AC 6/1/774-901, letter to Lady Chamberlain of 16 September 1932; ibid. to Lady Chamberlain, 5 October 1932.)

25 Bassett, *Democracy and Foreign Policy*, p. 287.

26 Ibid., pp. 5-6.

27 Cecil, *A Great Experiment*, e.g. pp. 230 and 234.

28 Cecil Papers, Add. 51112. Drummond nevertheless worked at Geneva in a direction which accorded with that of British policy.

Nevertheless, the element of self-contradiction in Cecil's public pronouncements on collective security in the inter-war years was pointed out as long ago as 1939 by E. H. Carr.[29] And Cecil's account of the Far Eastern crisis, published in 1941, contains enough confusion and inaccuracy to invite further inquiry. As a single example, one might take his statement that the Japanese accepted a ceasefire at Shanghai in May 1932 because the West showed they were 'prepared to take serious action', and his clear implication that similar determination would have forced Japan to back down in Manchuria. 'Nothing that occurred later', he writes, 'modified these conclusions.'[30] This glosses over (1) the fact that, whatever gestures they might make by sending a few more ships and men to Shanghai, Britain and the United States remained determined to avoid war and were not 'prepared to take serious action'[31]; and (2) the great difference in Japanese eyes at the time between Shanghai and their 'lifeline', Manchuria, on which there could be no question of any compromise or withdrawal.[32] Confusion is also apparent when Cecil writes (correctly) that 'force alone would have turned (Japan) from her purpose',[33] since this is not only opposed to the arguments he was advancing at the

29 *The 20 Years' Crisis* (London, 1962 ed), pp. 36–7.
30 *A Great Experiment*, pp. 232–3; this was written before Pearl Harbor.
31 The British determination not to fight over Shanghai – and her inability to do so in any case – is fully recorded in the Foreign Office, Cabinet and Cabinet Committee papers in the Public Record Office. As examples, see the discussion of the Far Eastern Committee of the Cabinet on 15 February 1932 (CAB 27/482); the Report of a Sub-Committee of the Committee of Imperial Defence on Economic Sanctions Against Japan, 2 March 1932 (CAB 24/228, CP 92 (32)); and the Annual Review, for 1932, by the Chief of Staff Sub-Committee of the CID, with a Report on the Far Eastern Situation (CAB 24/229, CP 104 (32)). Simon received advice from British observers in Shanghai and passed it on to the Cabinet to the following effect: that, despite the culpable nature of the Japanese action, once the fighting had started, 'from the point of view of the security of the Settlement it appeared better that the Japanese should succeed than the Chinese'. (Cabinet of 17 February, CAB 23/70.) For the severe limitations on what the US Government could contemplate doing, see, for example, Stimson's cable to Hugh Wilson, 26 February 1932 (*Foreign Relations of the United States, 1932*, III: Washington, DC, 1948, pp. 452–3). Hoover's views will be found in a contemporary memorandum printed in R. L. Wilbur and A. M. Hyde, *The Hoover Policies* (New York, 1937), pp. 600–1. In his *Memoirs* (New York, 1952), Hoover relies a great deal on Cecil's book in suggesting that it was the European powers which made sanctions impossible. This gloss on his own role at the time is put in perspective by Professor Rappaport's comment (*Henry L. Stimson and Japan, 1931–1933*: Chicago, 1963, p. 121) that 'Tokyo had only to look across the Pacific to realize that any bellicosity displayed by the Secretary of State was a mere façade'.
32 For an example of the indifference of the Kwantung Army towards League views on Manchuria, see the Chief of Staff's message to the Vice Minister of War, 4 June 1932 (International Military Tribunal for the Far East, Document no. 613, Exhibit 227); see also M. D. Kennedy, *The Estrangement of Great Britain and Japan* (Manchester, 1969), p. 194.
33 *A Great Experiment*, p. 332.

time, but also sits oddly in the same book as the argument on the effectiveness of *a show of force*, referred to above, and the implications of his emphasis that Japan was 'very vulnerable to economic sanctions'.[34]

Despite such later confusion, however, it was clear enough from February 1932 onwards that Cecil did find the Government's efforts entirely inadequate. This is one reason for concentrating on the earlier, and more uncertain, period, but there is a more important one: that it was on these early months that many critics of Britain and the League came to focus when seeking an explanation for the failure to halt Japanese expansion. William Martin, for instance, wrote that, had the urgent appeal to Japan from the President of the League Council in February 1932 been sent at the end of September or in October, 'il y a longtemps que l'effusion du sang serait arrêtée en Extrême-Orient. Il est maintenant bien tard pour faire reculer le Japon, dont toutes les forces impérialistes sont déchaînées.'[35] In a *Manchester Guardian* article on 22 January 1932, 'A Student of the League' declared that if that organization had stood firm in October, withdrawing all ambassadors and leaving Japan in 'complete moral isolation', then 'a few weeks or a few months of this treatment, plus the Chinese boycott, would have produced a Government and a frame of mind in Japan which would have made an honourable settlement . . . feasible'.[36]

34 Ibid., p. 225. It is interesting to read Cecil's view in 1941 of the need to clarify Article XVI for the future: 'the action is to be preventive rather than penal, and is only obligatory if it is reasonably likely to be successful' (ibid, p. 351). By 1946, Salvador de Madariaga was also stressing the unsatisfactory nature of sanctions as a means of international coercion: 'Sanctions are based on the false analogy between inter-individual and international relations. A man is attacked in the street. A policeman and half a dozen zealous citizens rush to defend him, collar the bully and land him in gaol. Can this scene be transferred to international life? Evidently not. Nations . . . are determined by the natural laws of their place to do certain things and avoid others . . . [And] sanctions – even so-called economic sanctions – hurt the punishing nation as much as – at times even more than – the punished' (*Victors, Beware*, London, 1946, pp. 129–30). In 1931–3, these were the arguments of the British Foreign Office, rather than of Senor Madariaga and his colleagues at Geneva. Gilbert Murray also came to see an economic boycott as an unsatisfactory instrument. (Script of a Home Service talk of 26 July 1955, in the Gilbert Murray Papers.) Sir Arthur Salter, too, who in 1932 urged Simon to take action against Japan, a country 'happily more susceptible than almost any other to the threat of isolation and severance of economic relations' (letter of 2 February 1932; PRO, FO 371, F590/1/10) was to observe in 1936: 'From the start [of the League] we should have faced the fact that it is no use whatever to think of imposing any kind of sanctions against an aggressor unless you are prepared, if necessary, to support that pressure by the use of armed forces.' Royal Institute of International Affairs, *The Future of the League of Nations* (New York, 1936), pp. 65–6.

35 *Journal de Genève*, 19 February 1932. Cf. A. Zimmern, *The League of Nations and the Rule of Law* (London, 1939), p. 428: 'The first week was undoubtedly the crucial period, and the Council meeting of September 25, in which Great Britain, represented by Lord Cecil, retreated from the Greco-Bulgarian precedent of the previous week, was the crucial *moment.*'

36 Although the *Manchester Guardian*'s own initial caution is often overlooked. See, for

Moreover Cecil himself came to see this as having been the decisive period. On 23 March 1932, he wrote to a friend that the flaw in Simon's House of Commons speech the day before was that it ignored the facts of Japanese aggression, together with the question of whether stronger action in the autumn would have prevented these events. The October and November meetings of the Council had above all been the time for taking a strong line, he added in a letter of 11 April. 'I think there is a great deal to be said for the proposition that it was too late for coercion when Simon arrived in Geneva,' (i.e. 6 February 1932).[37] In a sense, therefore, it is above all Cecil's own later opinions that lead one back to re-examine his views and his relations with London[38] in the autumn of 1931.

There is no question but that differences and uneasiness did exist in this relationship from the outset. In part, the uneasiness arose from circumstances unconnected with Japan. Cecil felt he had little in common with those forces in British politics which had swept to power under the title of a National Government; though nominally an 'independent Conservative' and a 'reluctant supporter' of the new Government, he found himself during the next 12 months increasingly disposed to join the Liberals.[39] In addition, Cecil felt strongly that his lack of an official position in the Government or Foreign Office was a grave handicap to his efforts as a representative at Geneva. On 19 November 1931, he wrote to Simon that he felt 'very much the ambiguity of the position as a kind of amateur without any real authority', adding, and then scribbling over, a final

---

example, its editorial of 30 September 1931: 'The League . . . has to face this danger under very great disadvantages, due not only to distance but to uncertainty as to whether the soldiers or politicians really rule Japan. It must act if peace is to be preserved, but it must act with circumspection.' And on 26 October: 'The League has done all it can for the moment.' Cf. the comment in the study by the Geneva Research Information Committee, *The League and Manchuria* (Geneva Special Studies, vol. II, no. 10, 1931) on the situation on 22 September: 'Speculation was rife, running from the "strong action" which many people, *unthoughtful of the consequences*, urged, to complete inaction . . .' (emphasis added).

37 Cecil Papers, Add. 51100, letters to H. St George Saunders.

38 'London' is used in the sense of 'predominant opinion in the Government and Foreign Office'. Though there were some differences between the two, they may be taken as one so far as Cecil was concerned.

39 See, for example, a letter to Philip Noel-Baker, 7 October 1932 (Cecil Papers, Add. 51107). There is a delightful letter in the Gilbert Murray papers (dated 1 December 1931)in which Lady Cecil describes to Lady Mary Murray her inability to keep her temper with people of 'our class – I mean people who dine late and all that – and are supposed to be educated [and] seem so often to go wrong about things that matter'. Such people tended to regard Cecil as a crank. On Cecil's previous relationship with Arthur Henderson and MacDonald, see D. Carlton, *MacDonald versus Henderson* (London, 1970), chs 1 and 4.

sentence to the effect that he was uncertain as to the backing he might receive from the Cabinet, and that he would be glad to get home again.[40] 'Everyone knows I have no power to speak for the government, except on direct instructions', he wrote to Simon on 2 February 1932. 'It is really and truly creating the impression that H.M.G. think very little of the League.'[41] It was a dilemma, for, as he was to explain to Philip Noel-Baker in connection with his agreement to attend the Disarmament Conference in 1932, if he turned down such employment as a delegate it would weaken his influence on public opinion and lend weight to the criticisms directed against 'unpractical' champions of the Covenant.[42] Interestingly enough, he was to attend the 1932 Assembly of the League, despite his unofficial status and despite the fact that on the Far East he was, in his own words, 'forced to confine himself to platitudes'.[43]

On their side, the Government had memories of Cecil's resignation over disarmament in 1927, and his continued battle for that cause from a position well in advance of that of Whitehall.[44] 'Need we consider [Cecil]?', MacDonald was to write to Simon at the end of 1932, when he was searching for someone to be given ministerial rank in order to deal especially with Geneva. 'Is he in sufficient sympathy with us? Would he work in a team . . .? Would he be acceptable to our colleagues?'[45]

In addition to this underlying unease, however, there were differences of emphasis over Manchuria, and differences in deciding what policy options were to be ruled out from the beginning. London did not contemplate the use of force, nor did Cecil. But on examination the former also speedily ruled out economic sanctions, partly because it was thought they might lead

40 FO 800/285 (Simon's private papers).
41 FO 800/286.
42 Letter of 21 July 1932, Cecil Papers, Add. 51107.
43 *A Great Experiment*, p. 234.
44 See, for example, Cecil's clash with the Admiralty over the Draft Model Treaty at a conference between the Foreign Office, Cecil, and the Chiefs of Staff, 24 July 1930 (CAB 21/348). Some of Cecil's remarks on that occasion are relevant to the Manchurian situation. 'In practice', he assured a disbelieving First Sea Lord, 'he considered that all nations would be bound to respect and obey the direction of the League, but smaller nations might not have their sense of duty so highly developed.' Later, however, he asserted that 'supposing a big country had definitely made up its mind to risk a war and had invaded another country, he did not think that it would in the least mind violating a further covenant'. In response to Mr Alexander's warning that, given additional powers, the League might wish to stop Britain sending the fleet to Singapore in an emergency, Cecil, according to the minutes, 'agreed, but added that unless we agreed, we would not be bound to accept the League recommendation. We might have excellent reasons for saying that this movement must be carried out, for reasons of national security.' The Japanese were to justify their shipment of additional troops to Manchuria in similar terms.
45 FO 800/287, letter of 23 December 1932.

to an armed response by Japan. In a Foreign Office minute of 27 October Sir John Pratt suggested that the Government

should ab initio discourage the idea that the application of sanctions is even a remote possibility. The League would practically have to bring about a state of war in order to have an excuse for applying Article XVI. Moreover, . . . the United States at the first whisper of the word 'sanctions' would publicly dissociate itself from further association with the League. [46]

Similarly the rough notes which Simon scribbled out at the Cabinet meeting of 11 November ran: 'Policy – conciliatory to Japan. To China. Don't rely *solely* on others: play your own part. Don't seek to transfer to Art. 16. To Japan: we don't *want* to apply sanctions.'[47] The Cabinet duly concluded that 'The League of Nations should be upheld. The Cabinet recognized, however, *inter se*, that the sanctions provided for in Article XVI of the Covenant were not suitable and could not in practice be applied in the present case.'[48] They also inquired of Simon 'whether Lord Cecil was going with me for the Council meeting in Paris next Monday: I said yes . . . It was intimated to me that the Cabinet expected me to put the British view and I said I certainly should'.[49]

Cecil was far from eager to press on to Article 16, as will be seen later, but he was not inclined to rule out this option so decisively. Nor was he as anxious to be circumspect over Japanese feelings as were leading Foreign Office officials,[50] endlessly reinforced in their view by Sir Francis Lindley from Tokyo. Thus, when Cecil urged in a private meeting of the Council on 19 November that it should make clear that Japan had not carried out her obligations, Sir Victor Wellesley[51] termed his remarks 'somewhat unwise' and Vansittart, agreeing, spoke to Simon about the matter.[52] Similarly, when Cecil raised the possibility of British and other neutral troops being used to help stabilize the situation in Manchuria, Wellesley minuted that 'we should have more to lose than any other Power as the

46 FO 371, F5949/1391/10, minutes to no. 664 of *Documents on British Foreign Policy 1919-1939* (hereinafter cited as DBFP), second series, vol. VIII. For a more detailed analysis of British policy in this period, see Christopher Thorne, 'The Shanghai Crisis of 1932', in *American Historical Review*, October 1970.
47 FO 371, F7596/1391/10.
48 CAB 23/69.
49 FO 371, F7596/1391/10.
50 From the outset, the views of Cadogan (Adviser on League of Nations Affairs) were closer to those of Cecil than to many of his superiors in the Foreign Office. See his dissenting minute among those commenting on the Council proceedings of 22 September 1931; FO 371, F5217/1391/10.
51 Deputy Under-Secretary of State.
52 FO 371, F6756/1391/10; minutes on DBFP vol. VIII, no. 754.

whole of our policy in the Far East rests very much on Japanese goodwill'. 'I entirely agree', added Simon. 'There is no possibility.'[53]

Cecil was well aware of this divergence, in the case of Lindley from the 'repeated' copies of the telegrams from Tokyo (which Cecil described to Simon as 'not very illuminating').[54] When his own policy had become clearer, he was to proffer it as a distinct alternative to that urged by the ambassador.[55] As for Wellesley, it was to his 'dead hand' and personal distrust of Cecil that the latter, in a bitter letter to Simon, traced the swift Foreign Office rejection of his neutral-troops proposal: 'He has shown himself for the last three or four years resolutely opposed to anything that may make the action of the League effective in China.'[56]

General Government and Foreign Office neglect of the League was a theme to which Cecil frequently returned.[57] So, too, was the need for more 'open' diplomacy. True to his fundamental belief in the inherent rightness and strength of public opinion, cherishing publicity as 'an immensely powerful guarantee against injustice and misunderstanding',[58] he urged on Drummond and others the great damage done to the cause of the League by the secrecy of the negotiations which took place over Manchuria during meetings of the Council.[59] Drummond disagreed – as of course did the Foreign Office. 'If we had tried to negotiate in public', he wrote, 'we should never have secured an agreed resolution.'[60] But Cecil's belief in the potency of his weapon was – as yet – unshaken. 'I am not at all convinced that all the bluff we heard from Tokyo about the indifference of Japanese public opinion was really genuine. Sooner or later she would have had to give way if public opinion had been strong enough.'[61]

Meanwhile as the inauguration of the Disarmament Conference in February 1932 drew nearer, the differences of opinion between Cecil and

53 FO 371, F6979/1391/10 (minutes on DBFP vol. VIII, no. 787; cf. no. 831). Wellesley was to write a memorandum on the Far Eastern Problem (6 February 1932; DBFP second series, vol. IX, no. 356) which Vansittart minuted as 'a powerful and reasoned statement, at least to a large extent, of a case for Japan' (FO 371, F1033/1/10).

54 DBFP vol. VIII, no. 787. In December Cecil described Lindley's attitude as having been 'quite inadequate right through this dispute' (ibid., vol. IX, no. 17, n.).

55 Ibid, vol. IX, nos 321 and 347.

56 Cecil Papers, Add. 51082, letter of 28 November 1931. Despite his clashes with Cecil, Wellesley hoped and believed that 'the forces of internationalism [would] in the long run triumph over those of nationalism'. Memorandum of 1 December 1930, 'A proposal for the establishment of a Politico-Economic Intelligence Department in the Foreign Office'; Ramsay MacDonald Papers, RM 1/39.

57 For example, in a letter to Simon on 1 February 1932, FO 800/286.

58 *A Great Experiment*, pp. 92–3. Cf. Carr, *The Twenty Years' Crisis*, ch. 3.

59 For example, DBFP vol. IX, no. 10.					60 Ibid., no. 34.

61 Ibid., no. 40 (letter of 31 December 1931). For the gulf between this image and reality, see for example, Ogata, *Defiance in Manchuria*.

the Government on that score were brought into the open, especially in connection with the question of whether he was to attend as a delegate.[62] In 1930, Cecil had concluded his dispatch covering the *Report of the Preparatory Commission for the Disarmament Conference* with the challenge: 'It rests with the Governments to give proof of their oft-repeated intention to reduce the burden of armaments and therewith the risk of war.'[63] Now, he doubted the wholeheartedness of at least some members of the new Government in his cause.

Yet his distrust on this score did not, apparently, embrace the Foreign Secretary, or the Prime Minister. He declined the invitation to be a delegate at the Conference, but added in a letter of explanation to MacDonald 'that if I had to work only with you and [Simon] I should have had no fear of serious disagreement'.[64] And it is in this sphere of political relationships, of individuals as opponents or allies, that some revision appears to be warranted on the Far Eastern issue. Before long Cecil was to criticize Simon in public, and in private to be sharper still – 'He is the worst Foreign Secretary since Derby in '76', he wrote to Murray in January 1933.[65] The strictures in *A Great Experiment* have already been mentioned. But in the early months of the crisis, and even for a while afterwards, Simon appears in much of Cecil's correspondence in a very different light, as a man with whom it was easy and pleasant to work, and with whom there was agreement on essentials.[66] To a letter of 19 December from MacDonald, thanking him for his efforts at Geneva and sympathizing with the problems of working 'in a team', Cecil replied: 'You speak of differences – but I am not conscious of any more than must almost inevitably occur on such occasions, – certainly there have been none to make it difficult for me to carry out the policy you and your colleagues decided on.'[67] His relations with Simon had been 'close and cordial', he added in the letter explaining his disarmament decision. 'It has been a great pleasure to me to work with you', he wrote to Simon on 25 February 1932, 'and

62 See the correspondence between Simon and Cecil from November to January, in FO 800/285 and 286.
63 Cmnd 3757.
64 Cecil Papers, Add. 51081, letter of 21 January 1932.
65 Gilbert Murray Papers, letter of 5 January 1933.
66 With Reading, too, Cecil's working relations appear to have been good, despite his later assertion that the former thought it 'of relatively small moment what happened in Manchuria'. Cf. a Foreign Office Minute by Reading of 28 October (in DBFP vol. VIII, no. 662): 'My impression is that if US would now take matters up where the L. of N. has left it there would be better hope of Japan moving in the right direction . . . We should get into communication forthwith with US', FO 371, F5950/1391/10; and Reading's letter to Vansittart on 21 October: 'A failure by the League to find some way round the difficulty would be nothing short of a calamity . . .', FO 800/226 – Reading's private papers.
67 Cecil Papers, Add. 51081, letter of 24 December 1931.

even on the rare occasions when we have not been absolutely in accord, I always felt, I hope rightly, that fundamentally there was no difference between us.'[68]

It might be suspected that such phrases represented no more than official and personal courtesy, the reflexes of someone of whom Simon wrote to MacDonald: 'I hold most strongly that his loyalty as a colleague, and, so long as he is a colleague, is beyond question.'[69] Cecil's letters to close friends suggest that this was not the case, however. On 13 November he wrote to Gilbert Murray that Simon was 'quite sound' on the Manchurian question.[70] Two weeks later he was dismissing a *News Chronicle* report 'which seemed to set up a kind of opposition between me and Simon' as 'the very reverse of fact',[71] whilst William Martin's *Spectator* article was 'fantastic nonsense'.[72] As late as 11 April, in a letter which has already been quoted in part, he not only recognized that it might have been 'too late for coercion when Simon arrived in Geneva', but added that 'My criticism of him, *so far as it goes, which is not very far*, is really with reference to the Paris meeting'.[73]

The question which naturally arises – why were professional relations between Cecil and Simon reasonably good (to put it at its lowest) in this period? – leads one to examine the former's analyses of and prescriptions for the Manchurian crisis at the time, the second area where some revision appears necessary. For despite the very real differences with London which have been noted above, it would appear that Cecil was often uncertain as to what could or should be done; that only *after* what he later saw as the vital period did he come to feel that a strong line should be taken immediately; that, like many others, he was for some time uncertain as to the strength of the case against Japan; that he was concerned to avoid or at least delay recourse to Article 16; and that by December he was not at all displeased or unhopeful at what the League had achieved.

As before, the public evidence for such conclusions must be treated with caution. Cecil was no doubt anxious to be seen as loyal to the Government's policies so long as he represented the country at Geneva,

68 FO 800/286.

69 FO 800/287, letter of 30 December 1932.

70 Gilbert Murray Papers.

71 Gilbert Murray Papers, letter of 28 November 1931. The article referred to concerned the decision (on which Murray had sought the advice of the two men in Geneva) not to hold a special meeting of the LNU on the Far East at that juncture.

72 Cecil Papers, Add. 51132, letter of 24 December 1931. In this case Cecil may have been referring especially to Martin's suggestion of a secret bargain with Japan, rather than to his own position.

73 Ibid., Add. 51100, letter to H. St George Saunders. Emphasis added. The Council met in Paris, rather than in Geneva, between 16 November and 10 December 1931.

and to reassure British supporters of the League that it was not failing in its task of restoring peace. His speech to a League of Nations Union meeting on 11 December may have come in this category, when, referring to the 'two great agencies of disorder and two great difficulties' with which the League had had to contend, 'Japanese militarism and Chinese anarchy', he assured his listeners that 'the justification of the League was complete. It was entitled to say, "we have prevented war, have made some attempt to secure justice, and have laid the foundations for what we believe to be a better state of things." '[74] In fact, in *A Great Experiment* Cecil describes such public views as 'much too optimistic', but adds: 'I notice in the letters I wrote at the time I was not, privately, very sanguine because I thought the Japanese had adopted not only the technical skill of their German military instructors but also their principles of international policy.'[75]

Not all his letters, as will be seen, bear out this statement. This is more surprising than the revelation that in the very early days, with little information to hand, Cecil misjudged events along with many others.[76] 'All the great Powers have been equally determined on trying to reach a settlement of the crisis', he wrote to Philip Noel-Baker. '. . . There is no doubt that the Chinese after their manner have enormously exaggerated what has been happening.'[77] The seriousness of the situation was more apparent by

74 *Manchester Guardian*, 12 December 1931.

75 p. 228.

76 On 10 September, Cecil told the Assembly that 'there had scarcely ever been a period in the world's history when war seemed less likely', and that Franco-German tension accounted for 'seventy-five per cent of the political unrest in the world'. *League of Nations Official Journal*, Special Supplement no. 93 (Geneva, 1931), pp. 59–60.

77 Cecil Papers, Add. 51107, letter of 25 September 1931. Cf. the recollection of Hugh Wilson (US Minister in Switzerland): 'There was no one member of the Council who was aware of the special rights of Japan in Manchuria . . .', *Diplomat Between Wars* (New York, 1941), p. 261. At the Council meeting of 22 September, Cecil recalled the occasion of the Greco-Bulgarian dispute as a model for League action (see J. Barros, *The League of Nations and the Great Powers*, Oxford, 1970). On 25 September, he agreed with the Japanese representative that 'primarily, the question of the dispute was a matter for the parties and not for the Council to deal with, unless it came before the latter under Article 15 . . .', the Council's task being only 'to safeguard the peace of nations'. By 23 October, however, he was stressing that 'the most essential thing is to try to find a fundamental cure for what is now amiss'. *League of Nations Official Journal* (December 1931), pp. 2270, 2284, 2348. The writer has not found evidence of any instructions from London which would account for Cecil's change of emphasis on 25 September. Although subsequent Foreign Office minutes rejected the Greco-Bulgarian parallel (FO 371, F5217/1391/10), the Cabinet on 22 September had approved what was already Cecil's intention: an attempt to secure a withdrawal of troops behind a certain line. CAB 23/68. Cecil appears to have overlooked his use of the Greco-Bulgarian model – that case had been dealt with under Article 11 – when later declaring that all would have been well had China and the League proceeded under Article 15.

The impatient observations of the *Manchester Guardian* on 10 October make ironic reading in the light of later recriminations: 'It is satisfactory to know that on this occasion (i.e. the

the evening of 18 October when Madariaga, Colban and Massigli joined Cecil in his hotel room to discuss what pressure might be brought against Japan if she persisted in occupying Chinese territory. Their report[78] has already been referred to as having (according to Cecil) alarmed Lord Reading, but it was not the purpose of the document to press for strong action at once. While suggesting that 'there is no power of effective economic pressure by any means short of those intended in Article 16', its concluding emphasis was that 'it would be very difficult to take any action, whether under Articles 10, 11, 15 or 16, unless the United States were at any rate benevolently neutral'. And on the possibility of withdrawing ambassadors from Tokyo, it observed:

It must, however, be admitted that apart from the Covenant it would seem doubtful whether such action as Japan has taken in China would normally be regarded as an adequate reason for interrupting diplomatic negotiations . . . (and) unless the United States were prepared also to withdraw their representative, the gesture would lose almost all its moral effect.[79]

As for the severing of economic relations with Japan by members of the League Council, 'it would be quite useless without the association of the United States and probably Russia'.

It was the need for patience that Cecil stressed at the public meeting of the Council on 24 October, calling on his colleagues to remember that they must not outstrip 'the public opinion of the world', which was their chief weapon. 'It is of the utmost importance', he declared, 'that our deliberations – conducted with all the speed that is possible, no doubt – should yet be rather behind than in front of the opinion of the world.'[80] By this criterion (if one were to allow that such a thing as 'world opinion' existed), the British Government deserved Cecil's subsequent approval rather than his censure. In private, too, he was far from anxious at the time to proceed with the application of Article 16 and sanctions, recognizing the hazards involved and advocating the use of Article 15 as a means of delaying any such embarrassment. He urged this on Simon in a letter of 13 November,[81]

Council meeting of 13 October 1931) Lord Reading will represent Great Britain, as Lord Cecil's diplomacy at the last meetings was so extraordinarily diplomatic that he appeared in one speech to be undoing what he had achieved in another.'

78 DBFP, vol. VIII, no. 664.

79 Cecil later wrote (*A Great Experiment*, p. 227) that at Paris Simon 'was not prepared . . . *even to urge that a diplomatic protest should be made by withdrawing the envoys of the League Powers from Tokyo*' (emphasis added).

80 *League of Nations Official Journal* (December 1931), p. 2360.

81 DBFP vol. VIII, no. 730. China had brought the crisis before the League under Article 11; she was to invoke Articles 10 and 15 on 29 January 1932.

and six days later reiterated that if the Chinese decided 'that it would suit them better to have an open state of war with Japan and (called) upon us and other members to do our duty under Article 16 – that would put us into an extremely difficult and dangerous position.'[82] He was writing the same thing on 8 December – 'it would be very awkward, in view of the existing domestic situation'[83] – and meanwhile arrived at what appeared to be an accurate assessment of the freedom of manoeuvre which the Japanese possessed:

The possibility of arriving at some settlement of this dispute depends entirely on what is the real policy of Japan. If she desires to establish what would be in effect a protectorate over Manchuria she will not agree to any withdrawal of her troops until that has been accomplished . . . There seems little doubt that a protectorate is in fact the policy of the Military party in Tokyo.[84]

The same emphasis on the perils of anything but a slow and moderate procedure appears in Cecil's letters to Gilbert Murray:

In any case (he wrote on 13 November), I rather incline to think that any violent or outspoken action on our part might be dangerous at this moment. The truth is that we must be content to move rather slowly because owing to the complex condition of affairs just now we cannot threaten.[85]

A week later, while agreeing that Manchuria was 'a very serious blow to the machinery which we have devised', he felt optimistic enough to add that 'if this League Commission [of Inquiry] goes through that will be something and indeed perhaps in the long run more than anything else that could have been devised'.[86] The League machinery was 'quite adequate' to deal with the issue 'on ordinary straightforward lines', he wrote on 28 November. Had the Chinese brought their case under Article 15, 'we should have had an inquiry which would, by now, have been well on its way and we should have taken whatever measures were necessary to render an actual clash unlikely'.[87]

82 Ibid., no. 754, footnote.　　　　　　　　　　　　83 Ibid., no. 831.
84 Ibid., no. 739 (memorandum for Sir John Simon, 16 November). After such an analysis, together with the letters cited below, there is a hint that the writer is covering himself in the parenthesis which occurs later in this memorandum: 'If anything in the nature of coercion is ruled out – as I gather it is . . .' On 13 January 1932, Cecil was to write to Austen Chamberlain that he had 'for a long time believed that economic blockade was impracticable except as a part of belligerent action'. Cecil Papers, Add. 51079.
85 Gilbert Murray Papers. Cf. the emphasis in *A Great Experiment* (p. 332): 'Not only was force not used to restrain the aggressor . . .'
86 Gilbert Murray Papers, letter of 21 November 1931.
87 Ibid., letter of 28 November. Philip Noel-Baker was similarly optimistic about the consequences of an inquiry. 'I am . . . sure that once the Commission was appointed and des-

Both Simon and Cecil were anxious to see 'some vindication of the moral authority of the League' in a situation where outright success was as yet denied them, and they were agreed that Britain should work for a satisfactory declaration of principle within the Council, rather than push ahead on her own.[88] Moreover, as the drafting progressed of what was to be the League Resolution of 10 December, Cecil was not urging that the Japanese must somehow be made to withdraw immediately:

The stumbling block is still the time for evacuation. It appears to me that there is good ground for saying that it would be improper for us to fix a time until we have heard what our Commission has had to say on the subject. The only difficulty is that that must mean a considerable delay, since it would take some little time to get the Commission set up.[89]

This readiness to contemplate at least some delay before the League would have to take further action was not due simply to Cecil's awareness of the reluctance of Britain (and France) to take effective steps to implement any immediate and drastic decision. A more straightforward reason is that he appears to have shared the widespread uncertainty over the extent to which Japan's guilt could be proved at this time. It was not until 11 December that the Minseito Cabinet in Tokyo gave way to one more clearly dominated by the military, and the crucial Kwantung Army drive on Chinchow, which secured the whole of South Manchuria, was not to begin until 23 December. (Chinchow fell on 3 January.) Meanwhile, Cecil was not asserting the view which one might expect from reading *A Great Experiment*.[90] ('No honest man could doubt that Japan had "resorted to war" . . . or that the other members of the League were bound to take action under Article 16 to assist China. But nothing had been done beyond sending the Lytton Commission to inquire.') On 26 November he talked in Paris to two leading members of the League of Nations Union, the Secretary, Dr Maxwell Garnett, and Vice-Admiral S. R. Drury-Lowe, who was on the Executive Committee. The Admiral immediately sent an account of the meeting to his Chairman, Gilbert Murray, saying he was 'very disturbed' by Cecil's views:

He personally thinks Japan is wrong; but that she cannot be charged with actually breaking the Covenant, though he admits she has acted against the spirit of it and

patched things would enormously improve. The Japanese would never dare to continue fighting and they would never dare to resist the operations of the Commission on the spot.' The two great weapons of the League were not being used: 'public discussion and the supply of impartial information' (letter to Murray of 7 December 1931, Murray Papers).

88 DBFP vol. VIII, nos 745, 789 and 795.

89 Ibid., no. 795 (letter to Simon, 27 November). 90 p. 231.

that she *has* broken Art. 2 of the Kellogg Pact. But there has been no actual break of any article of the Covenant. [At this point the Admiral had disagreed and cited Article 10 as having been broken.] Cecil says Japan can plead she has only acted to maintain order in same way (sic) as we acted in Shanghai by sending in an expeditionary force. He agrees that the Japanese military are in real control . . . Cecil agrees that Japan should withdraw but asks how it is suggested the League should turn her out? . . . As regards the Disarmament Conference he said he does not think it will be affected by what's happening and that it is in a way an argument for Disarmament! [91]

It is conceivable that Cecil was loyally striving not to give his listeners any fresh ammunition to use against the Government, and his sometimes strained relations with Garnett within the LNU might be adduced as a particular reason for care. But the conversation chimes with the note of caution already cited from Cecil's letters and reports, and if there was a particular motive behind his words on this occasion it was surely the one suggested by Gilbert Murray in his reply to Admiral Drury-Lowe: 'I am greatly disappointed about what you tell me about Cecil's attitude . . . I cannot help thinking that [he] is influenced by his great desire to defend the League against the charge of having failed completely.' [92] Many of Cecil's subsequent speeches and writings could be prefaced with this remark. Among them should be included, no doubt, those expressing qualified optimism when the 10 December Resolution had been passed, thereby salvaging a little of the Council's dignity. [93] In a letter to Simon two days before, Cecil had expressed his fears that 'the whole incident will greatly weaken the position we have hitherto taken up with the French that they are sufficiently protected by the clauses of the Covenant against German attack'. But he continued:

It has been a very exasperating experience, but if by good luck the Resolution goes through and there is no attack on Chinchow, the net result will be not so very bad

91 Gilbert Murray Papers. The British expeditionary force referred to (at one time it numbered 20,000 men) had been sent to Shanghai in 1927 during a period of acute disturbances in China. It is important to recall that the Covenant (unlike the Pact of Paris) did not prohibit the use of force, being concerned only with 'resort to war'. As in the Corfu incident, war was not declared between China and Japan in 1931–3, and diplomatic relations were not severed.   92 Gilbert Murray Papers, letter of 28 November 1931.
93 Briefly, a League Resolution of 30 September had called for a halt to the fighting and a Japanese withdrawal as soon as was practicable; on 24 October the Council had called upon Japan to withdraw by 16 November, and although Japan's sole dissenting vote rendered this Resolution inoperative, there was evident humiliation when she did not comply. The 10 December Resolution reaffirmed that of 30 September, called upon both sides not to aggravate the situation and set up (thanks to Japan's change of mind) a Commission of Inquiry. Japan ominously reserved the right to take 'police' action against bandits meanwhile.

and at any rate a great deal better than it looked as if it were likely to be three weeks ago.[94]

And in arguing the need for more publicity in a letter to Drummond on 18 December, Cecil implied that the League had done reasonably well:

. . . I recognize, that, *quite unjustly, as I think*, the Manchurian affair has done the League more harm than any other single event in its history. Now, I am convinced that if the public had really been able to follow what was happening, and how we have come from one point to another, *the great part of this discontent would vanish.*[95]

What had been lacking, he repeated to Drummond at the end of the year, was sufficient publicity to produce an overwhelmingly strong public opinion against Japan.[96] It was a refusal to admit the conclusion he himself had allowed for in 1919:

For the most part there is no attempt to rely on anything like a superstate; no attempt to rely upon force to carry out a decision of the Council or the Assembly of the League. What we rely upon is public opinion . . . and if we are wrong about it, then the whole thing is wrong.[97]

It was only when the Far Eastern crisis had run its course, and the Abyssinian one had followed, that some admission of miscalculation was forthcoming:

I put aside, personally, all hope of maintaining peace by objurgation or appeals or even the unassisted influence of world opinion. These influences which have ultimately great power in international affairs have never yet succeeded in preventing a war which has been determined upon by any powerful country . . . If we are to give the new [i.e. League] system fair trial . . . we must be as ready to make sacrifices for [it] as we used to be ready to make sacrifices for matters of 'honour and vital interest'.[98]

Here, too, there were disappointments in store.

94 DBFP vol. VIII, no. 831.
95 Ibid., vol. IX, no. 10 (emphasis added).
96 Ibid., no. 40.
97 Hansard, *Parliamentary Debates*, House of Commons, CXVIII, 990–2 (21 July 1919).
98 Cecil Papers, Add. 51083, memorandum on League policy, 26 May 1936, sent to Eden. For an illustration of the inner struggles experienced by pacific or pacifist supporters of the League as the likelihood of having to use force was borne in upon them, see Kingsley Martin, *Editor* (Penguin, 1969).

In the New Year the Japanese seizure of Chinchow and attack at Shanghai swiftly increased the frustration of those who championed collective security. Although willing to attend the Council meeting at the end of January, Cecil asked Simon for instructions with the rider: 'I confess the situation appears to me almost intolerable.'[99] From Geneva he then urged that Shanghai was 'a test case'; that if the Japanese were shown to be the aggressors there and would not withdraw, Britain should propose 'the simultaneous withdrawal of all diplomatic representatives at Tokyo'; and that if necessary a ban should be placed on imports from Japan.[100] There followed his public campaign referred to earlier. On their side the Cabinet heard from J. H. Thomas ('much more sympathetic than Sir John', in Cecil's eyes) that 'one of his difficulties [at Geneva] had been that Lord Cecil . . . was personally in favour of a more forceful policy by the League towards Japan'.[101]

In public, this widening gap between Cecil and the Government focused attention on the former as the man who must know the details of official short-comings. In private, it brought the warm appreciation of the US Secretary of State, Stimson.[102] Even so, there were clear limits to what Cecil thought could be done, and they were clearer in private than in public. He ruled out a direct blockade of Japan 'or other military measures against her' as 'quite impracticable'.[103] He believed that sanctions, operated in conjunction with the United States, would succeed 'without any risk of war', but that if the US could not cooperate 'it would be far better to wash our hands of the whole business'.[104] He had already recognized that, although the Americans might favour action, 'they prefer it to be taken by someone else rather than themselves',[105] and that 'the attitude of the United States and Russia is . . . a permanent source of weakness to the League'.[106] At the end of February he 'did not believe any suggestion for economic pressure had ever come from [the] American Government'.[107] And by March he was

99 DBFP, vol. IX, no. 74.   100 Ibid., nos 204 and 267.

101 CAB 23/70, Cabinet meeting of 10 February 1932. Thomas, armed with the weight of Dominion opinion and his Trade Union experience of the superiority of conciliation over sanctions, was a leading proponent in Cabinet of the view that Article 16 should be abolished altogether.

102 *Foreign Relations of the United States, 1932*, III, pp. 85–6 and 94–5.

103 DBFP, vol. IX, no. 267.

104 FO 800/286, letter to Simon, 26 February 1932. President Hoover ruled out any question of the United States joining in sanctions, other than that of non-recognition. See Richard Current, 'The Stimson Doctrine and the Hoover Doctrine', in *American Historical Review*, no. 59 (1953–4).

105 FO 800/285, letter to Simon, 27 November 1931.

106 Cecil Papers, Add. 51079, letter to Austen Chamberlain, 13 January 1932.

107 Gilbert Murray Papers, letter of 25 February 1932, containing a draft reply to a telegram Murray had received from a League supporter in the USA, suggesting that London was

ready to term a voluntary boycott of Japanese goods 'useless', since Japanese exports to Britain were negligible, while 'the richer class is very unsound, and even the poorer class is very ignorant'. He doubted whether it would be done in America very much.[108] Clearly it was taking time to mobilize enlightened public opinion. 'I should prefer now', he wrote in April, 'to defer any very strong action about Manchuria until the Lytton Commission has reported'.[109] Priority should now be given to a campaign to save the Disarmament Conference since 'it is as much as you can do to get the ordinary [LNU] branch secretary to understand one set of points. If you ask him to understand two, he will either muddle them both, or drop one of them.'[110] It is a suitably disillusioned note on which to leave Cecil's further experiences during the crisis.

One is led to conclude, then, that in the early months of the Far Eastern crisis, despite certain very real differences of approach and emphasis, the gap between Cecil and the Government was less wide than the former's written testimony would suggest. As he himself would doubtless have been the first to remark, the greatness of a cause does not of itself bestow upon its champion a flawless intellect, an unshakeable consistency, or an unrivalled prescience. Cecil's views took time to shape and contained contradictions. The emphasis of what he had to say was not identical in each of his spheres of operation – within the League, the Foreign Office and the League of Nations Union, for instance. The vehemence with which he expressed his own opinions increased – was enabled to increase, perhaps – as his access to secret analyses of the limitations forced upon British policy diminished. And, as is common, eventual certainties were projected unduly far into the past when the holder of them came to review events in later years.[111]

It is worth noting that over the Far Eastern crisis Cecil was not alone in some of these respects. Reference has already been made to the *Manchester*

---

obstructing Washington's desire to follow the League in imposing sanctions. The sender of the telegram had surrendered to wishful thinking following an interview with the Secretary of State, Stimson. Stimson Diary (Yale), 18 February 1932, and Newton D. Baker Papers (Library of Congress), boxes 147 and 149.

108 Cecil Papers, Add. 51107, letter to Philip Noel-Baker, 7 March 1932. And yet in his letter of 11 April to St George Saunders, cited earlier, Cecil concluded: 'That does not mean that in the last stage it may not have been more desirable to proceed by way of an unofficial boycott.'   109 Ibid, letter to Philip Noel-Baker, 29 April 1932.
110 Ibid., letters to Philip Noel-Baker, 22 March and 29 April 1932.
111 Cf. the examples given by Karl Deutsch and Richard Merritt, 'Effects of events on National and International Images', in H. Kelman (ed.), *International Behavior* (New York, 1966), p. 145: 'If messages or memories about past events do not directly reinforce a strongly held image, they may be selectively screened or distorted until they do so.'

Guardian's caution during September and October. Henry Stimson, whose exasperation was to know no bounds when others displayed little enthusiasm for condemning Japan, had been a leading advocate of restraint in the early days.[112] Herbert Hoover, who firmly opposed Stimson's musings on the desirability of employing economic sanctions, was later to project the intransigence of both himself and his Secretary of State further backwards than had been the case.[113] As for Cecil's shifting views on the efficacy of public opinion, there is something of a parallel to be found in Walter Lippmann's attitude to the doctrine of non-recognition. Having privately played some part in Stimson's decision to declare such a policy over the seizure of Manchuria, Lippmann publicly described it as a 'novel and far reaching' measure which had saved faces and might' save the situation: 'The world has in effect announced a campaign of passive resistance against the Japanese aggression.'[114] By 1934, however, he was arguing that part of the basis for an urgently needed settlement with Japan would have to be an American willingness 'to recognize that the revival of Russia as a great power in the Far East, the continuing weakness of China, *the separation of Manchuria*, and our withdrawal from the Philippines, are new elements in the situation . . .'[115]

The other examples of shifting opinion and uncertainty over the crisis which are to be found among Cecil's LNU friends are a reminder, however, that his own degree of confusion rested on more than simply the limitations of human memory or prescience. They reflected the underlying dilemma with which champions of collective security found themselves confronted by the Japanese action. Beneath their dismay and their anger, men who put all their trust in the League were under the same kind of pressures as those Americans in 1949 who believed implicitly in their country's omnipotence, and yet found the Communists in control of mainland China.[116] One had either painfully to revise a deeply held belief, or to find 'proof' of conspiracy and betrayal. In this case it was generally easier to maintain that Britain had thwarted what would otherwise have been a vin-

112 See, for example, *Foreign Relations of the United States, 1931*, III, p. 57.
113 Cf. *The Memoirs of Herbert Hoover, 1920–1933* (New York, 1952), pp. 366–70; E. E. Morison, *Turmoil and Tradition* (Boston, 1960), p. 383.
114 Lippmann, *Interpretations, 1931–1933* (London, 1933), pp. 207–9.
115 *Interpretations, 1933–1935* (New York, 1936), p. 339; emphasis added. Lippmann's 1931 analysis that 'the Powers are not in a position to do more . . . The Manchurian issue is beyond the resources of our civilisation' had been amended thirteen years later to the assertion: 'What we might have done, what the League might have done, if China had been able and willing to fight, no one can say. The fact is that China did not resist, and this is a significant and conclusive reason, far more significant than any other reason, why Japan was not stopped' (*Interpretations, 1931–1933*, pp. 189–90, and *US War Aims*, London, 1944, p. 9).
116 See N. Graebner, *The New Isolationism* (New York, 1956). Cf. Sir John Pratt, *War and Politics in China* (London, 1943), p. 223.

dication of the League than it was to recognize that 'Covenants, without the Sword, are but Words, and of no strength to secure a man at all'.[117] Cecil found himself in a situation which exposed the inherent limitations of the League. He could not conclude from the experience, however, that the objective and subjective preconditions necessary for the establishment of true collective security were unlikely to be met.[118] The League was not inadequate; it had been betrayed.[119]

E. H. Carr has already analysed, in *The 20 Years Crisis*, some of consequences of the fact that the League rested upon a body of Western, liberal-democratic idealism, its reliance on the rightness and strength of public opinion springing directly from the tradition exemplified by John Stuart Mill. In this respect, an essentially Eurocentric organization was at a disadvantage in 1931 for reasons more profound than the obvious one of sheer distance from the scene of the fighting. The gulf between Manchuria and Geneva did more than limit the League's supply of relevant information. Reliance on the sanction of public opinion and moral condemnation rests on the assumption that all men hold peace to be more desirable than war and will place the highest value on retaining the respect of their fellows in such matters. Similarly, belief in the deterring power of economic sanctions rests partly upon a system of values where pleasure will always be sought in preference to pain. Such considerations were alien to the middle-ranking officers who directed the Kwantung Army, and through that army, Japanese policy during this crisis; they were to be of little importance in the 1941 discussions which led to the decision to strike at Pearl Harbor, despite the unlikelihood of ultimate victory.[120] Cecil was endeavouring to use a weapon which, in the circumstances, was irrelevant.

117 Thomas Hobbes, *Leviathan* (Everyman edn) (London, 1924), p. 87.
118 See Inis Claude, *Swords Into Ploughshares* (New York, 1959), ch. 12. The underlying paradox has often been pointed out: that to achieve genuine collective security would require a degree of disinterested commitment among men and states that, if it were achieved, would render the machinery of such security unnecessary.
119 The basis for this reaction has been well summarized by Professor F. S. Northedge in a paper on 'British Opinion, the League and the UN', which he wrote for a Chatham House study-group in 1953: 'The liberal creed, and in relation to international affairs, its League of Nations idealism, were effective in unleashing two of the most powerful of human dispositions, the impulse towards a better human society, and the capacity for indignation and resentment when this impulse is frustrated' (p. 37). I am grateful to Professor Northedge for lending me his copy of this paper. Cf. the comments of Harold Nicolson in the Chatham House discussions, *The Future of the League of Nations*, p. 159.
120 See Nobutaka Ike (ed.), *Japan's Decision for War* (Stanford, Ca, 1967). Cf. R. A. Scalapino, *Democracy and the Party Movement in Prewar Japan* (Berkeley, Ca, 1962), p. 346: 'The history of Japan after 1931 represented the logical culmination of previous trends . . . It did not require a fundamental revolution to push the democratic movement aside in Japan, and, indeed, no such event occurred.' For examples of some inter-national or intertribal

The weapon was also, of course, weak in its own right. Supporters of the League were faced with the unwillingness of governments and peoples to risk another war over an issue where their own vital interests did not appear to be at stake, where the background to the dispute seemed confusing, and where the potential enemy had an overwhelming local military superiority. As for the United States in 1956 and the USSR in 1962 (though for reasons of vulnerability through weakness, rather than vulnerability despite strength), the option of raising the issue to the level of a major military confrontation was unacceptable. As for the use of economic pressure – even if the possibility were ignored of a consequent resort to arms by the determined transgressor – depression in the West harshly discouraged any resort to a weapon 'whose double-edged effect would be immediate and severe'.[121]

The League failed over Manchuria. The 'Stimson doctrine' of non-recognition failed too, steeped as it was in that American tradition which saw international politics in terms of moral absolutes, and anticipating as it did another failure, this time involving the whole of China. The League and the United States overlapped in their failure, and even had they coincided, the result would almost certainly have been the same. Given the state of the US economy and public opinion in 1931–3, supporters of a League which included the United States would simply have had one excuse the less.[122]

The League's failure was a consequence, not of betrayal, but of its inherent limitations.[123] In this light, Cècil's troubled arguments may be seen as an attempt to stave off, and then to explain away, the inevitable. It was a mental process which had its counterpart within public opinion, and which contributed significantly to the endangering of Britain's security in the 1930s. And yet without men such as Cecil and Murray (Madariaga's 'civic monks') to devote themselves to this unattainable cause, to refuse, with Leonard Woolf, to yield 'even to the logic of events', and to pursue 'the shadow of a shadow of a dream',[124] the inter-war years would have

---

consequences of contrasting value-systems, see Kelman, *International Behavior*, particularly the chapter by R. A. Levine on 'Socialization, social structure, and intersocial images'.
121 CAB 24/228, Report by a Sub-Committee of the Committee of Imperial Defence on Economic Sanctions Against Japan, 2 March 1932. Cf. the Chiefs of Staff Review for 1932: 'The position is about as bad as it could be . . . The whole of territory in the Far East, as well as the coastline of India and our vast trade and shipping, lies open to attack.' CAB 24/229.
122 This was also the opinion of Hugh Wilson: 'I think . . . we would have recoiled even farther from the obligations of the Covenant, just as Great Britain recoiled from a literal interpretation of Article X . . . ', *Diplomat Between Wars*, p. 334.
123 For a further discussion of the limitations involved, as demonstrated on an earlier occasion, see J. Barros, *The Corfu Incident of 1923* (Princeton, NJ, 1965), especially pp. 301ff.
124 Leonard Woolf, *The Journey Not the Arrival Matters* (London, 1969), pp. 168–72. Salvador de Madariaga, 'Gilbert Murray and the League', in Gilbert Murray, *An Unfinished Autobiography* (London, 1960), which provides a brief but brilliant study of Cecil as well as of Murray.

been infinitely the poorer. 'The League would be worth nothing if it did not sometimes attempt the impossible', wrote Vansittart in May 1931.[125] It might not have been the kind of tribute which supporters of that organization would have appreciated or accepted, but it acknowledged the lasting importance of the ideal embodied in the Covenant. Having questioned a portion of its contents, the writer would not dispute the title of *A Great Experiment.*

125 CAB 24/225, C.P.317(31).

10

The Quest for Arms Embargoes:
Failure in 1933

At the time of writing, the search for an agreement which would halt the supply of arms to the Middle East continues with mounting anxiety but little prospect of success. The embargoes imposed unilaterally by Britain in 1967 and by France more recently have disappeared into the limbo of lost causes. The equally vain attempts in Parliament to prevent British arms being sent to Nigeria are also fading rapidly from the public memory, while the sale of arms to South Africa by the Soviet Union and other states continues, regardless of a United Nation ban of 1963. No doubt there will be a spasm of renewed interest on that score if and when a Conservative government resumes British shipments to South Africa behind the debatable distinction which their party makes between arms required for external defence and those which could be used for the maintenance of *apartheid*.

The situation in which the National Government briefly attempted to place an embargo on the sale of arms to Japan and China in 1933 was not identical to that obtaining in any one of the above cases. Among the public, for example, feelings against arms manufacturers as 'merchants of death' and instigators of war were far more intense in the post-1918 period than they have been since 1945 (despite such obvious exceptions as, say, hostility in America towards the suppliers of napalm), while the concept of weapons as deterrents was much less widely accepted in 1933 than it has become in the nuclear age. Nevertheless there is a familiarity about many of the questions which presented themselves to MacDonald's government and their attentive public: how much weight should be accorded to moral considerations as against those of *realpolitik*? Would an embargo which covered the whole area of conflict penalize one contestant more than the other, and would a successful freezing of external supplies perpetuate,

Reproduced from *Journal of Contemporary History*, 5 (1970), pp. 129–49.

rather than diminish, instability? For how long should a single country continue to impose an embargo when others are rendering nugatory its practical effects? And behind these and other questions, what is the purpose of the action contemplated: to punish the guilty party in a conflict? To restore or maintain the balance of power and the prospects of peace in the area? Or simply to rid the national conscience of the guilt associated with 'blood money'?

The 1933 episode also serves as a reminder of the large number of considerations which can press in upon the foreign policy decision-maker, situated as he is within two overlapping environments, the domestic and the international, and having to accord and re-accord degrees of significance to such rapidly changing factors as the focus of public attention, the endeavours of pressure groups, and the responses and initiatives of other governments, as well as to longer-term ones such as the country's economic and military resources, or the state of its armaments industry in the face of new threats appearing over the horizon.

These particular elements happen to have been present in 1933, and some of them, like domestic opinion, have of course played an insignificant part on other occasions. But an examination of this case may reveal some of the difficulties which can face those responsible for halting or permitting the flow of arms at times when both the press and the public are inclined to view the issue in their own somewhat simplified terms.

The announcement of the British embargo at the end of February 1933 was made against a background of confusion and disillusionment in international politics. The United States and Japan were preoccupied with the political and social repercussions of the depression, while Europe was in addition being reminded of the fragility of the Versailles frontiers in the presence of a Germany now ruled by the Nazis. In Geneva, the Disarmament Conference, opened so bravely a year before by Arthur Henderson's 'refusal to contemplate even the possibility of failure', was now, in Eden's words to the Cabinet, 'tottering to its failure' over the incompatible demands of France and Germany, its participants 'deeply depressed at the prospect', and its experts still wrestling with such questions as the licensing of armaments manufacturers and the defining of an act of aggression.[1]

The hopes reposed in collective security had already suffered another severe blow from the apparent impotence of the League in the face of the

1 Eden to Simon and Baldwin, 24 February 1933 (Baldwin Papers, vol. 121); minutes of the Disarmament Committee of the Cabinet, 2 March 1933 (Public Record Office, CAB 21/379); Disarmament Committee, Papers (CAB 27/504)). All Foreign Office and Cabinet papers are hereafter cited under their classification in the PRO.

Japanese seizure of Manchuria following the Mukden 'incident' in September 1931. By January 1933, 'Manchukuo' had been established and recognized as an independent state by Tokyo, a development which the report of the Lytton Commission submitted to the League of Nations declared to be out of all proportion to Japan's original grievances and not based on the wishes of the population involved. Tokyo, however, was clearly not disposed towards conciliation. Japanese troops were now poised to take the neighbouring province of Jehol, and in a skirmish with the Chinese at Shanhaikuan provided a reminder of how easily the conflict might spill over, beyond the Great Wall, into the region of Tientsin and Peking. Yet however impotent the League might be, the moment was approaching when it would have to declare its position over the conflict and the Lytton Report, risking the secession of Japan in the process.

It was fully appreciated in London that the likely consequence of this deteriorating state of affairs was a return to what Vansittart described as 'the pre-war condition of the balance of power – but even worse'.[2] It was a prospect which threw into sharp relief the fears and hopes of the whole generation which had been scarred by the experience of 1914–18, and was as unwelcome to a Vansittart as it was to a Cecil, to a Baldwin as much as to a Lansbury.[3] Their proposed solutions differed widely, however, and never more so than over the question of armaments. Whereas Baldwin was slowly moving towards the notion of a British deterrent, Lansbury advocated more vehemently than ever the abolition of all weapons, unilaterally if necessary; and there were violent disagreements within the League of Nations Union between those like Cecil on the one hand, who supported the French idea of a force under the direct control of the League, and Austen Chamberlain on the other who, like the Foreign Office, regarded such a proposal as both impracticable and dangerous.[4]

Even so, the development of the Far Eastern crisis since the Mukden incident of 18 September 1931, had given rise to what eventually became a well-publicized discussion on the possibility of some kind of action over the sale of arms to that part of the world.[5] This may have been due in part to the

2 Minute of 26 February 1933 (Vansittart Papers).

3 In February, for example, Baldwin read to Tom Jones the plea of an acquaintance for a return to 'the old diplomacy'. To Jones' retort that 'the old diplomacy brought us to the Great War', Baldwin replied: 'Yes, I admit, it is an awful dilemma'. T. Jones, *A Diary with Letters* (London, 1954), p. 93.

4 See K. Middlemas and J. Barnes, *Baldwin* (London, 1969), especially ch. 28. For the French proposals advanced at Geneva in the autumn of 1932 see *Documents Diplomatiques Français, 1932–1939* (DDF), 1re Série, tome 1, nos. 286, 331; on the clash between Cecil and Chamberlain, see, for example, Chamberlain to Simon, 30 May 1932 (Austen Chamberlain Papers, AC 39/1-6), and Cecil to Chamberlain, 10 April 1933 (Cecil Papers, vol. IX).

5 The public manifestations are described at length in R. Bassett, *Democracy and Foreign Policy*

geographical scale of the conflict, which in Manchuria involved an area the size of France and Germany combined. More significant, however, was the nature of the fighting as exhibited to Western eyes at Shanghai between January and March 1932, involving as it did the use of tanks, aircraft and heavy artillery, and the destruction of civilian life and property in the suburb of Chapei. Correspondents had been filing reports which were calculated to shock their readers in a way which familiarity has subsequently rendered almost impossible:

In the middle of the war-torn area I saw an old Chinese woman sitting in an open field, weeping and wringing her hands, ignorant of all but the starkest externals of what was going on about her and entirely helpless to protect herself. Some distance to the right a Japanese soldier appeared . . . followed by several more behind. The leading soldier raised his rifle, aimed at the women and fired. He missed. The woman continued to weep, her face buried in her hands. The rifleman leisurely aimed again and fired. This time he scored with deadly accuracy. His bullet sent the helpless victim into eternity. His comrades pushed forward.[6]

It is not surprising that there should have been an increasing desire to have no hand in supplying weapons which might be used in such a fashion. But there was an additional reason why an arms embargo became attractive to many people, even when the Shanghai episode had been settled: the hope that here at least a way would be found of registering Britain's disapproval of the conflict as a whole and Japan's actions in particular. For by the end of 1932 it had become apparent to all but the most fervent champions of collective security that there was no possibility of either Britain or the United States resorting to economic sanctions in order to force Japan to disgorge Manchuria, however much some of the smaller states in the League might still clamour for action on these lines under Article 16 of the Covenant. Similarly, attempts to institute an unofficial boycott of Japanese goods as an alternative, while attracting a certain amount of support on the East coast of the United States, had scarcely got beyond the stage of enquiry and speculation in Britain, despite the private efforts of Gilbert Murray, Chairman of the Executive Committee of the League of Nations Union. Even Cecil had thought it 'useless' to attempt such a boycott.[7] Hence, an arms embargo was one of a dwindling number of gestures (the withdrawal

---

(London, 1952). The files of the press-cuttings library of the Royal Institute of International Affairs also contain a considerable amount of material.

6 *New York Times*, 24 February 1932.

7 For example, letters from Murray to the Executive Committee of the National Peace Council and to George Lansbury, 2 February 1932, and Lansbury's lukewarm and evasive reply of 3 February (Gilbert Murray Papers). Cecil to Philip Noel-Baker, 7 March 1932 (Cecil Papers, vol. XXXVII).

of ambassadors being another) which might still be made in what centre and left opinion found a highly frustrating situation.

It was not a gesture which was advocated with clarity and unanimity, however, and this no doubt contributed to the acquiescence which was to greet the eventual failure of the embargo. Two main categories of argument may be distinguished: that the ban should apply to both Japan and China as a means of restricting the scale of the conflict, or of bringing peace, or of freeing Britain from complicity in acts of destruction; and that it should apply to Japan alone, as a sanction against aggression and in support of the principles of the Covenant. Individuals and newspapers, however, are to be found wandering from one category to another, sometimes consciously, as the situation changed, sometimes in a muddle over ends and means.

Among those who at one time advocated an embargo on arms to both belligerents was Gilbert Murray, who described it in a letter to Cecil of November 1931 as one of the means of stopping the war 'without proceeding to the enormously heavy artillery of Article 16'.[8] In the same month, George Lansbury suggested in the Commons that this action should be urged upon all members of the League, and the General Council of the LNU followed suit, at least by implication, a few weeks later.[9] On 19 December the *New Statesman* called for such a policy in order that Britain should have 'no further share in shedding this blood', and during the following year both MPs and private individuals and groups continued to plead that the country should meet this 'acid test of [its] sincerity in desiring peace'.[10]

Already, however, the Japanese assault at Shanghai was increasing the demand for an embargo on arms to that country alone. In February, the Executive of the LNU proposed this as one of the penalties which should be inflicted on whichever of the belligerents (i.e. Japan) refused the West's offer of good offices to resolve the conflict, and a deputation discussed the situation with Simon at the Foreign Office.[11] Later in the month the *New Statesman* and the Independent Labour Party pronounced in the same sense, and the General Assembly of the Church of Scotland did so early in March.[12] A few people, notably Dr Maude Royden and her 'peace army'

8 Cecil Papers, vol. LXII.

9 Bassett, *Democracy and Foreign Policy*, pp. 27, 45. It is worth recalling that in a speech broadcast early in December, Cecil described the League as having had to cope with 'two great agencies of disorder . . ., Japanese militarism and Chinese anarchy'.

10 See, for example *Manchester Guardian*, 2 March and 20 May 1932, the latter issue containing a letter from the officers of various Cambridge University societies with a combined membership of 3000. Cf. Bassett, *Democracy and Foreign Policy*, p. 155.

11 FO 800/286.

12 *Manchester Guardian*, 3 March 1932; Bassett, *Democracy and Foreign Policy*, pp. 160–1. At the

went even further, attempting to prevent the departure of ships carrying supplies to Japan. And by February 1933, with the Lytton Report published and Japan as opposed as ever to conciliation, the ranks of those who discussed the possibility of instituting an arms embargo against her had swollen to include not only Lansbury and the Union of Democratic Control, but even Lord Lytton himself. [13]

The volume, though not the harmony, of these assorted voices reached its height during February, for it was then that the Japanese began their assault on Jehol, that the report completed by the League's Committee of 19 was adopted by the Assembly, and that the Japanese delegation withdrew from Geneva. On the 13th, the Executive of the LNU sent to the Foreign Office a resolution urging the Government to secure international agreement for the banning of arms supplies to any disputing state which refused to accept 'a decision or report by the League of Nations'. The idea of a different kind of international action – halting the flow of weapons to both Japan and China, as well as to Bolivia and Paraguay – was raised in the Commons two days later, and the *Daily Herald* (on the 16th), together with a joint meeting of the TUC General Council and Labour Party National Executive (on the 22nd) also proposed an embargo in respect of both parties to the Far Eastern dispute. In fact, the resolution passed by this last meeting provides a good example of the mixture of motives present at the time, for it went on to demand the application of a full economic boycott *against Japan alone* if that country rejected the League's proposals for a settlement; and as it became obvious that this was precisely what Japan intended to do, it was the concept of a *punitive* embargo against the aggressor which came to the fore. The *News Chronicle*, which had campaigned vigorously for this from February 20 onwards, was joined by the *New Statesman*, the *Manchester Guardian* and the *Daily Herald*. On the 22nd Lord Lytton appeared to speak in the same sense, though a day later he gave warning that practical considerations might require the embargo to be placed on China as well as Japan. In the Commons a small group of Conservatives, some connected with the LNU, put down a motion aimed at stopping supplies to Japan alone, and even *The Times*, which published a letter from Gilbert Murray on the subject on the 25th, supported the idea in a leader on the same day. Even so, it came as a considerable surprise (earlier ministerial answers having stressed that only international action could be considered) when, during a debate in the Commons on the 27th, Simon suddenly announced that the Government had decided, 'as from

---

Trades Union Congress in September, however, Bevin and others were to argue that it was impracticable to call for a ban on arms shipments to the Far East (ibid., pp. 225–7); *The Times*, 25 June 1932.

13 *Manchester Guardian*, 22 November 1932, 18, 21, 23, 24 February 1933.

today, and pending the opportunity of international consultation and
decision such as I hope for', not to issue further licences for the export of
arms to Japan or China.

Before examining the process by which the Government had arrived at
their decision, it is necessary to appreciate why they found themselves in an
exposed position over this issue in the first place. After all, armaments were
flowing into Japan and China from a considerable number of countries
besides Britain, the battle for orders among European firms being
especially fierce in China.[14] French supplies were arriving in that country
across her southern border, while the apparently substantial sales of French
arms to Japan was one element behind the persistent rumours of a secret
Franco-Japanese military understanding or even alliance.[15] Although it is
impossible to place any exact figure on such sales, the value of the shares
of firms like Hotchkiss and Creusot provides some indication of what was
taking place, leaping as they did in some cases from well under 1000 francs
in November 1931, to over 1500 francs by March 1932.[16] In the United
States the Administration refused to allow the Chinese to purchase
government surplus stocks, but the private supply of planes, weapons and
explosives continued.[17] Arms were also reported to be entering China from
or via the Soviet Union, with the Italians providing aeroplanes by 1933
if not earlier.[18] Weapons for the Far East were being shipped out of
Hamburg, some of them almost certainly coming from the Czech Skoda
works, and Heinkel were known to be building planes for China; several
other German firms were supplying munitions to both belligerents, despite
a denial by the German Embassy in Tokyo (which touchingly added that
its country was in any case permitted to manufacture only revolvers) and

14 See *Foreign Relations of the United States* (FRUS) 1932, IV, p. 588, where there is a
description of this competition given by a Belgian representative of the Fabrique National des
Armes de Guerre.
15 For examples of these rumours see FRUS, 1931, III, p. 387, and ibid., 1932, III, p. 170.
In February 1932, Simon had privately professed to believe that some such understanding
existed (State Department, file 793.94/4255), but by the late summer of that year Paris was
taking a firmly pro-League line, and rejected secret Japanese offers of an alliance (DDF, I,
nos. 3, 8, 148, 168, 202).
16 See *Le Populaire*, 26 February 1932; *Manchester Guardian*, 29 February 1932; *New York
Times*, 4 February 1932.
17 See FRUS, 1932, IV, p. 588; State Department file 793.94/4652; and D. Pearson and
C. Brown, *The Diplomatic Game* (London, 1935), p. 353. The fate of attempts to pass embargo
legislation in the United States is set out in R. Divine, *The Illusion of Neutrality* (Chicago,
1962).
18 FRUS, 1932, IV, p. 70; 1933, III, p. 285; State Department 793.94/4726.

various German import-export firms in China were selling arms with the encouragement of the German Ministry of Defence.[19]

Of what amounted, therefore, to a substantial trade, British firms had not secured a particularly large part, their sales for 1932 (as recorded by the Board of Trade) being worth only £500,000 to Japan and under £100,000 to China.[20] Licences issued during February 1933 covered only 20 rifles, 6,200,000 cartridges, 3 bomb racks, 3 bomb sights and 3 gun cameras (all to China), with an application being received shortly afterwards to sell 150 machine guns to Japan.[21] Britain's peculiar position sprang, not from the extent of her business, but from her government's powers of control. None of the other arms-manufacturing countries had a system of state regulation for such exports, with the exception of the US President's power to prohibit the sale of arms to China when conditions of domestic violence obtained there.[22] When, early in 1932, Senator Dill and Representative Fish introduced resolutions which would have allowed the banning of arms to any warring nation, they had been headed off by the State Department, and deputations from various peace organizations got no further.[23] In January 1933, the Secretary of State, Henry Stimson, managed to override the lobbying of armaments interests and to persuade President Hoover to ask Congress for the power to institute an embargo on arms which would 'be used in international conflicts'; but the request was held up in the Senate, and the House Committee on Foreign Affairs wanted to trim it to apply to countries of the American continent. By 22 February it was clear that nothing further would be done until the Roosevelt Administration had taken office.[24]

The British Government therefore stood alone, for under the Arms Export Prohibition Order of 1931, all overseas sales had to be licensed in Whitehall.[25] In consequence they were particularly exposed to the cry that they should 'give a lead' to the rest of the world. Less specific, but

19 State Department 793.94/4454, 4606, 4823, 5767; *New York Times*, 26 February 1932. The Chinese issued figures of German arms supplies for 1931 and 1932 amounting to 3.4 million Reichsmarks per annum, although the Foreign Ministry in Berlin - largely ignorant of the efforts of its Defence Ministry - claimed that Swedish, Czech, and Swiss material had been included in those totals. (I am grateful to my colleague, Dr John Chapman, for this information.)

20 Minutes of the Disarmament Committee of the Cabinet, 22 February 1932 (CAB 21/379).

21 *The Times*, 14 March 1933; for licences issued in March 1933, see *Manchester Guardian* of 17 April.

22 See FRUS, 1932, III, p. 452; 1933, III, p. 559.

23 *United States Daily*, 29 January–10 February 1932; Pearson and Brown, *The Diplomatic Game*, p. 352; State Department 793.94/4802.

24 FRUS, 1933, III, p. 231; Pearson and Drew, *The Diplomatic Game*, pp. 353–8.

25 The legal position is set out in *Documents on British Foreign Policy, 1919–1939* (DBFP), Second Series, IX, no. 427.

undoubtedly present, was also the Government's awareness that they were open to the accusation of indifference to the rights and wrongs of the Far Eastern conflict and to the cause of collective security, or indeed that they were simply and unashamedly pro-Japanese. However incomplete and inaccurate these charges, which have been repeated by historians, what must be noted is that by the end of 1932 they had become a commonplace in some sections of international, as well as of domestic, opinion. On 23 December, for example, following a disastrously equivocal speech to the League Assembly by Simon on the 7th, the senior American diplomat on the spot reported that 'the struggle at Geneva is seen as no longer between China and Japan or between the League and Japan, but rather between Great Britain and the League';[26] it was a comment which echoed that of Captain Liddell Hart in March, when he 'doubted whether the old idea of "perfide Albion" had ever been more wide-spread.'[27]

The dangers of seeming to confirm such criticism were apparent. As Sir John Pratt wrote in a Foreign Office memorandum of December: 'A false step now, or even the appearance of any hesitation might arouse the abiding hostility of the Chinese and severely compromise our position both with the League and in America'.[28] Thus, with considerable reservations over the undefined length of the commitment, the Cabinet had reluctantly come to accept by early February 1933 that they would have to join in a League declaration of non-recognition of 'Manchukuo', and that some-thing amounting to a condemnation of Japan could not be avoided at Geneva. The dilemma arose from what were seen as the 'embarrassing and even dangerous' consequences of such a condemnation – the blow to dis-armament hopes if Japan were to leave the League; the increased pressure for some kind of sanctions against that country; and the likelihood, repeatedly stressed by the British Ambassador in Tokyo, and agreed by all his Western colleagues, of Japan's 'running amok' in the Far East if economic measures were adopted against her, in a situation where the Chiefs of Staff and Committee of Imperial Defence had bluntly spelled out Britain's powerlessness to defend her trade, her possessions or her Commonwealth against a Japanese attack.[29]

At the same time domestic criticism, which had faded away after the Shanghai episode, had been mounting again since the publication of the

26 FRUS, 1932, IV, p. 451.
27 Letter from Philip Noel-Baker to Cecil, 7 March 1932 (Cecil Papers, vol. XXXVII); cf. *New York Times*, 19 September 1932.
28 FO 371, F74/33/10.
29 See, for example, Simon's memorandum for the Cabinet, 19 November 1932 (CP 404(32) in CAB 24/235); Cabinet Conclusions of 8 February 1933 (CAB 23/75); Chiefs of Staff Annual Report, March 1932 (CP 104(32) in CAB 24/229).

Lytton Report in September, and was no doubt all the more irritating for its crucial ignorance of the weakness, amounting almost to a confidence trick, of the country's presence in the Far East. Among these critics, the body most capable of causing the Government embarrassment over the condemnation of Japan was undoubtedly the LNU, which had Cecil and Grey as its joint Presidents (though their views on the crisis were markedly different), about 3000 branches with nearly a million members, and Gilbert Murray in the key position at the head of its Executive Committee. More than anything else, the embargo was seen by those who instituted it as a gesture towards domestic opinion, and therefore a series of communications between Murray and Simon – who were old acquaintances – in the immediately preceding period may be taken as a final and significant element of the background to the decision itself.

On 14 December 1932, Murray wrote to the Foreign Secretary to warn him

that opinion in the Union is greatly worked up over the Japanese crisis. They fear that you are going too far in the direction of conciliation . . . and that any failure to stand firm for the Lytton Report and the non-recognition of Manchu-Kuo will result in a betrayal of the League and the whole new order in international politics . . . Cecil and I used strong influence with the Council to prevent some public message of the sort being sent to you . . . Letters of indignation are pouring in daily.[30]

The result of this letter was an invitation for Murray to call on Simon at his home in Oxfordshire at the end of the month, when the Foreign Secretary went out of his way – including showing his visitor two confidential Foreign Office papers – to give a reassurance that the Government would not default over the Lytton Report, but also to explain the constraints within which British policy had to be formulated. Simon's subsequent note was that the talk had been 'fairly satisfactory', and he reinforced his efforts by sending Murray a copy of the remarks he had addressed to the representatives of China and Japan on the subject of the Government's readiness to pronounce on the merits of the dispute if conciliation failed. 'It is a relief to me to see your letter', Murray replied, 'and I shall now be able to reassure many of my friends on the Left, of course without quoting or hinting at my authority'.[31] In his own account of the meeting, written to Cecil, Murray accepted that 'with her trade disappearing, her unemployment increasing, and her currency off the gold standard, Great Britain simply dare not shoulder the responsibilities which she undertook when she

30 FO 800/287 and Murray Papers.
31 Letters of 29 and 30 December 1932 (Murray Papers).

was a strong power'. To this extent, Simon's message had clearly got home; but the writer added that nevertheless he felt 'that cowardice combined with trickiness is probably the worst policy'.[32]

Murray was as good as his word to Simon, and worked to secure a moderate resolution by his Executive which would not 'say beforehand what might be done if Japan refused to come into conference, because that seemed like assuming wrong action on her part'. He also declined to sign a petition being organized by Lord Davies (the leading Welsh member of the Union), which called for the application against Japan of Article 16 of the Covenant, and at Simon's prompting wrote to the editor of the *Manchester Guardian* to ask whether the Foreign Secretary's efforts at Geneva were not possibly being reported with undue harshness.[33] There were many in the LNU, however, who were straining to throw everything into the fight against the Government and the Japanese, as Davies' Welsh Executive Committee demonstrated when it passed and transmitted to the Prime Minister a resolution calling for an immediate embargo on arms to Japan, followed by the severance of all diplomatic, financial and economic relations if that country persisted in its refusal to comply with the League's recommendations.[34] If Murray was to restrain this mounting impatience, it was of some help that he could at least agree that there should be 'a great national agitation against the supply of arms to Japan'.[35]

In a letter of 26 January, he summarized for Simon's benefit – and with a clearly implied warning and call for action – the state of opinion among the members of the Union's Executive Committee. They were reluctant, he wrote, to take any steps which might 'weaken your hands in dealing with the crisis', or to encourage any action which might precipitate war or leave Britain unsupported. On the other hand they were unanimous in desiring an international agreement whereby no state would negotiate with 'Manchukuo' without first informing everyone else, a denial by Britain of all financial aid to Japan, and an arms embargo against that country. 'The feeling on this (last) point is extremely strong', Murray added. In conclusion he warned Simon that those on 'the Left' still favoured a resort to Article 16,[36] and on 31 January, in company with Austen Chamberlain, he again visited the Foreign Secretary. 'Gilbert Murray goes with me to

32 Letter of 4 January 1933 (ibid.).

33 Murray to Davies, 13 January; to Carruthers, 10 January; to Davies, 27 January; to Crozier, 23 January (Murray Papers); Simon to Murray, 18 January (FO 800/288); Murray to Simon, 21 January (FO 371, F 881/33/10).

34 FO 371, F 586/33/10; cf. a letter of 16 March to Murray from members of the LNU headquarters staff, calling for a stronger line to be taken (Murray Papers).

35 Murray to Davies, 27 January; cf. Murray to Salvador de Madariaga, 14 January (Murray Papers).

36 FO 371, F 881/33/10.

ginger me up', wrote Chamberlain to his wife, 'and I go with him to tone him down and we both go to keep the Union from taking violent courses.' On the day after the interview, Chamberlain reported that he thought he and his Chairman could 'hold the Union Committee with the material given them and prevent any follies', whilst Simon wrote to say that he was going further into the arms question, which was 'one of the most *intractable* of subjects.'[37]

Murray had got the Foreign Secretary moving in the required direction, helping him along by sending in his Committee's resolution on February 13, and by his letter in *The Times* on the 25th. But Simon was about to demonstrate once more the truth of Eden's later remark, that 'his brilliant analytical mind hated to take decisions. As a consequence he was tempted to dodge them, for which there was always an ingenious reason'.[38] Murray's cause – even in the modified form of an embargo on both Japan and China – would probably have been lost, but for the Chancellor of the Exchequer, Neville Chamberlain.

The question of what policy should be adopted over arms exports to the Far East had been wrestled with inside the Foreign Office during the Shanghai crisis, when the decision reached had been to prevent the supply of Government-owned stocks, but to continue to license private sales on the grounds that a unilateral prohibition would merely penalize British manufacturers to the benefit of their foreign rivals.[39] Simon now raised the issue again in a memorandum for the Cabinet, dated 18 February, which also reviewed the wider decisions which would have to be taken on the Far East in the coming weeks. Rejecting any resort to sanctions under Article 16, and pointing out that if Japan were to leave the League the prospects for disarmament would be worsened, the Foreign Secretary asked his colleagues what should be done in response to the likely pressure for an arms embargo, and appended the recent resolution on the subject by the LNU Executive.[40] This memorandum was discussed in Cabinet on the morning of the 22nd, when it was agreed that the draft report of the League's Committee of 19 should be endorsed by Britain, but that if

37 Austen Chamberlain Papers, AC/6/1/902–1062. Chamberlain himself favoured an embargo against both Japan and China; though aware that this was 'hardly fair to China', he believed that an embargo against Japan alone 'might lead to very dangerous complications'. (Letter of 25 February in ibid.)
38 Lord Avon, *Facing the Dictators* (London, 1962), p. 28. This trait of Simon's was widely observed and noted in the private papers of other members of the Government.
39 DBFP, IX, no. 427. The Bolivia–Paraguay case was a much easier one, and Britain proposed to America a joint arms embargo for those countries in January 1933.
40 CP 42(33), in CAB 24/238.

necessary the country would have to dissociate itself from any move to apply Article 16; as for arms supplies, this was referred to the Cabinet's Disarmament Committee which was meeting that afternoon.[41]

The possibilities and objections considered at this Committee were to dominate all subsequent discussion of the subject.[42] Simon's opening comments on the various alternatives were that to do nothing was a course 'he did not think parliamentary and public opinion would tolerate'; that unilaterally to stop supplies to Japan alone would increase that country's resentment against Britain – and, he noted (one feels with relief), would be going further than even the LNU resolution, which called on the Government to obtain an international agreement; that to declare Britain's readiness to join such an international embargo on sales to Japan 'would be approved by moderate supporters of the League', would force the issue into the open at Geneva and would involve cooperation with Washington, but would also raise the possibility of Japanese retaliation in the form of a blockade of China and the seizure of arms destined for that country; and that to stop the supply of arms to both Japan and China would be likely to injure the latter above all, since her domestic industry was the far less developed of the two. Each option, in other words, was open to objections on the grounds of danger or of ineffectiveness; but there remained the first consideration Simon had mentioned – the image of public opinion which was now embedded in the Foreign Secretary's mind and that of some of his colleagues, and which pointed towards the necessity of taking *some* action, however limited its effect.

The discussion which followed concentrated on practical matters, rather than 'the moral duty . . . to supply arms to the aggrieved nation', since 'the fact that the two countries concerned (were) China and Japan eliminated the possibility of taking any' such academic decision'. It was recalled, rather, that an embargo which embraced China might harm Britain's general trade with her, that America could not act until legislation had passed through Congress, and that British industry stood to lose orders worth about £1000 a day. This last point was stressed by Hailsham, the Secretary of State for War (who conveniently received a telephone message at the time to the effect that British firms were already sub-contracting abroad for fear of an embargo), and by Hankey in his capacity of Secretary to the Committee of Imperial Defence, a body which was gravely concerned at the decline in the country's armaments manufacturing capacity,

---

41 CAB 23/75. In describing the ensuing divisions of opinion within the Cabinet, I have been greatly and most kindly helped by discussion with Captain S. W. Roskill, RN, who has the (closed) Hankey Papers in his care and is writing a biography of that omniscient Whitehall figure. (This has now been published.)
42 CAB 21/379.

especially in the face of rising tension in Europe. [43] MacDonald's conclusion was that the matter would have to be discussed at Geneva, in spite of his disillusionment with the League: 'it was quite intolerable that a decision as to what the big States do should rest with such small States'. Finally Neville Chamberlain proposed a month's embargo, to be applied to Japan and China while negotiations were carried on with other arms-producing countries, and it was agreed to put a recommendation to this effect before the full Cabinet that evening. There it was modified under renewed warnings of the likelihood of losing large contracts and of increasing unemployment. Licences would be suspended without a time limit being specified, but two weeks was mentioned as a possibility. The small likelihood of securing an international agreement within such a period was not openly admitted, but must have been in many minds. [44]

Opinions in Whitehall and the Government were by now becoming more sharply defined. According to Hankey, permanent officials in the Foreign Office, Board of Trade and Service Departments were strongly opposed to an embargo, and these views were reflected in the Cabinet where Hailsham, Runciman (Board of Trade), Eyres-Monsell (Admiralty) and Betterton (Labour) were the strongest critics of the proposal. They were joined by Cunliffe-Lister (Colonial Secretary), who may have been influenced by considerations of Britain's need to maintain an air-defence industry especially – as Lord Swinton he was to transfer to the Air Ministry in 1935. MacDonald, for his part, although predisposed against the arms trade, was unwilling to place Britain in an exposed position in the Far East, and in any case was by now a tired and ineffectual man. Baldwin, too, was by his own admission a jaded figure, and was increasingly preoccupied with the distant threat from Germany. [45]

With Simon vacillating between the promptings of Murray and the advice of his own officials, the anti-embargo group would almost certainly have got their way had they not run into the formidable opposition of Neville Chamberlain. His position in the Cabinet was strong. As Chancellor, he had taken on the major responsibility of dragging the country out of its economic and financial crisis of 1931 (or what was thought to be one at the time), and had helped to salvage the stormy Ottawa Conference in the summer of 1932. Not only was he particularly

---

43 See the minutes of the CID for 6 April 1933 (CAB 2/5). For details, see the Ninth and Tenth Reports of the Principal Supply Officers' Committee (PSO, 350, 404), and correspondence in the Weir Papers. The conclusion was that 'our preparations for the turnover of industry from peace to war purposes are behind those of the principal Powers, including America'. Cf. CAB 27/551.
44 CAB 23/75.
45 See Middlemas and Barnes, *Baldwin*, p. 727.

well placed to play down, as he did, the economic importance of Britain's armaments trade, but as a leading advocate of the need to renew close relations with Japan, he could scarcely be accused of ignoring the dangers of alienating that country by an embargo. Above all, amid weakness and vacillation his forceful personality, however limited the vision behind it – and in some ways *because* of those limits – was able to pull a decision his way once his mind was made up, and on this matter he was clear. 'We cannot . . . fold our arms like those smug Americans', he wrote to one of his sisters on 25 February, 'and say we cannot help it if our people *will* sell ammunition and machine guns'.[46] Hankey noted him as saying that the arms industry was a beastly business, and that in time of war Britain could in any case obtain supplies from the United States. This distaste for selling arms was not peculiar to Chamberlain – MacDonald uttered similar sentiments – but the Chancellor wrote privately that only the rumbustious Dominions Secretary, Jimmy Thomas, followed his lead without wavering.

Chamberlain's fixity of purpose contrasted above all with Simon's equivocation. Having initially pointed in the direction of some kind of embargo, the latter, according to a delighted Hankey, was now 'got at' by Foreign Office officials and produced on 24 February a further memorandum for the Cabinet in which he questioned the decision taken two days earlier on the grounds that a fortnight was inadequate both for conducting international discussions and for suspending exports. Given his colleagues' initial reluctance to contemplate even a month's trial, the clear implication of Simon's paper (though characteristically it remained only an implication) was that in the circumstances the gesture contemplated was not worth making.[47] Reluctantly, MacDonald agreed to reconvene the Cabinet, which met on the 27th to hear the Foreign Secretary describe the disappointing preliminary replies which had been received from other countries – Belgium unwilling to join anything but a universal action, Holland specifying that oil would have to be exempted, the United States unable to act, at least until Congress met in mid-April, and only France responding favourably to the prospect of any step calculated to uphold the Covenant.

If the French reply faintly raised the idea of an embargo against Japan alone, a letter which was read out from the absent First Lord of the Admiralty swiftly ruled it out again. 'We cannot go into a scheme of this kind', wrote Eyres-Monsell, 'without dire risk of war', and he conveyed secret Admiralty intelligence to the effect that the Japanese had a plan for attacking Singapore, and possibly a force standing by at that moment to

46 Neville Chamberlain Papers.
47 CP 48(33) in CAB 24/238.

execute it in the event of a confrontation with Britain. The information may well have been inaccurate,[48] but it was the image and not the reality which counted, and its unsettling effects were reinforced by Hailsham's warnings on behalf of the War Office. There would be no gesture against Japan alone, even though those present agreed that this was what 'ought to be adopted on purely moral grounds if practical considerations could be disregarded'. But although it was also generally agreed that the most likely outcome was the continuation of arms supplies to the Far East, Chamberlain stuck out for the view that it was not morally defensible to shelter behind the likely refusal of other states to participate in an embargo; moreover Baldwin (to Hankey's disappointment) and Simon (to Hankey's disgust) failed to support Hailsham and Runciman. It was finally agreed, therefore, that a provisional and unilateral embargo covering Japan and China would be announced in the Commons that day, though without specifying a time limit and – more significantly – without taking the lead at Geneva in the matter, since the only course acceptable to the majority there would be the dangerous one of a prohibition against Japan alone.[49]

In other words, a gesture, but no more, would be made on behalf of the British public. This is clearly how the decision was seen by those who had taken it. 'I got my way about the Embargo', Chamberlain wrote to one of his sisters, 'as S[tanley] B[aldwin] said, by knowing my mind and sticking to it.' He had been surprised by the poor reception accorded the announcement abroad, especially in Japan, since she would scarcely be harmed; other states were no doubt annoyed because of their 'bad conscience', but the action 'was not taken to please them but to satisfy our own people'. In any case he thought that a Japanese victory was about to bring to an end the whole violent episode in the Far East.[50]

Chamberlain had got his way, but the opposition persisted in their efforts to have the decision reversed. Hankey wrote to the Chancellor to demonstrate once more the vital importance of Britain's armaments industry in the existing world situation, and at a meeting of the Cabinet's Disarmament Committee on 5 March Runciman cited five cases in which an arms contract had already been secured by French or US firms over the heads of the impotent British.[51] Once again, therefore, the matter came

48 Professor James Crowley, author of *Japan's Quest for Autonomy* (Princeton, NJ, 1966), has informed the writer that he has seen no evidence for the existence of such a plan or force in the Japanese archives.

49 CAB 23/75. In his Commons speech later in the day, Simon used a phrase which, taken out of context, was widely interpreted as meaning that Britain's main concern was to keep out of trouble. Even Murray felt obliged to write a surprised letter to *The Spectator*, though adding (correctly) that no doubt Sir John 'only meant that he was quite rightly determined not to get involved in war with Japan' (Murray Papers).

50 Letter of 4 March (Neville Chamberlain Papers). 51 CAB 21/379.

before the full Cabinet, on 6 March, and Simon reported on the further replies which had been received to Britain's inquiries abroad – all of them decidedly cautious, with a clear negative from Washington. This mounting discouragement swiftly exposed the half-heartedness which had underlain the initial decision. It was agreed that if a question were put in the Commons, it should be revealed that foreign firms were still executing orders for the Far East, and that if the Prime Minister were to find the attitude of other states unsatisfactory during his forthcoming visit with Simon to Geneva, he would inform the Cabinet with a view to the embargo being lifted. [52] The early termination of the gesture thus became a probability; a week later it was a fact.

For those in Britain whose main concern had been to escape from the evils of the arms trade, Simon's announcement on February 27 had been a moment for rejoicing. But those like Cecil who sought some constraint on the aggressor nation received the news with only modified rapture, accepting it as no more than a preliminary step towards some form of sanctions. [53] As for the right-wing press, it was highly critical of the blow to British industry and to Anglo-Japanese relations, while, as Chamberlain had noted with surprise, no one abroad seemed pleased with the decision either. The Japanese were indignant. The Chinese were angered by a move which was bound to penalize them more than Japan, and to their own tart remarks were added those of the British Chamber of Commerce at Shanghai. [54] In Washington there had been no change from Stimson's initial reaction when approached about the idea on 24 February: 'The world was delivering a most forceful judgment against Japan, and my hunch was that (it) might lose force if we attempted to couple it with ineffective material action'. An embargo, thought Stimson – even one against Japan alone – would hurt China above all; and in any event Congressional approval would not be forthcoming for some time. Hoover, especially, was at this time fairly quivering with apprehension at anything which might remotely look like a sanction against Japan, while the powerful Senator Borah declared publicly that the British move also discriminated against China: 'I don't care what London does: I am not for it'. [55] In Geneva, too, the move

52 CAB 23/75.
53 Lord Davies described it as 'a cowardly and probably futile effort to avoid "trouble" and evade the responsibilities in which we . . . are pledged under Article 16'. *The Times*, 1 March.
54 In a telegram to the China Association in London, the Chamber described the measure as one 'which merely penalized British trade and excites Chinese resentment'. China Association, General Committee Papers, 1933. Cf. FRUS, 1933, III, p. 219.
55 FRUS, 1933, III, pp. 204, 209, 217; *Manchester Guardian*, 28 February 1933. Walter Lippmann had written against the idea of an arms embargo a year before: *Interpretations: 1931–2*

had been received with the surprised assumption that it could harm only China, and was bound to be ineffective.[56]

Meanwhile the Japanese had turned what some had expected to be a prolonged battle for Jehol into a Chinese rout. The town fell on 4 March, and the whole province was in Japanese hands two weeks later. It was an added argument on the side of those who wished to forget about an arms embargo, as Simon found – and accepted – when he raised the subject with the French Ambassador on the 8th. De Fleuriau observed:

Mais c'est une affaire finie, il n'y a plus de guerre; en fait il n'y en a que ces opérations militaires auxquelles j'ai assisté en Chine, et ou un parti avance et l'autre recule sans se battre.

Sir John Simon m'a répliqué que, si les événements me donnaient raison, il n'y aurait pas lieu de continuer la discussion de l'embargo.[57]

Nor did Simon push the matter any harder in Geneva, telling the US Minister in Switzerland that Britain had acted only 'to draw attention to the matter', and 'emphatically' agreeing with Stimson's view that an embargo was serving no useful purpose.[58] On 12 March he despatched a telegram to the Cabinet, giving the opinion of MacDonald and himself that no international agreement would be forthcoming and that the decision of 27 February should therefore be rescinded.[59] This was endorsed by the Cabinet on the following day, discussion being concerned less with this matter than with the threatened breakdown of the Disarmament Conference. Baldwin announced the lifting of the embargo in the Commons that afternoon.

There was little reaction in the British press or in Parliament, though it was denounced by the *News Chronicle* as a 'weak-kneed surrender', and left individuals 'grieved at the reversion to a course that has no moral justification'.[60] Organizations like the LNU and newspapers like the *Manchester Guardian* had, after all, stressed that only *international* action would be adequate, and that, apparently would not be forthcoming despite Britain's example. The final comment from those who had hoped through an embargo to impose penalties on Japan may be left to Murray, who was

---

(London, 1933), p. 207. The *New York Times* dismissed the embargo on 2 March as ineffective, and probably deviously motivated.

56 *Manchester Guardian*, 1 March. Cf. *Le Populaire*, 1 March.

57 DDF, II, no. 383.

58 FRUS, 1933, pp. III, 232, 235.

59 CP 64(33) in CAB 24/239.

60 Letter to Baldwin from Vyvyan Adams, MP, 13 March (Baldwin Papers, vol. 120): cf. Bassett, *Democracy and Foreign Policy*, pp. 494ff.

to reflect on the difficulties involved in non-military sanctions in general during a broadcast in 1955 which he called 'Memories of the Peace Movement':

Events produced a League much weaker and a group of aggressors much stronger and more daring than we had anticipated . . . [and] boycott always proved an unsatisfactory instrument. It only worked as a threat when the victim was very weak. It meant great commercial loss to all who applied it faithfully, and offered immense temptation to any nation who broke it. Worst of all, if the war maker knew that the League would only use measures short of war, all he had to do was to treat such measures as an unpardonable aggression and threaten to meet them by a declaration of war. [61]

These and related problems had been present in the minds of those responsible for British policy in 1933. On that occasion, Murray and those for whom he spoke had at least achieved something which does not happen often in international politics: the deflection of a state's foreign policy away from its immediate economic and strategic interests for the sake of a moral consideration. What were termed in Cabinet 'practical realities' speedily reasserted themselves, however. And as was to be the case over Abyssinia three years later, the public appeared ready to acquiesce once some kind of gesture had been made. Denying arms to Britain's own forces continued for some years to appeal more widely and strongly than did denying them to others.

61 Murray Papers.

11

The British Cause and Indian
Nationalism in 1940:
an Officer's Rejection of Empire

This is a footnote to history, no more. It concerns an individual of no
fame, and in terms of the mighty events and issues of 1940, of little
account. The embarrassment he caused the British authorities was soon
removed; his encounter with the famous, in the shape of Nehru, was not
such as to earn a place in the history of India's struggle for independence.
One cannot even claim, as is the case with those recent, fascinating
reminiscences of *The District Officer in India*,[1] that the single man represents
many others whose experiences at the time were essentially similar: indeed,
the behaviour of the individual at the centre of the episode described below
was such as to make him extremely atypical. Nevertheless, history should
find room for the odd, as for the failure. Moreover, it will be argued below
that the issues faced in his own mind in 1940 by the young British officer
concerned were of significance if one chose to juxtapose his country's proclaimed war aims with its imperial presence in India; were seen in this way
by Indians themselves; and by 1942 were to be brought before the Government in London, not least in the context of American attitudes towards the
campaign for Indian independence.

In August 1940, Jawaharlal Nehru, as leader of the All-India Congress
Committee, had arrived in Bombay for a crucial series of meetings of his
Planning Committee.[2] Nehru and his colleagues were already at
loggerheads with the administration headed by the Viceroy and Governor-
General, Lord Linlithgow. Reacting strongly against Linlithgow's failure

Reproduced from the *Journal of Imperial and Commonwealth History*, 10 (1982), pp. 344–59.

1 R. Hunt and J. Harrison (eds), *The District Officer in India, 1930–1947* (London, 1980).
2 The records of the Planning Committee are in file G-22, part II, All India Congress Papers
(Nehru Memorial Library, New Delhi).

to consult them before declaring India to be at war with Germany in September 1939, Congress had made its support for Britain in her new struggle conditional upon a promise of independence for India soon after the war and the provision of places for Indians in the central government in Delhi meanwhile. When such pledges were not forthcoming from London, Congress governments in the provinces had resigned in October 1939.[3]

Now, in August 1940, Linlithgow had at last made a statement on constitutional matters. He offered, however, only the assurance that Dominion status for India was Britain's aim, that a representative body would be set up some time after the war to devise a constitution, and that in the meantime certain Indians would be invited to join the Viceroy's Executive and War Advisory Councils. It was not enough for Congress, whose forthcoming rejection was to be all the more fierce in that Linlithgow's statement had appeared to leave the way open for that eventual outcome which was being sought by Muhammad Jinnah and his Muslim League: a separate Pakistan. The consequence was to be the launching by Gandhi in the following October of a civil disobedience movement on the part of tens of thousands in the subcontinent. Nehru himself was to be arrested before the year was out.

It is relevant to the story which follows to note that Indian nationalists were correct when they cast doubt upon the intentions and goodwill of both the Viceroy and the Prime Minister in London. In his appeal to the Indian people to rally to the anti-Nazi cause in September 1939, Linlithgow had spoken of the dangers threatening 'our civilization'. His private belief, however, was that, far from sharing a civilization with Britain, India had 'no natural association with the Empire', from which it was 'alien by race, history and religion'; that Britain's role there rested ultimately upon force; and that the essential question (to which his own preferred answer was an affirmative) was 'whether . . . whatever the feeling of India, we intend to stay in this country for our own reasons . . .'.[4]

As for Churchill, he rejected all thought of independence for India and was strongly averse to venturing upon 'the slippery slope of concessions'. To him, 'the Hindu/Moslem feud' was to be welcomed as 'a bulwark of British rule' in the sub-continent, whilst his subsequent resistance to the

---

3 On the setting in terms of constitutional disputes between Britain and India at this time, see, for example, N. Mansergh (ed.), *The Transfer of Power, 1942–7:* vol. 1. *The Cripps Mission* (London, 1970); B. N. Pandey, *The Break-up of British India* (London, 1969); S. Gopal, *Jawaharlal Nehru.* vol. 1 (London, 1975); B. R. Tomlinson, *The Political Economy of the Raj, 1914–1947* (London, 1979). On the racial issue in particular, see C. Thorne, 'Racial Aspect of the Far Eastern War of 1941–1945, *Proceedings of the British Academy, 1980–81* (London, 1982).

4 See C. Thorne, *Allies of a Kind: The United States, Britain, and the War Against Japan, 1941–1945* (London and New York, 1978) p. 62.

proposal to send additional food supplies to India during the dreadful Bengal famine of 1943 was privately to be described by his Secretary of State for India, Leo Amery, as 'Hitler-like'.[5] It is also worth recalling the conclusion that was to be drawn by the new Viceroy, Lord Wavell, who took over from Linlithgow in 1943, after his initial discussions in London: 'I have discovered that the Cabinet is not honest in its expressed desire to make progress in India'.[6]

In short, though independence was in fact only seven years away, from an Indian point of view in the summer of 1940, and not without reason, there seemed little prospect of obtaining a satisfactory answer to that pertinent and 'crucial question' which the *Bombay Chronicle* (recalling the behaviour of the Western powers after the First World War) had posed in the previous September:

Is the present war imperialistic? Or, more accurately, is Britain's policy in it imperialistic? If Britain is out to maintain the status quo besides destroying Nazism, it follows that she wants to maintain imperialism, including her own in India . . . She has yet to establish her *bona fides*, and the [Congress] Working Committee rightly contends that 'if Great Britain fights for the maintenance and extension of Democracy, then she must necessarily end Imperialism in her own possessions and . . . the Indian people must have the right of Self-Determination . . . and must guide their own policy'. . . . The destruction of Hitlerism . . . must mean the end of the domination of one nation over another.[7]

During the August meetings of the Congress Planning Committee, Nehru was staying at the Bombay home of his sister, and on the day in question had returned there for lunch. He was interrupted in that meal, however, by an uninvited caller – a caller who made him forget for a while his haste to return to the Committee's afternoon session. For the man who presented himself at the door was no ordinary visitor. He was dressed in khadi: in the homespun shirt, loose pyjama trousers and cap worn by many of the natives of the subcontinent, a symbol of defiance against the purchase of imported clothing materials. But he was not Indian. He was a British Army officer, and he had come, not only to seek Nehru's advice, but to offer him his services.[8]

---

5 Ibid., pp. 5–6, 60–62, 345–6, 474.

6 P. Moon (ed.), *Wavell: The Viceroy's Journal* (London, 1973), entry for 8 October 1943, and passim; also, for example, Wavell to Ismay, 8 February 1944, Ismay Papers (King's College, London), IV/Con/2/3.

7 *Bombay Chronicle*, 16 September 1939.

8 This description of events is contained in Nehru to Gandhi, 2 October 1940, Nehru Papers (Nehru Memorial Library, New Delhi), Correspondence, vol. 26.

Convinced of the justice of the Indian nationalist cause and unwilling to play a part in the defence of an Empire whose existence he could not justify, the young Englishman was bent upon leaving the Army. He had, it seemed, disposed of his uniform and had sought out Nehru in the hope that the latter could somehow help him to stay in India as a private individual, and could make some use of him in the struggle for Indian independence. And as if this ambition were not remarkable enough in the circumstances of 1940 (when Britain was fighting for her very existence and acceptance of patriotic duty was the norm), the newcomer also revealed that he was descended from the general who had conquered Sind for the Empire a hundred years earlier, and who had subsequently become Commander-in-Chief of the Army in India.

Nehru's startling visitor was Second Lieutenant Charles Napier of the Northamptonshire Regiment. It is possible that he is alive today; but that is one of the questions which the writer is at present unable to answer.[9] Indeed, it is an incomplete inquiry which is being reported here, but perhaps one that, in its way, is all the more intriguing for that. It should also be emphasized at the outset that the actions taken by the authorities in India against Napier and recorded below appear in retrospect not only predictable but entirely understandable: in other words, that this is a story without villains. It concerns a confrontation between men of totally differing outlooks and priorities. At the same time, however, it provides something of a microcosm of an underlying dilemma concerning imperial policies in the context of a struggle fought in the name of freedom. The priority that had to be given to sheer survival in the early years of the war, together with a natural preoccupation with developments nearer home, concealed the dilemma from many in Britain; so, too, did the exigencies of military confrontation for many – probably most – of those who were to

9 Attempts to trace what happened to Charles Napier after 1941 have been made with the kind assistance of the Northamptonshire Regiment and of the historian of the Napier family, Mrs Priscilla Napier. Other lines of inquiry that have so far failed to bear fruit include ones directed to various banks and the Ministry of Pensions and National Insurance, as well as those pursued through the records of wartime deaths in the Services, of expatriate deaths in India up to independence, and of deaths in the United Kingdom from the end of the war onwards. Telephone contacts with every C. J. Napier listed in United Kingdom directories have also drawn a blank. As for documentary evidence on the 1940 episode itself, records of courts-martial for the period remain closed. On an India Office Library file – also closed – relating to Napier, see note 32 below. Subsequent to the publication of this article, I learned that Napier worked for the India Office Library for a period after the war, having taken a degree in Indo-Aryan at the School of Oriental and African Studies in London. He later returned briefly to India as principal of a public [i.e. private] school in Bihar, where his insistence on wearing khadi and speaking Hindi again apparently led to difficulties – this time with school governors and parents who were looking for an English Englishman, so to speak. The irony scarcely needs underlining.

fight the Japanese from and in Imperial territories themselves in South and Southeast Asia. Even so, there were those, both within and outside official circles, who were aware of the pressing need for new attitudes and policies towards the Empire: Duff Cooper and Ernest Bevin within the Government, for example; the Governor of Burma (Sir Reginald Dorman-Smith), Dr Margery Perham, and, subsequently, Lord Mountbatten as Supreme Allied Commander, South-East Asia.[10] What makes Charles Napier so unusual was his status and situation at the time, the early stage of the war at which he faced the issue, and the extreme nature of his conclusions and actions in that respect.

The 1940 episode is also of interest because of the very differing reactions that Napier produced in Nehru and Gandhi respectively, and because of Napier's own family connection with India's past: that is, his relationship (Nehru recalled it later as that of great-grandson, but that would seem likely to be a generation too few) to Sir Charles James Napier, GCB, veteran of the Peninsular War, conqueror of Sind in 1843, and Commander-in-Chief, India, until 1850. At first glance, such an ancestry might make the behaviour of Charles Napier in 1940 appear all the more bizarre, as well as ironic. In fact, however, his entertaining of radical political beliefs, together with his deep concern for the condition of the people of India, gave the young Second Lieutenant a great deal in common with his illustrious forbear. As Commander of the Northern District of England during the early phase of the Chartist demonstrations in 1839–41, Sir Charles, whilst determined to see that order was maintained, had privately sympathized with the 'legal political opinions' of that movement – 'very like my own!', he wrote to a friend. Moved to both sorrow and anger by the wretchedness and poverty of the mass of the people in the North, he had loathed the poor law and the 'cotton lords' alike, concluding that the country's overall prosperity lacked 'a foundation on [*sic*] sense or honesty'.[11]

In India, too, Sir Charles had regarded his victories over the Ameers who ruled Sind as an achievement on behalf of 'the liberties of the people' and against those who exploited them. At the same time he was fiercely critical of that mismanagement and rapacity which he saw as the hallmarks of the East India Company, whose administration of India still had a few years to run. The Company's Court of Directors, he was to write publicly, had 'milked the cow . . . for a hundred years . . . and given her no sustenance'. More radically still (though this time in private), he reflected whilst campaigning in Sind that Britain had 'had no right to come [there]' in the first place. After a series of clashes with Lord Dalhousie, the

10 See, for example, Thorne, *Allies of a Kind*, pp. 10, 58, 61, 221, 343–6, 459.
11 Lt Gen. Sir W. Napier, *The Life and Opinions of General Sir Charles James Napier* (London, 1857), for example, pp. 19, 39, 51, 75, 145.

Governor-General, during which he strenuously warned that the Indian Army was being driven towards revolt by the Government's indifference and insensitivity, Sir Charles resigned as C.-in-C. in 1850 – seven years before the Mutiny. 'All in India now', he declared in print, 'is sacrificed to Mammon!'[12]

For all his radical opinions, Lieutenant-General Sir Charles Napier retired as something of a national hero. Whatever his distaste for much of the current order of things, he had not turned away from his military duties in the service of the Empire, and indeed had achieved great success in that cause. Second Lieutenant Charles Napier, on the other hand, not only chose 90 years later to reject the prevailing assumptions about the British ruling presence in India, but refused to have any further part in that presence. Inevitably, he was brushed aside; unknown and virtually unnoticed, though at least at peace with his conscience.

In 1940, Napier was 25, having been born in Portrush in Northern Ireland in 1915.[13] Apparently he had joined the Army as a private before entering Sandhurst in September 1938. In other words, he had elected to become a Regular soldier, for conscription had not then been introduced. At Sandhurst, after taking the abbreviated two-term course which was being run in the threatening international circumstances of the time, he passed out on 3 July 1939. Joining the Northamptonshire Regiment, he left Britain for India in September.[14]

The First Battalion of the Northamptonshires – the 48th Regiment of Foot – had already been in India for some years, and in 1939 was in Bihar Province, engaged in internal security duties. 'In the city of Patna', records the Regimental History, 'the troops had frequently been subject to great provocation and even to attack by anti-British elements there, so much so that they had been forbidden to visit in parties of less than four'.[15] Early in 1940, the Battalion moved to Jhansi in the United Provinces, roughly in the centre of India, and was to remain there even when other units of the 10th Infantry Brigade, to which it belonged, left for the Middle East under Brigadier (as he then was) William Slim. By then, the Northamptonshires

12 Ibid., for example, pp. 245, 263, 275, 290, 354, 404; Lt Gen. Sir Charles James Napier, *Defects, Civil and Military, of the Indian Government* (London, 1853), for example, pp. 33–4.

13 Copy of birth certificate obtained from Oifig an Ard-Chláraitheora, Dublin.

14 *India Army List, 1940*; interviews with Major Terence Molloy, MC, and Major M. R. Haselhurst, retired officers of the Northamptonshire Regiment who were fellow-Second Lieutenants of Napier's in India.

15 W. J. Jervois, *History of the Northamptonshire Regiment, 1934–1948* (Northampton, 1953), ch. VII; interview with Brigadier D. E. Taunton, CB, DSO, DL, who in 1940 was a Captain with the Regiment in India, and was subsequently to be its Commanding Officer.

had had to find a new Commanding Officer, when the existing and much-admired incumbent of that post was recalled for new duties in the United Kingdom in May. One may surmise that when Major A. O. F. Winkler was promoted to Lieutenant-Colonel to fill the gap, Charles Napier was far from pleased, as the former made no secret of his racially based contempt for Indians.

Regimental life at Jhansi is recalled by then-subalterns as having been relaxed, with little or no expectation that a new war would break out in the Far East. Officers were not given to discussing any wider political issues associated either with the European conflict or the existence of Empire; the life and atmosphere of the Mess appear to have been of that unreflective and extrovert variety which anyone who has been in the Services – or has read, say, Paul Scott's *Raj Quartet* – would expect. Inevitably, Charles Napier, his mind increasingly preoccupied with the Indian nationalist cause, was something of a solitary figure in this setting. (This state may also have owed something to his having been several years older than would usually have been the case for someone in his position as junior subaltern.)[16] His colleagues regarded him as being an efficient platoon commander, and as they recall it, he did not choose to argue his political views with them. Nor did he make anything of his Napier ancestry. But he kept largely to himself, and, more remarkable still, displayed much zeal in learning native languages. All subalterns had to attend a class in Urdu, a requirement which most of them fulfilled with distinctly modified rapture. Napier, by contrast, obtained additional tuition for himself.[17]

It was when he was detached from Regimental duties, however, that the views which Napier had been forming came fully into the open. He was sent to be an instructor at the Training School for British and Indian officers at Mhow, some 280 or so miles away to the south-west and roughly half-way between Jhansi and Bombay. In this new setting, he would probably have been much more free to act as an individual than had been the case in his Regimental surroundings. He took to wearing khadi when off duty, and to visiting the bazaar in Mhow in order to talk there with Indian shopkeepers and others. As Nehru subsequently recollected the description of his situation that Napier gave him in Bombay: 'He did not fit in with his brother officers. He was more serious and intellectual and he felt

16 In reflecting on the episode, I have been helped and stimulated by the views of Colonel Hugh Toye, who served in India during the war and subsequently had special responsibilities concerning captured members of the Indian National Army which, under Subhas Chandra Bose, fought alongside the Japanese. [See his *The Springing Tiger: A Study of a Revolution* (London, 1959).] I must emphasize in relation to all my interviewees, however, that I alone am responsible for the opinions offered in this article.

17 Interviews with Majors Molloy and Haselhurst.

drawn towards India, especially the poorer classes . . . I think he gave a good part of his salary to the poor.'[18]

Central India was a region that at the time was causing the authorities some concern from the point of view of ensuring civic calm and rallying support for the war effort. Earlier in the year, for example, Military Intelligence had reported that German propaganda broadcasts in Hindi were 'attracting considerable notice'. In Mhow itself, there were some desertions in August from the newly formed Indian 5th Labour Corps. The instigator, it was believed, was a grocer who had a shop in the British Infantry Bazaar, who was subsequently sentenced under the Defence of India Rules.[19]

Whether because of his visits to the bazaar, or because he began to make known his opinions in the Training School Mess, Napier now came into confrontation with his Commanding Officer at Mhow, Brigadier P. G. Westmacott. That the exchange between the two men took place across a wide gulf can be inferred from one of the passages in the written summary of his position and views which Napier drew up in August at the other's request.[20] Having condemned the intolerance and hypocrisy that he found in the attitude of his fellow-countrymen towards the religious beliefs held by Indians ('I am not a Christian, but neither do I pretend to be one'), he added somewhat opaquely: 'I deplore my unacceptability in the eyes of my Commanding Officer, a thing which no decent Englishman would do, be he Christian or no.'

Napier's residual belief in a quality termed English 'decency' was not accompanied by admiration for 'the average Englishman', whom he regarded as all too satisfied with the possession of 'an effete mind in a healthy body': a 'suet-headed mentality' that, together with a hypocritical indifference to spiritual matters, he saw as being 'in direct opposition to the Oriental view of life'. And indeed, the line of criticism that Napier developed in his written statement went wider still, to encompass the whole of 'modern European civilization'. It was that civilization, he argued, which had created in 'the ordinary man' 'an inability to think and a distrust of those who can' and which had led to the existing 'mad struggle generated by greed and fear' among the European states themselves. In such a time of war, it provided men with work and a sense of purpose; but in peace 'there is unemployment, starvation and misery'.

18 Nehru to Gandhi, 2 Oct. 1940, loc. cit.
19 Military Intelligence report, 22 Jan. 1940, Fortnightly Reports of Political Agents, Central India, R/1/29/2148, and report for first two weeks of August 1940, ibid., R/1/29/2120 (India Office Library, London).
20 Statement attached to Nehru to Gandhi, 2 October 1940, Nehru Papers.

The scope and unqualified nature of this condemnation doubtless owed something to the youthfulness and sense of isolation of the writer, quite apart from the passion that his cause itself had aroused in him. It is obvious that his root-and-branch dismissal of 'modern European civilization', together with his brusque explanation of what had brought about the war of 1939, invited from his superiors an equally abrupt and total rejection of what he wished to say.

Yet it is worth recalling in passing that during the inter-war years no small number of thinking people in Europe, shocked by the apparently senseless carnage of 1914–18, or by the widespread social distress that followed, or both, had come to the conclusion that something was profoundly wrong with their 'modern civilization' and had urged the need for drastic change in one direction or another. For Arthur Koestler and others, it was Soviet Communism that appeared to offer the hope of redemption.[21] For an Arnold Toynbee ('men and women all over the world', he wrote in 1931, 'were seriously contemplating the possibility that the Western system of society might . . . cease to work . . . [as a result of] a spontaneous disintegration . . . from within'),[22] it was a return to the values and order of an earlier European era that was needed. And for some, such as the French writer, Romain Rolland, it was to the East that European man should turn in order to rediscover that spirituality which had become buried beneath what another critic, Lewis Mumford, termed 'purposeless materialism [and] superfluous power'.[23]

The belief that radical changes within European societies were essential was also shared by many of those involved in the fight against Nazi Germany. Where Napier differed was in his unwillingness to subordinate a rejection of certain features of the existing order to the requirements of defeating Germany. Undoubtedly, too, he was out of step with most of his fellow-countrymen in his criticism of their national characteristics, particularly in that summer of 1940, when pride was inseparable from defiance in the face of threatened destruction. He was by no means the first, however, to discern as a feature of the English what Ralph Waldo Emerson had called their 'impatience of . . . minds addicted to contemplation', and Hippolyte Taine their possession of heads containing 'many facts but few ideas'.[24]

21 See R. H. S. Crossman (ed.), *The God That Failed* (New York, 1954).

22 A. Toynbee, introduction to his *Survey of International Affairs, 1931* (Royal Institute of International Affairs, Oxford, 1932).

23 R. Rolland, *Inde Journal, 1915–1943* (Paris, 1960), passim; L. Mumford, *Technics and Civilisation* (London, 1946), p. 273.

24 R. W. Emerson, *English Traits, Representative Men, and Other Essays* (London, 1951), pp. 39ff.; H. Taine, *Notes sur l'Angleterre* (Paris, 1872), ch. VIII.

The decisive factor for Napier in 1940, however, was neither the general nature of European civilization nor the characteristics of the Englishman. It was his conviction that there was no justification for British rule in India. The Empire, he asserted in the statement requested by his CO, was no more than 'an association for the making of money, propagated by merchants in England under a hypocritical screen of "Empire glory and the betterment of the native races" '. The British had failed to ensure that the people of India had sufficient to eat; but quite apart from such considerations, 'a country should be ruled by its inhabitants, because freedom is the most important thing of all'.

Such views, Napier suggested, were 'incompatible with the retention of my commission', and towards the end of his statement he emphasized that his wish to leave the Army was no impulsive and unconsidered gesture. He was prepared to give up his more-than-adequate income, 'prepared to leave a profession on which I have always been keen and to cut myself off from such friends and relations as I have in England. Prepared is not the right word. Hoping would be more appropriate.' It was a step that he wished to take, even though 'every Indian in the bazar' (sic) had advised him against it and had made it plain that those of them whose livelihood depended on the British would not risk taking action in an attempt to secure independence. He concluded:

I am well aware that anything I may do will make scarcely a ripple in an ocean which at the present time is as near to being churned with blood as ever before. But if one must join in the general fight in this mad world, it is surely a feeble creature who would not fight for what he believes to be right, even if he must do it without a bank balance. Freedom is more important than food.

In Nehru's eyes, Charles Napier's statement of his beliefs was a 'very fine' thing. He himself, after all, had not long before been expressing in private the view that the Anglo-German war was 'a purely imperialist venture on both sides' in which he would 'hate to see India entangled'.[25] 'My heart went out to this young and terribly sincere boy', he wrote to Gandhi, and six weeks later his visitor's face 'haunted' him still.

Whilst impressed by Napier's desire to work for the cause of Indian independence, however, Nehru felt that he must above all save him from the charge of desertion which could obviously arise at any moment. Furthermore, he argued, it was within the Army itself that he could do most good, by seeking to awaken in others an awareness of the justice of

25 Nehru to Gandhi, 24 January and 4 February 1940, Nehru Papers, Correspondence, vol. 26.

India's demands. He suggested, therefore, that Napier should travel to Jhansi (whither he had apparently been instructed to return from Mhow) and, having changed out of khadi, report to his Regimental Commanding Officer. He would then be in a position to face the authorities over the issues raised in his written statement, without additionally inviting the grave charge of desertion.

Napier accepted Nehru's advice and left for the station, promising that he would maintain contact. Six weeks later, however, Nehru had still heard nothing from him, and it was now, in early October, that he wrote to Gandhi to describe the incident, enclosing a copy of Napier's statement and raising the question of whether he had advised the young man correctly. Gandhi's reaction, however, was very different from his own. He replied simply:

My dear Jawaharlal,
. . . Your letter about Napier with enclosure. I am sending it to the Viceroy. It is a pathetic case.[26]

And send it to the Viceroy he did. Linlithgow in turn passed on the papers to the Commander-in-Chief, commenting blandly in a letter to Gandhi: 'These are difficult cases, as the Pandit [i.e. Nehru] clearly recognized, and I think, if I may say so, that the advice he gave was eminently sensible and in the best interests of the officer concerned.'[27]

Gandhi's remarkable response to the affair is probably best understood in terms of a strong aversion to anything smacking of disloyalty to a person's own nation or sworn duty. (For example, he was to deplore the actions of those members of the Indian Army who, after being captured by the Japanese, fought alongside the latter as the Indian National Army, with the proclaimed intention of securing independence for their homeland.) Whatever his motives, however, his action in revealing the details of Napier's visit to Nehru could have served to bring serious trouble upon the head of the young Englishman. In fact, by the time Gandhi wrote to the Viceroy, Napier was already awaiting Court Martial, having been placed under arrest as soon as he arrived back in Jhansi around the end of August.[28] His statement of political beliefs had also been forwarded already to the C.-in-C. by his Commanding Officer at Mhow. Even so, the inten-

26 Gandhi to Nehru, 6 October 1940, Nehru Papers, Correspondence vol. 26.
27 Linlithgow to Gandhi, 11 October 1940, Linlithgow Papers, MSS.Eur.F. 125/122 (India Office Library, London).
28 Napier's own summary of events following his visit to Nehru is set out in a letter to Nehru dated 5 October 1940, and smuggled out from his place of arrest in Mhow, where he awaited Court Martial. Nehru Papers, Correspondence, vol. 54; also interviews with fellow-officers of his Regiment, as above.

tions behind Napier's visit to Nehru, as well as the fact of their meeting itself (unless the intelligence services already knew of it) were now revealed to the authorities, thanks to Gandhi. Since the Court Martial had not yet been held, it therefore remains possible that the old man's unfeeling initiative did indeed make matters more difficult for Napier.

At this point we encounter one of the unanswered questions referred to earlier: what was the exact charge brought against Napier, and what evidence was assembled in that connection?[29] Whatever the precise case against him may have been, he had to wait the best part of two months before it was heard. He had been sent back under arrest from Jhansi to Mhow, where the Court Martial was to take place. There, his conditions were, in his own words, 'fairly comfortable'. And although he was apparently ordered not to speak native languages, and 'at one period was forbidden to write to any Indian at all', he found means (through Indian soldiers or cleaners, perhaps?) of evading the censor in order to write to Nehru early in October.

Apologizing 'that when you have a continent to worry about, I should add one more person to that number', Napier summarized the reasons why, although he had returned to Jhansi as advised, he had nevertheless felt obliged to reject Nehru's suggestion that he should remain in the Army. In a British regiment, he wrote, one could do 'no good at all' on India's behalf, among either the officers or the men. Had he been able to transfer to an Indian regiment, things might have been different, but such a move was impossible. In any event, there remained a more fundamental objection:

You can hardly expect me, holding the views I do, to remain in the service, for the very reasons which you outline in your biography [sic] when you say that Congress supporters cannot enter the Indian Army because they are not prepared to take the oath of allegiance.

Had the opportunity arisen, Napier continued, he felt that he could have made some small contribution to the cause of Indian independence. 'Admittedly I should be considered eccentric, but what harm from that if

29 Did the accusation arise solely from the statement handed to the CO at Mhow? That would seem unlikely. Did it relate to things Napier had said or was alleged to have said, during his visits to the bazaar at Mhow, and thus involve, say, the preaching of sedition; or was it limited to unbecoming conduct? Did his intention to desert when he went to Bombay come to form a part of the case? And, a related question: did Napier know that his arrest might be at hand when he sought out Nehru? Writing six weeks after the event, Nehru recalled only that his visitor had been 'due to report at Jhansi the next morning', and that his own advice had been based on 'the chance of getting him back to Jhansi in time if he took the next train'.

one is sincere.' (And what, for example, was so absurd about his wearing khadi, when it was 'comfortable, clean, hygenic, cheap, normal to the country and suitable to the climate?') He realized now, of course, that he was not going to be able to remain in India in a private capacity. But that, too, 'comes no more into my calculations than it does into those of Congress if you decide at the present time to stand out for free speech. You decide what you ought to do, and then you proceed to attempt to do it.' His brother officers, he acknowledged, 'naturally either think me mad, or else completely despicable.' But even if he had been unable to make them 'do any thinking', he could at least 'abstain from doing harm' at Mhow, where he had been engaged in training young Indians to 'ape . . . the least intelligent portion of the British race'. 'I hope', he concluded, 'that you decide to stand out against the policy of pressing India willy-nilly into the war – but whatever you do, I sincerely wish you success in it'.

Napier's Court Martial eventually took place, and evidently he was found guilty. He was not informed of the sentence of the court, however, until he had been placed some three weeks later, and still under arrest, on a ship in Karachi that was about to leave for the United Kingdom.[30] (This has been corroborated by the then-subaltern who had the duty of escorting him to Karachi.) Possibly the authorities were anxious to ensure that there was no further contact between the young officer and Indian nationalists. That nationalists besides Nehru did, indeed, already know about the case can be inferred from Napier's ability to smuggle out his letter to the Congress leader in October. Moreover, the railway route to be taken by the prisoner and his escort beween Jhansi and Karachi was changed at the last minute by Military Intelligence, apparently because they believed that groups of Indians were waiting to see Napier along the way.[31]

The sentence of the court, conveyed to Napier just before the ship sailed, was that he was to be 'Dismissed the Service'. His own description of the sentence, in a subsequent letter to Nehru, was the ambiguous one of 'cashiered from the Army'; but a note in an official file, which chimes with the recollections of his subaltern-escort, makes it clear that the more severe penalty of 'cashiering' was not resorted to.[32] In short, he had been found

30 Napier's account of events following his Court Martial is in the letter, dated 20 January 1941, that he wrote to Nehru whilst on board ship en route to the United Kingdom. Nehru Papers, Correspondence, vol. 54.

31 Interview with Major Haselhurst, who (as a 2nd Lt) had the task of escorting Napier to Karachi.

32 I am grateful to staff of the India Office Library who summarized for me 'non-sensitive' factual material contained in a file relating to Napier: Public and Judicial (Separate) Collection, 394/1941. This file, created when Napier returned to the United Kingdom, is closed for 75 years, and a request by the present writer to have this status reconsidered has so far failed to produce results. The reason for the closure is probably that papers in the file

'unsuitable' rather than culpable. And it remained possible that he would be called up for war work or into the ranks of, say the RAF on his return to the United Kingdom. He himself, however, thought it 'very likely that I shall be arrested on landing under the Emergency Regulations, in which case I shall be provided with a billet in the Temple of Swaraj [i.e. imprisonment] until the end of the war'.

This forecast was made in a letter to Nehru which Napier wrote in January 1941 as he travelled homewards. He also took the opportunity to take issue with Nehru over the latter's public expressions of confidence in the mass of the British people as having no wish to hold India in subjection. 'The public-school class', he wrote, were 'firmly in favour of Empire, mainly on the grounds of tradition', whilst 'the lower classes' were content to echo such views in the knowledge that they, too, had long benefited from Britain's exploitation of Imperial markets. Given also a widespread 'racial and colour prejudice' and a general contempt for non-violent doctrines as being 'weak and unmanly' (he himself, he acknowledged, was 'prepared to use violence when I consider other means impracticable'), there were few in Britain, he argued, who had sympathy for India's cause. His own hope, however, continued to be 'to do some good' and, if he were not re-arrested, 'to return to the East in the near future'.

What did happen to Charles Napier when he arrived back in the United Kingdom in 1941? It appears that the authorities in Liverpool confiscated some notebooks and Indian political pamphlets that he had brought back with him, and that other officials were concerned to ensure that he did not return to India.[33] From this concern, together with the moving of his bank account to Richmond in Surrey in early 1942, it can be inferred that he was not in fact imprisoned, and it is possible that he was required to undertake some new form of war service. But for the moment that is as much as the writer can say.

What is clear in retrospect, however, is that Napier was naive in ever believing that he would be allowed to stay in India and help the cause of independence after resigning his Commission. A Government of India under Lord Linlithgow, faced with nationalist agitation that was to culminate in the 'Quit India' movement in 1942, was not going to tolerate what it could regard only as disloyal trouble-making from within the ranks of the British themselves. And although in 1940 Japan had yet to enter the

---

identify certain members of the intelligence services at the time. The file does not, apparently, contain details of Napier's court martial.

33 There is no indication of the contents or whereabouts of the notebooks and pamphlets that had been confiscated.

war and create India's moment of supreme peril, the general conviction that Britain herself needed to mobilize every scrap of her resources – including Imperial ones – made it doubly certain that views such as Napier's would not be tolerated, that he himself would be removed from the scene with all speed, and that the affair could be hushed up as far as was possible. In the words of a retired senior officer who has been consulted about the episode: 'He really chose to buck an entrenched system at precisely the wrong moment!'

Napier's response, no doubt, would have been that for him it was the right and only moment: that it was there, in the India of 1940, that he was forced to confront his own beliefs, and that the proclaimed principles for which Britain was already at war served to underline what he had come to see as a dealing in double standards. The sense of isolation which he felt whilst arriving at such a crisis of conscience was doubtless heightened by his recent and existing environments at Sandhurst and in a Regimental Mess. In this connection, it is worth recalling the observations made by a C.-in-C. India six years earlier. On the eve of his retirement from that post, Field Marshall Sir Philip Chetwode had declared:

I am horrified, as I travel up and down India, at the number of officers, senior and junior alike, who have allowed themselves to sink into a state of complete brain sickness. Their narrow interests are bounded by the morning parade, the game they happen to play, and purely local and unimportant matters . . . [They] are quite unaware of the larger aspects of what is going on in India around them, and still less of the stupendous events outside this country that are now in process of forming an entirely new world. [34]

It was probably his immediate, military environment, too, which helped Napier to arrive at conclusions concerning the attitudes towards Empire of the British people as a whole which in retrospect are open to considerable qualification. Attachment to imperial possessions was less widespread and less strong than Napier believed. Nor did he anticipate those leftward shifts of opinion during the war in this and other respects which have been surveyed in, for example, Paul Addison's *The Road to 1945*, Professor Louis' *Imperialism at Bay*, and the present writer's *Allies of a Kind*. [35]

At the same time, however, it must be emphasized that in the setting of 1940 it would not have been the reactionaries and the narrow-minded alone who would have regarded Napier's behaviour as bizarre and a menace.

34 Quoted in B. Bond, *British Military Policy Between the Two World Wars* (Oxford, 1981), p. 68. And see, e.g., I. Stephens, *Monsoon Morning* (London, 1966).
35 P. Addison, *The Road to 1945* (London, 1975); W. R. Louis, *Imperialism at Bay* (Oxford, 1977).

That has been the retrospective conclusion of virtually all those with whom I have discussed the episode who were in India at the time. Philip Mason, for example, who in 1940 held a senior post in the Indian Civil Service, and who subsequently became Director of the Institute of Race Relations in London and an outstanding historian of British India,[36] has reflected that, had Napier's case come his way at the time,

I don't think I should have been sympathetic with his *position*, though I might, I hope, have felt sympathy with his personal dilemma. But I should have felt, I think, that a war is no time for indulging personal idiosyncracies. Did he really want the Germans to win? Would it have been for India's good? . . . I think most of us in Government service, however liberal in long-term views about India's future, would have taken that kind of view.[37]

One can only speculate, of course, as to what would have followed had India been granted what Congress was demanding in 1939–40 – and, we must add, had the fast-widening gap between Congress and the Muslim League been bridged sufficiently to make some form of stable administration possible. That only a self-governing India could put her full effort into the war was one of Nehru's arguments in 1942, when the arrival of the Cripps Mission brought matters to a head, just as it was the cry of various Americans, in and out of official positions.[38] Let it merely be said here that one can deplore the reactionary, racist and callous attitudes of Churchill towards India at the time without necessarily being convinced that to have met all the wartime demands of Congress would have assisted the allies to defeat Germany and Japan, or have been of benefit to India herself.

Whatever one may think of the timing and tactics of Charles Napier's defiance in 1940, however, or of the sweeping nature of some of his assertions, his sincerity and concern for the people of India surely remain evident. (In the 'closed' official file, referred to above, that was opened on him after the confiscation in Liverpool of his notebooks and pamphlets, a note explaining why he had been sent back to the United Kingdom described him as being entirely sincere, though of course misguided.) If he appears to have gravely underestimated the significance of what was at stake between Britain and Hitler's Germany (as did Captain Basil Liddell Hart, for example, among others),[39] at the same time he perceived, as did few of those about him in the Army, those related issues concerning the future of Britain's Empire which by 1945 would have come much more to the fore.

36 See his memoirs, *A Shaft of Sunlight* (London, 1978).
37 Letter to the author, 11 December 1979. Dr Mason's reflections on the affair have been of great value – although, again, the views expressed in the article are those of the writer alone.
38 See Thorne, *Allies of a Kind*, pp. 240-4.
39 See B. Bond, *Liddell Hart: A Study of His Military Thought* (London, 1977).

(As early as January 1943, indeed, the Army's Directorate of Education would be ready to distribute in its *British Way and Purpose* series a pamphlet on colonial policy which contained the assertion: 'Self-government is better than good government, and we are pledged to train the colonies in self-government.'[40])

Moreover, Napier was correct in sensing that Britain's role in India was being called in question more profoundly than ever before. The nature of this situation was appreciated by many of the younger members of the Indian Civil Service who had come out from British universities in the 1930s, and their reactions were often positive.[41] But awareness of this kind seems to have been rare in military circles. One senior officer, Field Marshal Lord Wavell, has rightly received much praise for grasping the serious state of affairs when he became Viceroy in 1943, and for striving, against Churchill's fierce opposition, to develop immediate, wartime initiatives over constitutional issues. (This was all the more remarkable in that, at the time of the Cripps Mission in 1942, Wavell, then Commander-in-Chief, had strongly defended the constitutional status quo.) By the same token, should not a junior officer be given some credit at least for having divined in 1940 that the circumstances of war, far from enabling the nationalist issue to be put aside, were thrusting it forward, rather?[42]

What Napier in his private and extreme way seems to have sensed, and what Wavell three years later was urging upon London, was that time was not on Britain's side in India. In this connection, it is worth mentioning that, in his statement for his CO in 1940, Napier questioned how long Britain would be able to go on relying upon the loyalty of the Indian Army in the context of increasing nationalist demands. In that the great bulk of that Army did remain loyal during the war, and indeed (for all Churchill's private sneers) performed valiant service, the question might appear to have been absurd. And yet, after the defeat of Japan, Wavell was to be much exercised by the mounting clamour within India over Britain's use of Indian units to hold in check the nationalist movements of fellow-Asians, notably in Indonesia. Meanwhile, during the 1941–45 Far Eastern War,

40 Directorate of Army Education, *The British Way and Purpose*, vol. 3, January 1943.
41 See, for example, Hunt and Harrison, *The District Officer in India*.
42 This does not mean, of course, that Wavell's responses can be likened to Napier's, or vice versa. The latter's freedom from the responsibilities of high office permitted him to adopt an extreme stance, based on principle and personal conviction, of a kind entirely denied to someone in Wavell's position, even had the wish to act thus been present. And when Wavell sought to tackle the political problems confronting him, he was to do so with an awareness of their complexity – not least where Congress/Muslim League hostility was concerned – which went far beyond the Congress-orientated assumptions of Napier in 1940. (See Moon, *Wavell: The Viceroy's Journal*, passim.) Differences in age, experience and role, quite apart from ones of personality, make such a contrast entirely understandable.

some 20,000 or so members of the Indian Army had, after their capture by the Japanese, agreed to fight alongside them (and under the eventual leadership of Subhas Chandra Bose) in the Indian National Army. And although the INA was bitterly scorned by many of the Indian soldiers who remained loyal to the Raj, when its survivors eventually returned home after Japan's surrender they came to be treated as heroes rather than as traitors. Nehru himself, who in 1942 publicly deplored the notion of collaborating with the Japanese, found it expedient in 1946 to describe the wartime efforts of the INA as 'a brave adventure' which had sprung from 'a passionate desire to serve the cause of Indian freedom'.[43]

Political issues apart, Charles Napier's wish to identify himself with the people of India will no doubt appear to some as having led him into romanticized forms of behaviour, such as wearing khadi. (One of the earlier British champions of Indian independence who sought to identify with the people of that country, Mrs Annie Besant, had also been dismissed by many contemporaries as being simply odd.)[44] But although he was, obviously, a young man of passion in a hurry, his letters indicate that there was much more to Napier than that.

Further inquiries may make it possible to remove some of the uncertainties surrounding the affair. One item of curiosity, however, will never be ticked off the list. The reader will have noted in passing how closely some of the 1940 Napier's condemnations of British policy and performance in India, and of unemployment at home, echoed those of his distinguished ancestor a century before. Both men, too (although the circumstances were of course far from identical), questioned the reliability of the Indian Army as an instrument of continuing British rule. Even Second Lieutenant Napier's emphatic readiness to give up his income calls to mind the reason given by Sir Charles for being unwilling to contemplate a peerage in the 1840s: that to accept the government pension that would be needed for its upkeep would mean 'ending my career by robbing my starving fellow-countrymen'.[45]

Yet we know, too, how Sir Charles Napier accepted and prosecuted his duty to fight the enemies of the Crown. How, then, one wonders, would the old General have judged the case had his shade been present in that courtroom in Mhow in 1940?

43 On the INA, see Toye, *Springing Tiger*, K. K. Ghosh, *The Indian National Army: Second Front of the Independence Movement* (Meerut, 1969); J. C. Lebra, *Jungle Alliance: Japan and the Indian National Army* (Singapore, 1971). For Nehru's views of 1942 and 1946, press statement of April 1942, A.I.C.C. Papers, G-26, part II; statement of 10 October 1946, ibid., file 60/1946.
44 See E. Halévy, *Imperialism and the Rise of Labour, 1895–1905* (London, 1961), p. 183.
45 W. Napier, *General Sir Charles James Napier*, p. 455.

12

Britain and the Black GIs: Racial Issues and Anglo-American Relations in 1942

In the House of Commons on 29 September 1942, Winston Churchill found himself faced with a highly embarrassing question from Tom Driberg, Independent MP for Maldon, Essex. Was the Prime Minister aware, asked Driberg, 'that an unfortunate result of the presence here of American forces had been the introduction in some parts of Britain of discrimination against Negro troops'? Would he therefore 'make friendly representations to the American military authorities asking them to instruct their men that the colour bar is not the custom in this country and that its non-observance by British troops or civilians should be regarded with equanimity?' The issue needed dealing with firmly and constructively, Driberg declared, rather than pretending that it did not exist. And when Churchill expressed the hope that 'without any action on my part the points of view of all concerned will be mutually understood and respected', he was reminded by the Communist MP Willie Gallacher that he had already received from Gallacher a copy of a letter written by a group of men in the armed forces, in which they reported being lectured by an officer on the undesirability of mixing with Negro troops in London.[1]

There was all the less likelihood that the Government could avoid this issue in that it had been aired in the press not long before. Earlier in September the *Sunday Pictorial*[2] had heard from angry parishioners of

This essay originally appeared in abridged form in the *Sunday Times* magazine and was reproduced, with the references reinstated and by courtesy of the Editor, in *New Community* (Journal of the Community Relations Commission), 3 (1974), pp. 1-10, from which it is reproduced here. Crown Copyright documents from the Public Record Office, on which much of this article is based, appear by permission of the Controller of Her Majesty's Stationery Office.

1 *Hansard*, House of Commons, vol. 383, cols 670-1.
2 *Sunday Pictorial*, 6 September 1942.

Worle, in Weston-Super-Mare, following a talk to local women by the wife of the vicar. In her own words, this lady had suggested to her audience the following six-point code of behaviour:

1   If a local woman keeps a shop and a coloured soldier enters she must serve him, but she must do it as quickly as possible and indicate that she does not desire him to come there again.
2   If she is in a cinema and notices a coloured soldier next to her, she moves to another seat immediately.
3   If she is walking on the pavement and a coloured soldier is coming towards her, she crosses to the other pavement.
4   If she is in a shop and a coloured soldier enters, she leaves as soon as she has made her purchases or before that if she is in a queue.
5   White women, of course, must have no relationship with coloured troops.
6   On no account must coloured troops be invited into the homes of white women.

The *Sunday Pictorial's* reaction had been to assure the visiting Negro 'that there is no colour bar in this country and that he is as welcome as any other Allied soldier. He will find that the vast majority of people here have nothing but repugnance for the narrow-minded, uninformed prejudices expressed by the vicar's wife. There is – and will be – no persecution of coloured people in Britain.' Even so, other incidents were coming to light. Early in October, for example, the manager of an Oxford snack-bar was writing to *The Times* to record his shame at the humiliation forced on a Negro soldier who had called in search of food and had presented an open letter from his commanding officer. The letter explained that Private X was:

. . . a soldier in the US Army, and it is necessary that he sometimes has a meal, which he has, on occasions, found it difficult to obtain. I would be grateful if you would look after him.[3]

The soldier in question was one of the 170,000 US ground and air troops who were in or en route to the United Kingdom by the end of 1942[4] – a number far less than originally planned, being reduced by the demands of the Pacific and Mediterranean theatres, but enough to make a sizeable impact on the British scene from the summer of that year onwards. By June, baseball was being played in London's parks; by the autumn, with

3   *The Times*, 2 October 1942.
4   M. Matloff and E. M. Snell, *Strategic Planning for Coalition Warfare*, 1941–42 (Washington, DC, 1953), ch. XVI.

the aerodromes of the US Army Air Corps beginning to form small islands of American life in the British countryside, over 100,000 workers were being employed to build further bases and camps for the visitors.[5] The arrangement between Washington and London had been that up to about 10 per cent of these incoming troops could be black, and in fact by the time Driberg and Gallacher raised the question in the Commons between 11 and 12 thousand Negroes had already arrived.[6]

From the beginning the British press had been loud in its welcome for the Americans as a whole. 'We feel stronger', declared *The Times*, 'not only physically but even more in spirit, for their presence among us.' Suggestions for ways of organizing local hospitality filled the correspondence columns, the *News of the World*, for example, believing that 'every British home is waiting for a lead in this urgent obligation to our American comrades and cousins.'[7] Behind this expansiveness there lay on the British side reasons going beyond the obvious requirements of wartime partnership. Already there was talk of the need to win the peace as well, with continuing and extensive transatlantic cooperation being seen as vital if a more lasting basis for international relations was to be created. In this sense, the fostering of ties on a personal level might help to prevent a post-war retreat into renewed isolation on the part of the United States – something that seemed all the more ominously possible with the Republican gains in the Congressional elections of that November. As *The Times* put it:

If the Americans and Englishmen can seize this opportunity to sit down together round the same hearth, and the American can be enabled to see how life is lived in England, and the Englishman to hear how it is lived in America, the foundations of the future will be well and truly laid.[8]

This need to become aware of the history and way of life of one's new Ally was being widely emphasized, and sometimes anxiously so. Stereotypes of the visitors derived from 'the gangster-infested cinema' must go, as must all notions of innate English superiority. Professor Denis Brogan, writing in the *Spectator* about the deterioration of Anglo-American relations since Pearl

5 See, for example, *News of the World*, 21, 28 June 1942; *The Times*, 6 July, 10 August, 29 September 1942.
6 Cabinet minutes, 31 August 1942, CAB 65/28; Grigg memorandum, 31 October 1943, WP (42) 441, CAB 66/29. All Cabinet, Foreign Office and Premier papers in Public Record Office, London.
7 For example, *The Times*, 6, 15 July, 3, 11 September, 26 November, 22 December 1942; *News of the World*, 2 April 1942; *Daily Express*, 4 July, 13, 19 August, 21 October 1942. US Army surveys later in the war suggested that American troops were more appreciative of Britain the longer they stayed there.
8 *The Times*, 29 July 1942; cf. ibid., 30 December 1942.

Harbor and the Blitz, was one of those who felt obliged to remind his readers that 'the United States is a foreign country and the Americans . . . in short are non-English – a state of affairs to which they are wholly reconciled.'[9]

That grounds did exist for disagreement and misunderstanding was obvious enough. Anyone who doubted this in terms of general outlook would encounter strong evidence to the contrary early in the following summer, when Gallup Polls in the two countries asked which of the United Nations had up to then made the greatest single contribution towards winning the war, the British sample answering the Soviet Union (50 per cent), Britain (42 per cent), China (5 per cent) and the United States (3 per cent); as against the American response which placed the United States first (55 per cent), followed by the Soviet Union (32 per cent), Britain (9 per cent) and China (4 per cent).[10] Meanwhile in 1942 there were also grounds for concern about more immediate and local friction. Jibes that were to become familiar, about Americans being 'over-paid, over-sexed and over here', pointed to the kind of issue that could give rise to trouble, and Vernon Bartlett wrote to *The Times* to give examples of malicious rumours that he had come across, including the tale to be heard in pubs of Americans asking to be served with their beer 'as quickly as the British got out of Tobruk'.[11]

Where Negro troops were concerned, however, difficulties by no means arose solely from the kind of aversion expressed by the vicar's wife who was quoted earlier. On the contrary, a greater danger appeared to lie in the very warmth of the welcome which many people were ready to give to these soldiers – a response which threatened to conflict with the patterns of behaviour and expectations brought over with them by white Americans. Thus, the highest-ranking Negro in the US Army, Brigadier-General Benjamin O. Davies, was reported in October as saying that 'all the coloured troops he had talked to had been profuse in their praise of the way in which they had been received by British soldiers and the British public'; but at the same time he admitted that 'there had been resentment on the part of some white American troops against the way in which British people had entertained coloured troops.'[12]

It was, indeed, in this respect, rather than that of hostility by their own people, that the British Cabinet had to face a difficult issue involving inter-Allied relations. In the United States the social upheavals caused by the war were helping to raise more acutely than ever the question of Negro rights and opportunities, as Gunnar Myrdal was soon to highlight in his book, *An*

---

9 Letters in *The Times*, 25, 28 July 1942; *Daily Express*, 3 August 1942; *Spectator*, 3 July 1942.
10 Gallup Poll archives, by kind permission of Dr H. Durant.
11 *The Times*, 22 August 1942. Cf. *News of the World*, 1 November 1942.
12 *The Times*, 14 October 1942.

American Dilemma. But although President Roosevelt, under the threat of large-scale demonstrations, had set up a Fair Employment Practices Committee to combat job discrimination, he was far from giving either this Committee or the Negro cause as a whole his strong and consistent support. [13] And although Eleanor Roosevelt for her part was quick to take up with General Marshall and others cases involving Negro troops, the U.S. Army remained organized on a segregated basis, apart from the allocation of white officers to Negro units. [14] (In Britain, the Negroes had their own camps, canteens, clubs, hostels and so forth.) In this matter, the American Secretary of War, Henry L. Stimson, has been described as 'virtually a reformer' when set alongside the senior ranks of his Army; nevertheless he could assert early in 1942 that 'the Negro still lacks the particular initiative which a commanding officer of men needs in war . . . Also the social intermixture of the two races is basically impossible.' [15] This attitude was in keeping with Stimson's earlier observation, when Governor General of the Philippines, that he had found only one Filipino politician with 'a sufficiently Anglo-Saxon mind' to be thought of as possibly capable of ruling over the islands. [16] 'We are faced', he wrote in his diary at the beginning of 1942, 'with the insoluble problem of the black race in this country.' [17] And in the following September, he noted that Arthur Sulzberger of the *New York Times*, who had been in Britain for three weeks, felt that 'the fact that the English treat our colored people without drawing the race line was sure to make trouble in the end.' [18] Shortly before, John Foster Dulles had come back from a visit to Britain with the same worry. [19] Roosevelt himself, according to Stimson, was likewise concerned when the latter told him of Sulzberger's alarm:

I told him of the current dangerous situation in the USA and the difficulties which we [i.e. the Army] are having, and then I told him that Mrs Roosevelt notified me of

13 Reports sent to the President by the Bureau of Intelligence during 1942 were reminding him – if it were needed – of how wide and deep was the antipathy towards Negroes among his fellow-whites. Roosevelt Papers, PSF, box 170.
14 See, for example, N. Wynn, 'The impact of the Second World War on the American negro', *Journal of Contemporary History* vol. 6, no. 2, 1971; Ulysses Lee, *The Employment of Negro Troops*, US Army in World War 2, Special Studies (Washington, DC, 1966); F. C. Pogue, *George C. Marshall: Ordeal and Hope* (New York, 1966), pp. 15–16.
15 J. M. Burns, *Roosevelt, The Soldier of Freedom* (London, 1971), pp. 265–6.
16 Stimson Diary (Yale University), 17 January 1929. Stimson modified his views a little later in the war. See H. L. Stimson and M. Bundy, *On Active Service in Peace and War* (New York, 1948), p. 463.
17 Stimson Diary, 13 January 1942.
18 Ibid., 24 September 1942.
19 Dulles Report on June–July visit to UK, Institute of Pacific Relations Papers, box 374 (Columbia University).

her coming trip to the UK and asked him if he would not caution her on the subject of making any comments as the different treatment which Negroes received in the UK from what they received in the US. He was very much interested in this whole subject and very sympathetic to our whole attitude, and told me he would pass the word on to Mrs Roosevelt.[20]

It was here, in other words, that there lay the sting in Driberg's question to the Prime Minister, when he suggested that the US Army authorities should be reminded 'that the colour bar is not a custom in this country'.

Various members of the Government had seen the problem coming some while before it arrived on the Cabinet's agenda. The President of the Board of Trade, Hugh Dalton, for example, after talking to an official from the Ministry of Information early in July, had speculated that white Americans might set about Negroes in the streets or public houses, when the British public were likely to take the part of the Negroes.[21] The Cabinet itself learned early in August that Eisenhower was proposing to segregate his black troops in a limited number of areas where special arrangements could be made for them, but even so, disquiet was expressed when the subject was brought up again at the end of the month.[22] The Foreign Secretary, Anthony Eden, thought that 'various difficulties' might arise if the full ten-per-cent allocation of these troops continued to be sent – he suggested that their health might suffer from the rigours of an English winter – and that the Government would be justified in pressing Washington to reduce the flow as far as possible. This was in fact done before long by means of a private word with Roosevelt's close adviser, Harry Hopkins.[23]

Meanwhile, however, in the absence of a policy decision at Government level, lesser authorities had already felt obliged to give some guidance in the matter to those in contact with the Negroes. Thus, after consulting senior US officers in the area, the Major-General responsible for administration in Southern Command had issued to District Commanders and Regional Commissioners a set of 'Notes On Relations With Coloured Troops'. The document began by surveying the history and position of the Negroes in America, depicting 'a bond of mutual esteem' between black and white in

20 Stimson Diary, 2 October 1942.
21 Dalton Diary (London School of Economics), 5 July 1942.
22 Cabinets of 10 and 31 August 1942, CAB 65/27.
23 Foreign Office file FO 371/30680, A11660/G. Hopkins to Marshall, 19 August 1942, Hopkins Papers, box 136 (Roosevelt Library).

the southern states, where 'the white man feels his moral duty to [the Negro] as it were to a child'; in many ways, therefore, the Negro in the south was happier than his freer but socially isolated brother in the north. Wherever they lived, however, they possessed certain fundamental characteristics which had to be borne in mind when dealing with them in a British context:

While there are many coloured men of high mentality and cultural distinction, the generality are of a simple mental outlook. They work hard when they have no money and when they have money prefer to do nothing until it is gone. In short they have not the white man's ability to think and act to a plan. Their spiritual outlook is well known and their songs give the clue to their nature. They respond to sympathetic treatment. They are natural psychologists in that they can size up a white man's character and can take advantage of a weakness. Too much freedom, too wide associations with white men, tend to make them lose their heads and have on occasions led to civil strife. This occurred after the last war due to too free treatment and associations which they had experienced in France.[24]

There followed specific advice on the need to take account of this 'mental outlook' and to 'conform to the American attitude'; to avoid making 'intimate friends' with Negroes and to refuse to listen to those 'few political extremists [from the United States] who endeavour to make the colour question a means to stir up political trouble.'

This monument to white arrogance was appended to a memorandum prepared for the Cabinet early in October by the Secretary of State for War, Sir James Grigg. Grigg outlined the problem as he saw it by contrasting the US Army's 'combination of equal rights and segregation practiced in the Southern States' with the British public's 'natural inclination to make no distinction between the treatment of white and coloured troops and . . . to regard such distinctions as undemocratic . . . [and] as racial discrimination which will give rise to bitter resentment.' There was also the difficulty that members of the Government – including the Minister of Information in a *Sunday Express* article (20 September) – had recently been urging the public that there must be no colour bar where British subjects from the colonies were concerned, an exhortation that could easily be read as applying to coloured visitors as a whole. Yet there had already been instances of white Americans walking out of canteens and public houses on seeing Negroes being served there. Moreover, Grigg added, 'the coloured troops themselves probably expect to be treated in this country as in the United States, and a markedly different treatment might

24 Appendix to Grigg memorandum, 3 October 1942, WP (42) 441 in CAB 66/29.

well cause political difficulties in America at the end of the war.' The morale of Britain's own forces would also suffer if there were 'any unnecessary association between American coloured troops and British women'. Therefore, while suggesting that there should be 'no official discrimination' against Negro troops beyond that instituted by their own Army, Grigg proposed to follow the lines of the Southern Command document, and to allow British officers to interpret the facts of the American colour question 'so as to educate the personnel of the Army, including the ATS, to adopt towards the USA coloured troops the attitude of the USA Army Authorities'.

This last suggestion of Grigg's at once became the focal point for a flurry of memoranda by some of his colleagues – even though various members of the Cabinet such as Attlee and Bevin, who might have been expected to join in, did not do so, at least on paper. In fact it was two decidedly non-socialist members of the Government who were quick to take issue with what Grigg had in mind. As Secretary of State for the Colonies, Viscount Cranborne (later Marquess of Salisbury) deplored the idea of seeking to guide British citizens into the ways of the Americans. Such a move, he felt, was likely to cause serious resentment among coloured people already in Britain, as well as those in the colonies; it could also lead to a reaction among the general public 'gravely prejudicial to Anglo-American relations'. 'I cannot believe', Cranborne wrote, 'that thinking Americans would wish us to adopt their ideas and prejudices any more than they would ours.'[25]

Within the Foreign Office, and against the inclinations of Eden himself, opinion tended to lean in Grigg's direction rather than Cranborne's. 'The really important thing' wrote the Parliamentary Under-Secretary of State, Richard Law, 'is that we should not have avoidable friction between the two armies, and that American troops should not go back to their homes with the view that we are a decadent and unspeakable race.'[26]

But Cranborne did find support from that least-loved of politicians, Lord Simon, the Lord Chancellor. 'The British attitude to coloured people', Simon declared, 'is in fact widely different from the American attitude.' Public houses were exactly that – for all the public; Service clubs and similar establishments run by bodies like Toc H and the Salvation Army could not and should not be segregated; the British Empire was mainly a

---

25 Cranborne memorandum, 2 October 1942, WP (42) 442, CAB 66/29.
26 FO 371/30680, A9731/G.

coloured Empire. He concluded with a plea for equality – although the implication was of equality on sufferance:

There is a profound British conviction underneath the surface that if a coloured man behaves himself he is entitled to the same treatment as a white man . . . and I believe that the great mass of American coloured men are perfectly well conditioned. In any case, barring American coloured troops from canteens, clubs, etc., will not reduce the risk of association with white women in the least – rather the opposite. [27]

This last, sexual aspect of the matter which Grigg and Simon had raised had also been troubling other minds for some time, as the Home Secretary, Herbert Morrison, made clear when he added his contribution to the debate. Some of the Regional Commissioners, he reported, had expressed considerable apprehension over the presence of black troops and their association with the civil population, 'particularly with British women'. Certain Commissioners, wrote Morrison, had indicated that some women 'appear to find a peculiar fascination in associating with men of colour', with resulting resentment among the white Americans and the spreading of rumours which were likely to impair the morale of British servicemen. On the other hand, reports from senior police officers showed that 'on the whole the American coloured troops . . . have behaved well and that, apart from isolated incidents, there have been no difficulties created by [their] association . . . with the civil population'. Chief Constables had already been instructed that their forces should exercise no discrimination and should not encourage anything of that nature on the part of licensees of cinemas, public houses, restaurants etc. Moreover, General Eisenhower had expressed himself as being in complete accord with such a policy, and had even managed to avow that it matched that of his own Army.

Morrison, therefore, while seeing the case for 'giving some warning to the members of the ATS and other women's Services', came down against Grigg's proposal and warned of the controversy that would ensue if and when such instructions leaked out. [28] In this he was supported by Brendan Bracken, the Minister of Information, who reproduced for the benefit of his colleagues a letter which he had sent to Grigg in September. He had written then:

I am sure that the American policy of segregation is the best practical contribution to the avoidance of trouble. Let us second it in every way. But . . . I cannot believe that we ought by any process, visible or invisible, to try to lead our own people to

27 Simon memorandum, 9 October 1942, WP (42) 445, CAB 66/29.
28 Morrison memorandum, 10 October 1942, WP (42) 456, CAB 66/29.

adopt as their own the American social attitude to the American negro; nor should we succeed . . . A wrong step would be disastrous . . .[29]

On the Prime Minister's instructions the matter now came before the Cabinet on 13 October, one last contribution on paper being received beforehand from Stafford Cripps, then Lord Privy Seal, who produced a series of revisions to Grigg's draft circular, omitting all generalized analysis of the Negro character, together with the suggestion that the British Services should adopt the American approach.[30] This draft by Cripps proved broadly acceptable to the majority of Ministers present at the meeting.[31] Grigg's original proposal, it was felt, went too far; the American authorities must realize 'that Britain had a different problem as regards her coloured people and that a *modus vivendi* between the two points of view should be found'. Nor should the US Army expect the British authorities, civil or military, to assist them in enforcing a policy of segregation, while there could be no question of restricting admission to such places as canteens, public houses and cinemas. On the other hand it was generally agreed by the Cabinet that the attitude of the US Army 'was a factor of great importance', and that 'it was desirable that the people of this country should avoid becoming too friendly with coloured troops'. Apparently the only Minister to protest against this last conclusion was again Cranborne, who spoke with the colonies in mind. Sir Alexander Cadogan, the Permanent Under-Secretary at the Foreign Office, who was present, recorded in his diary that Cranborne gave as an illustration the case of one of his coloured officials at the Colonial Office, who was now barred from his usual lunch-time restaurant because it was patronized by American officers; to this the Prime Minister apparently rejoined: 'That's all right; if he takes his banjo with him they'll think he's one of the band.'[32]

All members of the Cabinet were talking at once, according to Cadogan, but eventually it was decided that Cripps, Grigg and Morrison should prepare confidential guidelines for the Services and also approve a suitable article for publication by the Army Bureau of Current Affairs. Their draft, having been shown to Eisenhower on Churchill's instructions, was endorsed by the Cabinet a week later,[33] for distribution to senior officers of the Army, RAF and ATS, together with 'such Editors as the Minister of Information thought appropriate for their confidential information'. The press were to be asked not to make any reference to the existence of the

29 Bracken memorandum, 12 October 1942, WP (42) 459, CAB 66/29.
30 Cripps memorandum, 12 October 1942, WP (42) 460, CAB 66/29.
31 Cabinet of 13 October 1942, CAB 65/28.
32 D. Dilks (ed.), *The Diaries of Sir Alexander Cadogan* (London, 1971), p. 483.
33 Cabinet of 20 October 1942, CAB 65/28; WP (42) 473, CAB 66/30; PREM 4, 26/9.

instructions and not to draw attention to the ABCA article when it appeared.

Some traces of the original Southern Command notes were still present in the new 'Instructions as to the advice which should be given to British Service Personnel', notably when they surveyed the position of Negroes in the United States. The general approach, however, was now that there was no reason to adopt what was called 'the American attitude', but every reason to respect it and to avoid arguments on the issue. 'The Americans are making a great experiment in working out a democratic way of life in a mixed community . . . even if we have different views on how race relationships should be treated in our own country and in the Empire.' Members of the Services should therefore 'be friendly and sympathetic towards coloured American troops – but (should) remember that they are not accustomed in their own country to close and intimate relations with white people'. Everyone should be on his guard against rumours and trouble-makers, while

for a white woman to go about in the company of a Negro American is likely to lead to controversy and ill-feeling. It may also be misunderstood by the Negro troops themselves. This does not mean that friendly hospitality in the home or in social gatherings need be ruled out, though in such cases care should be taken not to invite white and coloured troops at the same time.

A similar approach, though less explicit advice, was adopted in the article on 'The Colour Problem as the Americans See It', which appeared in a December issue of the Army's *Current Affairs*.[34] Additional emphasis was placed here on the measures already taken by President Roosevelt's administration to improve the Negroes' lot in the United States, and on the existence of 'comparable problems within the British Commonwealth'. Looking forward to a world 'where discrimination loses its offensive aspect of superiority and subservience and becomes merely a means of respecting and preserving what is best in each', the article went on to recognize the special view of the war which the American Negro and others might have as a result of existing discrimination:

Since the primary object of the present struggle in which the United Nations are engaged is to preserve freedom in its broadest sense, it is clear that to the coloured people this war may have an even deeper meaning than it has to us. They are our comrades in war and they must remain our comrades in peace.

34 *Current Affairs*, 5 December 1942.

This linking by *Current Affairs* of Negro rights in the United States with wider issues of race and freedom was not uncommon in 1942. Obviously the Nazi doctrines and practices regarding the Jews were themselves sufficient to carry the question of race into the broad area of war aims. At the same time, however, the extension of the conflict into Asia in 1941 had precipitated a new emphasis on matters of colour and in particular of white dominance and imperialism. It was above all with these Asian (and to a lesser extent African) issues that the Negro question tended to be associated. An American bishop, for example, had recently declared that his country could not 'with a clear conscience sit down at the world council-table to deal with the relations of Empires to subject peoples unless she takes drastic steps to apply Christianity to race relations within her own borders'.[35] Similar ideas were being vigorously expressed by Wendell Willkie, the defeated Republican presidential candidate of 1940.[36] 'I venture to think', wrote Gandhi to Roosevelt in July 1942, 'that the Allied declaration that [they] are fighting to make the world safe for freedom of the individual and for democracy sounds hollow, so long as India, and for that matter Africa, are exploited by Great Britain, and America has the Negro problem in her own home.'[37]

In 1942, however, it was Great Britain, far more so than the United States, that found herself in the dock over these matters, charged by widespread opinion in America and Asia with exploiting and seeking to perpetuate her colonial empire in a manner completely at odds with the higher aims of the war and the equality of all peoples. There were, of course, greatly divergent attitudes within the British Government in this respect – Grigg, for example, was far apart from someone like Ernest Bevin – but it was above all the voice of Churchill that was heard by the world. Clement Attlee might publicly avow that the Atlantic Charter (in which Roosevelt and the Prime Minister had stated their respect for 'the right of all peoples to choose the form of government under which they will live') applied to 'all races of mankind'; but this was swamped by Churchill's denial that the Charter affected the pace of the movement towards self-government within the British Empire.[38] Turmoil in India in 1942 and the failure of the Cripps mission to reach agreement with the Congress Party in the spring of that

35 *Spectator*, 28 August 1942.
36 See, for example, Willkie's speech of 26 October 1942, widely reported the following day, and E. Barnard, *Wendell Willkie, Fighter for Freedom* (Marquette, Michigan, 1966). Cf. H. R. Isaacs, *No Peace for Asia* (1967 edn, Cambridge, Mass.), pp. 10ff.
37 *Foreign Relations of the United States*, 1942, vol. I, p. 677.
38 For the debate within Whitehall on the applicability of the Atlantic Charter, see, for example, PREM 4, 43A and 50/3.

year had further focused attention on British policies, while the military *debâcles* in Malaya and Burma had helped spread the conviction that it was a rotten structure which the Government in London was seeking to prop up.

Thus, in the United States, Wendell Willkie returned from a tour of Asia and the Middle East calling for firm promises of freedom for the peoples of these regions, a theme he was to elaborate in his best-selling book, *One World*. American columnists like Drew Pearson were busy belabouring the British empire and in the Senate Committee on Foreign Relations there were calls for the Administration to use its power of the purse to force a change in British imperial policies.[39] Chiang Kai-shek, too, had publicly advised Churchill's Government to grant India self-government, and in official circles in Washington there were fears that London's failure to comply might contribute to the loss to the Japanese not only of India but of China as well. Such consequences were again seen as having strong racial implications. 'Psychologically', wrote a senior State Department official, 'Japan might well obtain such a secure place as the leader of the Asiatic races, if not the colored races, of the world, that Japan's defeat by the United Nations might not be definitive.'[40]

Were there faint echoes here, perhaps, of the fear that had been quite widely expressed in the United States in the early part of the century, that an expansionist Japan might find sympathizers among America's Negroes?[41]

The National Association for the Advancement of Colored Peoples was among the American bodies championing the cause of Indian nationalism, while in 1942–3 small pro-Japanese Negro cults were unearthed in a few American cities. 'Write on my tombstone', one Negro draftee was said to have declared, 'Here lies a black man, killed fighting a yellow man for the protection of a white man.' Writing in 1942, Gunnar Myrdal observed: 'In this war there was a "coloured" nation on the other side – Japan. And that nation had started out by beating the white Anglo-Saxons on their own ground . . . Even unsophisticated Negroes began to see vaguely a colour scheme in world events.'[42]

39 See, for example, *Foreign Relations of the United States*, 1942, vol I, p. 606. Cf. A. H. Vandenberg (ed.), *The Private Papers of Senator Vandenberg* (London, 1953), entry for 1 July 1943.
40 Hamilton memorandum, 17 June 1942, *Foreign Relations of the United States*, 1942, *China*, p. 71.
41 See A. Iriye, *Pacific Estrangement* (Cambridge, Mass., 1972), p. 159.
42 G. Myrdal, *An American Dilemma*, vol. II (New York, 1944), p. 1006. In the words of one of the Bureau of Intelligence summaries sent to Roosevelt in March of the same year, 'the fundamental patriotism of Negroes . . . should not be allowed to obscure the frustration, pessimism, cynicism and insecurity which appears to characterize their attitude toward the war.' Report of 16 March 1942, Roosevelt Papers, PSF, box 170.

Racial groupings and potential conflicts of various kinds were thus well to the fore in a good many official minds on the Allied side in 1942. Churchill himself, on the occasion of Chiang Kai-shek's visit to Delhi and elsewhere early in the year, had privately voiced fears of a 'pan-Asian malaise [spreading] through all the bazaars of India'.[43] Roosevelt for his part had even put to work a professor of the Smithsonian Institution – and was burbling away in private in his harebrained fashion – on the possibility of bringing about a cross-breeding of European and various Asian races in the Far East in order to produce a stock less delinquent than the Japanese, whose skull pattern, less developed than that of the Caucasians, might be responsible for their aggressive behaviour, or so the professor and the President thought.[44]

As for the British Government, they were well aware of the need to justify their country's continued rule over its colonial peoples, and were soon to be engaged in an urgent search for a public declaration of principles on the subject to which the US Government, it was hoped, could also subscribe.[45] (At the level of officials, an inter-departmental committee was set up to find the best methods of 'bringing home to the American people the fact that the organization and principles of the British Empire are such that on moral and material grounds the United States can and should cooperate with it.')

There were growlings by Churchill and others in private (and Grigg, more anxious than most to placate the United States over Negro segregation, was surprisingly among those who most fiercely resented American interference over the Empire, believing that in Burma and India alike Britain should after the war 'retain quite unashamedly the ultimate authority').[46] But Britain's growing material dependence on the United States and the perceived need to retain her cooperation after victory made it impossible to ignore criticism from that quarter. As Richard Law of the Foreign Office observed in a paper for the Cabinet on his return from Washington and New York, one could scarcely throw back the problems of Harlem and Alabama in resentful exchange for interference over India and Southeast Asia, since the Americans could easily retort that there was no comparison in terms of practical interest. Even so, Law, like others in London, found these allies more than a little alarming. 'It is easy to understand what [American] critics of the Administration mean', he wrote, 'when they speak of "the lunatic fringe" at Washington. For these people

43 Churchill to Linlithgow, 3 February 1942, PREM 4, 45/3.
44 Campbell to Cadogan, 6 August 1942, PREM 4, 42/9, and Thorne, *Allies*, pp. 158-9, 167-8.
45 See, for example, PREM 4, 42/9. Also note the frequent defence of colonial and racial policies in the Army's *British Way and Purpose* pamphlets at the time.
46 Grigg memorandum, 5 January 1943, PREM 4, 42/9; Grigg to Churchill, 7 April 1943, PREM 4, 50/3.

are not men of the world. They are children, playing with bricks, and "making the world over".'[47]

Meanwhile Britain's imported racial question in the form of Negro troops was not removed by well-meant Government advice. Before the end of 1942, the National Association for the Advancement of Colored Peoples was causing embarrassment in Whitehall by asking for a denial of the rumour that Britain had bowed to southern white prejudice in the US Army by seeking to reduce the number of Negroes crossing the Atlantic.[48] And a year after the War Office's document had gone out, the Prime Minister's kinsman, the Duke of Marlborough, who was serving as a liaison officer with the US Army, came in private to 10 Downing Street to raise the matter again.[49] His concern on this occasion, however, was what he saw as the threat posed by Negroes (there were now 35,000 of them in the United Kingdom) to the local civilian population, especially in matters of violence and sexual assaults. Churchill's immediate and anxious demands for facts and figures revealed that in crimes of this nature convictions against black Americans were proportionately far higher than they were against whites; so too was the incidence of venereal disease. Even so, allegations against Negroes had often been unsubstantiated on inquiry, and the Secretary of State for War (who ascribed the crime figures to 'the natural propensities of the coloured man') was obliged to conclude that 'unless more definite facts of bad behaviour can be supplied, it is very difficult to ask the Americans to take any action'. Moreover, the local US Army authorities were inclined to put part of the blame on 'the behaviour, on occasions, of the British civilian population, and in particular on some sections of the female population'. Several instances had been reported, for example, of civilians taking the part of Negro soldiers against white US officers and military police patrols.[50] Grigg concluded:

Although in the Army we have managed to foster a reasonably sane attitude, the outlook of the public at large is very much less understanding . . . There is a danger that grave mischief will be done to Anglo-American relations unless we realise that before the problem can be solved we may have to face the question of changing our attitude towards the colour problem.

47 Law memorandum, 21 September 1942, WP (42) 492, CAB 66/30.
48 FO 371/30680, A11660/G.
49 Letters and memoranda of October 1943, PREM 4, 26/9. Cf. *Hansard*, House of Commons, vol. 397, cols 1231–2.
50 For similar occurrences in Bristol on 15 July 1944, see FO 371/38511, AN 3006/6/45.

Eventually, the course of the war and the consequent departure to the Continent of most of the American troops, black and white, produced its own solution. During their stay in Britain the Negroes had evoked strongly contrasting approaches to questions of race and colour among both officials and members of the public; they had also brought with them a vivid, and for the Government uncomfortable, reminder of white dominance within the United States. Potentially, they had provided the material for a fierce retort when white America, official and non-official, began putting pressure on Britain for her imperialism and racial chauvinism.[51] It was the kind of ammunition, however, that could not readily be used against a dominant ally when fighting for one's life. Meanwhile for many of those in high places on both sides of the Atlantic, and not only for a Grigg or a Stimson, the assumption still was that the world which would emerge from the war would continue to be a white man's oyster.

51 Strong, but private, comments by British officials and politicians on aspects of American imperialism during the war can be found in, for example, PREM 4, 42/9. For wider examinations of the main issues noted in this essay, see the author's *Racial Aspects of the Far Eastern War of 1941-1945* (London, 1982) and *The Issue of War* (London, 1985; pb. edn re-titled *The Far Eastern War. States and Societies, 1941-45* (London, 1986)); also e.g. J. W. Dower, *War Without Mercy. Race and Power in the Pacific War* (New York, 1986).

13

En route to Estrangement: American Society and World War Two in the Global Setting

'The United States is . . . separate, aloof, more alone than even the most cynical or pessimistic observers might have predicted in the heyday of American post-war power.' So argues Sanford Ungar when introducing a recent collection of essays which employs the term 'estrangement' to sum up the United States' current relations with the rest of the world, including its allies.[1] And this term, 'estrangement', has been borrowed here, so to speak, as the point of departure for an essay that will attempt to place the experience of the Second World War in the context of 'the shaping of modern America' – although this does not mean that the perspective or the main argument of the present paper are the same as those to be found in the volume in question. It is no doubt true that American attitudes have shifted considerably since the mid-1960s and 'the heyday of American post-war power', and that the United States is more 'estranged' now, 20 years later, than it was then. What the essay that follows focuses upon, however, is an 'estrangement' that, in essence, was present even when many West Europeans in the late 1940s and 1950s were welcoming the clearly hegemonic role which the United States was assuming within the new alliance structures of the time; an 'estrangement' that, fundamentally, was as old as the Republic itself, but which in certain ways, and paradoxically, had been reinforced rather than reduced during the years when a war of global proportions was bringing both the United States of America and Americans into closer and more lasting contact with the rest of the world

This essay was written for a conference on 'World War Two and the Shaping of Modern America', held at Rutgers University, NJ, in April 1986 and is reproduced here by kind permission of the organizer of that conference, Professor Warren Kimball.

1 S. J. Ungar (ed.), *Estrangement. America and the World* (New York, 1986), p. 14.

than ever before. The 1980s have indeed witnessed a widening of the gulf; but viewed within the perspective and on the levels being adopted here, such a development becomes merely one of degree only, and is in no way surprising.

To some extent this essay represents a departure from its author's previous historical exercises. 'Presentism', as it is called – from which the historian is never completely free, of course, but which in the normal way is to be eschewed as far as possible – is here, by request, unashamedly to the fore. Here, too, within a small space, is sketched little more than the outline of a broad historical thesis: a thesis covering so wide a canvas, indeed, that there can be no hope in the present setting of noting, let alone doing justice to, the many qualifications and nuances that should be attached to it. Nor will any attempt be made here to assemble and assess the kind of detailed documentary evidence that formed the basis of, for example, the writer's study of Anglo-American relations during the war, *Allies of a Kind*, or even the weight of supporting references to published and unpublished material concerning numerous wartime societies around the world that figured in his complementary study, *The Issue of War*.[2] What follows is no more than a broad argument which puts forward one perspective (it does not proclaim it as the *only* perspective) within which to view the United States' experience in and responses to the conflict of 1937/39–1945, together with 'modern America's' subsequent relations with the rest of the world.

This being said, some of the difficulties and dangers attendant upon such an exercise need to be acknowledged and spelled out a little more fully before proceeding with the main argument itself. In this respect, the costs, as well as the potential benefits, of generalization are obvious enough. As for the 'presentism' referred to – strongly embedded as it is in much American historiography, and engraved as it is in the very stones of the National Archives in Washington, DC, both manifestations of the Republic's political culture – the accompanying danger of approaching and interpreting a past era in terms of the preoccupations and assumptions of the present should also be evident. ('Our practicalism, presentism, and lack of tragic experience', suggests Karl Nelson, 'have long conditioned us to write and read our history as if we had become what we are because we had earlier decided to be this way.'[3]) Beyond this, however, the paper that follows – indeed, the entire conference for which it is written – must also conjure up certain underlying questions concerning the relationship

2 C. Thorne, *Allies of a Kind. The United States, Britain, and the War Against Japan, 1941–1945* (New York, 1978); Thorne, *The Issue of War. States, Societies, and the Far Eastern Conflict, 1941–1945* (New York, 1985).
3 K. L. Nelson (ed.), *The Impact of War on American Life: the Twentieth Century Experience* (New York, 1971), p. 1.

between the disciplines of history and sociology, and the possibility of achieving a synthesis of the two: questions which, while being borne in mind throughout, can here receive no more than an acknowledgement in the form of references to a few of the works which examine them at length.[4] More hazardous still is the particular requirement of a subject such as the one here being addressed: that is, that is must lead us into the problem-strewn fields of both comparative sociology and international relations, together with the possible connections between them – an area whose difficulties and potential have been examined by the present writer in a separate essay.[5]

Quite apart, then, from the underlying problem of how to 'combine the sociologist's acute sense of structure with the historian's equally sharp sense of change', in the context of this particular exercise there needs to be at the outset an emphasizing of the obvious: that in comparing the experiences and responses of the United States to war with those of other societies, we are in certain ways unable to place like alongside like, and that in each case the developments observed must be viewed in the context of and relative to the entire culture and value-system in question;[6] that the societies caught up in the Second World War were coming to that shared event from widely differing situations, and that, even as between the United States on the one hand and the industrialized, liberal-democratic states of Western Europe on the other, there existed not only significant differences in social, economic and political structures, but a contrast in political cultures that was already fundamental.[7]

Such pre-war contrasts – which as between the United States and numerous other countries involved in the war were obviously greater still

4 For example, P. Burke, *Sociology and History* (London, 1980); F. Braudel, *On History* (trans. S. Matthews; London, 1980); P. Abrams, *Historical Sociology* (Shepton Mallet, 1982); T. Skocpol, *States and Social Revolutions* (Cambridge, 1979).

5 'Societies, sociology, and the international. Some contributions and questions, with particular reference to total war', essay number 3 above. See also, for example, Skocpol, *States and Social Revolutions*; B. Moore, *Social Origins of Dictatorship and Democracy: Lord and Peasant in the Making of the Modern World* (London, 1967); A. Giddens, *The Nation-State and Violence* (Cambridge, 1985); W. Eberhard, *Conquerors and Rulers. Social Forces in Medieval China* (Leiden, 1965), ch. 1.

6 See, for example, M. Mead, 'The comparative study of cultures', in *Anthropology: A Human Science* (Princeton, NJ 1964), and Lucian Pye's thesis that 'cultural variations are decisive in determining the course of political development', in his *Asian Power and Politics. The Cultural Dimensions of Authority* (Cambridge, Mass., 1985).

7 On underlying American–West European differences as they existed in the inter-war years, see, for example, B. D. Karl, *The Uneasy State. The United States from 1915 to 1945* (Chicago, 1983), and F. Costigliola, *Awkward Dominion. American Political, Economic, and Cultural Relations with Europe, 1919–1933* (Ithaca, NY, 1984); and on the European-American contrast in general, for example, S. P. Huntington, *American Politics. The Promise of Disharmony* (Cambridge, Mass., 1981).

– constitute only one of the many variables which came to affect the ways and degrees in which the conflict of 1937/9–1945 left its mark, others – to cite only two – including the manner of initial involvement in the war, and the nature, extent and length of that involvement thereafter.[8] Nevertheless, for all its difficulties and limitations, a comparative perspective on the American experience of the period is not without its intellectual justification. The conflict itself, after all, was not the only connection linking the states and societies concerned. One does not have to accept, say, the (reductionist) 'world system' paradigm of Wallerstein or the Marxist premises of Wolf regarding 'the social system of the modern world'[9] in order to acknowledge that strong ties of a structural and economic kind were by 1937/9 encompassing virtually all societies around the globe; that, whatever the differences in their individual cultures, patterns of organization, and stages of industrialization and urbanization, many of those societies were by then alike in having to face problems relating to the spread of modern science, technology and industry, to the development of what Robert Gilpin has termed 'a world market economy', and to the spread of what was being called (in a blanket phrase that itself, of course, begs certain questions) 'mass society'. Alike, too, and as a consequence of developments of this kind, they were being confronted with issues concerning, *inter alia*, the relationships between government and governed, order and freedom, *laissez-faire* and intervention, society and the individual. To put it more vividly (albeit more narrowly), the private reflections of the distinguished American journalist, Raymond Clapper, on the mail he was receiving following Henry Wallace's 1942 speech on 'the century of the common man' could have applied, *mutatis mutandis*, to any one of a large number of societies which were embroiled in the war:

People are groping for some way out of the dilemma of the modern world . . . The people who come along with some ideas as to how to control the machine and make it work for us are the ones who will be listened to.[10]

8 On such general questions concerning war and society, see, for example, essay number 3, 'Societies, sociology, and the international'; Nelson, *Impact of War*, Introduction; A. Marwick, *War and Social Change in the 20th Century* (London, 1977). Also, on the US in particular, A. A. Stein, *The Nation at War* (Baltimore, Ma, 1980), and M. Stohl, *War and Domestic Political Violence. The American Capacity for Repression and Reaction* (London, 1976).

9 I. Wallerstein, *The Modern World-System. Capitalist Agriculture and the Origins of the Capitalist World-Economy in the Sixteenth Century* (New York, 1974); E. R. Wolf, *Europe and the People Without History* (Berkeley, Ca, 1982). Cf., for example, T. Skocpol, 'Wallerstein's World Capitalist System', in *American Journal of Sociology*, vol. 82, March 1977, and Giddens, *The Nation-State and Violence*, pp. 161ff.

10 Clapper to Landon, 29 May 1942, Clapper Papers (Library of Congress), box 50. On the wider issues and perspectives involved, see, for example, Thorne, *Issue*, chs 2, 3, 8 and 9; A. Giddens, *The Class Structure of Advanced Societies* (London, 1973), and *A Contemporary Critique*

Wartime developments within a single society have to be seen in relation to the specific culture and structures concerned. But often it is indeed only when such a relative perspective has been applied – to take one instance, as regards the position of women[11] – that certain broad similarities and patterns sometimes begin to emerge across even those divisions commonly drawn between, say, 'Western' and 'Asian' societies. Not that, in the argument which follows, it is the similarities of wartime experience and response between the United States and the rest of the world that are being emphasized. Rather, the stress is upon differences and contrasts in this respect. The point being made here, however, is that the underlying issues which (largely unseen or unacknowledged) were facing Americans in these years were less peculiar to the Republic than was generally conceived at the time.

The argument itself is of course being advanced by someone who, for all, say, his close friendships among Americans and his admiration for the dynamism and anti-authoritarianism of their society, nevertheless stands outside the Republic in terms of his own nationality and socialization. Such an external viewpoint may have its advantages in the present context; but it should also be recognized at the outset, not least by the writer himself, that it is likely to entail, too, problems of empathy and communication. We can acknowledge, as has David Strauss with reference to French critics of American society in the 1920s,[12] that foreign reservations are by no means necessarily based, as tends to be assumed, upon ignorance or incorrect information. None the less, not being American, not being *committed* to the United States of America as a citizen, is likely to leave its mark. Is the difference one that is also sometimes exacerbated by a difficulty, on the American side, in standing outside the Republic, so to speak, and viewing it from there? Does it have some relevance for the present paper when we find Salman Rushdie concluding, at the recent PEN congress in New York, that what had been heard there were 'two ideas of America which have been quarrelling. The first is . . . an idea of America held by Americans, and the other is an idea of America held by everyone else'? Is it relevant when, say, a London reviewer of a biography of Norman Mailer judges

of Dialectical Materialism (London, 1981); E. Gellner, *Nations and Nationalism* (Oxford, 1983); R. Gilpin, *War and Change in World Politics* (Cambridge, 1981); A. J. Latham, *The International Economy and the Underdeveloped World, 1865-1914* (London, 1978); S. Giner, *Mass Society* (London, 1976); M. D. Biddiss, *The Age of the Masses* (London, 1977).

11 See Thorne, *Issue*, pp. 77-9, 257, 266-9, and the more detailed works referred to there.

12 D. Strauss, *Menace in the West. The Rise of French Anti-Americanism in Modern Times* (Westport, Conn., 1978), p. 3. And see, for example, Reinhold Niebuhr, *The Irony of American History* (London, 1952), p. 21: 'We find it almost as difficult as the Communists to believe that anyone could think ill of us, since we are as persuaded as they that our society is so essentially virtuous that only malice could prompt criticism of any of our actions.'

that the tapes upon which the book was based reveal 'the insularity of much American intellectual life'; or when the United States is depicted in London also as 'a nation with the best information technology in the world, but with no ideas of what is going on outside its own borders'; or when a good many European historians, including the present writer, see much American writing on recent international history as being conceived on the basis of a series of simple, bilateral relationships – between the United States on the one hand and this or that country on the other, like the design of a rimless wheel, a set of spokes radiating outwards from an ever-crucial and all-absorbing centre?[13]

To pose such initial questions is not to ignore or devalue the immense and enviable capacity for self-criticism among Americans themselves. For, notwithstanding the ethnocentric complacency that lay behind much of the 'modernization' theorizing and belief in 'the end of ideology' in the 1950s and 1960s (notwithstanding the assumptions of a Brzezinski, say: 'For better or for worse, the rest of the world learns what is in store for it by observing what happens in the United States'[14]), there have not been wanting Americans to suggest that since 1945 their state and nation have become 'estranged' from much of the remainder of humankind.

In this context, the term 'estrangement' is not alluding to that conscious and deliberate distancing of one's society and body-politic from the entanglements and corruptness of the rest of the world which had been a marked feature of the Republic's history before the war and which continued to exercise an attraction for many thereafter. The concern of the American protesters being referred to, as of the present essay, is with an unwitting 'estrangement' in terms of social and political priorities; in terms of assumptions and values which go deeper than the mere existence of foreign governments and regimes that align themselves with the United States, than the continuing vitality of market forces and incentives around the globe, or than the evident aversion of so many peoples to Soviet-style communism. 'With unfailing consistency, we have since the end of the Second World War intervened on behalf of conservative and fascist repression against revolution and radical reform. In an age when societies

13 See respectively *Times Literary Supplement*, 7 February 1986; *Sunday Times* (London), 28 July 1985; *The Times* (London), 27 July 1984; and for example the comments by Kathleen Burk in 'What is diplomatic history?', *History Today*, July 1985, and by David Reynolds in 'The origins of the Cold War: the European dimension', *Historical Journal*, 1985, no. 2. See also, for example, L. Hartz, *The Liberal Tradition in America* (New York, 1955), p. 29; P. A. Cohen, *Discovering History in China: American Historical Writing on the Recent Chinese Past* (New York, 1984), and the relevant articles in the 120th anniversary edition of *The Nation*, 22 March 1986.

14 Z. Brzezinski, *Between Two Ages. America's Role in the Technetronic Era* (New York, 1970), p. 31; and see, for example, Costigliola, *Awkward Dominion*, passim.

are in a revolutionary or prerevolutionary stage, we have become the foremost counter-revolutionary, status quo power on earth. Such a policy can only lead to moral and political disaster.'[15] Hans Morgenthau's cry in 1974[16] is merely one of many, that have come from a variety of positions along the political spectrum, and not simply from the so-called 'New Left'. Selig Harrison, for example, has drawn out in detail the extent to which, for all the aid and alliances linking the Republic to various states in Asia, its policies and the assumptions behind them have helped create a 'widening gulf' between itself and nationalists in that part of the globe. 'We find the world too complex to be understood, managed or even fully observed', reflects George Ball; '. . . we fail even to recognize the fundamental differences in our national situations and requirements [*vis-à-vis* Western Europe].'[17] Or again, we can note the relevance for the United States' external, as well as for its internal, relationships, and for what follows, of the recent findings of Robert Bellah and his colleagues:

Americans, it would seem, feel most comfortable in thinking about politics in terms of a consensual community of autonomous, but essentially similar, individuals, and it is to such a conception that they turn for the cure of their present ills. For all the lip service given to respect for cultural differences, Americans seem to lack the resources to think about the relationships between groups that are culturally, socially, or economically quite different . . . The radical egalitarianism of an individualist society has its own problems. For such a society is really constituted only of autonomous middle-class individuals. Those who for whatever reason do not meet the criteria for full membership are left outside in a way unknown in a hierarchical society.[18]

15 H. Morgenthau, 'Repression's friend', *New York Times*, 10 October 1974, as quoted in Huntington, *American Politics*. And see for example J. L. S. Girling, *America and the Third World. Revolution and Intervention* (London, 1980).
16 To suggest that this particular, all-embracing description and condemnation might need some qualifying is not, of course, to embrace the remarkable counter-thesis advanced by Samuel Huntington, for whom 'the message [before the late 1960s] of the superiority of liberty . . . was there for all to see in [America's] troop deployments, carrier task forces, foreign aid missions, and intelligence operatives'; who suggests that 'the destruction of Chilean democracy in 1973 might have been avoided' if the United States had intervened more forcefully in that country's electoral process in 1970. *American Politics*, pp. 252–3, 259.
17 S. S. Harrison, *The Widening Gulf. Asian Nationalism and American Policy* (New York, 1978); G. W. Ball, *The Past Has Another Pattern* (New York, 1982), pp. 468–9, 480. See, for example, J. Kwitny, *Endless Enemies. The Making of an Unfriendly World* (New York, 1984); R. J. Barnett, *Roots of War. The Men and Institutions Behind U.S. Foreign Policy* (London, 1973); M. P. Rogin, *Ronald Reagan, the Movie and other Episodes in Political Demonology* (Berkeley, 1987); E. Stillman and W. Pfaff, *Power and Impotence. The Failure of America's Foreign Policy* (New York, 1966).
18 R. N. Bellah et al., *Habits of the Heart. Individualism and Commitment in American Life* (Berkeley, Ca, 1985), p. 206. And see, for example, Niebuhr, *Irony of American History*, pp. 28, 36: 'Since America developed as a bourgeois society, . . . it naturally inclined toward the bourgeois ideology which neglects the factor of power in the human community and equates

More particularly, the broad argument being advanced in this essay can be related directly to the reflections on the war years themselves provided by some of those participants who were interviewed by Studs Terkel for his '*The Good War*': by Joe Marcus, for example ('We knew all the answers. We knew how Third World countries could develop best. We were the papa. We were in charge. It seeped all through our society'); or by Paul Edwards ('We had 20, 25 years of greatness in our country, when we reached out to the rest of the world with help . . . Now we're being pinched back into the meanness of the soul that had grabbed a new middle class that came out of poverty, as I do').[19] The argument can also be seen as connecting directly with the analyses provided by Stanley Hoffmann of the 'exceptionalism' of the Republic and its society ('We Americans', declared the *Saturday Evening Post* as the war neared its end, 'can boast that we are not as other men are'[20]), its continuing post-war quest for primacy and 'expectation of universal relevance', its Manicheism, its 'craving for simplicity', and its 'fascination [with] force and muscle'.[21]

'The idea of a world in which the United States would be merely one actor like any other, or even a great power like so many others in history, remains intolerable.'[22] In order to obtain a full understanding of current characteristics of this kind, penetratingly observed by Hoffmann, we would of course need to explore much further back, much wider and deeper, than simply as far as the Second World War. Indeed, a thorough explanation could scarcely stop short of an analysis of the making of American society

---

interest with rationality . . . We can understand the neat logic of either economic reciprocity or the show of pure power. But we are mystified by the endless complexities of human motives and the varied compounds of ethnic loyalties, cultural traditions, social hopes, envies and fears which enter into the policies of nations, and which lie at the foundation of their political cohesion.'

19 S. Terkel (ed.), '*The Good War*'. *An Oral History of World War Two* (New York, 1984), pp. 329, 572–3.

20 Quoted in G. Perrett, *Days of Sadness, Years of Triumph. The American People, 1939–1945* (New York, 1973), p. 418.

21 S. Hoffmann: *Gulliver's Troubles, or the Setting of American Foreign Policy* (New York, 1968); *Primacy or World Order. American Foreign Policy Since the Cold War* (New York, 1978); *Dead Ends. American Foreign Policy in the New Cold War* (Cambridge, Mass., 1983). In relation to the last characteristic, see, for example, the argument of Huntington, quoted earlier, on 'carrier task forces', etc. Are there things to be learned, also in this regard, not only from the 'gun culture' of the Republic, but from its literature? See, for example, Leslie Fiedler in *Love and Death in the American Novel* (New York, 1975, p. 28) on '. . . the dark vision of the American – his obsession with violence and his embarrassment before love . . .'. The relevance of the recent enthusiasm for the primitivism of such cinematic offerings as *Rambo, Rocky IV, Red Dawn* and *Star Wars* needs no underlining.

22 *Dead Ends*, p. 83. Note how misplaced, in the era of Reaganism, appear the expectations regarding the 'Europeanization of America' to be found in Peter Schrag, *The End of the American Future* (New York, 1973).

and American political culture from their earliest days: of reminders concerning, for example, the causes and consequences of the absence of a radical social revolution in American history,[23] and the underlying reasons why, generically speaking, in Huntington's words, 'change and reform in America can go only so far and no further';[24] why to be American is to define oneself in terms of an evangelizing creed, is to 'be' an ideology, as Richard Hofstadter once put it; why socialism has never commanded a significant degree of acceptance within the Republic; why an outburst of social and political protest such as Progressivism was itself largely conservative in essence; why there was no alliance in the 1890s between agrarian radicalism and urban labour, and why, in Michael Rogin's phrase, 'class action [in America] was a substitute for a general challenge to the industrial capitalist system'. In terms of more specific historical antecedents, we would need to examine why and how Progressivism itself faded away around the time of the First World War; why the New Deal, limited from the outset in its radicalism and its collectivism (Roosevelt and the Brains Trust, observes Rosen, 'neither envisaged nor promoted the welfare state'), soon lacked the momentum which might have been imparted by a widespread 'sense of an emergency based on a critical change in the nature of Western industrialism', with Roosevelt himself, perhaps, as Karl sees it, 'sharing to some extent in the conservative reaction', and, 'like most Americans' in the 1930s, perceiving 'little relation between domestic attitudes and the events being played out abroad'.[25]

This 'exceptionalism' of the 1930s was in no way new, of course; merely all the more at odds with the reality of a world of increasingly 'penetrated' states and interdependent societies. In the present context, it is particularly interesting to note the extent to which the 1914–18 war, too, had been perceived, in Karl's words, 'as foreign, hence alien to the American experience', and hence, again, bearing in its frightful course no message for the Republic regarding 'a threat to traditional liberal democracy in the logic of science or in the complex demands of technological advance'. (Indeed, as Rogin among others has emphasized, the war had played an

23 See, for example, Barrington Moore, *Social Origins of Dictatorship*, pp. 112-3; S. P. Huntington, *Political Order in Changing Societies* (New Haven, Conn., 1968), pp. 98-9, 135.
24 Huntington, *American Politics*, p. 107, and M. H. Hunt, *Ideology and U.S. Foreign Policy* (New Haven, 1987).
25 A. Rosen, *Hoover, Roosevelt, and the Brains Trust. From Depression to New Deal* (New York, 1977), p. 303; Karl, *The Uneasy State*, pp. 130, 175, 215; M. P. Rogin, *The Intellectuals and McCarthy: the Radical Specter* (Cambridge, Mass. 1967), chs 6-8. And see, for instance, Huntington, *American Politics*, p. 90; Hartz, *The Liberal Tradition in America*, passim; E. A. Shils, *The Torment of Secrecy. The Background and Consequences of American Security Policies* (London, 1956), pp. 94ff; Davis, *Prisoners of the American Dream*.

important part in diminishing the fervour of Progressive hostility to the big corporations, 'as business seemed to cleanse itself by cooperating voluntarily in the national interest'.) The contrast which Karl rightly goes on to draw is with 'European proponents of a new industrial order' who 'did not accept a fixed relation' between that same liberal democracy and the rapidly accelerating material changes of the time: some of them, of course, abandoning that political belief and goal altogether, but others seeking 'to redefine democracy in terms of revolutionary new conceptions of mass society'.[26]

It is within settings such as these that we can begin to appreciate the extent to which, even before the onset of the Second World War, and even if we leave aside for the moment the 'non-Western', 'non-industrialized' societies of the world, the United States stood apart: a symbol of hope and promise to many, of course, but apart none the less. Living in the United States, wrote the French intellectual André Siegfried (anticipating the similar conclusions of a number of more left-wing compatriots after 1945), 'taught me more about Europe than long years spent on our continent. We became conscious of a reality which escapes us here [in France]: that there exists a European spirit of which the American spirit is often the perfect antithesis.'[27]

It is also within such perspectives that we can better understand the misgiving in 1940–1 of the young American diplomat John Carter Vincent, as his own country was drawn closer to direct involvement in the rapidly spreading international conflict that had been precipitated by Nazism and Japanese militarism. As he rightly saw it at the time, behind the 'smokescreen of battles', 'great social forces were at work', representing the culmination of decades in which 'there has been a growing dissatisfaction on the part of the subordinate majority with the static dominant minority'; a dissatisfaction which was 'gradually translating itself into a dynamic revolt against anti-social national sovereignties and anti-social free capitalism'. Vincent's fear, however, was that the United States was 'going into this war blindly trying to preserve something that is already spoiled in half the world'. Its government, he wrote privately, looked like taking the country into the fight without first establishing those crucial prerequisites of 'social reform and social objectives' that would enable the United States 'to come out of the war . . . prepared to construct something worthwhile'.[28]

26 Karl, *The Uneasy State*, p. 33; Rogin, *The Intellectuals*, p. 203. For one interpretation of, for example, British political responses to the experience of the 1914–18 war, see K. Middlemas, *Politics in Industrial Society. The Experience of the British System Since 1911* (London, 1979), chs 3–5. In the general context, see Costigliola, *Awkward Dominion*.

27 Quoted in Strauss, *Menace in the West*, pp. 203ff; and see ibid., ch. 16.

28 Quoted in G. May, *China Scapegoat. The Diplomatic Ordeal of John Carter Vincent* (Washington, DC, 1979), pp. 59, 62.

It was a shrewd and prescient analysis. And in effect, what Vincent was foreseeing was the United States' road to estrangement. Whether, in the light of the distinctive features of the Republic's political culture, of its history and of its forthcoming experience of the war itself, an alternative road was ever a realistic option, as the young diplomat himself seemed to think, is another matter.

At this point it becomes important to emphasize what is *not* being said or implied in the overall argument. Above all, there are two features of the war years themselves that are not being overlooked, for indeed it is in the light of them that the broad historical picture being sketched here, if accepted, takes on an aspect of the tragic rather than, say, of planned or wanton wrongdoing. The first of those two features is the considerable amount of goodwill towards the rest of the world that existed among Americans at the time. Even when one has allowed that, for example, implications of what even then was being referred to as US 'economic imperialism' can be discerned in, say, the pages of Wendell Willkie's *One World*; even when one has noted the ignorance and national-centred assumptions that surrounded, for instance, so much American rhetoric concerning China and the Chinese,[29] or the degree of self-delusion accompanying the Office of Strategic Services (OSS) reports that the peoples of Southeast Asia were 'enthusiastically pro-American';[30] even when the element of over-confidence amounting to arrogance is apparent in the conviction within official circles, reported back to London in 1942 by an observer familiar with and admiring of the Republic,

that the United States stands for something in the world – something of which the world has need, something which the world is going to like, something, in the last analysis, which the world is going to take whether it likes it or not . . .[31]

– even so the existence of a genuine desire to assist and benefit others remains apparent.

In this context, Theodore White's later reflections on General Stilwell's wartime approach to the problems encompassing Chinese politics and military matters are doubtless pertinent: 'He came', wrote White in the

29 See, for example, M. Schaller, *The U.S. Crusade in China, 1938–1945* (New York, 1979); H. R. Isaacs, *Scratches on our Minds* (New York, 1963); K. E. Shewmaker, *Americans and Chinese Communists, 1927–1945* (Ithaca, NY, 1971); W. I. Cohen, *America's Response to China* (New York, 1971); Thorne, *Allies*, passim, and *Issue*, ch., 6.
30 See the OSS Research and Analysis reports quoted and cited in Thorne, *Issue*, p. 204.
31 Richard Law, Cabinet paper of 21 September 1942, WP(42)492, CAB 66/30, Public Record Office, London.

1970s, 'of a tradition . . . of Americans who felt so strongly that we were the good people that wherever they went they were convinced that they, as Americans, brought virtue. Nor could Stilwell conceive that what was good for America could possibly be bad, or wrong, for other peoples.'[32] At the same time, however, the second of our two features must be borne in mind. For it is clear that large numbers of people, within a great variety of nations around the world, did indeed look to the United States during the war for inspiration and assistance, not simply in terms of their own immediate burdens and desires, but in the hope of seeing 'a better world' overall emerge from the pain and devastation of these years.

In this regard, it remains at least very possible, for example, that the borrowings from the Declaration of Independence contained in the corresponding proclamation for Vietnam issued by Ho Chi Minh in September 1945 represented something more than a mere tactical search for political advantage.[33] Certainly, if it was Churchill (alongside the Red Army at Stalingrad) who for many epitomized defiance against tyranny and militarism, it was Roosevelt above all who was widely seen, in the words of one (socialist) New Zealand newspaper in 1944, as the leader who was 'trusted as a friend to bring into being a better world by curbing the activities of those who would stay the march of progress'.[34]

There remain two other initial riders to be recorded before the core of the argument is put forward. The first is that that argument is not to be taken as suggesting that substantial social change failed to take place within the United States during the war years. The details of those changes are available in a number of major studies,[35] will doubtless be the subject of other papers and debate during the present conference, and will be placed within a comparative perspective later in this essay itself. What is called for at this stage is simply an initial acknowledgement that, during the war, large numbers of black and female Americans, for example, obtained jobs (both within and outside the country's armed forces) and obtained levels of real income that in both instances had previously been denied them; that the Servicemen's Readjustment Act of 1944 in particular (the 'GI Bill of Rights') was to facilitate major changes in the fields of educational opportunity, career prospects and housing; and that the overall distribution

32 T. H. White, *In Search of History* (New York, 1978), p. 178.
33 Declaration of Independence of the Democratic Republic of Vietnam, together with Ho Chi Minh's accompanying speech, as printed in *La République* (Hanoi), 18 October 1945 (Bibliothèque Nationale, Paris). And cf., for example, C. Fenn, *Ho Chi Minh* (New York, 1973), pp. 83-4, and S. Karnow, *Vietnam. A History* (New York, 1983), p. 138.
34 *The Standard* (Wellington), 16 November 1944; and see Thorne, *Issue*, p. 235.
35 For example, J. M. Blum, *V Was For Victory. Politics and American Culture During World War II* (New York, 1976); R. Polenberg, *War and Society. The United States, 1941-1945* (Philadelphia, 1972); Perrett, *Days of Sadness*; Karl, *The Uneasy State*.

of the vastly enhanced national income shifted significantly in a more equitable direction[36] – a shift whose consequences, like those of the 1944 Act, are amply testified to in individual and family terms in the recollections obtained by Studs Terkel.

The final initial qualification concerns, not American society but those others with which, here and elsewhere, it can be compared within the context of the war. And what is not being suggested or implied in this regard is that either widespread calls during these years for fundamental social reform, or the enactment of preliminary measures aimed in that direction, or both, were necessarily a prelude to sustained and wholly successful post-war endeavours in that same sense. True, when measured against the pre-war political economy and social structure in each case, the changes that were in the making in China and Yugoslavia, say, were great and enduring indeed. True, in Britain, also, the reforms initiated by the wartime coalition government and the larger achievements – themselves made possible by the experience of war – of the Labour ministries of 1945–51 were to have lasting social consequences,[37] just as, obviously, the removal of imperial rule in territories such as India and Indonesia – again, greatly hastened and facilitated by the war – was both to represent and to provide the setting for further, major change. To say as much, however, is not to ignore the extent to which reforming hopes and intentions that were present during the war years were to be frustrated thereafter: to which, for example, the 're-making of British society' failed to materialise;[38] to which the excitement and expectations of Resistance intellectuals in France had come to be superseded by despair and resentment by the 1950s;[39] or – to adopt a wider perspective – to which the wartime and immediate post-war assumptions on the part of Nehru and others concerning the brotherhood of Asians were soon to fade away as Hindu stood bloodily against Moslem and as Indians took up arms against those same Chinese who earlier had been proclaimed heroic partners and 'the embodiment of Asia's hopes for the future.'[40]

---

36 See, for example, the tables reproduced in Perrett, *Days of Sadness*, pp. 353–4, and in D'A. Campbell, *Women At War With America: Private Lives in a Patriotic Era* (Cambridge, Mass., 1984), pp. 168, 182.

37 See the outstanding assessment by K. O. Morgan, *Labour in Power 1945–1951* (Oxford, 1984).

38 See, for example, A. Bullock, *Ernest Bevin: Foreign Secretary* (London, 1983), p. 703.

39 See, for example, S. Hoffmann, *France: Change and Tradition* (London, 1963), and J. D. Wilkinson, *The Intellectual Resistance in Europe* (Cambridge, Mass., 1981).

40 On wartime Indian perceptions of China, see Thorne, *Issue*, pp. 169–71. On broad post-war developments see for instance G. Krishna, 'India and the International Order – Retreat from Idealism', in H. Bull and A. Watson (eds), *The Expansion of International Society* (London, 1984), and S. N. Hay, *Asian Ideas of East and West* (Cambridge, Mass., 1970), p. 329.

These circumscriptions being registered, what, then, remains as the central thrust of the argument in regard to the war years themselves? It can be summarized in three propositions. The first is that the overall American experience of the war differed substantially from those of well-nigh all the other societies that were directly involved. The second – closely associated with the first, but more important – is that Americans in general failed to perceive the underlying significance of the war in terms of the wider and deeper social, economic and political problems that, *mutatis mutandis*, faced and increasingly linked virtually all societies of the time, and that in this they stood apart from large numbers of people (whatever their particular perspectives and prescriptions might be) of other nations around the world. And the third (and again closely connected) proposition is that the predominant American response to the experience of war was not only fundamentally different in its mood and its direction from those which came to the fore in other societies, but also (taken in conjunction, of course, with those pre-existing differences of situation, political culture and outlook referred to earlier) helped widen the gap, mental even more than material, that was to separate the Republic from so much of the rest of the world in the post-war era.

Little space need be devoted here to the contrast in material experience of the war between 1937 and 1945 that set the United States apart from well-nigh every other state and society directly involved. (The qualification 'well-nigh' is included to allow for the fact that, in certain respects only, the experience of Canada, say, was not wholly dissimilar.) The continental territory of the Republic suffered no assault at enemy hands. It was neither occupied nor bombed. On the contrary, as John Morton Blum has put it, the great majority of the American people were 'fighting the war on imagination alone'.[41] What is more, the war years witnessed a significant increase in prosperity for most Americans, with consumer purchases of goods and services rising by 12 per cent between 1939 and 1944, average real weekly earnings in manufacturing industry, for instance, climbing in the same period from $24 to nearly $37 (inflation being notably kept under control), and the average daily consumption of calories increasing by 4 per cent at the same time. Again, as a proportion of the total population the number of Americans who lost their lives as a result of the war was small in comparison to, say, Britain or New Zealand, and almost minute when placed alongside the figures for the Soviet Union, China, Germany and Japan. More people died in the Bengal famine of 1943 (attributable to the war at least in considerable degree) than the total of American losses, twice as many Russian civilians in the seige of Leningrad alone, two-thirds

41 Blum, *V Was For Victory*, p. 16.

as many people in the Netherlands, even. Or, to take another, often related, measure, where the average daily calorific consumption in the Netherlands in the middle of 1944 (it was to drop sharply in the ensuing winter) was 1,500, among the French around 1,100 and in the North of Italy just over 1,000, for the American military in the Pacific areas it was 4,758 – a figure substantially higher than that for the neighbouring Australian armed forces, for example, and over twice that for their Japanese counterparts.

As Paul Edwards has summarized the contrast for Terkel in retrospect:

While the rest of the world came out bruised and scarred and nearly destroyed, we came out with the most unbelievable machinery, tools, manpower, money.[42] The war was fun for America – if you'll pardon my bitterness. New gratifications they'd never known in their lives . . . And the rest of the world was bleeding and in pain.[43]

'The trauma of war', comments Stein, 'lingers in other societies in a way that it has not in the USA, save, of course, for the South in the late nineteenth century. Unlike Europeans, Americans do not have an ingrained sense of the ramifications of war.'[44] And in relation to American literature, Fiedler likewise concludes: 'The rise and destruction of Nazism we have recorded in old newspapers and new textbooks as documented truth, actuality; but we have lived its course in our viscera and our nerves as a bad dream in which, though we die for it, we cannot really believe.'[45]

The second of the propositions summarized above involves a contrast that is less susceptible to precise demonstration and measurement, but is of greater significance. We have already noted in passing Professor Karl's judgement on the extent to which Americans had perceived the 1914–18 war as having little or no bearing upon the problems and further development of their own society. And where the new international conflict was concerned, despite the much greater degree to which the United States

42 In the period which saw US gross national product soar from $88.6 billion to $198.7 billion (1939–45), US output of manufactured goods rise by 300 per cent (1940–4), US overall productive capacity increase by around 50 per cent and agricultural productivity by over 25 per cent (1940–4), Britain, for example, lost around one-quarter of its national wealth, Chinese production and currency alike were well-nigh ruined, and France, for instance, was by 1943 paying to Germany almost one-third of what had been the total national product five years earlier.
43 Terkel, '*The Good War*, pp. 572–3. On the contrasts cited, and others, see for example, A. S. Milward, *War, Economy and Society, 1939–1945* (London, 1977); G. Wright, *The Ordeal of Total War, 1939–1945* (New York, 1968); A. Werth, *Russia At War, 1941–1945* (London, 1964); A. Calder, *The People's War, 1939–1945* (London, 1969); Thorne, *Issue*, ch. 8.
44 Stein, *Nation at War*, p. 5. And see D. M. Kennedy, 'War and the American character', *The Stanford Magazine*, Spring/Summer 1975.
45 Fiedler, *Love and Death*, p. 481.

was involved, both contemporary surveys and subsequent historical analyses suggest that an essentially similar detachment, indifference, or unawareness predominated among the population of the Republic. For all the efforts of press, radio, cinema and propaganda services, a large proportion of Americans remained largely ignorant about the world beyond their shores. (Sixty per cent of those polled in 1942 were unable to locate either China or India on the outline map provided.) Large numbers of those who were obliged to go overseas in uniform signally failed to empathize with the unfamiliar cultures and societies – those of the 'slopeys' of China and the 'wogs' of India, for example – they found there. ('Our men', wrote the outstanding front-line correspondent, Ernie Pyle, '. . . are impatient with the strange peoples and customs of the countries they now inhabit. They say that if they ever get home they never want to see another foreign country.'[46])

What is more, of those at home in the United States questioned by Gallup Poll in September 1942, 40 per cent were declaring themselves as not knowing 'what this war is all about', essentially the same picture emerging from other surveys conducted by the Office of War Information, where officials like Arthur Schlesinger Jr and Archibald MacLeish who sought to foster a wider perspective and awareness among the public at large were before long driven either to resign or to sink back in despair.[47] What stood out among US soldiers, reported the researchers of the Army's Information and Education Division, was 'an absence of thinking about the meaning of the war' beyond that of 'a defensive necessity'; and again: 'except for a very limited number of men, little feeling of personal commitment to the war emerged [from our surveys].'[48]

More impressionistically, Raymond Clapper (who was among those observers who judged the British public to be taking 'all the inconveniences' of war 'much more in their stride' than his fellow-Americans) privately declared himself to be in full agreement with the friend (George Carlin, general manager of the United Features Syndicate) who, on noting that a woman had been placed in a sanatorium as a mental patient and 'wouldn't admit to herself or anyone that the war is actually going on', reflected that 'most of the population has taken the same attitude, even if

46 See, for example, Isaacs, *Scratches on our Minds*, pp. 37, 176ff., 317; Blum, *V Was for Victory*, pp. 65ff; J. Israel, 'Southwest Associated University', in P. K. Sih (ed.), *Nationalist China During the Sino-Japanese War, 1937-1945* (Hicksville, NY, 1977); E. Taylor, *Richer by Asia* (London, 1948), and *Awakening From History* (London, 1971).

47 See for instance R. Dallek, *Franklin D. Roosevelt and American Foreign Policy, 1932-1945* (New York, 1979), p. 350; A. M. Winkler, *The Politics of Propaganda. The Office of War Information, 1942-1945* (New Haven, Conn., 1978), pp. 5-6, 40ff, 54, and passim.

48 S. A. Stouffer et al., *The American Soldier: Adjustment During Army Life* (Princeton, NJ, 1949), ch. 9.

they are not in sanatoria'.[49] 'Few faced the underlying issues [of the war] squarely', concluded Merle Curti subsequently, '. . . [with] business advertisements in the press and on radio imply[ing] that the country was fighting in order to get back to bigger and better bathtubs, radios, and automobiles.'[50] And Blum has observed in similar vein:

There were . . . few Americans, in office or out, who believed that reconstruction was a legitimate part of the cost of war, few who believed that equality of sacrifice – so much discussed during the war – applied to the rebuilding of the societies the war had rent . . . Weary of the memory of depression and of the demands of a foreign war, rather bored with politics, international or domestic, the American people accepted victory and prosperity as a sufficient achievement of the safety and security their hearts desired.[51]

Now both historical evidence and common sense suggest that in other societies, too, large numbers of people – probably the majority – tended to be concerned, day in day out, with the immediate, practical requirements of living and surviving. Among peoples and armies other than those of the United States, of course, ignorance of and indifference to the foreigner was not uncommon. But at the same time it is also evident (as will be seen from the kinds of study cited earlier in regard to the material consequences of the war beyond America, and the kind of detailed evidence put forward in the present writer's *The Issue of War*)[52] that in many of those other societies the war *was* widely seen, however confusedly, as having great significance in terms of the socioeconomic and political issues facing peoples and polities in the mid-twentieth century, in terms of both the domestic and the wider, international settings.

In order to sustain this last suggestion, we do not have to rely upon such obvious and (it might be thought) atypically extreme developments as those

49 Notes in Clapper Papers, box 37, and Carlin–Clapper correspondence, August 1942, in ibid. box 50. And see for example Carl Becker to Max Lerner, 11 March 1942, in M. Kammen (ed.), *'What Is the Good of History?' Selected Letters of Carl L. Becker, 1900–1945* (Ithaca, NY, 1973), p. 285.
50 Curti, *The Growth of American Thought*, as given in Nelson, *Impact of War*.
51 Blum, *V Was for Victory*, pp. 312, 332; and see for example polls recorded in H. Cantril and M. Strunk, *Public Opinion, 1935–1946* (Princeton, NJ, 1951).
52 See also e.g. P. Addison, *The Road to 1945. British Politics and the Second World War* (London, 1975); A. Calder and D. Sheridan (ed.), *Speak For Yourself. A Mass-Observation Anthology, 1937–1949* (Oxford, 1985); H. Michel and B. Mirkine-Guetzévitch (eds), *Les idées politiques et sociales de la Résistance* (Paris, 1954); M. Selden, *The Yenan Way in Revolutionary China* (Cambridge, Mass., 1971); J. D. Spence, *The Gate of Heavenly Peace. The Chinese People and Their Revolution, 1895–1980* (London, 1982); J. M. Halpern, 'Farming as a way of life. Yugoslav peasant attitudes', in J. F. Karcz (ed.), *Soviet and East European Agriculture* (Berkeley, Ca, 1967); P. Auty, *Tito. A Biography* (London, 1970); W. R. Roberts, *Tito, Mihailovic, and the Allies, 1941–1945* (New Brunswick, NJ, 1973).

that were taking place in Yenan, say, or in the areas of Yugoslavia where Tito was coming to hold sway, or in association with the urgings of Nehru and the Congress within India (not forgetting the home thoughts from abroad of Subhas Chandra Bose). Even among the inherently conservative Dutch, for example, there developed within the working class during the war years 'a broad radical trend . . . [which was] manifested in restiveness and rejection of the existing social and economic order'.[53] As for the Anglo-American contrast, among the British the concern to see fundamental domestic reform was widespread among the middle class and the professions, as well as the working class,[54] while Merle Curti, in developing his argument that among Americans during these years there existed 'little broadly based patriotic understanding of the larger meaning of the war', found a marked difference between the teaching materials and opportunities for discussion that were provided for members of the armed forces in each of the two countries.[55] 'You have only to hear the troops discussing the Beveridge Report [the report published in Britain at the end of 1942 which called for the creation of a comprehensive system of social security organized by the state] . . . to know that the masses are on the move'.[56] Harold Laski, writing thus to Roosevelt at the end of 1942, can scarcely be described as a disinterested observer of social change; but the contrast, as summarized by Karl, is manifest: 'If British [war-time] planners were anticipating a wave of radicalism at the war's end, American planners were learning to anticipate the opposite.'[57]

The reformist movements that were developing so strongly in Britain and elsewhere had their origins in situations and ideas that antedated the war itself, of course. The new international conflict, however, not only gave them the opportunity for rapid growth; it was itself widely seen as reinforcing the need for drastic change, both domestically and beyond. And it was within such a context that, viewed from abroad, the United States could already be seen to be at odds with the way things were moving

53 J. C. Blom, 'The Second World War and Dutch society', in A. S. Duke and C. A. Tamse (eds), *Britain and the Netherlands,* vol. VI: War and Society (The Hague, 1977); and see, on attempts to refashion the basis of Dutch political life, J. Bank, *Opkomst en ondergang van de Nederlandse Volks Beweging* (Deventer, 1978).

54 See, for example, Morgan, *Labour in Power*, pp. 31, 41, 86, 109, 156, 285.

55 Curti, *American Thought*. For the radical nature of some British Army discussion papers distributed to troops, see Directorate of Army Education, *The British Way and Purpose* (London, 1944).

56 Laski to Roosevelt, 27 December 1942, Frankfurter Papers (Library of Congress), box 75.

57 Karl, *The Uneasy State*, p. 215. Cf. Niebuhr, *Irony of American History*, p. 29: 'Every free nation in alliance with us is more disposed to bring economic life under political control than our traditional theory allows. There is therefore considerable moral misunderstanding between ourselves and our allies'.

elsewhere. It was, wrote Eden's Private Secretary in London, 'an old-fashioned country, . . . fearful of political and economic change', its business and political elites siding 'naturally with the Right and Right Centre in Europe', yet being faced now with a Europe that was 'moving Leftwards', if not in a Communist, at least in a 'Beveridge' direction.[58] As the same *Standard* newspaper in New Zealand that so warmly hailed the person of Roosevelt expressed it early in 1944:

While we in New Zealand have feelings of the deepest gratitude to our great ally . . . for the magnificent part it is playing in the war, . . . and while we desire the closest relations between the United States and ourselves after the war, there are features of American commercial life that are deeply repugnant to the vast majority of New Zealanders.[59]

For Indians and others, Britain's continuing imperial rule represented an oppressive anachronism that stood in the way of the new world that must emerge from the war. But in terms of its own domestic political and social developments, Britain itself could be seen as pointing the way towards the kinds of change that were required. 'The world is going left, as it must', proclaimed the nationalist *Bombay Chronicle* when hailing the landslide victory of the Labour Party in the 1945 election. 'The movement is both clear and irresistible.'[60] 'A new spirit is abroad in the world', declared the Burmese nationalist leader, Aung San, on the same occasion, 'and the peoples are coming into their own.'[61] True, for those who had looked only to Winston Churchill as the embodiment of British society, the move in an essentially collectivist direction that was embodied in the triumph of Attlee and his colleagues had not been anticipated. (To many Americans, including Harry Hopkins, James Forrestal and others in Washington itself, it came as a decided shock.[62]) The reality, however, was that long before the election itself Churchill, while still accepted as war-leader by the great majority of the British people, had been, in Paul Addison's phrase, 'cut off like an island from the shore' by the advancing tide of reconstruction – reconstruction that was already finding its expression in measures taken by a Coalition government which was 'prov[ing] to be the greatest reforming administration since the Liberal government of 1905–14'.[63]

58 J. Harvey (ed.), *The War Diaries of Oliver Harvey, 1941–1945* (London, 1978), entries for 7 January, 20 September, 1 December 1942 and 14 June 1943.
59 *Standard* (Wellington), 20 January 1944.
60 *Bombay Chronicle*, 27 and 28 July, 8 August 1945.
61 Quoted in Maung Maung (ed.), *Aung San of Burma* (The Hague, 1962).
62 See Thorne, *Allies of a Kind*, p. 511.
63 Addison, *Road to 1945*, pp. 14, 126.

The United States – still, of course, as already emphasized, a symbol of liberty for many people around the world; still an inspiration to many foreigners for its hustling, 'can-do' approach to obstacles and its seemingly limitless productive capacity – did not (could not?) offer the world the example of 'a great reforming administration' during the war years, as Vincent had feared would be the case. Again, given the space available, we need only refer here to the kinds of detailed studies which others have provided on the limited nature of social reform and the continuing strength of reaction in various areas of American life. For example, it is instructive to place the wartime experiences of the Congress of Industrial Organizations (CIO) unions and of US labour organizations generally alongside those of their British counterparts, or, in terms of major figures from the world of labour, to contrast the crucial position of Ernest Bevin within the London administration (symbolizing as it did a very different basis of collaboration between government, private industry and unions) with the relatively insignificant role played by Sidney Hillman in Washington. ('The National War Labor Board', comments Dr Lichtenstein, 'which most businessmen mistrusted as a bastion of New Deal labor liberalism, proved to be one of the administration's most effective tools in regulating industrial conflict in a way that ultimately strengthened corporate hegemony.'[64])

Other aspects of American society will no doubt be examined in detail elsewhere in the present conference: the position of women, for example, on which D'Ann Campbell, while demonstrating how, in the armed forces and industry, 'the men simply would not allow the women to leave their private sphere', has argued at length that the war years 'did not mark a drastic break with traditional working patterns or sex roles';[65] or the position of black Americans, for whom the lowering of some barriers during these years served only, amid heightened prejudice, to bring them up against more fundamental ones that remained in place, so that for many, in James Baldwin's phrase, as the second of the 'double Vs' continued unachieved, 'a certain respect for white Americans faded'. 'Many of the men I have talked to', wrote Walter White to his NAACP (National Association for the Advancement of Colored Peoples) staff while on a tour of service units in the Pacific area in 1945, 'believe that their fight for democracy will begin when they reach San Francisco on their way' home.' For large numbers of blacks, concluded one of their number who continued to serve as a career officer, the war years in the armed forces had been 'a racial nightmare'.[66]

64 N. Lichtenstein, *Labor's War At Home* (Cambridge, 1982), p. 4; and see Davis, *Prisoners*, ch. 2.
65 Campbell, *Women at War*, pp. 46; 83; and see e.g. Perrett, *Days of Sadness*, pp. 343–5.
66 White memo., 12 February 1945, NAACP Papers (Library of Congress), box 583;

This is not the place to pursue the overall question of whether it can be said, as Stein has argued, that for all the heightened nationalism fostered by the war, 'domestic disunity' increased within the United States between 1941 and 1945, with 'cohesion decreasing . . . as a function of mobilization'.[67] More to the immediate point is, for example, the contrast between the reception of the Beveridge Report in Britain and the fate of those reports of a broadly similar kind (*After the War – Full Employment* and *After the War – Toward Security*) which, after long gestation, were put forward by the National Resources Planning Board in 1942–3. For not only were these reports, and the Board which had spawned them, fiercely denounced in Congress and on Wall Street as 'socialist, fascist and medieval', but polls showed that the public at large had 'little general interest in the report [on improved social security]', which 'generated some suspicion among those who actually knew what it was about'. As Karl observes, 'to a society committed to the virtues of self help and a faith in boundless opportunity', the idea that the state might have to assume an ongoing responsibility for citizens unable to escape from extreme poverty 'was appalling' – not simply because it could be associated with socialism or Marxism, but 'because [it] called for national programs to eradicate local and regional differences'.[68]

It must again be emphasized that such particular issues and choices must be seen in the context of the culture, political culture and history of the society concerned. Nor is it the intention here to argue, say, that American society *should* have turned in a 'Beveridge' direction during the war, whether in relation to its own long-term well-being or to some overriding moral and social value. Indeed, as has been indicated earlier, given the history and political culture of the Republic, together with its distinctive experience of the war itself, one might well conclude that the enhancement of conservatism within its borders during these years was inescapable. The point being made is simply that in adhering to the concept of the autonomous individual as 'the fundamental element' in its democracy, and in rejecting nationwide, state-centred solutions to the socioeconomic problems of the mid-twentieth century world, the United States was distancing itself from the major trends of the time, viewed in the global context.

Besides the long-term reasons for this choice by American society as a whole, which have been alluded to above, there are obviously more

---

Baldwin quoted by R. Dalfiume, 'Beginnings of the Negro Revolution', in Nelson, *Impact of War*; M. P. Motley (ed.), *The Invisible Soldier. The Experience of the Black Soldier in World War II* (Detroit, 1975).

67 Stein, *The Nation at War*, pp. 42, 53 and passim. See also Stohl, *War and Domestic Political Violence*.

68 Karl, The Uneasy State, pp. 214ff.

immediate, structural shifts within the Republic during the war years themselves which are relevant: not least, the ways and degrees to which international conflict was enhancing the standing, profits and predominance of large business organizations, including those which were developing close connections with a newly confident and assertive military elite.[69] ('One would hardly recognize the cowed and submissive men of the 1930s', writes Samuel Huntington, 'in the proud and powerful commanders of the victorious American forces, [for whom by 1944–5] civilian control was a relic of the past which had little place in the future.'[70]) Such developments were, of course, profoundly disturbing to confirmed New Dealers like Harold Ickes (Secretary of the Interior) and (less prominently) Bruce Catton. Indeed, in 1943 Ickes went so far as to confide to the British ambassador that he believed the Republic 'might be headed for an era of fascism following the war', in which event he thought Britain and the Soviet Union would – and should – 'come to an understanding'.[71]

Even by the time he was recording this in his diary, however, Ickes and his political values were themselves, to adapt Lenin, 'the wave of the past'. The extent to which Roosevelt, as President, did or did not remain privately committed to an extension of the reforms which had been introduced between 1933 and 1937 must remain uncertain and the subject of strong debate. (Or to put it another way: how much should be read into his call, in January 1945, for a second Bill of Rights?) And doubtless some will reject Blum's conclusion that 'he did not seriously question the general desirability of the political state of the world as it had existed in his early manhood'.[72] What is apparent, none the less, is that the President had no intention of seeking to challenge his fellow-Americans to act upon the view of the worldwide international conflict as signalling the need and providing the spring-board for radical social change in the United States and beyond.

69 See e.g. Blum, *V Was for Victory*, pp. 105ff, 145; Polenberg, *War and Society*, pp. 139, 219, 237; A. D. Kaplan, 'Big enterprise in a competitive system', in Nelson, *Impact of War*. Businesses employing less than 500 workers accounted for 52 per cent of manufacturing employees in 1939, 38 per cent in 1944. Corporate profit after taxes, $6.4 billion in 1940, reached $10.8 billion in 1944.

70 S. P. Huntington, *The Soldier and the State* (New York, 1957), pp. 335–6. On, for example, the significant role and foreign policy submissions of the head of the Army's Services of Supply, Lt General Brehon Somervell, see Thorne, *Allies of a Kind*, pp. 288, 336, 390 and 433, and Thorne, *The Issue of War*, pp. 255, 297. The contemporary analyses put forward by C. Wright Mills, however much they may need amending in retrospect, are obviously relevant. See also M. S. Sherry, *Preparing for the Next War: American Plans for Post-War Defense, 1941–1945* (New Haven, Conn., 1977), p. 24 and passim.

71 Ickes Diary (Library of Congress), 22 March, 4 and 14 June, 5 and 26 July 1942, 3 April 1943, 1 January 1944; B. Catton, *The War Lords of Washington* (New York, 1948). And see Thorne, *Issue*, pp. 255, 295.

72 Blum, *V Was for Victory*, p. 259.

'Tommy, cut out this New Deal stuff. It's tough to win a war': Roosevelt's private remark to Corcoran in 1940[73] anticipated his public assertion four or so years later that 'Dr New Deal' was no longer required. Nor, beyond the 'ringing generalizations' of his State of the Union message in January 1945, did he provide clear proposals for an alternative basis for social reform in the era that lay ahead.[74]

This retreat of Roosevelt's – begun well before Pearl Harbor – mirrored a profound wartime shift on the part of the country as a whole in an essentially rightwards direction: a development signalled by, for example, the mid-term elections of 1942 and 1946, by the dropping of Henry Wallace as Vice President in 1944, and, among the clerisy, by the acclaim accorded the publication (also in 1944) of Hayek's *Road to Serfdom*; a development which entailed the rejection of some form of collectivist response to the problems of industrialized, mass society, and which had by 1944, in Karl's words, reduced Roosevelt's own leadership in matters of domestic policy to 'pure form'.[75] The country was 'going rightist again', noted Eric Sevareid at the end of 1943, his perceptions of his own society sharpened by his overseas travels as a correspondent.[76] 'We are getting some of those radical boys out of the way', asserted James Byrnes, Director of Economic Stabilization, 'and more will go.' By 1944, an Archibald MacLeish was reduced to bewailing 'the tragic outlook for all liberal proposals, the collapse of liberal leadership, and the inevitable defeat of all liberal aims'.[77]

Despair, however, was far from being the predominant mood of the time. The country's enhanced prosperity and massive success in the war itself could bring a well-nigh feverish sense of confidence in its train, as Theodore White discovered as he toured war zones in the Far East: 'A sense of the American purpose as Triumph over Evil became unshakeable in me', he recalled later, 'almost maniacal, as I began to flick around the map of Asia which was opening to our conquests'.[78] The power of the dollar, Henry Morgenthau informed his staff, was going to ensure that it would be Franklin Roosevelt who not only should but could 'write the peace treaty'.[79] 'It will be a long, hard war, the Secretary of the American

---

73 Terkel, '*The Good War*', p. 318.

74 Karl, *The Uneasy State*, p. 222.

75 Ibid. And see, for example, Polenberg, *War and Society*, pp. 73ff, 91ff, 189ff.

76 Sevareid notes, 22 December 1943, Sevareid Papers (Library of Congress), box D3. And see, for example, Clapper to Howard, 24 June 1942, Clapper Papers, box 50.

77 F. L. Israel (ed.), *The War Diary of Breckenridge Long* (Lincoln, Nebraska, 1966), entry for 9 September 1943; Winkler, *Politics of Propaganda*, p. 71. And see for example, J. M. Blum (ed.), *The Price of Vision. The Diary of Henry A. Wallace, 1942–1946* (Boston, 1973), p. 381 and passim.

78 White, *In Search of History*, p. 223.

79 J. M. Blum, *Roosevelt and Morgenthau* (Boston, 1970), p. 490.

Asiatic Association had written privately on the morrow of Pearl Harbor itself, 'but after it is over Uncle Sam will do the talking in this world',[80] and three years later there could seem every reason to conclude that he had been entirely prescient. 'The good fortune of the world', proclaimed the *Chicago Tribune* on that exact anniversary (8 December 1944), 'is that power and unquestionable intentions [now] go together'. And at the war's end itself (15 August 1945), the *New York Herald Tribune* was voicing a widespread sentiment when it concluded, with a sense almost of awe, and of grave responsibility:

Every American faces himself and his countrymen with a new confidence, a new sense of power . . . We cannot if we would shut our eyes to the fact that ours is the supreme position. The Great Republic has come into its own; it stands first among the peoples of the earth.

The 'militant nationalism' of the time, as Merle Curti was to term it, is entirely understandable in retrospect, even when it can be seen that the accompanying assumptions often embraced a failure to appreciate or accept the extent to which it was the Soviet Union that had brought about the military defeat of Nazi Germany, and the reality of the Soviet Union as an emerging super-power.[81] Nor, for all the internal divisions and conflicts that are apparent in retrospect, is it at all surprising that these years also witnessed a greatly increased emphasis on 'Americanism', thus making the war, as Philip Gleason sees it, 'the central event in the shaping of Americans' understanding of their national identity for the next generation'.[82]

What this involved, of course, as Gleason himself, Huntington, and many others have emphasized, was a reinforcing of that identity in terms of 'a set of universal ideas and values'. Thus it meant, also, a reinforcing of the assumptions and expectations that all peoples of the world were, in a sense, potential or nascent Americans,[83] an outlook nowhere more remarkably demonstrated than in the person of that erstwhile champion of cultural relativism, Margaret Mead, who was now, in 1953, to proclaim the conviction

80 Chevalier to Hornbeck, 8 December 1941, Hornbeck Papers (Hoover Institute), box 6.
81 See A. W. DePorte, *Europe Between the Superpowers* (New Haven, Conn., 1979), ch. 6.
82 P. Gleason, 'American identity and Americanization', in S. Thernstrom (ed.), *Harvard Encyclopedia of American Ethnic Groups* (Cambridge, Mass., 1980).
83 Lucian Pye's contention (*Asian Power and Politics*, p. 28) that, 'several generations of Americans [having been] taught by the texts of Margaret Mead and Ruth Benedict . . . that it is wrong to be ethnocentric', 'Americans are probably the only people in the world who know the anxieties of saying something inconsistent with cultural relativism' is an unintended gem.

that American civilization is not simply the last flower to bloom on the outmoded tree of European history, . . . but something new and different, . . . because the men who built it have themselves incorporated the ability to change and change swiftly as the need arises. As we have learned to change ourselves, so we believe that others can change also, and we believe that they will want to change, that men have only to see a better way of life to reach out for it spontaneously. Our faith includes no forebodings about the effect of destroying old customs and . . . we do not conceive of people forcibly changed by other human beings. We conceive of them as seeing a light and following it freely. [84]

At the time she was writing, *The Quiet American* was taking shape in the mind of Graham Greene. 'What America has got abroad is power', argued C. Wright Mills in 1952; 'what it has *not* got at home or abroad is cultural prestige'. [85] With the triumph of 1945 did indeed come a vastly increased involvement in the world beyond its shores on the part of the United States. But as Michael Howard has put it, resembling 'a secular church, or perhaps a gigantic sect', its earliest concern having been, 'like those sects which played so large a part in its foundation . . . to keep itself unspotted from the infections of the world, to create an inward-looking community whose members could practise and bear witness to the faith', the Republic could immerse itself and operate within the international system 'with a clear conscience only if it could remake that system in its own image'. [86] At the same time, for reasons which include those pointed to by Robert Bellah and his colleagues in the extract quoted earlier, the Republic as a society, and not simply its policy-makers, inevitably experienced profound difficulties when it came to dealing with other societies, or sections of them, that were moving in a direction that was radically different from its own predominant and inherent middle class conservatism, and that were inspired by values at odds with those individualistic, *laissez-faire* lodestars by which American lives were defined and steered. As Bruce Catton bitterly expressed it soon after the war: 'commitment to the status quo at home, where reaction had found its voice again', became 'by logical extension commitment to the status quo abroad as well'. [87]

Such a development is not to be seen, as Catton himself tended to view it at the time, as the result, essentially, of maneouvrings on the part of the 'dollar-a-year' men from the major corporations who had crowded into positions of power and influence in wartime Washington, and (as he

84 M. Mead, *New Lives For Old* (New York, 1961), p. 19; cf. her earlier warnings in *Anthropology: A Human Science*, p. 142.
85 Mills, 'Liberal values in the modern world', in L. Horowitz (ed.), *Power, Politics and People. The Collected Essays of C. Wright Mills* (New York, 1963).
86 M. Howard, *War and the Liberal Conscience* (Oxford, 1981), p. 116.
87 Catton, *War Lords of Washington*, p. 306. And see A. Wolfe, *America's Impasse. The Rise and Fall of the Politics of Growth* (Boston, 1981).

argued) had thus been able to thwart the will and intentions of the President. That 'fear of change [which] kept our war from being a people's war', to which Catton also referred,[88] is to be seen more fundamentally (*pace* Margaret Mead) as a deeply rooted characteristic of American political culture in general: one that was brought strongly to the fore by the circumstances of the war years, as it was to come to the fore again in the aftermath of defeat in Vietnam. At bottom, it is here that we find the reasons why – in the Philippines and in South Korea, for example[89] – the enhanced might of the United States was quickly employed to prop up the 'haves' against the 'have-nots' (which frequently meant supporting wartime collaborators with the enemy against those who had actively resisted): here, in American conservatism and 'autism' when faced with different cultures and with values that point towards radical social reform, rather than in conspiracy theories relating to this or that group, or in a reductionist economic determinism.

If a fundamental insensitivity to the nature and values of other societies was to be a continuing feature of US dealings with the outside world after the war – and it is itself a comment that Henry Kissinger, who displayed that insensitivity (*vis-à-vis* peoples, that is, rather than regimes) to an outstanding degree was and continues to be widely thought of among Americans as shrewdly knowledgeable about that world[90] – it was not solely power and a sense of power that fuelled its accompanying assertiveness. For all the immense increase in confidence brought about by wartime developments that was noted above, an underlying lack of that very commodity supplied its own agitated impulsion. 'This nation', observed Aline Caro-Delvaille in a penetrating article published in *Le Monde* in September 1945,

88 Catton, *War Lords*, p. 310.
89 See, for example, B. Cumings, *The Origins of the Korean War. Liberation and the Emergence of Separate Regimes, 1945–1947* (Princeton, NJ, 1981), p. xxiv and passim; L. E. Bauzon, *Philippine Agrarian Reform, 1880–1965. The Revolution That Never Was* (Singapore, 1975); B. J. Kerkvliet, *The Huk Rebellion. A Study of Peasant Revolt in the Philippines* (Berkeley, Ca, 1977), pp. 65, 110ff; G. K. Goodman, 'The Japanese occupation of the Philippines: Successful collaboration of invading and indigenous power elites', in *Journal of International Studies*, Sophia University Institute of International Relations, Tokyo, vol. V, no. 2, 1982, and 'The Japanese occupation of the Philippines: the Commonwealth sustained', 1985 seminar paper, University of Kansas; C. M. Petillo, *Douglas MacArthur: the Philippine Years* (Bloomington, Indiana, 1981).
90 On Kissinger's approach to international affairs, Stanley Hoffmann's critique is invaluable. Seymour Hersh, Oriana Fallaci and Joseph Heller have also, in their various ways, helped reveal various facets and provided appropriate commentaries; nor, as the respectful, deferential audiences continue to gather – in London and Tokyo, as well as Washington – have the passing years lessened the timeliness of Anthony Lewis' *New York Times* observation: 'That we honour a person who has done such things in our name is a comment on us.'

'is profoundly unsure of itself'.[91] The reaction – not simply to hostile forces and Soviet tyranny, but to an apparent rejection of America's universal values, to the unfamiliar, to the foreign and to the complex – was often one of fear.

In this connection, it is perhaps not unduly fanciful to imagine the bewilderment of a visiting Venusian if, having learned of the Republic's unparalleled wealth and resources, together with its recent military triumphs around the world, he or she had arrived in Washington, DC in 1948 to read, say, the secret conviction of the National Security Council's staff that any step back from the 'struggle for power' with the Soviet Union would result in 'eventual national suicide';[92] or to learn two years later that the Chairman of the National Resources Board was sure that the country was 'losing . . . [the] war of survival' in which it had become engaged.[93] Hysteria over the 'loss' of China in 1949; the posture of the world's most powerful state in the 1980s, a sumo wrestler, as it were, perched on a chair at the sight of a socialist Nicaraguan mouse appearing 'on its doorstep' (which is to say, approximately the distance away which separates London from Albania): it is not only Venusians who might stare in wonder. But such sights are not beyond explanation and understanding, of course, even if seasoned observers can still be taken by surprise momentarily – as was Oriana Fallaci, for example, when Alexandros Panagoulis (a man of 1775, one might have thought, if ever there was one) was denied entry into the Republic because he had dared to seek to destroy one of Kissinger's tame dictators.[94] And this understanding would have to take in, of course, an underlying uncertainty, at times fear, regarding the oft-proclaimed strength and solidarity of American society itself.

Such fear had been manifested in the widespread 'Red Scare' that followed the ending of the First World War: it was above all 'the forces of disorder' within, as Herbert Hoover termed them, that could see to it that 'society would crumble' – this last a phrase from Woodrow Wilson, who, even in 1910, to quote Lloyd Gardner, had seen, as he thought, 'the looming clouds of revolution gathering over America', and whose main concern in 1914, well before the Bolshevik challenge was flung down, had been, as he himself avowed privately at the end of the war, the United States'

---

91 *Le Monde*, 9 September 1945. Cf. Fiedler (*Love and Death*, p. 503), on 'the brutality and terror endemic in our life', and Alonzo L. Hamby, (*Liberalism and its Challengers. FDR to Reagan*, New York, 1985, p. 70) on 'a new and *insecure* middle class, determined to protect its gains . . .' after the war. Emphasis added.
92 NSC 7, 30 March 1948 (National Archives).
93 NSC 100, 11 January 1950.
94 See Oriana Fallaci, *Interview with History* (Boston, 1976), pp. 343–4, and Fallaci, *A Man* (London, 1981), p. 233.

'imminent danger of civil discord'.[95] The 'great common experience' of the 1941–5 war, with its accompanying films which portrayed the trans-ethnic oneness of the people of the Republic, did not remove the bases for such anxiety. The 'great fear' of McCarthyism was to feed on a profound inner social doubt, as well as upon a 'paranoid style' in the country's politics and the desperate strivings of Republican elites for power.[96] 'Our democracy', asserted the authors of that secular hymn to American values, NSC 68, 'possesses a unique degree of unity'. But they felt impelled to warn, none the less, how easily the Soviet enemy might 'turn to its own uses the most dangerous and divisive trends in our own society'. In Rogin's words, 'the fear of a disintegrating consensus is endemic in American politics'. 'Our interventionist policy', shrewdly observed Stillman and Pfaff in the mid-1960s, 'arises [in part because it is] a kind of social cement – a national mission, nearly a messianism, which expresses an American need for world identity that will confirm our national identity. It is a disguise for our insecurity and violence, a mask . . . It may be that we have used a fifth of a century of Cold War as a means of avoiding self-confrontation'.[97]

That such paranoia and fear of change within both the domestic life and external relations of the Republic have been deplored and resisted by Americans themselves scarcely needs underlining, although at a conference concerned with the Second World War a visiting Briton, with some youthful memories of 'the Blitz', may perhaps be permitted a salute to the memory of Ed Murrow in particular. Nor is it to be forgotten, even when all allowance has been made for the exercise of self-interest and political calculation on the part of Washington, and for 'revisionist' analyses of the mainsprings of West European recovery after the war,[98] that the impulse of generosity and a desire to help others less fortunate did figure in the creation of the Marshall Aid programme during these same years of alarm and reaction. The anger of those Senators who realized too late that they had

95 See L. C. Gardner, *Safe for Democracy. The Anglo-American Response to Revolution, 1913–1923* (New York, 1984), pp. 37, 161, 170, 203, 235, 245, 258, 260, 279, 346, and passim, and Gleason, 'American identity'.
96 D. Caute, *The Great Fear. The Anti-Communist Purge Under Truman and Eisenhower* (New York, 1978); R. Hofstadter, *The Paranoid Style in American Politics* (New York, 1967); Rogin, *The Intellectuals*. Note also Rogin's observation (p. 9) on various 'pluralists' who had been identified with the cause of reform during the Second World War: 'These hopes soon exhausted themselves as the cold war and the rise of McCarthyism deadened [their] radical impulses . . .: the country now had to be defended against attack from without and within . . . [and they] now sought values in traditions of mainstream America with which they could identify. They attributed to peripheral, radical movements the diseases they had previously located at the heart of the American ethos.'
97 NSC 68, 14 April 1950; Rogin, *The Intellectuals*, p. 33; Stillman and Pfaff, *Power and Impotence*, pp. 183, 189.
98 See A. S. Milward, *The Reconstruction of Western Europe, 1945–51* (London, 1984).

allowed through a bill which, in the words of one of them, might 'infect our impressionable American youths with foreign isms' could not prevent the Fulbright Act of 1946 from widening the horizons of foreigners and Americans alike. [99] Nor, again, was the raucous degree to which 'reaction had found its voice again' by the 1950s to prevent an answering shout of reformist indignation and creativity from reverberating around the country and bringing about substantial social reform in the 1960s and early 70s.

And yet the central propositions of this paper remain in place none the less. It was, after all, during that very period of 'credal passion' in the 60s, as Huntington chooses to call it, that some of the Republic's dealings with the outside world were to epitomize its inability to come to terms with social radicalism and the anthropologically alien, just as the attitudes of many of its citizens towards the 'gooks' on the far side of the Pacific were merely to reflect a racism that had been embedded in its own history from the outset. [100] Even in domestic terms, the underlying and essential conservatism of American society was not to break, ready still to surge to the fore once more in the 1980s. 'We ended a war', reflected Tom Hayden in 1977, 'toppled two Presidents, desegregated the South, broke other barriers of discrimination. How could we accomplish so much and have so little in the end?' Three years later, there came the landslide victory for a movement having 'at its core', in Walter Dean Burnham's words, 'the repeal of both the theory and the practice of social harmony that [had] dominated public policy . . . for the past half-century . . .: a one-sided class struggle on behalf of the rich . . .' [101]

It is not being suggested, of course, that it was the experiences and responses of the Second World War that by themselves created that gulf between the Republic and so much of the rest of the world which has widened further still in the era of Reaganism. As was emphasized earlier, much longer-term characteristics appertaining to the country, its society and its political culture were already, well before Pearl Harbor, pointing towards such an estrangement amid the technological economic and social circumstances obtaining in the mid-to-late twentieth century. Indeed, such characteristics were to ensure that, even after 1945, the other, and

99 See, for example, H. Johnson and B. Gwertzman, *Fulbright The Dissenter* (London, 1969), ch. 3.
100 See R. Drinnon, *Facing West. The Metaphysics of Indian-Hating and Empire-Building* (New York, 1980). Also, for example, R. Smith, *Vietnam and the West* (Ithaca, NY, 1971); F. Fitzgerald, *Fire in the Lake. The Vietnamese and the Americans in Vietnam* (New York, 1972); R. Hofstadter and M. Wallace (ed.), *American Violence: a Documentary History* (New York, 1970), pp. 283ff.
101 Hayden article in *Time*, 15 August 1977, as quoted in Huntington, *American Politics*; W. D. Burnham, *The Current Crisis in American Politics* (New York, 1982), p. 14; J. Krieger, *Reagan, Thatcher, and the Politics of Decline* (Cambridge, 1986).

sought-after, form of 'estrangement' that was alluded to earlier in the essay was to retain its attraction within the United States itself: that is, the desire to distance the Republic from corruption and entanglements overseas, even though the world had first to be made 'safe for America to leave it', as the phrase had it;[102] even though, in the mid-1980s, that 'regression to an idealized golden sanctuary in the past' represented by the Star Wars fantasy[103] ('a magic solution', as a former Secretary General of the United Nations has described it: 'a return to former invulnerability if only sufficient dollars are allocated and an adequate number of weapon systems produced'),[104] cannot yet guarantee a secure escape.

Viewed in retrospect, nevertheless, the war years throw a particularly strong light on the longer-term process of estrangement. The international conflict itself, encompassing so many of the world's peoples, brought into sharper focus (for those who chose to see it) socioeconomic pressures and problems as well as opportunities, of a kind that cut across the familiar divisions of nation and state. And while, in their own ways and in relation to their individual cultures, political cultures and pre-war situations, most of the societies involved, to put it crudely, turned 'leftwards' in consequence, American society turned further to the right – a course upon which it had already been embarked, as Karl and others have emphasized, since the early, aberrant years of the New Deal. To put it another way: whereas the war greatly heightened the politicization of the great majority of the societies that were caught up in it, within the United States it served to reinforce the characteristic which the events of the mid-1930s had briefly disrupted, whereby, in Burnham's words again, 'the entire weight of our social, no less than our political, history in this century has been in the direction not of rediscovering politics but of suppressing it'.[105]

The opportunity which Vincent had perceived to be present on the eve of Pearl Harbor had not been seized – although it will be apparent that to the present writer it is very doubtful that a realistic option of the kind the diplomat had in mind had indeed been present. 'We have scarcely begun to develop theories of social change', Manfred Halpern was to write in the 1960s, 'that would allow us to understand the fundamental revolutions now

102 See, for example, N. Graebner. *The New Isolationism: a Study in Politics and Foreign Policy Since 1950* (New York, 1956).
103 E. P. Thompson (ed.), *Star Wars* (London, 1985), p. 138. And see, for example, J. Chase, 'A quest for invulnerability' in Ungar, *Estrangement*.
104 K. Waldheim, *In the Eye of the Storm* (London, 1985), p. 245. Cf. Senator Fulbright's comment in 1954 on the Bricker amendment: 'We have come to this constitutional crisis . . . because in our desperation to escape the world that we can never escape, we are seeking some device of magic that would enable us to accomplish an impossible end.' Johnson and Gwertzman, *Fulbright*, p. 278.
105 Burnham, *The Current Crisis*, p. 197.

in progress in the world'.[106] Perhaps if not major theories, then some beginnings of empathy might conceivably have merged from the turmoil and devastation of the war years; but the great majority of Americans did not experience, perceive or conceptualize the event in that way. Where goodwill and concern for the rest of humankind emerged, it tended to take the form, as it did for Pearl Buck, for example, of a desire to see 'the American way of life prevail in the world';[107] of a conviction, with Margaret Mead, that other societies would 'see the American light and follow it freely'. And as a consequence of such crude and unwitting wartime arrogance, boosted as it was by the scientific, technological and industrial marvels of those years, the mental gap between the United States and those other societies was ultimately to widen all the more.

We thus come back to the paradox that was suggested at the beginning of this essay: that during the very wartime period when the United States was being brought more closely and in many ways inextricably into contact with the rest of the world, its 'apartness' from that world was in certain fundamental respects being reinforced. Looked at in another way, within that 'presentist' perspective which this conference has called for, it can be suggested that an examination of American experiences of and responses to the Second World War, set alongside those of the other societies involved, can contribute to our understanding of three further paradoxes – tragic in essence – which have come to figure prominently in the post-war world. (It scarcely needs saying that the post-war years have not been wanting in other tragedies or other seeming contradictions, as exemplified, for example, by the gulags, the endemic repression and the foreign invasions of a power whose proclaimed belief and goal lie in freedom for the workers of the world.)

The first paradox is that of an American society, composed as it is of an extraordinary range of ethnic groups originating from virtually every corner of the globe, which has none the less been remarkably 'tone-deaf', so to speak,[108] when listening to and dealing with societies, cultures and

106 M. Halpern, 'The morality and politics of intervention' (1963), in K. W. Thompson (ed.), *Moral Dimensions of American Foreign Policy* (New Brunswick, 1984), p. 82.

107 Buck speech of February 1942, reported in material in the Hornbeck Papers, box 40. Contrast this expectation of Miss Buck's, directed above all towards Asia, with, for instance, calls among Asian clerisies in the 1980s for a revival of 'our bright, old culture' and the rediscovery of 'an Asian-Pacific identity' (whatever that may be), in place of seeking to ape 'Western civilization' with its 'negative', as well as helpful, influences. See, for example, A. J. L. Armour (ed.), *Asia and Japan. The Search for Modernization and Identity* (London, 1985), passim; also Pye, in *Asian Power and Politics*, passim, and C. Thorne, *American Political Culture and the Asian Frontier, 1943–1973* (London, 1988).

108 Cf. Studs Terkel's recent reflections on the well-peopled '51st state' of the Republic, 'Catatonia': *Talking to Myself. A Memoir of My Times*, (London, 1986), pp. 317ff.

political cultures other than its own. The second is the paradox lying behind Morgenthau's outcry in 1974: of an American society which, so long associated with the causes of freedom and equality and so often the home of generous instincts towards all humanity, has none the less come to be identified in many parts of the world with repression, exploitation and social inequality beyond its borders.[109] But it is the third paradox that is potentially the most tragic of all. For it is embodied in the situation that has developed in our own time, whereby the society which for no small reason was once proclaimed and seen as 'the last, best hope of mankind' has contributed significantly, through a conjunction of its exceptionalism and its autism, its evangelicalism and its technological and political millennarianism, its escapism, its confidence and its fear,[110] to processes which have brought humankind in its entirety to within touching distance of destruction.

109 See, for example, Walter LaFeber's superb survey of US relations with Central America, *Inevitable Revolutions* (New York, 1983), and Kwitny, *Endless Enemies*.
110 See Anthony Lewis in the *New York Times*, 20 July 1969: 'What we lack is any agreed moral basis for [the] solution [of our earthly responsibilities], a common vision of the good society. Perhaps we are twentieth century Vikings, driven, conquering without humanizing qualities. We would know the stars but do not know ourselves.' Cf. Fulbright again, in 1964: 'The American people [appear to] prefer military rockets to public schools and flights to the moon to urban renewal. In a perverse way, we have grown rather attached to the cold war. It occupies us with a stirring and seemingly clear and simple challenge from outside and diverts us from problems here at home which many Americans would rather not try to solve . . .'. Johnson and Gwertzman, *Fulbright*, p. 285. On the mounting US scientific and technological millennarianism of the 1960s, see W. A. McDougall, . . . *The Heavens and the Earth. A Political History of the Space Age* (New York, 1985), and the apprehensive contemporary observations of an 'insider', E. B. Skolnikoff, *Science, Technology, and American Foreign Policy* (Cambridge, Mass., 1967), pp. 302ff. Also M. L. Smith, 'Selling the moon. The US manned space program and the triumph of commodity scientism', in R. W. Fox and T. J. J. Lears (eds), *The Culture of Consumption. Critical Essays in American History, 1880-1980* (New York, 1983).

Index

Coastal Defense or Blue Water." *U.S. Naval Institute Proceedings* 102, no. 879 (May 1976).

White, Gordon. "The Politics of Social Stratification in a Socialist Society: The Case of China, 1959-69." Ph.D. dissertation, Stanford University, 1974.

White, Lynn T. "The Liberation Army and the Chinese People." *Armed Forces and Society* 1, no. 3 (Spring 1975).

Whiting, Allen S. "The Use of Force in Foreign Policy by the People's Republic of China." *The Annals of the American Academy of Political and Social Science* 402 (July 1972).

Periodicals

China News Analysis. Hong Kong.

China News Summary. Hong Kong, British Regional Information Service.

China Topics. Hong Kong, British Regional Information Service.

Chinese Communist Affairs: Facts and Features. Taipei (ceased publication ca. 1968).

Chung-kung Yen-chiu [Studies on Chinese Communism]. Taipei.

Current Scene. Hong Kong, U.S. Information Service.

Far Eastern Economic Review.

Fei-ch'ing Yueh-pao [Chinese Communist Affairs Monthly]. Taipei.

Issues and Studies. Taipei.

Union Research Service. Hong Kong.

Index